THE
LIBRARY
OF THE
BRITISH
MUSEUM

RETROSPECTIVE
ESSAYS ON THE
DEPARTMENT
OF PRINTED
BOOKS

Edited by
P. R. HARRIS

THE BRITISH LIBRARY
1991

Jacket illustration:
The Arch Room, 1841 [Maps C.26.f.7].

© 1991 The British Library Board
First published 1991 by
The British Library
Great Russell Street London WC1B 3DG

British Library Cataloguing in Publication Data
A catalogue record for this title is
available from The British Library.

ISBN 0-7123-0242-5

Designed by John Mitchell
Typeset by Bexhill Phototypesetters in 9½pt Garamond
Printed in England by
Cambridge University Press

CONTENTS

PREFACE

In a speech delivered in October 1943 on the rebuilding of the House of Commons after it had been destroyed by bombing, Winston Churchill said: 'We shape our buildings, and afterwards our buildings shape us'.

By 1997 the former library departments of the British Museum will have moved from the building which has influenced their development for the past 160 years, and they will in the future be moulded by the form of the new building which will house the British Library at St Pancras. Many practices which have evolved in response to the design of the British Museum building will soon become unexplained oddities. It therefore seems desirable to place on record some aspects of the history of the Library and its work as it has developed for more than a century and a half, in particular while there are still persons available who can remember the institution as it was forty or fifty years ago.

The desire to record in print the way in which the books have been arranged and accommodated since the earliest days was what originally inspired this volume. In 1954 Mr F. J. Hill submitted a thesis for a Fellowship of the Library Association under the title 'Shelving and Classification of Printed Books in the British Museum, 1753–1953'. A copy of this thesis has long stood on the reference shelves of the North Library, and has proved an invaluable resource both for staff and for readers who wanted information about the placing system of the library. Since his retirement, Mr Hill has brought his study up to the present time – no small task considering the many changes that there have been in the arrangement of the Library during the past forty years.

Given the imminent move to St Pancras, it was thought of interest to study in detail how the move from Montagu House to the present British Museum building was planned and executed in the 1830s and early 1840s. This is the topic of the second essay. When this move had been completed, one of Antonio Panizzi's major tasks was to secure adequate money for acquisitions, and this involved a detailed description of what the aims of the Library should be in the field of collection development. He had already set out his priorities in a report to the Trustees dated 12 October 1837, but in the early 1840s he planned and supervised a detailed survey of the weaknesses and strengths of the collections. The findings of this survey were included in a report which was printed in 1845. This convinced the Government that a major increase in the purchase grant was needed. In the third essay, Miss Ilse Sternberg outlines how, during the 122 years between 1837 and 1959, the acquisitions policies of the Department of Printed Books were elaborated, and what resources were available to implement the plans which were drawn up.

Important as purchases, gifts and exchanges were and are, the bulk of the material received by the Library has arrived as a result of the operation of the deposit provisions of various Copyright Acts. The revolutionary effect which Panizzi had in this area after he became responsible for copyright deposit in 1850 is well known. At the cost of great personal unpopularity he enforced the British Museum's rights, despite considerable opposition from some publishers. A key episode was his campaign against H. G. Bohn from 1850 to 1853, which is here studied by Dr Manley.

One of the greatest achievements of the Department of Printed Books has been the provision of a printed catalogue of its holdings. The initial printing, which was carried out between 1880 and 1905, was an enormous task; but equally important was the work of keeping the catalogue up to date by inserting entries for accessions into the large guard volumes which contained the pasted-down columns of the original catalogue. The constant and precise task of maintaining the catalogue is the theme of Dr King's first contribution. In 1987, Mr A. H. Chaplin produced an invaluable account of the catalogue (in his *GK: 150 Years of the General Catalogue of Printed Books in the British Museum*), and since to some extent this covers ground which is also covered by Dr King, it is only fair to record that the latter's typescript reached the editor of this volume over a year before Mr Chaplin's history of the catalogue was published.

The sixth contribution deals with a part of the collections, the history of which has long been shrouded in mystery – the pornographic material known as the Private Case collection. In the past 25 years this material has been made more readily available to the readers, largely as a result of a campaign by Mr Peter Fryer, who in 1966 published a book entitled *Private Case, Public Scandal*. Mr Fryer believed that this collection was established after 1856, while others who had worked on Private Case material considered that it was set up even later. Mr Paul Cross, in his detailed study of the history of the Private Case, proves that the collection dates back to 1841.

The volume concludes with a second contribution by Dr King, which is different in character from the other six essays. It contains some of his memories of the 42 years which he spent as a member of the staff of the Library from 1934 to 1976. Although some other members of the staff have written briefly of their experiences in the Library, this is the largest body of reminiscences to be printed since Robert Cowtan published his *Memories of the British Museum* in 1872. Official records are indispensable when writing the history of an institution, but how often does the historian long in vain for the non-official version of the story.

A former member of the staff, and the author of the standard history of the Library, Arundell Esdaile, entitled a volume of essays and verses which he published in 1940 *Autolycus' Pack*. This present volume too is a miscellany, but the editor does not think of himself as another Autolycus – 'a snapper-up of unconsidered trifles'. At the present stage of the Library's history when so much is changing, and a number of tried and tested procedures are being discarded, an attempt to record some of them is needed – '*Colligite fragmenta ne pereant*'.

P. R. HARRIS
May 1990

NOTES ON CONTRIBUTORS

PAUL J. CROSS joined the staff of the British Library in 1986. He has worked in the Placer's section and in the Divisional Office of the Humanities and Social Sciences Division.

P. R. HARRIS was on the staff of the Library from 1947 to 1986. From 1966 he was in charge successively of the Acquisitions Branch, the English and North European Branch and the West European Branch. His booklet on the Reading Room was published in 1979.

F. J. HILL was on the staff of the Library from 1947 to 1984. From 1957 he was in charge of the Subject Index. He edited a completely revised edition of Arundell Esdaile's *National Libraries of the World* (1957).

DR ALEC HYATT KING was on the staff of the Library from 1934 to 1976. From 1944 he was in charge of the Music Room (later called the Music Library). His books include *Some British Collectors of Music, c.1600–1960* (1963), *Printed Music in the British Museum* (1979), *A Wealth of Music in the British Library and the British Museum* (1983), and *Musical Pursuits* (1987).

DR K. A. MANLEY is on the staff of the Institute of Historical Research of London University. He is the editor of *Library History*.

ILSE STERNBERG has been on the staff of the Library since 1973. She is in charge of Overseas English Collections.

LIST OF ILLUSTRATIONS

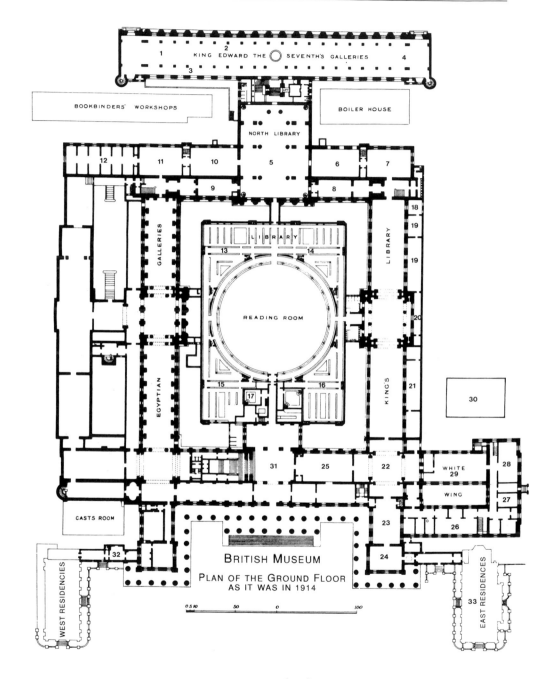

KING EDWARD THE SEVENTH'S GALLERIES

BOOKBINDERS' WORKSHOPS

BOILER HOUSE

NORTH LIBRARY

GALLERIES

EGYPTIAN

LIBRARY

READING ROOM

LIBRARY

KING'S

WHITE

WING

CASTS ROOM

WEST RESIDENCIES

EAST RESIDENCIES

BRITISH MUSEUM

PLAN OF THE GROUND FLOOR
AS IT WAS IN 1914

1 Music Room on the mezzanine floor above (from *c.*1920).

2 Map Room on mezzanine floor above (from *c.*1920).

3 State Paper Room (later called the Official Publications Library) on subground floor below.

4 Copyright Receipt Office on subground floor below (*c.*1920–1974).

5 North Library (originally called the Large Room); built 1838, enlarged 1914, remodelled 1938.

6 One of the Reading Rooms, 1838–57; subsequently the Music Room, 1860s–*c.*1920; then used by cataloguing staff and called the Old Music Room; now called Room A1. On the floor above, after the rebuilding of the 1930s, was created Room A2, which was used by staff working on the revision of the General Catalogue (GK II) until the 1950s. It was subsequently used by other cataloguing staff.

7 One of the Reading Rooms, 1838–57; subsequently the Catalogue Room until the 1950s; then the Title Room until the 1970s; subsequently used by acquisitions staff and called Room T1. On the floor above, after the reconstruction of the 1930s was the Title Room, until it was moved to the floor below in the 1950s. Subsequently used by cataloguing staff and called Room T2.

8 The Banksian Room (Room B1); this contained the Banksian Library until the 1960s, and was also used by acquisitions staff. On the floor above, after the reconstruction of the 1930s, was Room B2 which was used by cataloguing and acquisitions staff. Above that was Room B3 which housed the Catalogue Shop from the 1930s.

9 The Cracherode Room (Room C1); this accommodated the Cracherode Library, and was also used by cataloguing staff. On the floor above, after the reconstruction of the 1930s,

was Room C2 which was used by the staff of the Subject Index, and subsequently by cataloguing staff.

10 Supplementary Room 1 (Room S1). During the 1930s three more rooms (S3, 5 and 7) were built above.

11 Supplementary Room 2 (Room S2). During the 1930s three more rooms (S4, 6 and 8) were built above.

12 The Arch Room. Unchanged since it was built *c.*1840.

13 NW Quadrant. Built 1857; rebuilt in the 1930s.

14 NE Quadrant. Built 1857; rebuilt in the 1930s.

15 SW Quadrant. Built 1857; destroyed by bombing 1941; rebuilt in the 1950s.

16 SE Quadrant. Built 1857. An extra floor was built on top *c.*1920.

17 Site of the Copyright Receipt Office, 1857–*c.*1899.

18 Keeper's (later Principal Keeper's) Office. Built 1847.

19 Keeper's Ante-Room.

20 Hebrew Library.

21 Oriental Library. (Rooms 19–21 which were built in the 1840s were originally called the Long Room.)

22 Manuscripts Saloon.

23 Manuscripts Middle Room.

24 Manuscripts South Room. (The Middle and South Rooms were used as the Reading Rooms from 1827–38.)

25 Grenville Library.

26 Manuscripts Students Room.

27 Copyright Receipt Office, *c.*1899–*c.*1920.

28 Newspaper Reading Room, *c.*1885–1932.

29 Newspaper storage room, *c.*1885–1932.

30 The 'Drill Hall'.

31 Front Hall.

32 Director's Study, 1856–early 1930s. (Subsequently the Director had his study in one of the West Residences.)

33 Duty Officer's Flat. (Also known as the Rota Flat.)

THE SHELVING AND CLASSIFICATION
OF PRINTED BOOKS

F. J. HILL

I · THE FOUNDATION; THE LIBRARY IN MONTAGU HOUSE

THIS ACCOUNT OF one aspect of work in the British Museum Library and the British Library was derived from numerous sources, many of which are listed in the notes. To these were added personal accounts and reminiscences, particularly from the older members of the staff. In the late 1940s and 1950s almost all the Library staff were still accommodated in the original Bloomsbury building; contact with colleagues was easy and frequent, and much interest and assistance were forthcoming and most gratefully received. Especially helpful were C. B. Oldman, Principal Keeper of Printed Books from 1948 to 1959, and A. F. Johnson, who for many years was the Placer of books.

The history of the British Museum Library and its principal collections to 1943 is to be found in Dr Arundell Esdaile's *The British Museum Library* (1946), and, to the advent of the British Library, in Edward Miller's *That Noble Cabinet. A history of the British Museum* (1973). The present work aims to show how the collections of printed material received at the foundation and subsequently were housed and arranged, how specialised collections have been formed and accommodated within the Library, and how the Library as a whole has been contained, organised, and made accessible. After more than two centuries as part of the British Museum, ownership of the Library collections passed to the British Library in 1973, although at the time of writing (1989) the collections are still largely housed in the building of the British Museum. The problem of housing this vast and ever-increasing mass of material was a major factor in the creation of the British Library, and the completion of the first stage of a new library building, planned for the early 1990s, will bring relief to Museum and Library alike.

The Act of foundation of 1753 names two collections of printed books, that of Sir Hans Sloane (1660–1753), physician, scientist and collector, with his manuscripts and other material, and that of Major Arthur Edwards.[1] Sloane's library, rich in works on medicine and science, contained much material on other subjects as well, and until 1800 it formed the greater part of the working collection of printed books. But among Sloane's books, and in collections added later to the library, there were many duplicates, and until 1832 sales were held to dispose of unwanted items. A manuscript catalogue of Sloane's printed books, with his pressmarks, is preserved in the Library (Sloane MS 3972c), and makes it possible to identify at least some of his volumes: the pressmarks consist of a letter and a number (e.g. R. 2355 in Gruterus (J.) *Iani Gruteri Pericula, id est, elegiarum libri IV*, 1587, 1213.l.5.(2.)). Other books from Sloane's library can be identified from alchemical and astronomical signs, used as a code to record the price paid for books.[2]

Major Arthur Edwards, a Fellow of the Society of Antiquaries, died in 1743, and left £7,000 to erect a building to house the library formed by Sir Robert Cotton. This had become Crown property in 1700, had been damaged in a fire at Ashburnham House in 1731, and had been subsequently removed to Westminster School. Edwards also left his own printed books, nearly 4,000 in number and mainly antiquarian in character, to be added to the Cotton collection, and both were incorporated into the Museum by the Act of foundation. A report, dated 13 August 1756, drawn up by Matthew Maty, the Keeper of Printed Books, with the help of Henry Rimius, and submitted to the Trustees before the removal of the books to the Museum, gave the number of volumes as about four thousand.[3] A catalogue prepared for the Trustees by the Reverend Richard Widmore exists in manuscript (C.120.h.2); the arrangement is first by language, then size, and finally by author. Each entry includes a number, but the numbers are not consecutive and do not appear to be connected with any subject classification in the original arrangement. From the pressmarks it is possible to identify some of the books, which are now dispersed in the Old Library.

Examples are:

Solleysel (Jacques de) *The Compleat Horseman or Perfect Farrier* (London, 1717) 779.f.1.
　　Pressmark in book and in Widmore's catalogue: 2535.

S., J., *Capt. Fortification and Military Discipline* (London, 1688,89) 534.d.22.
　　Pressmark in book and in Widmore's catalogue: 3656.

At its foundation the Museum was established in Montagu House, Bloomsbury, which had been rebuilt after a fire in 1686. The public were not admitted until 1759, the period following the purchase of the house in 1754 having been taken up with the removal and arrangement of the collections.

A report presented to the Trustees' Committee on 3 July 1755 stated that the 'admeasurements' of the various collections of printed books and manuscripts were:

Sr Hans Sloane's Books	4,600 ft superficial
Harleian Collection	1,700 do

[3]

Cottonian Library	384 do
Major Edwards's do.	576 do[4]

Twelve rooms on the ground floor, together with two other rooms, were allotted to the Printed Books, while the Manuscripts and Natural History collections occupied the first floor, an arrangement which left sufficient space for accessions of printed books for the next seventy years. Sloane's printed books filled the range of six rooms on the north side of the house, and further small rooms at the west end were used for the printed books of the Royal Library, which had been given by George II in 1757, and at the east end for shelving gifts received and books deposited by the Stationers' Company. Major Edwards's books were in a room to the east of the vestibule in the south front; he had requested in his will that they should be placed 'in some By-room or Corner' of the building to be provided for the Cottonian Library. The Trustees had ordered the books to be numbered before their removal, and the numbers to be entered in Widmore's catalogue; but those of Sloane, if not Edwards's as well, were rearranged on removal. The former had been inspected at Chelsea by a committee of the Trustees, and found 'disposed in a Very Irregular Manner, with little regard either to the Subjects or even size of them', and it was resolved on 13 December 1755 'That the Books in Sir Hans Sloane's and Major Edwards's Libraries be placed upon the Shelves according to their respective Faculties, observing the Sizes of the said Books within the said Faculties, and placing Sir Hans Sloane's Mss. either in a Separate Room, or in distinct divisions of the Shelves of the same Room Separate from the Printed Books.' The rearrangement was not to be commenced until shelving had been constructed and staff appointed to carry out the work.[5] The books of the Old Royal Library have numerical pressmarks dating from before their removal from St James's Palace, while a later system, introduced by the librarian Richard Bentley about 1694, appears in the early catalogues.[6] No new pressmarks were given to printed books of the Old Royal Library before 1790; the Old Royal and Cotton manuscripts are still shelved by the pressmarks which they already had when received in the Museum.

Of the other important collections received before the arrival of the King's Library in 1828, five were retained intact and are still shelved as entities. These are the Thomason Tracts, purchased by George III for the Museum in 1762, the plays bequeathed by David Garrick in 1779, the library of the Reverend C. M. Cracherode bequeathed in 1799, the collections of Charles Burney, purchased from his executors in 1818, and the works (mainly on natural history) bequeathed by Sir Joseph Banks in 1820. The books on British biography bequeathed by Sir William Musgrave in 1799, were originally kept together but they were later dispersed.

[4]

The library formed by George III and given to the Museum in 1823 by George IV (the King's Library) still occupies the gallery erected to receive it; it was placed there on its arrival in 1828. The Grenville Library (bequeathed in 1847) was also allocated a special room in which it is still housed. Later benefactions, however, have rarely consisted of entire collections, and none has been comparable in size. With ever-increasing pressure on space, special rooms have not been given to them. The majority have special catalogues.[7]

The difficulties and delays involved in the compilation of the general author catalogue of printed books have been related by Esdaile, Miller and A. H. Chaplin (in his *GK: 150 years of the General Catalogue*, 1987). Not until the printing of the General Catalogue between 1880 and 1905 was this problem solved. No subject guide was available until G. K. Fortescue's *Subject Index*, which listed selectively additions to the Library from 1881. During the first century of the existence of the Museum, readers were often taken to the shelves to help them find books on particular subjects, and Thomas Watts, when Placer, complained to Panizzi (the Keeper) about the frequent interruptions to his work resulting from this. Moreover, the historical value of keeping collections of books intact, and the encouragement which it gave to potential benefactors, had not yet been fully realised. It was natural therefore for the printed books to be arranged by subjects and a scheme with broad groupings was compiled by the Reverend Samuel Harper, Keeper of Printed Books, 1765–1803, and the Reverend Samuel Ayscough, Assistant Keeper, 1787–1805. Ayscough had already compiled classified indexes to the Sloane, Birch and Additional manuscripts in the Museum, (1782), to the *Monthly Review* (1786), and to other works. Harper's and Ayscough's 'synthetical arrangement' for the Printed Books, to replace the original arrangement used when Sloane's and Major Edwards's books were brought to the Museum, was ready for use by 1790, and the reshelving and pressmarking of the books went on until about 1805.[8] The result was that the foundation collections were dispersed, though an undated note by Sir Henry Ellis (Keeper of Printed Books, 1806–12, of Manuscripts, 1812–27, and Principal Librarian, 1827–56) attempts to preserve the record of their provenance, as follows:

> *Explanation of the Stamps in the Museum Books*
> The Square black mark denotes Sir Hans Sloane's Books only.
> The Books purchased have an Oval Mark in Red.
> The Books presented have a square mark in Yellow.
> The Blue square mark denotes the Royal Collection.
> The square Mark Red, Major Edwards's Books.
> Dr Birch's Books the square Mark Green.
> Mr Cracherode's the mark red, with C.M.C.[9]

[5]

Unfortunately the same stamps were later used for other material, so that their evidence on the provenance of books is not conclusive.

The outline of the 'synthetical arrangement' appears in print in the *Synopsis of the Contents of the British Museum* (first edition, 1808), and shows the distribution of subjects between the fourteen rooms which the Library then occupied. It was as follows:

Room	I	Philology, memoirs of academies, classics, descriptions of museums.
	II	Cracherode Library.
	III	Poetry, novels, letters, polygraphy.
	IV	History (ancient and modern), geography, travels.
	V	Modern history continued.
	VI	Modern history continued, biography, diplomacy, heraldry, archaeology, numismatics, bibliography.
	VII	Medicine, surgery, trade and commerce, arts, mathematics, astronomy.
	VIII	Medicine continued, natural history.
	IX	Politics, philosophy (moral and natural), chemistry, natural history.
	X	(The Reading Room) Ecclesiastical history, jurisprudence, divinity.
	XI	Divinity, continued.
	XII	Sermons, political tracts, King's Pamphlets (i.e. the Thomason Tracts).
	XIII	Acta Sanctorum, Musgrave's biographical collection, reviews, music.
	XIV	Parliamentary records, gazettes, newspapers.

Together with this outline was included an 'analytical syllabus', occupying eleven pages; it had five main classes: Theology, Jurisprudence, Sciences and Arts, History, and Belles-Lettres, with a total of 176 sub-divisions. Examples of the sub-divisions are:

	Room	*Cases*
THEOLOGY		
Sacred Writings		
Text and versions of the Scriptures	XI	AA*, BB, CC, DD, DD*
	XII	A in part

Commentators on the Old and New Testaments	XI	W, X, Y, Z
Sacred criticism on the text, style, divine authority, etc., of the Scriptures	XI	V
BELLES LETTRES		
Rhetoric		
Treatises on rhetoric	I	M, S, N
Orators, ancient and modern	I	O, P
Poetry		
Works on the origin and art of poetry	I	Q above
Greek poets	I	Q below, R

At the end is added the note 'In this analytical syllabus the Cracherodean Library has been omitted; the greater part of the books in that collection being alphabetically arranged.'

Many books still bear the Montagu House pressmark in pencil, or, less frequently, in ink, on the titlepage. Examples are:

Allen (Charles) *A.M. A New and Improved History of England*
   (London, 1793)   597.b.10
   Montagu House pressmark 5 I a.

Hume (David) *the Historian. Histoire d'Angleterre*
   (Amsterdam, 1769)   597.c.11
   Montagu House pressmark Gal. 5 B e.

Pisani (Ottavio) *Astrologia* (Antverpiae, 1613)   798.l.20
   Montagu House pressmark 7 EE k.

In these pressmarks the figure indicates the room, the capital letter refers to the press, and the small letter to the shelf. The prefix Gal. indicates galleries in some of the rooms. At this time and for many years after, the books were not labelled, and bore the pressmark on the titlepage or half-title only. Then, as now, open access for readers was limited to books on the reading room reference shelves; the 1818 *Synopsis*, describing the situation of the Library, says firmly 'Strangers are not admitted into these apartments, as the mere sight of the outside of books cannot convey either instruction or amusement'.

Accessions from copyright deposit and gift were not numerous during this period, with the exception of Cracherode's 4,500 volumes; the library of Sir Joseph Banks, some 16,000 volumes, bequeathed in 1820, remained at his house until room could be found for it in 1827, when it was placed, not on the ground floor of Montagu House with the other printed books, but in rooms V–VII on the first floor where manuscripts had been accommodated until their removal to the new building. The right to legal deposit, under successive Copyright Acts, which had passed to the Museum with the gift of the Old Royal Library in 1757, was very ineffectively exercised at this time. The books were collected on behalf of the Library by the Stationers' Company, and the few items received were added to the Old Royal Library, the books of which were not dispersed until about 1790. At first, books received by legal deposit were stamped on the spine with a rose and crown, to show that they had been acquired by the royal privilege. The latest publication so stamped which has been traced is one of 1810 (854.b.19.) though according to Baber the practice continued until 1814.[10]

II · THE KING'S LIBRARY AND THE NORTH WING

Measures to provide a new building, with more space both for readers and collections, and to reduce the risk of fire which prevailed in Montagu House, were considered by the Trustees in 1821. Two years later, the library formed by George III (the 'King's Library') was acquired, adding 65,000 books and 19,000 pamphlets to the 125,000 volumes already in the building, and an extension became imperative. Robert (later Sir Robert) Smirke drew up plans for the present building which was to replace Montagu House, and form the four sides of a quadrangle. The east wing, including the King's Library, was erected between 1823 and 1826, and the books were brought from Kensington Palace (to which they had been moved from Buckingham Palace) in 1828.

It was some time before the presses in the King's Library were glazed, and still longer before all the books were adequately repaired and bound. They were arranged by the Reverend H. H. Baber, Keeper of Printed Books, 1812– 37, and for the first time in the Museum the presses were numbered, rather than lettered: the shelves continued to be distinguished by a small letter, and, again for the first time, individual books received separate numbers.

As the collection was a historic entity, no provision was made in the shelf marking for accessions to be added. The books are in 304 presses, arranged by subject and size. On the east side, starting from the south, the subjects are history, beginning with geography and universal history, ancient history, ecclesiastical history, and continuing with the history of individual countries. The sequence is broken by nine presses in the centre of the room containing early editions of the classics, Caxtons and other early printed books, and plays. Then follow the remainder of history, antiquities, manners, customs, monuments, numismatics and inscriptions, heraldry, biography and literary history, the transactions of learned societies, and pamphlets. On the west side, from the south, the arrangement is theology, law, philosophy; a further collection, in the centre bay, of editions of the ancient classics; then, in the northern half of the west side, fine arts, useful arts, sports, literature, miscellaneous writers, plays and tracts. The arrangement of books in the gallery corresponds roughly to that on the ground floor. The manuscripts received with the King's Library, originally housed with the printed books, gave rise to a violent dispute between Panizzi and Madden (the Keeper of Manuscripts), and were finally removed to the Department of Manuscripts in 1841. The geographical collection, both printed and manuscript, was housed in table cases on the floor of the room, and later removed to the Map Room. (*See* VIII, below.)

In 1833 the Trustees succeeded in obtaining Treasury sanction for the erection of the North Wing, which was completed to Smirke's plans in 1837. A scheme for the removal of the library, now numbering about 163,000 volumes from Montagu House to the new wing, was drawn up by Baber and dated 24 June 1837, three weeks before his retirement. In it he was able to make use of experience gained when he had arranged the Burney and the Colt Hoare collections and the King's Library. His proposals, which remained effective for a century and a quarter, have had a wide and enduring effect on the form of the Library, providing as they did a basis for the later work of Watts. (For the details of his plan *see below* pp.10–12.)

He concluded that the most suitable system of pressmarking would be a continuation of the numerical one introduced for the King's Library, though using only press and shelfmarks, and without numbering the books individually. Though a general classified arrangement was desired for the bulk of the Library, the value of individual collections was already more fully appreciated than in the past. Sir Henry Ellis, then Principal Librarian, in his evidence to the Select Committee of 1835, was asked whether the retention of such collections intact was not prejudicial to good arrangement and classification. He replied that there was no objection to it, as long as individual books could be readily found: it was not desirable, however, to construct a new building with the primary view of preserving such collections intact.[11]

The work of superintending the removal fell to Baber's successor, Panizzi. Those of Baber's recommendations which were adopted were: the arrangement by size of the books, the formation of reference collections, and the shelving together of the tracts. Happily, the Cracherode, Banksian, and Colt Hoare collections were not dispersed. For the removal, additional assistants were recruited, among them being William Brenchley Rye, George Bullen, Edward Edwards, John Humffreys Parry, and Thomas Watts. The work was mainly organised by Watts. It was begun in January 1838 and the actual move was completed by the middle of 1840. It was so efficiently performed that only books actually in transit were at any time unavailable to readers.

The system by which the books were reclassified was compiled by Watts, and still remains effective for the books concerned, which form the collection now known as the Old Library. Their original arrangement in the north wing is shown in printed plans preserved in the Map Library, which give the press-numbers in each room.[12] There are two plans, one for ground floor presses, and one for those in the gallery, and each bears the manuscript note 'Library as arranged after its completion at the end of 1838'. Printed notes state, for the gound floor presses 'The numbers on the cases commence on the left hand side of the doors as you proceed from the Royal Library,' and for the gallery presses, 'The numbers commence on the cases on the east side of the north east angle in each room'. The Supplementary Rooms and the Large Room (now the North Library) had presses in projecting bays on the ground floor, with the gallery running round the outer wall only; the Arch Room had not yet been built. A manuscript copy of the classification scheme shows how subjects were grouped in each room. The arrangement was as follows:

Ground Floor

1–216	King's Library	
305–364	Reading Rooms (later the	Reference books. These pressmarks
365–430	Catalogue Room and Old Music Room respectively)	are now eliminated, except 305–309 containing a long series of works on ecclesiastical law and church history, which, however, have been moved to this pressmark more recently, and are not a survival of the reference collection in the old reading rooms; and 356.m.1.–358.b.5. (with gaps), now in the Official Publications Library, a series of Bills, Petitions, Acts, etc., of Great Britain, and probably part of the original reference collection.
431–462	Banksian Room	Part of Sir Joseph Banks's library; the remainder, with other books on natural history, being in the gallery of this room.
463–656	Large Room	Bibles, theology, law, philosophy, mathematics, medicine, art, topography, geography, history,

		numismatics, archaeology, heraldry and genealogy, encyclopaedias, biography, bibliography, philology, collected works, drama, large books, (mainly illustrated, 645–651), and Latin and Greek classics.
657–688	Cracherode Room	Cracherode Collection and other material.
689–841	Supplementary Rooms	A further series of books classified in the same way as those at 463–656, but with more detail in some sections (*see* Appendix B).

Gallery

217–304	King's Library	
842–890 ⎫ 891–952 ⎭	Reading Rooms	Theology, modern Greek, sermons, prayers, law, Romansch language, French dialects, Armenian. French Revolution Tracts, miscellaneous tracts and series, B tracts, theatre, periodicals.
953–990	Banksian Room	Geology, natural history, natural science, miscellaneous works, periodicals, agriculture, astronomy, topography and travels, geology (Banks's books, 953–965).
991–1066	Large Room	Poetry, English and classical, classical drama, Bibles, theology, political economy, commerce, education, chemistry, cookery, medicine, sports and games, music, art, topography and travels, history, poetry.
1067–1104	Cracherode Room	Poetry (continued), fiction, romances, epistles, rhetoric, literary history (pressmarks 1095–1104 not used).
1105–1159	First Supplementary Room	Bibles, theology, law, philosophy, political economy, chemistry, geology, agriculture, natural history, hospital reports, fiction, libraries, series.
1150–1213	Second Supplementary Room	Poetry, medicine (here with 17 subdivisions, unlike earlier pressmarks

[11]

for this subject), history and politics, biography, speeches, collected works, fiction, children's books, philology.

Thus the Old Library, other than special collections and reading-room books, occupied presses 463–656 and 689–1213. The classification is repeated four times, twice on the ground floor and twice in the gallery; with small books in the gallery and larger ones below. The press numbers in the gallery were distinct from those on the ground floor, though the subjects were grouped together. This differs from later practice in the Iron Library, where a pressmark could be continued from an upper floor press to one below. The ground floor of the reading rooms was occupied with reference books, and the gallery with a miscellaneous assortment of infrequently used works. The pressmarks in the gallery of the Large Room were continued into the Cracherode Room, where the ground floor contained Cracherode's books. There were, then, in fact two sequences of classification, that in the Large Room, and that in the Supplementary Rooms.

In this arrangement no pressmarks were provided for accessions, and a further sequence had to be commenced at once for them. It might be expected that all books brought from Montagu House would be found in the first classified sequence (presses 463–644 and 991–1095), but this is not the case; they are in fact found in both sequences, in the third sequence (to be mentioned below) and also in the Iron Library. There must have been a good deal of rearrangement at various times, and early sequences of books have later accessions mingled with them.

The North Wing provided space for only 20,000 volumes more than the old house, and accessions were now arriving at the rate of 4,000 to 5,000 volumes annually. The wing was extended by the completion in 1841 of the Arch Room – the only part of the North Wing still remaining substantially unaltered in appearance and structure. All the Arch Room presses were originally unglazed but those on the ground floor have since been glazed and used for special collections. The shelf numeration continued that of the second Supplementary Room:

Ground Floor: 1214–1349
First Gallery: 1350–1499
Second Gallery: 1500–1699

The scheme follows the general plan of the earlier ones, with two subject sequences originally on the ground floor, and one in the lower gallery. Many of the books are copyright accessions of the nineteenth century, but there are earlier works mingled with them, including those already mentioned, bearing Montagu House pressmarks. Others bear earlier Old Library pressmarks, and were moved to relieve congestion elsewhere, or to conform more closely with the classification, e.g.:

> *Tryphiodorus* London, 1791
> Montagu House pressmark: I. Q. i.
> Then at 997.k.22. (Aeschylus; this is incorrect, so removed to 1348.h.15. [Greek verse].)

Others again have been removed from the Iron Library, showing that at one time the Iron Library was reserved for modern books, and that there was some transfer of older books to the Old Library, and also that older books received were placed in the Old Library, e.g.:

> Clarke (R.) *The Life of Horatio, Viscount Nelson*, 1813. Donated, 1882, and placed at 10817.bb.14. (British naval and military biography). Removed about 1905 to 1452.f.12.

The open shelves which now remain in the Arch Room (1350–1457 on the first gallery; 1342–9 and 1470–1499 on the second) include the only books in the north wing still shelved where they were placed on their arrival in the library over a century ago. Pressmarks from 1500 were not taken into use until 1964, when they were allotted to non-rare accessions published before 1900, regardless of subject and language, subdivision being according to size.

In the arrangement of the Old Library, the smallest books were placed on the topmost shelf of each press, with successively larger ones on the lower shelves. For books too large to be accommodated in this way, a further series of pressmarks was introduced, 1700–1899, with about twenty-three subject-divisions, corresponding approximately to those in the rest of the Old Library. Large books are encountered much more frequently in some subjects than in others, so not every subject is represented in this series. A manuscript copy of the shelf arrangement survives in the Department of Printed Books. A further expedient occasionally adopted when placing large books was to duplicate an existing pressmark, that for the large volumes being distinguished by an asterisk.

The only significant additions made in recent years to the Old Library were accessions of Welsh fiction at 872 (now discontinued, as accessions are placed at new pressmarks in the General Library), and English and foreign books printed before 1640 and not sufficiently valuable to be kept in locked cases. These were added at the end, in presses 1471–1482 from about 1930 until about 1965. Incunabula were removed from the Old Library, and from other open shelves, by Proctor (*see below*, p.32), and they, together with some other books, particularly items from the Old Royal Library, were transferred to secure storage. Series still in progress and requiring additional space at intervals have also been removed. Others again were evidently transferred to the General Library in or shortly before 1914 from shelves in the Large Room, when it was reconstructed to form the North Library, e.g.: Jerome, *Omnia opera*, (Parisiis, 1609), from the Old Royal Library; later at 1013.h.9.; now at 3670.e.10. Otherwise the Old Library remains in content much as it was in 1850. But the North Wing contains the main staff workrooms of the Department of Printed Books, and the great increase in staff numbers since the construction of the wing, particularly since 1945, led to the removal of most of the books, and reconstruction of the rooms. Again, the more valuable books have been placed in secure storage, while the remainder are dispersed in various parts of the North Wing and the Iron Library.

The North Wing, when completed, had space for 240,000 volumes, and the total length of shelving in the building was about thirteen miles. The Arch Room could only accommodate the intake of a few years, while with the introduction of the steam printing press and the energetic application of the Copyright Act by Panizzi from 1850, the number of publications received increased enormously. Great numbers of volumes lay awaiting shelving. As an immediate palliative, the Long Room (Fig. 1) was constructed against the east wall of the King's Library, and completed about 1850. This was the last of Sir Robert Smirke's work at the Museum: it was designed to hold 85,000 volumes, and with its iron gallery and shelving on two floors was a modest forerunner of the Iron Library designed by his brother, Sydney. But it was at best an afterthought, and Watts, then Placer, said that the architect had cobbled the Museum. Nevertheless, it was effective and inconspicuous. The books were removed by stages from the northern half of the Long Room between 1938 and 1970, and the area was converted into offices for the Department of Printed Books.

Placing – the arranging of accessions in subject order on the shelves – was at first carried out by the Keeper of Printed Books, Watts being the first Assistant to whom the task was delegated. Realising that the classification which he had already drawn up to receive the Library from Montagu House did not allow the addition of accessions in the places most suited to them, he drew up a further scheme, which remained in use until 1964. Watts's classification (which is described in Richard Garnett's *Essays in Librarianship and Bibliography*, 1899), covers presses 3000–12991, and has ten principal divisions: Theology, Jurisprudence, Natural History and Medicine, Archaeology and Arts, Philosophy, History, Geography, Biography, Belles-Lettres, and

1 The Long Room, built in the 1840s (*Illustrated London News*, 7 June 1851).

Philology. The schedules were never officially published, as the staff used manuscript or typewritten copies, amended as necessary, but the complete list of headings and subheadings was set out by John Macfarlane in *Library Administration* (London, 1898), where they numbered 515. As space became increasingly scarce, subheadings were amalgamated, though a few new ones were introduced; the total number at the end was 380. Presses were numbered consecutively within each subdivision, and spare numbers left at the end of each to permit future growth, proportioned originally by estimation, which gave the classification the name 'Elastic System'. Its date of origin is reflected in the ample subdivision accorded to such subjects as theology, jurisprudence and history; medicine is unsatisfactory by modern standards, while engineering, science, etc., have very little subdivision. Within the press or presses allotted to individual subjects, arrangement was simply by size, and in order of accession. Each shelf was distinguished by a letter or letters, but individual books were not further identified by number or letter, so that it was possible to arrange the contents of a shelf in logical order, and to insert later accessions without having to alter the marks. This still applies to books in the Reading Room and North Library, but in the General Library it led to confusion, particularly with tract volumes, in which a number of slim items are bound together, and located by further numeration within the volume. The addition of 'third marks', or numbers for individual books was therefore begun in 1875, and completed early in the present century, apart from works in progress, which remained without third marks until shelved apart in 1911. (Panizzi had had 'third marks' added to the books of the Old Library in the 1840s.)

There is no subject notation in the classification apart from the pressmarks themselves. The system has no mnemonics, but the same order, in greater or less detail as required, is preserved in all headings having geographical subdivision. These are: religious controversy, church history, religious biography (grouped, with theological bibliography, under theology), law, archaeology, politics, education, history, topography, biography, poetry, drama, collected works, fiction, and philology. An outline of the classification, with examples of the varying degrees of subdivision, is given in Appendix D. There was no subject index to the schedules, beyond an outline in manuscript but the printed *Subject Index of Modern Works added to the Library of the British Museum* provided a guide to previous practice.

Another classification scheme prepared for the Trustees was intended to be used in the proposed classed catalogue of printed books, which was begun in 1824, but abandoned ten years later. Its author, the Reverend Thomas Hartwell Horne, was well-known as a bibliographer, and the work, entitled *Outlines for the Classification of a Library*, was printed for the Trustees in 1825. It was a modified form of the scheme which Horne had already used in his classed catalogue of the Harleian Manuscripts, but it was not, in its printed form, expressly suited to shelf arrangement. In a foreword, Horne traced the growth of earlier classification systems, such as those of Bacon and Naudé: his own was based on that of Brunet. In its principal classes it resembles Watts's 'Elastic System', except that the order of the third and fourth classes (philosophy and arts) is reversed. The principal classes are: religion, jurisprudence, philosophy, arts and trades, history, and literature. But the 'Synthetical Arrangement' of Harper and Ayscough, Horne's *Outlines*, and Watts's 'Elastic System', while they have features in common, and a common origin, do not represent successive stages in the development of a system. That Watts owed much to Brunet is shown by a comparison between the two (*see* Appendix C), but here again there was evidently no intention on the part of Watts to do more than profit from the experience of Brunet, for frequently, in main classes and in detail, there are differences which could not have arisen in a deliberate attempt to follow Brunet.

Accessions were placed by Watts according to the 'Elastic System' in the Long Room. Although the idea of fixed location was firmly established in the Museum, it was seen that movement of the books would be necessary at some time, and, both here and later in the Iron Library, the presses were made of a standard size (but unfortunately not in the North Wing when it was rebuilt in the 1930s). They were numbered, and the numbers, with shelfmarks, applied to the books. Had it been realised that the numeration could have been applied directly to the books, leaving the presses unnumbered, greater flexibility would have been available when any part of the book stock had to be moved. In fact the movements, especially frequent after the Second World War in the face of congestion, reconstruction, and war damage, made it impossible for each new number to commence in a new press, and the presses themselves ceased to be numbered, except in the King's Library and the Arch Room.

III · THE IRON LIBRARY; PLACING PRACTICE; PROPOSALS FOR A NEW BUILDING

In 1852 the Trustees took steps to provide further space for the Library, which had grown from 235,000 volumes in 1838 to 435,000 in 1848, and in 1857 the Reading Room and surrounding Iron Library were completed. The details of their planning and construction have been given by Esdaile:[13] the Iron Library had an estimated capacity of 1,300,000 volumes on twenty-five miles of shelving, and the Reading Room 60,000 volumes, of which 20,000 were on

[17]

2 The North-West Quadrant of the book-stacks, built 1857, showing the moving presses hung from the girders, in front of the original presses, and the gridded iron floors which allowed light to filter down from the glass roof to the basement (BL Archives).

open shelves directly accessible to readers. Panizzi's estimate that the Iron Library would contain the accessions of the next thirty years was correct, after which further space was provided by introducing moving presses (1887), giving room for an additional 900,000 volumes (Fig. 2). The moving presses were fitted in front of fixed presses in the ironwork, and each bore the same number as the fixed press it covered, distinguished by 0 as a prefix. The moving press was drawn forward or pushed sideways to give access to the fixed shelves behind it.[14]

The next step came in 1920, with the construction of an extra floor above the South-East Quadrant, but similar treatment of the other quadrants was

3 One of the Supplementary Rooms, as rebuilt in the 1930s, showing the moving presses hung from the girders (BL Archives).

considered impracticable because of the difficulty of imposing a further load on the existing structure. In 1931, therefore, the Supplementary Rooms were converted into additional stacks by inserting three intermediate floors, the eight rooms thus created being equipped with moving presses, which provided the equivalent of 3,000 single-sided presses. Unfortunately the narrow clearance between the presses installed often caused the movement of one to displace or even damage books in the next (Fig. 3). Alternate presses were therefore removed, reducing the capacity of the rooms by almost one half, but even so they were not satisfactory, the shelves being too narrow for the books of the general library. A certain proportion of wider fixed shelves had been provided, but Watts's classification did not make provision for broken sequences to accommodate large books. The presses were left moveable at first, which made access difficult, and books continued to be displaced, particularly from incompletely filled shelves. All the presses were therefore unhung in 1955–56 and arranged in fixed rows on the floor, with adquate gangways and lighting, but later still all the storage shelving was removed, and the rooms converted into staff working areas.

Reconstruction of the Iron Library was begun in 1932, the books from areas of building work being removed temporarily to the newly equipped Supplementary Rooms. By 1939, two of the four quadrants had been rebuilt with additional floors, independent of natural lighting, and providing greater protection from fire and dirt (Fig. 4)[15] It had been expected that the reconstruction of the quadrants would provide space for the accessions of the remainder of the twentieth century, but this estimate soon proved too optimistic.

Congestion in the Library became more and more serious. The rows of books on some of the deeper shelves were doubled, and many books were stored out of sequence in basements in the original Smirke building and in the King Edward VII building, causing difficulties and delay in the service to readers. It was impossible to place some accessions with their subjects, and the problem was on such a scale that the usual remedy – using temporary shelving erected near at hand until a rearrangement of the part of the Library affected should provide more space – could not be applied. A new series of pressmarks, commencing with 20,000, was therefore introduced in 1931, when space became available in the reconstructed Supplementary Rooms, and books which through lack of space could not be placed with their subject were shelved there. There was no classified arrangement, except that children's books were placed together. Some large series were removed to the 20,000 pressmark from congested parts of the Library. Because growth points in the General Library became successively unavailable, the later 20,000 presses contain a far wider range of subjects than the earlier. But in 1940 the number of books added began to diminish, and ceased soon after, since space had become available in the first of the reconstructed quadrants. The number of volumes remaining at the 20,000 pressmark is roughly 20,000.

In the years following the end of the Second World War, when available space had been reduced by war damage, and the task of replacing destroyed stock was being energetically pursued, congestion was dealt with by adding temporary shelving at growth points, and by a general process of easing out – a virtual rearrangement of the whole of the General Library, leaving space at the end of each subject for the estimated accessions of ten years. This was finished by 1955, by which time the South-West Quadrant which had been destroyed in 1941 had been rebuilt. New permanent shelving was installed in the North-East Quadrant (the shell of which had been completed at the

4 The North-West Quadrant of the book-stacks, as rebuilt in the 1930s (cf. Fig. 2)
(BL Archives).

beginning of the war) and improvements made to the South-East Quadrant, which was still awaiting reconstruction. But the decision in 1975, after many years of debate and delay on the part of successive governments, to construct a new building for the Library at St Pancras, brought a final halt to any major improvements to the Library accommodation at Bloomsbury.

As already mentioned, parallel sequences of pressmarks were used to shelve books on the same subject in gallery and ground floor presses of the North Wing. The Iron Library in its original form had three floors, the General Library occupying the first and ground floors. In a large part of this area the presses on both floors, and occasionally even in the basement (being separated only by iron gratings) were treated as single units. This continued the practice of parallel shelving in the North Wing, but was inconvenient for placing accessions. First floor shelves were lettered from a to dd, those below (on the ground floor) from de to g, or occasionally to m, and basement shelves, when the sequence was continued to them, from r to z. The rest of the basement was occupied by Periodical Publications, large volumes from the Old Library (presses 1700–1899), and some presses of large volumes from the General Library. In the reconstructed quadrants, the General Library for the most part occupied the first and lower floors, those above being used for Periodical Publications and Academies.

The placing procedure practised under Watts remained virtually unaltered until about 1960.[16] After the preceding operations of receiving, registering, stamping, and cataloguing, the accessions, with their 'titles' or handwritten catalogue entries, were taken daily to the Placer's room. Items for which there was already a pressmark (such as parts of series and numbers of periodicals) were either sent directly to the shelves after registration and stamping, or to the cataloguers if any alteration to their existing catalogue entry or any analytical entry to part of the contents was required. After this, they were taken to the Placer and shelved at the pressmark already allotted to them. Some minor items were not catalogued separately, but gathered under collective entries in the General Catalogue (informally known as 'dumps') of which many examples are to be found under the heading 'Collections' in the General Catalogue.

Items for the Map, Music, or State Paper Rooms which came to the Placers were set aside and sent to the staff concerned, though most of their acquisitions were received directly. New periodicals were set apart for attention as described below. New fiction and any material for secure storage were also set aside. The remainder was then sorted into twenty-nine subject groups, for which pigeon holes were provided in the Placer's room. This material was removed daily to corresponding subject points in the stacks, still known as 'tables' though after the actual tables provided in the iron stacks had been removed, spare shelves were used instead. The Placer visited each table in turn, further subdividing the books and placing them at the growth points at the end of each subject. Each table was visited about once a week. Finally the Placer's staff gathered up the books which had been placed, matched them for height with an available shelf in the subject, and gave each the next pressmark for that shelf, writing the pressmark in pencil on the half-title. The marking indicated which was the last book on the shelf, so that if recent additions were away being labelled, their pressmarks would not be used again.

The book, now bearing its pressmark, was sent to be bound (if necessary) and labelled, while the 'title', also bearing the pressmark, was returned to the Catalogue Room to be included in the next printed list of accessions. Books were labelled as early as 1826, with press and shelf marks, and in the Keeper's annual report of 1827 it was stated that about half of the books had been so labelled.[17] Later, however, labelling was discontinued, but when it appeared that this caused delays in the service to readers, labelling was reintroduced by Winter Jones. Some books in fine bindings are not labelled.

Reconstruction of the South-West Quadrant, which had been completely destroyed in an air raid in 1941, with the loss of very many books, was completed in 1955. It was expected at the time that the restored and enlarged quadrant would accommodate accessions until 1980, and that by then the first part of a new building for the Library would be available. But in fact space was once again at the point of exhaustion by 1960. Until then the 1753 foundation Act of the British Museum had required library material to be kept within the Bloomsbury site, the only subsequent exception being the news-papers housed at Colindale. The legal requirements were accordingly altered by the British Museum Act, 1963, and storage space was made available in vacant buildings of the Royal Arsenal at Woolwich. Little-used material was to be sent there, and the first consignment, from the State Paper Room, with some material designated for the Science Reference Library, was transferred in 1962. Items from the General Library began to be moved in 1972. By 1985 there were 94 kilometres of shelving at Woolwich and in the following year the accommodation there was virtually full. Another building at Micawber Street, London, N1., was taken into use in 1984, largely for the Science Reference Library. Other material, mainly from the Department of Oriental Manuscripts and Printed Books, was moved to buildings in the vicinity of the British Museum, particularly that erected in Store Street in 1963–65 for the National Central Library. Transport was provided to bring outhoused material to the reading rooms.

The first material to be outhoused included such categories as foreign government publications, a large proportion of children's literature, miscella-neous annual reports, uncatalogued foreign theses, and modern British fiction. But much material in moderate demand subsequently had to go, to leave space at Bloomsbury for the most-used items. At first, selection of material for outhousing was made on the basis of staff experience, but later readers' applications for books were analysed by computer to determine categories the removal of which would cause least inconvenience to readers, and there was some adjustment between the classes of material at Bloomsbury and those at Woolwich.

Watts's classification for the Iron Library in its original form had 515 subject headings, and could provide a practical source of subject information through direct access to the shelves (in practice restricted almost entirely to Library staff) in the early years of the Iron Library. When new subjects were encountered, new pressmarks were at first created, but as pressure on storage space increased, the reverse became the case, subjects being combined to reduce the number of entry points, and the amount of shelf space which had to be left vacant. In 1953 there were 380 subject headings in use. The Placer's view at that time was that classification of post–1880 material in the general stacks (to which there was no open access) was unnecessary, because of the existence of the Subject Index. In 1960 the number of subject headings was reduced to 44. In 1964 all available space within Watts's classes – the 'growth points' – was closed up, and a new series of pressmarks, still based on Watts, but reduced to twenty classes only, was introduced. In 1970 the number was again reduced, to eleven (*see* Appendix E). The pressmark included elements for the subject and size of the book, with a running number for each volume, and could be allocated without having to take each book to the shelf, effecting a great economy in labour. A distinguishing prefix, X, was included, with a further prefix, O, for non-periodical series and works in progress. A suffix, S, was also included where books needed attention from the binders. The same numeration, with the prefix P, was given to new periodicals from 1964, though here the number of subject divisions was twenty-six. The basic classification was retained because it was felt that this would help in the arrangement of book-stocks and the provision of subject areas and reading rooms when the Library was removed to a new building. In the Iron Library as originally arranged the pressmarks ran in numerical order through the building, so that any press could easily be found. Since then, shortage of space and reconstruction work have caused many books to be moved out of sequence, and by 1975 there were almost three hundred breaks in sequence, greatly increasing the work of the staff.

Plans for the redevelopment of the south bank of the Thames in the vicinity of Waterloo Bridge were drawn up after the Festival of Britain in 1952, and included a new scientific reference library which would incorporate the library of the Patent Office, and would be located in a proposed new science centre. The decision in 1960 that the new library (called the National Reference Library of Science and Invention – NRLSI) would form part of the British Museum removed the possibility that deposit under the Copyright Act might be split between two independent institutions. Preliminary work for the new library was carried out in the British Museum between 1960 and 1966, and included the selection of material from the stock and accessions of the British Museum suitable for transfer to the new library. In 1966 the Patent Office Library was transferred from the control of the Board of Trade to the British Museum and became the Holborn division of NRLSI. The NRLSI staff which had been working in the British Museum building, and the book stock which they had accumulated, were transferred to part of Whiteley's department store in Bayswater, west London. At first, books acquired expressly for NRLSI, and those selected from the general accessions, were given a general library pressmark, preceded in the printed catalogue entry by the words 'South Bank'. The books were to be given additional shelfmarks and catalogue entries, for NRLSI use when removed to NRLSI, and as the stocks of NRLSI were expected to be largely limited to recent publications, it was arranged that books withdrawn from its stocks would be transferred to the pressmarks originally allocated to them in the General Library.

The Patent Office Library, opened in 1855, has always had a high degree of open access, and this was retained after it became part of NRLSI, together with the original shelf classification, though much material is now outhoused. It is located in Southampton Buildings, Chancery Lane, London, WC2, and covers the physical sciences and related technology, engineering and commerce, including the patent collections. The non-inventive sciences – the life and earth sciences, astronomy, pure mathematics and medicine – formerly in Whiteley's building at Bayswater are available at the Aldwych Reading Room, Kean St, London, WC2, where there is further book storage.

A classification for the non-inventive sciences has been developed from that formerly used in the Patent Office Library, and adapted for a wider subject coverage. The scheme is hierarchical, and a major feature retained is the collocation of technologies and related sciences. In general the class marks do not exceed two letters plus two digits. Because of open access a high level of specificity is maintained, with an average of five to ten, and not more than twenty items in any one class on the open shelves. There are separate sub-collections for special publishing formats, e.g. serials, abstracts, and mono-graphs, within which the majority of works are classified by subject. These collections are indicated by prefixes to the shelfmarks. Exceptions are patents, which are arranged by countries, and trade literature, which is under the names of manufacturers.

The question of extending or rehousing the Library was discussed by the

Trustees of the British Museum and the British Library Board on the one hand and successive governments on the other for many years, and between 1945 and the 1960s plans were formulated for a new building opposite the main front of the Museum. Later, however, environmental objections were raised and a site in Euston Road next to St Pancras station was therefore acquired for a building to house the whole Library, except the Newspapers and the Lending Division; it was to be erected in stages, the first planned to be complete by 1991. Building work began in 1982 but in 1988 the government announced that only the first stage of the new building would be completed, while the remainder of the site would be used for other purposes. It is therefore expected that only some of the administrative offices of the Library, and the collections of manuscripts, printed books (in part) and Oriental printed books and manuscripts, together with the Science Reference and Information Service will be accommodated in the new building but that other services at present outhoused in London locations will not. In July 1988 a decision was still to be reached as to how the reference books are to be classified. For the Science Reference and Information Service, more open access will be available than at present.

In every library a balance has to be struck between conservation and exploitation, and much thought had been given to the possibility of increased open access in the new building. If accepted, this would have affected accommodation and storage space, staff provision, security and conservation. A working party investigated the suitability of the classification schemes available, and the contribution that the Library might be able to offer in the field to other libraries in Britain and abroad.[18] The present view, however, favours rapid service from closed stacks, and to this end material known or expected to be in frequent demand will be housed in close proximity to the reading areas, with less-used items in more distant areas, and perhaps outhoused. There are to be no classified arrangements for books added to the general collections, except music and works on the visual arts. Rare books will be shelved separately, under secure conditions, and will include all books printed before 1870.

Most of the stock acquired by the Library since 1975 has been separated into size categories in line with the St Pancras shelving plans, and a new shelfmarking system was adopted for all acquisitions placed from 1 April 1986. In formulating new shelfmarks, care has been taken to avoid the likelihood of confusion with existing shelfmarks, to make them as short as possible, or split into a number of parts which are easy to use. Possible confusion between figures and letters is avoided, and the shelfmarks will be suited for expansion and automation, so that factors such as language and bibliographical form (e.g. paperbacks) can be indicated if required. Further details of the shelfmarking plan for the new library are given in Appendix G.

The difficulty of shelving economically in the North Wing books too large to be placed either on the gallery or the ground floor presses in their correct subject group, and its solution by using an additional series of pressmarks has already been mentioned (*see* p.13). After the construction of the Iron Library, these books were transferred to its basement, but by 1940 the shelves allocated were full. Furthermore, the basement of the Iron Library, where dust constantly settled after falling through the gratings of the upper floors, was no suitable place in which to keep fine large books, nor indeed any books. After the reconstruction of the Large Room in 1907–14 to form the North Library, presses became available in its lower gallery, and here, from about 1922, a new series of presses, marked L.R. (Large Room), was begun. There was no subject arrangement; suitable books were placed in order of accession, with some transferred initially from other pressmarks. There were a few continuations, for which space for growth was left. A few books are still added to the L.R. sequence, though it is no longer shelved in the North Library. A parallel sequence, pressmarked L., was begun about 1955.

When presses 1700–1899, which were used for large books not of sufficient importance to be placed at L.R., became full, the pressmark Cup. 1247 was introduced; it was not a cupboard, despite the prefix, and had no connection with press 1247. The pressmark was in fact chosen arbitrarily, so that books placed there would be sent only to the North Library, where the tables (larger than those in the Reading Room) were more suitable for them. This series now extends from Cup. 1246 to Cup. 1285, and is shelved in the upper floor of the Circle which surrounds the Reading Room, and in the South-East Quadrant, both of which areas have suitably large shelves. One further sequence of pressmarks, 14000–14001, was begun about 1860, and used until the end of the century, with a few later additions; it is split between two locations in the South-East and North-West Quadrants, to obtain suitable shelving, and contains books measuring up to two feet in both height and width. Many are atlases or volumes of illustrations, some having accompanying volumes of text, shelved elsewhere in the General Library.

Even larger books, up to three feet in height, and three foot six inches in depth, are shelved at Cup. 645 – again apparently a purely arbitrary choice of pressmark, begun after the reconstruction of the Supplementary Rooms in 1931. Most of the works shelved there are guard-books or large volumes of plates. Wooden uprights provide a partial remedy against sagging. Valuable books too large to be stored upright in cases were in the nineteenth century kept flat on the shelves of table cases. Shelving units with rollers at the front edge of each shelf for horizontal storage have been installed in recent years in the Sub-Basement and Circle Basement. This prevents sagging, and since

1978 a programme of relocating material shelved upright, and over eighteen inches in height has been followed, but this work requires much staff time. Nevertheless, it has been possible to move runs of up to thirty books from the Old Library. When smaller numbers are moved, pressmarks have to be altered, with greater demands on staff time. Two new locked areas of shelving ('pens') were brought into use in 1980 for large volumes requiring secure storage.

Shelving unusually small books has been much less difficult. Many were placed on the open shelves of the Old Library, and some remain on open shelves, e.g. at I.X. (editions of the *Imitatio Christi*), where the smallest is two inches high, and at 944.a.–f., where there are seven shelves of miscellaneous small books received between 1908 and 1932. A number of small books, mainly early, but including copyright accessions of the nineteenth century, is kept at C.18.a., where they were probably placed during the last century; many others formerly with them have been removed to a miniature case at C.17.b.10., which contains volumes varying in height from three-quarters to two and a quarter inches; the most numerous are almanacs, with some Bibles, liturgical works, and other books. Three other sets of miscellaneous books varying in height roughly from one to three inches and kept in cases are those at 528.m.23. (about one hundred volumes, assembled in a miniature case from about 1890, some having been transferred from open shelves, and a few recent additions); at 600.i.23 (83 volumes in two miniature cases); and in Case 0 (this is a smaller set, commenced about 1905, and with no recent additions). Since 1980 books not more than three inches high have been placed at Cup.550. Among special collections of small books may be noted the travelling library of Sir Julius Caesar (1558–1636), 44 volumes of the classics, ranging from two and a half to four and a half inches in height, and kept in a case in the form of a large volume (C.20.f.15–58); and the almanacs collected by Edward Arnold, the largest five and a half inches high, and kept in a special case at C.97.f.6.

Tracts and pamphlets have been treated in a variety of ways. In Montagu House, as well as the Thomason and other special collections of tracts, there were numerous separate volumes of small items bound together. They were shelved in room 13, and numbered consecutively, and they are now at the pressmark T., within which their original numeration is preserved. Panizzi, giving evidence before the Commissioners in 1849, expressed the view that pamphlets should be bound separately, on the grounds that the use of one item in a tract volume caused avoidable wear to others, and his aim was to break up the tract volumes already in the Library.[19] This proved too expensive, however, and small works on a single subject or related subjects continued to be bound in convenient numbers in separate volumes, each item being distinguished by an addition to the pressmark (the 'fourth mark'), so that, if the pressmark of a tract volume were, for example, 3305.a.2., that of the fourth item in the volume would be 3305.a.2(4.). This has the disadvantage that, very occasionally, different works in a single volume may be required at the same moment by different readers, and there has been a return to the former practice of binding items separately. Except in the case of important items, the 'temporary' style of binding is used (*see below*, p.34). The pressmark PAM., at which many pamphlets were formerly placed, was eliminated about seventy years ago.

Single sheets, leaflets, and other similar items are almost invariably kept mounted in guard-books, of which there is a large number, mainly in the 1700 and 1800 pressmarks of the Old Library. A manuscript index is kept by the Placer of the subject for which each guard-book is intended; the bulk of the material so placed is catalogued, but there are a few guard-books for items not considered important enough to merit individual cataloguing, and these are listed in manuscript indexes. Such important single sheets as fragments of fifteenth century printing are bound separately and treated in the same way as a complete book.

Some academic dissertations, of which the Library has a large number, are outhoused under the pressmark DISS. They are placed by universities, and subdivided chronologically, so that, although the majority are not entered in the General Catalogue, they can be found easily. Others, on the shelves of the General Library, are catalogued in the usual way. A similar arrangement is applied to academic programmes.

Other material in the General Library which is not shelved according to Watts's classification includes some novels, anonymous books for children, works in progress, and annual reports. Novels by English authors were shelved in a separate sequence for about fifty years during the nineteenth century, and bear the running number which distinguishes them stamped in gold on the back: in the catalogue the number is preceded by the initial N. and the series runs from N.1 to N.2572 and in date roughly from 1817 to 1863. It was then discontinued, and novels were placed at the appropriate pressmark in the class Literature, until a second series, NN (New Novels) was commenced. This ran from 1912 to 1949, and from NN.1 to NN.40051. A third series, NNN, was commenced in 1950. The series AN, for American novels, ran from AN.1 to AN.3766: many in the series were transferred from the pressmarks 12702 to 12730 in the General Library. This series was only used between 1918 and 1937 however, and American fiction was then all placed in a subdivision of the class Literature.

Anonymous books for children, published in Britain, have not been catalogued since 1910. They are shelved by the names of publishers, and within three size groups, in receipt order; a title index is maintained on slips. A similar title index is maintained for illustrated comic papers, and they are shelved in a single numerical sequence, with the prefix CAR. (Cartoons). Chapbooks, particularly those received in tract volumes or in numbers forming part of a single donation or purchase, receive a single entry in the catalogue, or may be added, if appropriate, to an existing collection in the Library; they are recorded individually in yet another card index, and are given a general library pressmark.

Works published in successive parts, whether to be completed in a definite number of parts, or to be continued indefinitely (e.g. as a publisher's series), are distinguished from periodicals, academic and other journals, transactions, and other works bearing a regular date of publication. The former are known in the Library as works in progress. At one time they were placed with other works on their subject, space for future growth being left on the shelf. This proved uneconomical in space, however, and Richard Garnett suggested that they might be shelved separately, but this was not done until 1911; the W.P. pressmark appears for the first time in the accessions list for April of that year. They were kept, until about 1925, in the Old Copyright Office in the White Wing, and after that in the Iron Library, at first in the additional floor constructed in 1920 above the South-East Quadrant, and now for the most part housed in the basement of the South-East Quadrant and the circle surrounding the Reading Room. Until 1951 a single numerical sequence, prefixed W.P. was used, and as works ceased to be in progress they were removed to the appropriate pressmark in the General Library, and the W.P. pressmark thus vacated was reallocated. In theory, responsibility for closing such works rested with the cataloguing staff; in practice, many came prematurely to an end, and could only be weeded out by systematic inspection of the shelves. This was very difficult after the Second World War, owing to the shortage of staff, and the effects of war damage, together with the demise, from the same cause, of many works in progress. To make the detection of defunct works easier, from 1952 a new series of pressmarks was begun each year, distinguished by an additional letter, W.P.A. representing works commenced in 1952, W.P.B. those in 1953, and so on. Two sequences of numbers were used for each year, one for octavo and one for larger volumes, but this arrangement had to be discontinued after W.P.D. (1955). Instructions issued in 1983 were that where works were of sufficient importance to merit individual entries in the catalogue they were to be given separate pressmarks and not placed together as a series.

From its foundation the British Museum possessed outstanding collections of rare and valuable books, both in the libraries received in their entirety (such as the Sloane, Old Royal, Cracherode, King's, and Grenville) and in smaller groups of books and individual items acquired. Secure storage has been provided for these for over a century in the form of locked cases, though Panizzi told the Royal Commission of 1847–49 that only a few select books were kept in this way, and that he was experiencing difficulty in having additional presses glazed, as the Trustees were reluctant to allocate funds for the work.[20] Because of this, it was not possible at that time to admit the public to the Grenville Room or the King's Library. Now, the larger collections shelved entirely in cases are the King's Library, Grenville, and Cracherode; the Ashley Library is also in secure storage. For other select material, there are cases numbered 1–129 in the North Library, Service Passage, and Arch Room, with further cases available to receive the accessions of some years, at the present rate. Cases 1–16 contain incunabula and other valuable books removed from the King's Library before the cases there were glazed, Cases 17–24 more rare books, many of them from the Cracherode collection, and similarly placed there before the whole collection was kept under lock and key. The remaining cases are used for various classes of valuable material, e.g. Cases 35, 36, 51, 52, 110, and 111 for Bibles and Liturgies, Case 101 for the publications of the Roxburghe Club, Cases 102–105 for fine modern British printing, and Cases 122–123 for British books printed before 1641. Many of the books in these cases had previously stood on the open shelves of the Library; systematic placing of newly acquired valuable books in cases does not seem to have been practised before about 1860, and the transfer of valuable books to cases appears to have begun later.

Cases with a table top were also formerly in use, but most of them were removed during the reconstruction work of the 1930s. They shared the pressmark of the nearest press, with the prefix Tab. The same applied to the cupboards formerly in the Library, though the cupboards themselves have gone, and the books, except the large volumes at Cup. 600–652 and 1246 onwards, mentioned above, are kept in 'pens' – closed areas of stack introduced about 1955. The main Cup. series appears to have been developed from 1938, and was used for material which would have run the risk of theft or mutilation if left on open shelves. It included erotic material and works on sex, limited editions and private presses, transparencies and sound recordings.

Valuable accessions are now all shelved in secure conditions, either in a case, or pen. Books which in time will appreciate in rarity and value are earmarked to enable them to be moved en bloc to secure storage when desirable. Other accessions published before the end of the nineteenth century are also placed in the Old Library, at 1570 and subsequent pressmarks. For material requiring a higher degree of segregation there is a pressmark P.C. (private case). Confidential and suppressed books are also kept apart.

Incunabula were gathered together by Robert Proctor in the cases of the westernmost bays of the Arched Room between 1893 and 1903, and arranged in what has become generally known as 'Proctor order' – a chronological sequence of countries, towns, and presses. The method of pressmarking is described by A. W. Pollard in his preface to the first volume of the *Catalogue of Books printed in the XVth Century now in the British Museum* (1908). There is a single numerical sequence of pressmarks from 1–57000, with blocks of numbers allotted to individual printers, and other numbers left free for allocation to future discoveries. The pressmark so given is prefixed by the initial I, followed by another letter indicating the height of the book, A for those under nine inches in height, B for nine to fourteen inches, and C for those over fourteen inches. Each category is shelved separately, and a number allotted to a book in one is not used in either of the others.

Proctor's allocation of numbers was not satisfactory in every case, and where a comparatively large number of works of the same printer have been added since Proctor's time, some rearrangement has been required. Second copies receive the same number as originals, distinguished by adding a further lower-case letter. The incunabula in the King's and Grenville Libraries, which he was not allowed to move, Proctor indicated in his arrangement by dummy boards bearing details of each book, with its pressmark.

There are many special collections in the Library which have been formed by an individual, deal with a single subject, or for other reasons are of interest as entities, and are shelved as such, most of them in cases or other secure storage. Some have their own pressmarks, while others are located within the appropriate subject in the general library; they are listed in Alison Gould's *Named Special Collections in the Department of Printed Books* (1981). A list of special pressmarks indicative of subject, provenance, etc., is given in Appendix F. R. C. Alston in *A Topical Index to Pressmarks in use in the British Museum Library, 1823–1973* (1986) lists further manuscript and printed sources to special categories of subject, provenance, or form.

Most of the books transferred from Montagu House to the North Wing in 1838–40 remained on open shelves, even after the reconstruction of the North Wing in the 1930s. In the years from 1945, the rooms were subjected to increased pressure for staff accommodation, and the presence of the old library books, many of them rare and valuable, added to the space problem, while the environmental conditions were very unsuitable. Eventually, outhousing other material from the general library made more suitable space available in the quadrants, and in the upper gallery of the Reading Room, to which the books were removed, and much of the shelving in the workrooms was taken down.

To protect fine bindings and fragile items, special boxes are made in the Library bindery to fit individual books. Case books (which include all books from the King's, Grenville, Cracherode, and Ashley Libraries, incunabula, and other valuable material) are not sent into the Reading Room but are read in the North Library, where the larger tables lessen the risk of damage, and closer supervision is possible. Books to be read in the North Library, but not sufficiently valuable to be placed in a case, were formerly marked by a blue pressmark label instead of the usual buff or white one. Only books added to the L.R. pressmark now receive blue labels, but the rule still applies to books already bearing them. Where a photographic reproduction of a case book is available, it is issued to readers rather than the original, and a distinctive label on the back of the original indicates the existence of the copy to the staff fetching the book.

Storage of microforms presents no difficulty as regards space or equipment. Roll microfilm is kept on narrow open shelves, in cardboard boxes, identified with a running number, which is also added to the film, using a perforating punch. Where more than one bibliographical item is included in a single film, the catalogue entry for each receives a further identification number. Much wear and tear has been caused to books since 1945 by the very great increase in microfilm and other photographic copying. Increasingly stringent controls have become necessary, especially in the case of old or rare books and other fragile material, and current policy favours the production of stock negatives of works where the demand for photocopies is at all substantial.

Panizzi told the Royal Commission of 1847–49 that he had tried to withhold from readers fine and rare books, and material not yet bound, because of the risk of damage, but that there had been so many complaints that the practice had been discontinued.[21] It was still the custom, however, to withhold books in the King's or Cracherode Libraries if there was another copy in the Museum, and he thought that the same should apply to the Grenville Library. At present this rule applies only to the Grenville Library, but to preserve books in the other special collections, and to encourage the use of other copies when available, the following order of precedence is observed for entries of multiple copies in the General Catalogue:

1 Perfect copies precede imperfect.
2 Books on the open shelves of the Reading Room or North Library precede others.

3 Copies placed as part of a series precede copies placed apart.
4 Copies on open shelves precede copies placed in secure storage.
5 King's Library and other case copies precede Grenville.
6 Copies on ordinary paper precede those on fine or large paper.
7 Copies without manuscript notes precede those with them.

Where there is conflict between two of these principles, 1 overrides 2, and so on.

In the past all binding was carried out in the Museum bindery, but by the 1970s volume of work and of arrears had become so great that arrangements were made for the more routine work to be sent to HMSO binderies outside the building or to private contractors, leaving the Museum bindery more free to deal with the binding and repair of early or rare books.

Books to have a permanent place on the reference shelves of the Reading Room or North Library are rebound in half leather; substantial works in the General Library are usually bound as necessary, in buckram or leather, according to size. For rare or valuable books more elaborate styles are used, while pamphlets and items likely to be little used receive a so-called 'temporary' binding, consisting of paper boards with a cloth back, so that if later they require a more substantial binding, the temporary one can easily be replaced. During the nineteenth century a code of colours for bindings, depending on the subject of the book, was used, but it was later discontinued, and attention to colour is now restricted to preserving consistency in successive volumes of the same work. All paper-covered books were formerly bound after placing, as were the completed volumes of the majority of periodicals and academies, but from 1970 some of this material remained unbound, the paperbacks being simply labelled, and the periodicals and academies being stored in boxes holding the equivalent of about twelve volumes each.

Locked cases and pens provide some degree of protection against theft and malicious damage, but can do nothing to improve environmental conditions, which will be possible only when the Library is moved to a new building. Deterioration in modern paper and the effects of atmospheric acid on some leather bindings throw a very great burden on the binding resources available. Since 1977 rare books in need of repair have been segregated, to protect them from further deterioration. The establishment in 1984 of the National Preservation Office within the Library, with the support and co-operation of other institutions facing similar problems will, it is hoped, facilitate research and the exchange of information, promote co-operative projects, and seek additional sources of finance for the work.

While as much protection and care as the resources of the Library permit are devoted to rare books in the collections, it has to be recognised that all 'rare' books cannot be physically assembled and isolated from the remainder of the stock. Examples are to be found in almost every part of the collections, and every year thousands more books become 'rare'. This is borne out by the fact that of about a quarter of a million books lost in the bombing in 1941, it has been possible only to replace about half in the original after nearly fifty years. (Others have been replaced by microform copies.) Proposals for the storage of rare material at St Pancras are outlined in Appendix G.

V · REFERENCE BOOKS: DUPLICATES; BOOKS REMOVED FROM SHELVES

The first Reading Room was opened in the basement of Montagu House soon after the establishment of the Museum, and various other rooms in the house were subsequently used in turn; but not until 1827 when the two rooms to the south of the Manuscript Saloon were allocated to this function (the present Middle and South Rooms) was any collection of reference books provided (Fig. 5). Panizzi told the Commission of 1847–49 that Baber (Keeper of Printed Books, 1812–37) was accustomed to act on the advice of Cates, the Superinten-dent of the Reading Rooms, and place in the rooms any work which was requested, as far as space permitted.[22]

In 1838 new Reading Rooms at the east end of the North Wing were opened, and here there was space for a larger number of reference books, 10,000 volumes in all, available directly to readers, without the use of ladders. Panizzi also stated that the reference books needed rearrangement, but that this would cause difficulty to readers, who knew their locations, since there was as yet no catalogue of reading room reference books. In fact, certain readers used deliberately to misplace books, so that they alone knew where to find them.[23]

When the present Reading Room was opened in 1857, space became available for a reference collection of 20,000 volumes on the ground floor open shelves. They were assembled by W. B. Rye, (who became Keeper of Printed Books in 1869). Attention was given in the first place to 'dictionaries, encyclopaedias, atlases, gazetteers, catalogues, the leading works in art, science and literature, and the most important collections in the various branches of learning,' while many other works were included, which were not strictly works of reference, but which experience had shown to be in constant demand by readers.[24] The collection has been under more or less constant revision ever since. Additional free-standing presses were introduced at the end of the rows of readers' seats to accommodate a large number of

5 The Middle Room of the Department of Manuscripts which was used as one of the reading rooms of the Library from 1827–38 (BL Archives).

bibliographies. Those marked BB were installed in the late nineteenth century, and those marked AA in the 1960s. An author catalogue, with subject-index, of the reference books in the Room was compiled by Rye and published in 1859; it was revised at intervals, the fourth and last edition appearing in 1910. Working copies inlaid on large paper with accessions pasted in were maintained in the Room until 1950, when they were replaced by a card catalogue. At the same time, the books in the Reading Room galleries which had been included in the printed catalogue were omitted, as they no longer formed part of the reference collection. They had originally been selected as being in frequent demand by readers, and had been placed in the Reading Room to be available when the service of books from the Iron Library was interrupted by darkness or fog, electric light having been installed in the Reading Room some time before its introduction into the iron stacks.

The principal pressmarks now in the Reading Room are: for open-access books in the wall presses on the ground floor, 2000–2121; in the first floor gallery, 2200–2410; in the second floor gallery, books from the old library. Among other open access books in the Reading Room are the bibliographies in the free-standing presses at AA.A.–AA.T., and BB.A.–BB.T. There are also a few *ad hoc* shelfmarks, such as Dir. for directories. The sequence of open-access reference books is continued at 2122–2183 in the North Library gallery. The arrangement of the general reference collection in presses 2000–2121 at first followed closely that of the General Library, and the location of subjects and even individual books was shown in detail on a printed plan. Successive rearrangements have departed from Watts's scheme, however, and the main approach to the collection is now by way of the alphabetical subject catalogue on cards, maintained in the Reading Room. A selection of bibliographies, not on open shelves, but collected together for possible open access in the new building, has been assembled at 2701–2787 since 1960.

The Large Room in the centre of the North Wing was first used only to house books in the presses which surrounded the room and, at ground level, projected to form a series of bays on each side. During the Great Exhibition of 1851 (according to the *Illustrated London News* of 7 June of that year) it was opened to the public, and used as an exhibition gallery for the Department of Printed Books, as the King's Library was at a later date. When it was first used as a reading room is not clear. Panizzi had told the Commission of 1847–49 that readers coming for new books interrupted the work of those wanting older and more serious books, and that a separate reading room should be provided for them.[25] In 1907–14, during the construction of the King Edward VII Gallery, the Large Room was extended northwards and renamed the North Library; it underwent a further reconstruction in 1936–38. The greater table space available for each reader and the better facilities for supervision than in the Reading Room cause the North Library to be used for the consultation of valuable, bulky, or unbound material, while readers requiring seats for a continuous period are accommodated at one end of the room. Locked cases occupy the greater part of the walls at ground floor level; there is, however, a small reference collection, largely of works relating to historical bibliography, but including a copy of the printed edition of the General Catalogue. In the gallery presses is a continuation of the reference works from the Reading Room (presses 2122–83), other bibliographies and reference books, and some books in locked cases.

The value to the Library of duplicate copies of rare books, or of books subjected to exceptional wear and tear, was very early recognised, and was drawn to the attention of the Select Committee of 1835 by Sir Henry Ellis, the Principal Librarian.[26] It was, of course, of even greater significance in the days when photographic reproduction was not available as an important contributor to the reduction of wear and tear. In general, a duplicate copy is provided of most books on the open shelves of the Reading Room and North Library, and of other works in constant use. Books received by copyright deposit are not usually placed on open shelves, duplicates being bought for the purpose, so that the copyright material is preserved as a permanent record of the literary and publishing output of the country. Other duplicates of importance are those of rare or valuable books, when a little-used and well-preserved copy is particularly useful for exhibition purposes. Staff reference collections, particularly in connection with cataloguing work, can call for other duplicates, though if the demand by staff is not great, a book may be removed provisionally from the stacks to a workroom, its temporary whereabouts being indicated by a marker at the original pressmark. Other Departments of the British Museum and the British Library (although they have been able to use the resources of the Department of Printed Books) have also formed their own collections of reference works. Where these include works not present in the Department of Printed Books, entries for them have sometimes been made in the General Catalogue.

Panizzi stated his view to the Commissioners in 1847–49 that duplicates should be used to form a loan collection, and this finally came about with the incorporation of the National Central Library and the National Lending Library for Science and Technology into the British Library in 1973. It has been the rule that duplicates received by copyright deposit and not required for use in the Library shall be destroyed: those acquired by other means, however, can be discarded, and are sometimes given away or used for exchange. Garnett referred in 1895 to the then current practice of offering them to other libraries.[27] The sales of duplicates, held frequently in the early years of the Museum, included many volumes from the foundation collections, and were discontinued in 1832.

Other reasons for the absence of books from their pressmarks are, use by reader or member of staff, exhibition, photography, binding, removal to another pressmark, misplacement, and theft. Books may remain in use to a reader or member of staff as long as required, unless required for a more urgent purpose, with the provision that all books must be returned to shelves during the annual closed week, when shelves are checked as completely as staffing permits, and missing books noted. The removal of a book for a reader or staff member is marked on the shelf by a duplicate copy of the application slip. Other indicators are left for photography, binding, etc. Case, King's, and Grenville books are recorded in a register when issued for use, and the shelf boards used to issue them are in a numbered set, the absence of which from their box indicates at a glance the number of books in use. For issues to staff of case and other rare books, the normal type of shelf board is used.

A book misplaced among ten million volumes is a serious problem, the main hope for its recovery lying in its being observed during the closed week check, during the removal of books from one press to another, or in the course of the normal service of books. In addition, the staff who fetch and return the books develop a considerable insight into the way in which a pressmark may be misread, and where a mislaid volume may have come to rest. As for losses of books, it has always been the rule to withhold from open shelves books of smaller size than octavo, which has helped to keep down losses from the reading rooms. But the design of both North Wing and Iron Library, through which access is necessary not only for staff employed in that area, but also for considerable numbers of other individuals, makes satisfactory control very difficult. From 1950 staff entry to some areas of stack was restricted, but a higher degree of security must await a new building.

VI · PERIODICAL PUBLICATIONS AND ACADEMIES

Many of the periodicals and academies (i.e. serial publications and some monographs of learned societies) received in the Museum before Watts's time formed part of the King's and Banksian Libraries, where they are still to be found, with pressmarks appropriate to those collections. Others had been placed with monographs on the same subject, or in shelves allocated to encyclopaedias and series, and this continued after the removal from Montagu House to the North Wing. But the continuing growth in bulk of the periodicals, and in the number of new titles received, made it necessary to shelve the new items elsewhere. Watts therefore drew up a table of pressmarks on a subject basis, which, as in the case of the General Library classification, was considered to be the best approach in view of the lack of other subject guides to periodicals at that time. No copy of the original schedules survives, but the headings used until 1964 are given in Appendix H. There are some differences from the General Library classification; for example, genealogy and heraldry are preceded by anthropology and ethnography, while philology comes earlier than in the General Library, but the basic principle is the same. The notation is similarly in the form of numerical pressmarks, from 1 to 7000, preceded by the initials P.P., while individual periodicals are indicated by groups of one to three letters following the number: e.g. P.P.4183 ahz. is followed by P.P.4183 ai. Sub-series, supplements, etc., are indicated by the use of further figures: e.g. P.P.2076 a/3. In some sections, notably that dealing with economics and trade, the number of pressmarks originally allocated proved inadequate, and it was necessary to encroach on neighbouring subjects. Writing in 1851 when the system was newly introduced, Winter Jones hinted at some periodical publications being arranged by place of publication, in the same way as the first series of Academies (*see below*, p.41), but no trace of such an arrangement survives.[28]

The practical value of the detailed subject arrangement of periodicals diminished as the number of separate publications increased and more classified lists and bibliographies became available. From the inception in 1880 of the British Museum Subject Index, new periodicals were given subject entries in it. In 1964, to economise in shelf space and staff labour, a new series of pressmarks for periodical publications was introduced, with a numerical notation preceded by the letter P, and having only twenty-six classes (Appendix E). Some periodicals are divided between Bloomsbury and the Woolwich repository, or between Bloomsbury and the Science Reference and Information Service Library, with different pressmarks for the different locations.

In Watts's system, the first part or parts of a periodical or academy to be received in the Library after registration and stamping were sent for cataloguing, and thence, with the titles or catalogue entries in manuscript, to the Placer. With the use of a shelflist and subject index, a pressmark was allotted, and the part or parts sent to the shelves, while the titles were sent for entry in the accession registers for periodicals and academies. One register contained entries for material deposited under the Copyright Act, and the other for that received by purchase or donation, and against the entry for each item its pressmark was added. In this way, further parts arriving could be pressmarked immediately upon registration, and were sent directly to the shelves, unless they contained articles of sufficient importance to merit analytical entries in the General Catalogue or Subject Index, in which case they passed through the hands of a cataloguer and the Placer in the usual way. The shelflist used for allocating pressmarks latterly had two supplements and was partly in bound and partly in loose-leaf form. Amalgamation into a single series, using a visible index, would have greatly simplified the task of placing periodical publications.

Directories were once shelved in the old Newspaper Room in the White Wing. In some cases their full pressmarks were given in the General Catalogue, but often the only indication appearing there was N.R. (Newspaper Room) or J.R. (Journals Room), and a handlist had to be consulted before an item could be found. When the Newspaper Room was closed and a reading room for newspapers opened at Colindale in 1932, the directories were removed to shelves at the appropriate pressmark among the Periodical

Publications. Alteration of their pressmarks, however, to conform with the general classification for periodicals, was not carried out until 1950–52, in preparation for the re-editing of the heading 'Directories' in the new edition of the General Catalogue. This catalogue heading, with two subdivisions, one for localities, and the other for trades, professions, etc., provides a guide to the whole collection of directories.

When the subject arrangement for periodical publications was introduced, many of the Academies in progress were included in it. Their number was still small, but between 1837 and 1850 vigorous steps were taken to improve the holdings, and the number of titles represented increased four- or five-fold. A new scheme for shelving them was introduced, apparently between 1860 and 1870: as with periodical publications the basis of the pressmark is a number, preceded in this case by the abbreviation Ac. In their arrangement, the fundamental principle was to keep together all publications of each Academy and its subordinate bodies (e.g. the colleges and research institutes of a university), and there were two main groups of pressmarks, one arranged topographically, for institutions, such as universities, not having set limits to the subject range of their activities, and a second subdivided by subjects, for institutions concerned with specific subject fields. In this, as in the arrange-ment of periodical publications, the influence of the lack of adequate subject guides at the time is clear. The lack of a detailed subject-index to the classification made it difficult to add new entries in their correct place, and here again the problem was aggravated by the nature of the shelf-lists, which finally had three supplements, in a mixture of bound volume, loose-leaf, and card form. From 1965 no new titles have been added to the Academies pressmarks, but continuations are still added to them. New serials were then placed with periodical publications, and, later, monographs at the appropriate subject heading in the General Library. Finally the pressmarks Ac and P were replaced by one series pressmarked Z, in preparation for the move to St Pancras (*see* Appendix G).

The first section of the Academies classification, that arranged topographi-cally, is covered by pressmarks Ac.1–1997. The general layout is similar to that of the topographical and biographical sections of the General Library classifi-cation; within countries, subdivision is by towns, arranged alphabetically. Individual Academies were at first entered under the place in which they were situated, but later there were very many exceptions to this, as the available pressmarks in some parts of the schedules became exhausted. The arrange-ment of the second part of the scheme, by subjects, which follows the classification of the General Library, is given in Appendix I.

Each Academy was given a number which formed the pressmark of the first of its publications to be entered; those entered subsequently were distinguished by the addition of /2,/3, etc. Where individual parts of a series were not numbered, they were distinguished by further numbers (2), (3), etc.; and finally, subordinate institutes of an Academy, or further Academies in the same locality, were distinguished by the addition of one to three lower-case letters to the pressmark, so that an Academy pressmark in its most elaborate form is, for example, Ac.2691 dia/3 (7). It is necessary in sending for material from an Academy or periodical pressmark, to specify the dates and numbers of the parts required. The pressmarking of periodical publications and Academies was separate from that of accessions to the General Library, and was carried out by a separate group of staff.

Before the reconstruction of the Iron Library was begun in 1932, the Academies, apart from those in the second gallery of the Reading Room, were shelved in the second floor of the circle which immediately surrounds the Reading Room; the periodicals, except a few also in the second gallery of the Reading Room, were more widely dispersed, mainly in the basement of the Iron Library. At present, with a very few exceptions, the Academies occupy the second floor of the reconstructed Iron Library. The periodicals at Bloomsbury are mainly on the third and fourth floors, but a large number, especially those popular or trivial in character, or in little demand, are at Woolwich.

At one time, under Panizzi, unbound parts of periodicals were withheld from readers. This was a cause of frequent complaint, and in the 1880s Professor Dziatzko suggested that a separate reading room should be provided for them.[29] Subsequently, unbound parts of a selected number of periodicals were kept in the North Library for consultation: the present rule is that all unbound parts are available to readers, but only in the gallery of the North Library. No room has been available which might be satisfactorily converted into a periodicals reading room, though one was opened experimentally from 1960–64, for Slavonic periodicals only. When this was closed because the area was required for staff use, the latest issues of a number of periodicals were made available on open access in the gallery of the North Library. This experiment was terminated after a few years because of theft of and damage to the periodicals concerned.

VII · OFFICIAL PUBLICATIONS

Until the latter part of the nineteenth century, the official publications of governments and government departments were largely dispersed among the collections of the General Library. In 1885 the Newspaper Room in the White Wing was opened, and British Parliamentary Papers and a few Departmental Papers were kept with the London newspapers in or near the room.

Cataloguing of state papers was begun by Frank Campbell in 1884–1900, but little was achieved towards a satisfactory classified arrangement for them. British Departmental publications were arranged by the department of origin, and entered in an index kept in the Newspaper Room. The Indian and colonial official papers were in 1893 moved to the Banksian Room; others, including the American publications, were shelved in the upper gallery of the Arch Room.

After the First World War, many British official documents formerly included in Parliamentary Papers began to be issued separately, and the bulk of the official publications increased rapidly. It became clear that readers using them required advice and service of a more specialised nature than that provided in the Reading Room. When therefore the Newspaper Room was closed on the removal of the London newspapers to Colindale in 1932, a temporary reading room for official publications was opened in the White Wing; it was replaced two years later by the State Paper Room in the lower ground floor of the King Edward VII building (now the Official Publications and Social Sciences Library), and material was assembled there from the previous scattered storage points. Facilities for a limited number of readers were provided, but as the demands for storage grew, the reader space had to be withdrawn, and material was sent into the Reading Room to be used. Additional shelving in the North-East Quadrant and East Tangent was occupied, and more improvised in the King Edward basement. By 1964 material was being stored at Woolwich, and by 1988 more than half the stock was outhoused. Outhousing does not involve an alteration of pressmarks.

The system of pressmarks in its original form depended on a primary division into two classes, European and non-European state papers, indicated by the initials E.S. and S. respectively; further subdivision was by countries and government departments, blocks of numbers being allocated for the purpose, but in drawing up the schedules insufficient numbers were provided in many instances, causing congestion and shelving of items without regard to the classification. In about 1895 Campbell introduced two further main classes, I.S. (Indian) and A.S. (American), which were later subdivided geographically, but the classification remained unsatisfactory. It was recast after the Second World War, the main classes being: B.S. (British), C.S. (Colonial and Commonwealth), I.S. (Indian), A.S. (American), L.A.S. (Latin American), and S. (others). Other pressmarks which embrace large amounts of material in the Official Publication collections are U.N. (League of Nations, United Nations, and other international organisations). O.G. (Official Gazettes), and L.C.C. (London County Council). Since 1976, only British and United States Federal publications have been given individual pressmarks for each item.

[43]

Detailed shelf-lists in loose-leaf form are maintained, and additional press-marks are made from these as required. The wide variety in the size and shape of official publications makes close arrangement by size impossible, but by using adjustable steel shelving of ten inches, twelve inches, or fourteen inches in depth, satisfactory results are obtained. Some material is bound, a proportion of the small items being gathered in tract volumes, but by far the greater part is stored in brown paper parcels. The output of publications by governments and their departments tends to expand or contract very considerably, and without any warning, while departments and agencies are created or abolished equally unexpectedly. This makes allotting shelf space for official publications a difficult task, and occasions frequent easing-out or rearrangement. Further details of the classification of Official Publications are given in Appendix J.

VIII · MAPS

From the earliest years of the British Museum its collections have included maps and charts, and the number of items, small at first, began to grow significantly when the deposit of Ordnance Survey maps commenced in 1801. The library of Sir Joseph Banks (received in the Museum in 1827), included maps, while the outstanding acquisition in this field was the topographical collection of George III, presented with the rest of his library in 1823 (it arrived at the Museum in 1828), and containing over 50,000 items. In about 1840 the Trustees decided that the map collection should be systematically developed, and Panizzi pointed out to them the importance of cataloguing the material already in hand. The work was begun by William Hughes between 1841 and 1843 and continued by R. H. Major, who was appointed an Assistant in 1844 and placed in charge of maps. Major also drew up a classification for the maps, which was used until 1988. Further details are given in Appendix K. By 1848 all had been catalogued, mounted, and arranged, while extensive purchases continued to be made, under the direction of Winter Jones who became Keeper of Printed Books in 1856.

When the topographical collection of George III came to the Museum in 1828, it was placed in table cases in the King's Library. For the King's Maritime Collection, however, after the greater part was transferred from the Admiralty in 1844, there was no suitable space, and it remained on the floor in the King's Library until the Long Room on the east side of the King's Library had been completed, and the collection was moved to it. Items in the guard books, comprising maps and topographical views, both manuscript and printed, are arranged and numbered according to a regional classification. Those too large for the guard books, which measure twenty-four and a half by eighteen and a half inches, are stored (either rolled or flat) in table cases. All material of this kind is represented by dummies in the guard books. The rolls are arranged by countries, in alphabetical order. (Some items from the King's Maritime Collection which had been retained by the Admiralty in 1844, were handed over to the Map Library in 1952 and in 1988.)

Another important collection preserved in part in the Map Library is that of plans of London formed by Frederick Crace (1779–1859), and purchased in 1880. It was originally kept in the Department of Prints and Drawings, where the views are still preserved, but the plans were later transferred to the Map Room, and are kept in 19 portfolios. Crace's system of pressmarking, used in the printed catalogue of the collection (1878), was retained by the Museum.

Because of their size and fragile nature, maps require special storage conditions to make them available for use, while keeping wear and tear at a minimum level. A wide variety of methods has been employed at various times in the map collections of the British Museum and the British Library, examples of all of which may still be found. Maps may be printed or drawn on vellum, paper, or other materials. Those on paper may be reinforced with linen or other backing material, or laminated with nylon tissue. They may be attached to rollers, or framed under perspex.

Sheet maps may be bound in atlases or other volumes, or mounted in guard books, all of which, apart from their size, present no exceptional storage problems. For the largest volumes horizontal storage is desirable. Maps not so bound have in many instances been folded to enable them to be economically stored in solander cases of uniform size.

Writing in 1851 in the *North British Review* Winter Jones said that the general collection of sheet maps was classified and arranged geographically, and stored vertically in light millboard cases, like solander cases.[30] Where they were shelved at first is not clear; after the construction of the Iron Library the maps were housed in the basement of the South-East Quadrant, where working space for staff and readers was also provided. A new Map Room (now the Map Library) was included in the King Edward VII building, and the map collection was moved there in 1915, providing improved facilities for staff and readers, as well as greatly increased shelf space. The Map Library later became greatly congested, however, despite the removal of much bulky material, such as bound volumes of large-scale Ordnance Survey plans, to the King Edward basement. After the move to the King Edward VII building, many of the maps still unbound were dissected, mounted, and stored in a series of solander cases measuring twenty-two by fourteen inches, a larger size than that previously in use. Dissection involves cutting folded maps, and mounting the cut pieces on a cloth backing with sufficient space between them to enable the fold to be limited to the backing material. This indeed reduces wear and makes it possible to store material in boxes of uniform size, but it also makes it more difficult to use maps, and particularly to measure distances, and it was discontinued in the 1950s, when it was appreciated what damage was being done to material, some of which was early and valuable.

Until 1988 the classification of maps was continued according to the regional arrangement introduced by Winter Jones and Major, and accessions within each class were added in order of acquisition. Some large maps are still rolled for storage, on cardboard cylinders of four inches in diameter, and protected by linen covers, the ends being closed with tapes. Maps on vellum, and others which are to be kept flat are stored in portfolios. Other sheet maps which have not been folded or bound are kept flat in drawers. The largest portfolios in use measure thirty-six by fifty-six inches, and the largest drawers thirty-three by forty-two inches. Portfolios are stored on shelves, but no classified arrangement is maintained. The King's Topographical Collection is in guard books, which were rebound in the 1950s; the King's Maritime Collection, hitherto in portfolios, is gradually being transferred to guard books.

The Library possesses the full range of Ordnance Survey maps and plans on all scales and of all editions, and – a particularly valuable source of information for historical geographers – the surveyors' drawings made for the first Ordnance Survey one-inch map, presented by the Ordnance Survey in 1956. These have been issued in microfiche facsimile with a detailed commentary (Research Publications, Reading, 1989).

Atlases are pressmarked and shelved in the same way as books in the General Library, the pressmark having the prefix 'Maps'; they were originally arranged in classified order, but this is no longer applied, new material being added simply according to size and in order of acquisition. Suitably deep shelving is used for large volumes with locked cupboards for valuable material. Mounting and repair of maps is carried out in the Library bindery. A few rare items, such as the map of the world by Contarini, 1506, are mounted between sheets of perspex. The catalogue of printed maps includes descriptions of atlases, and of selected maps in books in the General Library.

Printed and photographic facsimiles of maps, of which there are a large number, are catalogued and stored with sheet maps, without distinction beyond a note of their nature in the catalogue entry. Before the separation of the British Library from the British Museum, there was some exchange of material with the Department of Prints and Drawings, engraved maps being received and topographical engravings given up. There was no arrangement of this kind with the Department of Manuscripts, but the Map Library and the

Department of Manuscripts are now both included in the Special Collections Directorate of the British Library, which may be expected to facilitate liaison.

In the second half of the nineteenth century and the early part of the twentieth, when the maps were in the South-East Quadrant, they occupied 188 presses; originally the only pressmark used was the abbreviation S (shelf) followed by two numbers, indicating the shelf and the position of the item on it: some material bore at this time the pressmark 'Gallery', indicating that the collection was not confined to the basement of the Quadrant. Major's regional classification was used for the arrangement of the sheet maps from the 1840s until 1988. After sections devoted to general collections of maps of the world, scriptural geography and ecclesiastical geography, with a chronological division into the three classes, ancient, medieval and modern, subdivision is progressively by continents, countries, etc. General maps are followed by special maps, e.g. railway maps, educational maps, etc. The notation is purely numerical, running from 1 to 98,580, with abundant gaps left for new subdivisions to be added. The classmark of a sheet map has two components, the first number being that of the class or sub-class, and the second is a running number (to distinguish maps in the same class) e.g. 63510. (70.). Political changes since Major's time made alterations necessary, while in cases where alteration would have been difficult, e.g. the former Austrian Empire, the old arrangement was retained, and additional numbers created for the new political and administrative areas.

It became necessary to abandon Major's scheme in 1988 because the perennial task of interfiling new accessions at the correct point in the geographical sequence, while simultaneously spacing out a growing collection of about 1¾ million maps held in two different buildings, proved to be impracticable. The collection has always been a closed one, with readers gaining access to maps via individual catalogue entries. Shelf-lists were never in a form that could have been made available to readers. The old system will be retained for further editions of existing holdings, so that the various editions of a single sheet will continue to be stored together.

Since 1 March 1988 new accessions have been arranged by a much simplified system. This has three categories related to the expected number of sheets in each set:

1 Maps X.1, etc. (for single sheet maps).
2 Maps Y.1, etc. (for series maps in sets of 49 sheets or less).
3 Maps Z.1, etc. (for series maps in sets of 50 sheets or more).

Each category follows a single numerical sequence, new accessions being added as required. The automation (in 1988) of the post-1975 accessions means that machine-readable records will be available for all material catalogued under the new system, with geographical headings and coding making it possible for all material for a given region to be selected.

In the shelving of British Admiralty and foreign nautical charts, the numeration given in the appropriate official list is retained and used as a pressmark, as explained in the introduction to the *Catalogue of Printed Maps, Plans, and Charts,* 1885. For map series of the Ordnance Survey and Geological Survey, only the abbreviations O.S., and G.S. appear in the caalogue, individual maps being identified by means of graphic indexes. The modern Ordnance Survey series, which are unbound, also bear the abbreviation O.S., and sheets are identified from index maps and filed by sheet numbers. However numerous sets have been incorporated in the geographical classification system.

Because of the great demand, six-inch county maps and large-scale plans of London have, for many years, been on open access. Shortage of storage space since the Second World War has made outhousing necessary, and by 1988 more than half the collection was stored in a repository at Micawber Street.

IX · MUSIC

Although the *Synopsis of Contents of the British Museum* (1808) refers to the music collection and its location in rooms 7 and 13, the first formal move towards organising the material appears to have been taken in 1812, with the appointment of the Rev. James Bean as part-time Assistant for the task. Bean died in 1826, and no identifiable trace of his work remains. In 1841 Thomas Oliphant joined the staff to catalogue manuscript and printed music, and introduced the primary division, still maintained, between vocal and instrumental music. The shelf-lists which survive, dating from 1844, were begun by him.[31] Previously, some entries had been made in the general catalogue for music in the foundation collections and later eighteenth-century acquisitions, but there were no entries for items in the King's Library, and later acquisitions, including copyright deposits, were only partially catalogued. A start was made on rearranging and binding the music already in the Museum, which was in some disorder, and, with the effective application of the Copyright Act under Panizzi, the number of accessions increased.

After the opening of the new Reading Room in 1857, the music was assembled in the western of the two former reading rooms in the North Wing (known until the 1960s as the Old Music Room). In 1885 William Barclay Squire joined the staff and reorganised the music, clearing arrears of cataloguing and introducing a system of selective cataloguing. Sheet music of importance was bound in tract volumes, while light and ephemeral items were not bound, but parcelled in batches covering the accessions of ten yearly periods, and arranged in alphabetical order of composers; each vocal item was entered in a title index. Parcelling ceased in 1980, and from 1981, when automated cataloguing was introduced, all newly published items were fully catalogued. Work also began on cataloguing items previously in parcels.

To protect valuable material, Squire introduced a series of locked cases, each bearing a number, preceded by the initial K (to avoid confusion with the cases used for printed books, which have the initial C), while within the cases, shelf and third marks were allocated as in the General Library.

Adequate space for the music was available until the completion of the King Edward VII building, and in 1922 the music was removed to the room in that building which it still occupies. The room is equipped with adjustable steel shelving, thirteen feet high, and fourteen and half inches, or, more frequently, seventeen inches deep. Shelves are not of uniform length. The total length of shelving available, one and three-quarter miles, was fully occupied by 1953. Until the arrival of the Hirsch Library in 1946–47, it was estimated that there was space for the accessions of some thirty years, but additional temporary storage is now in use, pending the availability of the new library building.

The system of pressmarking used for music was devised by Oliphant; it aims particularly at conservation of space, which it achieves very effectively. There are nine size categories within each of the two main divisions of vocal and instrumental music, distinguished by the letters A-i and a-i respectively. N for collected editions and P for outsize works were introduced subsequently. The use of letters helped in most instances to avoid confusion with General Library pressmarks. Within each category the volumes are placed in numerical order, individual items within a tract volume receiving a further distinguishing number. Blocks of numbers in each size category are allocated as required to individual composers whose works bulk large in the collection, and an alphabetical card-index of names enables further accessions to be appropriately shelved. Subsequent editions of works (other than those in tract volumes or parcels) receive the same pressmark as the earliest edition in the collection, with a distinguishing letter added. There has been no move to rearrange the music according to one of the more modern classification systems; there is no open access to the shelves for readers except for the reference collection in the music reading area (*see below* p.50) and the present arrangement is very well suited for service by staff. The general catalogues and indexes of music provide guides to composers and titles, while there is for music published before 1800 an index for both vocal and instrumental works, and for accessions from 1884 a card index listing arrangements for individual intruments or groups of instruments, and dances. (Both were discontinued about 1960.)

There is no accommodation for readers in the Music Library, and in the past music was usually sent into the Reading Room or North Library for consultation. There is now a music reading area in the Official Publications Library. No pianos or other instruments, or sound-proof rooms are available for the performance of music. The only sound recordings in the British Museum Library were those issued in conjunction with printed books, and there were no facilities for playing them. Sound recordings are not subject to legal deposit in Great Britain. The incorporation of the British Institute of Recorded Sound (now the National Sound Archive) into the British Library in 1983 has added a great quantity of recorded music to the collections together with the means to play it.

The Royal Music, which had been roughly catalogued by Squire while it was still at Buckingham Palace, was deposited on permanent loan at the British Museum in 1911 by King George V, and given outright to the Museum in 1957 by Queen Elizabeth II. The arrangement is Squire's, manuscripts, printed music and printed books being shelved separately, according to size. The collection is contained in locked cases in a room off the Music Library.

Accounts of the Hirsch Library, the only other major collection of music preserved as a unity in the British Library, and its arrangement, have been written by A. H. King, the Superintendent of the Music Room at the time of its receipt.[32] As catalogues of part of the collection had been published by Hirsch before its sale, it was decided, when the collection was received in the Museum, to retain his classified arrangement and pressmarking, both for music and printed books. A special stamp was prepared and impressed on each item. Material not in Hirsch's catalogue and further additions presented by him between 1946 and his death in 1951 were shelved in a second sequence. The more valuable items were placed in cases, and the remainder in locked storage areas. It is proposed to provide a special area for it in the stacks of the new library building. In both Royal and Hirsch collections, works on music are included, as well as music itself. Other books on music, however, are placed in the General Library, though there is in the Music Library a small number of reference works, primarily for staff use.

X · NEWSPAPERS

Because of their bulk and weight, particularly in bound volumes, and the lack of durability in wood-pulp papers, the maintenance of the newspaper collections of the Library has during the past century presented great problems, which have only in the last twenty years been eased by the application of selective microfilming. The growth of the collection reflects very closely the development of the newspaper itself. The forerunner of the newspaper was the single sheet or small pamphlet of the seventeenth century, which gradually increased in size as improvements were made in typography and communications. There were, however, three major barriers to increased size and wider circulation: stamp duty, paper duty, and advertisement tax. Abolition of these between 1855 and 1861 quickly brought expansion in newspaper publishing, while an even greater stimulus was to follow, twenty years later, with the introduction of wood-pulp paper and the linotype. Evening papers became general during the 1890s, and in 1896 appeared the *Daily Mail*, first of the halfpenny dailies. Since 1900, however, despite further growth in the size and circulation of newspapers, the number of titles has decreased through amalgamation or discontinuation. The high capital investment now required to commence publication of a national newspaper makes the appearance of new titles a rarity, but the development of free local newspapers (financed entirely by advertisements) in recent years has increased the quantity of material which has to be dealt with.

Nearly all the newspapers of the earliest period, 1619–41, in the Department of Printed Books, together with many later numbers, were received in the collection of Dr Charles Burney, purchased in 1818. Next in chronological order is the collection of tracts formed between 1640 and 1661 by George Thomason: both collections are bound in tract volumes in chronological order – the arrangement most useful to the student. The Burney volumes are numbered in three sequences; the two which contain the more valuable items, of the seventeenth and eighteenth centuries, are now kept in locked cases. Individual items are found from a manuscript handlist. Nineteenth-century newspapers from the Burney collection are now at the Colindale Newspaper Library: accessions of earlier newspapers are added to the Burney volumes at Bloomsbury. To reduce wear and tear on the originals, all the Thomason tracts and the Burney newspapers have been microfilmed, and the films, or prints made from them, are issued for use by readers.

The advance in newspaper production already outlined, and the systematic application of the Copyright Act by Panizzi, led to a rapid increase in the intake of newspapers during the middle years of the nineteenth century. Until 1869 they were delivered at the Stamp Office of the Inland Revenue, and retained there for three years, an inconvenient procedure, especially if on their eventual receipt at the Museum any parts were missing. When the North Wing was built in the 1830s the newspapers were moved from Montagu House to rooms in the basement below the Large Room (the present North Library). In

1849 Panizzi complained to the Royal Commission that, without consulting him, the Trustees had planned additional space for the newspapers in the basement at the south-west corner of the Large Room; this was very inconvenient in relation to the exiting storage area, and not suitably placed for service to the reading rooms.[33] Some time after the completion of the Iron Library the newspapers were removed to deep shelving in its basement, probably in the circle surrounding the Reading Room. No pressmarks appear for newspapers, other than foreign ones, in the catalogues; the foreign ones were allocated Periodical Publications pressmarks between 9,000 and 10,000, probably because, being so much smaller in bulk than the British newspapers, they could be placed with other periodicals.

The size and growth of the newspaper collection was a constant problem for the Trustees during the latter half of the nineteenth century, and various solutions were suggested. In 1870 a proposal by Earl Stanhope that only a selection of the newspapers received should be retained and bound was rejected, but it was decided that only the first edition daily of each newspaper should be kept. Three years later the collection amounted to 27,475 volumes, with an annual increase of about 1,200 volumes: the rate of increase of both British and foreign material was rising and it was estimated that space was available for the accessions of eight years. The Trustees decided that, in view of the growth of the collection and the problem of shelving, the newspapers should be separated from the Museum, and their preservation entrusted to a new department, and it was ordered (20 June 1874) that the Principal Librarian should inform the Treasury of the matter, and enquire whether a newspaper repository could be provided elsewhere.[34] No immediate action resulted, however, beyond the improvisation of further temporary storage.

In 1882 the Principal Librarian reported that there was space for the accessions of only one more year. To erect a new building elsewhere would be uneconomical and inconvenient: for practical purposes it might suffice to retain a selection of newspapers, but the responsibilities of the Museum under the Copyright Act prevented this. Relief was obtained by using space formerly occupied by the Natural History collections, which were removed to South Kensington between 1880 and 1883, and by the availability of the White Wing, opened in 1885, where adequate storage for newspapers was provided in the basement and the north side of the ground floor, together with reading rooms for newspapers (the Newspaper Room), and for old journals (the Journals Room).[35] Sets of the principal daily papers were shelved in the corridor leading to the Newspaper Room, and in the room were sets of the *London Gazette*, illustrated papers, such as the *Graphic*, and various trade papers.

By 1900 congestion was again acute, with space for two years only: a bill brought into Parliament proposing to transfer to local authorities local newspapers issued since 1837 was withdrawn, and in 1902 an Act was passed (2 Edward VII.c.12) enabling the Trustees for the first time to store part of the Library in a subsidiary repository. In 1895 a writer in the *Library* had envisaged a country repository 'before the end of the next century . . . where the dead books of the National Collection will be stored,'[36] and a decade after the writing of these words the Colindale repository was taken into use for English provincial, Scots and Irish newspapers published since 1800, though there were no facilities for readers, the newspapers being brought to Bloomsbury to be read. London newspapers continued to be stored in the White Wing and later also in the basement of the King Edward VII building, completed in 1914, and foreign newspapers in the basement of the Iron Library, and later in the King Edward basement. By 1922 the Colindale repository was full and new newspapers were all being shelved in the King Edward basement. In 1932 the Colindale repository was enlarged, and redesignated the British Museum Newspaper Library, a reading room was added, and the post-1900 London and foreign newspapers were moved there.[37] Some three hundred presses of material formerly handled by the Newspaper Room staff remained at Bloomsbury, including the Burney collection of newspapers before 1800, and others of the same period, a duplicate set of *The Times*, and playbills and directories. The newspaper reading room in the White Wing was closed.

Pressmarks allotted at various times to the directories, reference books, etc., used with the newspapers, include N.R. (the Newspaper Room in the White Wing), J.R. and F.J.R. (Journals Room and Foreign Journals Room). At Colindale the principal London national newspapers (on the 'London floor') are shelved by title. No pressmarks are given in the catalogue, but they are included in the shelf-list used by the library staff. Other London journals are shelved by year, and the volumes numbered within each year to assist in locating items. British provincial and Irish newspapers are shelved by years from 1961, all titles for a single year being shelved together. Here again, no pressmarks are given in the catalogue, and the library staff work from a shelf list.

Some British national newspapers are microfilmed on receipt, and the films made available to readers, thus reducing wear on the originals. The originals are bound, as are smaller journals and those periodicals which are kept at Colindale because of their content, format or frequency of publication.

Provincial newspapers after 1985 are not bound, but microfilmed, or obtained on film. Originals are wrapped in acid-free paper and stored in out-house accommodation near the Newspaper Library. Originals of some foreign newspapers are discarded after microfilming. In 1986–87 the number of microfilm frames (negative) made for archival purposes was 1,675,702. This released one hundred and twenty-four feet of shelving, and a further two hundred and sixteen feet were released by purchase of microfilm to replace originals. Five hundred feet were taken up by new accessions. The total amount of shelving occupied by March 1987 was 80,991 linear feet, containing approximately 600,000 volumes and parcels.

The old repository built in 1903 was almost completely destroyed by a bomb in October 1940, when 10,000 volumes of provincial and Irish papers were destroyed, and a further 15,000 damaged. It had two floors of 300 feet by forty feet, with steel shelving seven feet six inches in height, three feet wide, and two feet deep, in which three tiers of volumes could be accommodated. The 1932 stack is of six floors, each two hundred and sixty-four by fifty feet, with similar shelving: volumes salvaged from the wreck of the old repository were stored in temporary buildings erected in 1950. In 1956–57 a further extension to the Newspaper Library was built. Since then, problems have been partly solved by outhousing, and by selective discarding of microfilmed material.

XI · SHELF-LISTS

The absence of any satisfactory subject guide to the Library before the introduction of the Subject Index by Fortescue has already been mentioned. Readers were occasionally taken to the shelves in the early years of the Museum to help them find the material they needed, but as the size of the collections increased, particularly after the construction of the Iron Library, this became increasingly impracticable, since it could only be done by the Placer in person, and brought complaints from Watts when his routine work was interrupted. Compilation of shelf-lists (that is, sets of catalogue entries arranged in order of pressmark) began about 1807, and in May 1827 Baber reported to the Trustees that they were almost complete.[38] Shelf-lists of the King's Library were produced, but only two volumes survive. Work began on a new series of shelf-lists for the General Library from 1840 onwards (after the move from Montagu House) but it seems that they were never completed. Some of the lists which were produced are preserved in the Placer's archive (as are the surviving King's Library shelf-lists). From the time of the adoption of the guard-book form of catalogue about 1850, a shelf-list was produced in card form, additional copies of the transcribed titles being mounted on cards for this purpose.

When the General Catalogue was printed between 1880 and 1905, additional copies ('fourth copies') of each title were similarly mounted, and accessions titles treated in the same way, so that a complete shelf-list on cards was built up. It was used for a time as a classified catalogue, but its bulk and the limited subdivision of Watt's classification caused its value to diminish with the growth of the Library. In the end it was of practical use only as a shelf-list and as a means of tracing cross-references in the alphabetical catalogue, since all cross-references were filed with the main title for a work in the set of fourth copies. The fourth copies were of very great value in identifying books destroyed in the air raids of the Second World War, so that replacements could be sought. The addition of entries was discontinued in 1970.

The shelf-lists of Periodical Publications and Academies are described above, pp.40–42.

XII · CONCLUSION

The first eighty years of the British Museum's existence lay in a leisurely age, the conduct of the Library following traditional principles hardly altered since medieval times, until (in Esdaile's words) the Parliamentary Enquiry of 1835–36 goaded a backward and sleepy institution into a recognition of modern needs. Then followed the tremendous expansion of the collections, renewal and enlargement of the buildings, and reorganisation of methods under Panizzi which was to set the standard for the next hundred years. In the decade following the end of the Second World War that period finally ended. The buildings of the Library had suffered grievous damage from air raids, and despite the fact that the reconstruction of the South-West Quadrant provided much more space than its predecessor, storage was exhausted at many points in the Library. Until then the Acts governing the Museum had forbidden the storage of any material beyond the limits of the buildings at Bloomsbury or Colindale (though the war-time evacuation of some of the rare book collections was an exception). A new Act was therefore passed in 1963 and outhousing began in 1964 with storage at Woolwich Arsenal and a van service to bring material for use at Bloomsbury. The workrooms, especially those in the North Wing, were too small and very inflexible, and had to be supplemented with improvised and temporary accommodation in the Museum building and elsewhere. Against all this was the expansion of the collections, staff and services of the Library, and the other departments of the British Museum, with the need for still more space. In addition, the classification system, established as a personal tradition by the scholarship and phenomenal memory of Thomas Watts, had completely outlived the conditions for which it was designed.

Such are the difficulties in an institution of the size and antiquity of the British Museum, where staff and financial resources are limited, and divergence from established practices likely to cause a great deal of additional work and expense. Moreover the concept of the functions of a national library has been radically altered in modern times, particularly because of the development of the computer. In the United States of America, the Library of Congress, fortunate in its circumstances and resources, has been able to extend its services as a national library, and has provided a pattern for the establishment or reconstitution of other national libraries (e.g. at Canberra and Tokyo) in the twentieth century as the British Museum did in the nineteenth century.

It is to be hoped that the facilities provided by the new building at St Pancras will enable the Library to add to the important contributions it has made in the past to the world of librarianship. Certainly the books will benefit from being stored in controlled environmental conditions where physical deterioration will be greatly reduced and the burden on the resources of the Library will thus be lightened; and the facilities of a modern building will enable the staff to take full advantage of the very great advances which are taking place in the field of information technology.

NOTES

1   J. S. Finch, Sir Hans Sloane's printed books, in *The Library*, series 4, vol. 22 (1941), 67; F. C. Francis, The Sloane collection of printed books, in *British Museum Quarterly*, vol. 18 (1953), 4–5.

2   M. A. E. Nickson, Sloane's codes: the solution to a mystery, in *Factotum*, no. 7 (1979), 13–18.

3   BM Archives (Trustees' Committee minutes) CE 3/1, 117–21.

4   Ibid., 37.

5   E. Miller, *That Noble Cabinet* (1973), 49; BM Archives (Trustees' General Meeting minutes), CE 1/1, 71.

6   A note on old pressmarks on printed books in the British Museum Library is to be found on pp. 289–91 of *The Lumley Library. The catalogue of 1609. Edited by Sears Jayne and F. R. Johnson* (1956).

7   Alison Gould, *Named Special Collections in the Department of Printed Books* (1981).

8   A. Esdaile, *The British Museum Library* (1946), 340.

9   Ellis's note about the stamps is on f.288v of a scrapbook which he compiled entitled 'British Museum Cuttings and Extracts to c.1862'. It is in the archives of the British Museum.

10   A. Esdaile, op.cit., 357.

11   *Report from the Select Committee on the Condition, Management and Affairs of the British Museum*, (Parliamentary Papers, House of Commons, 1835, vol. VII), questions 481, 508.

12   Maps C.26.f.7 (formerly Maps 2.d.4).

13   A. Esdaile, op.cit., 117–20, 363–4.

14 R. Garnett, Movable shelving at the British Museum, in *Library Journal*, vol. 12 (1887), 261–2; R. Garnett, A New book press at the British Museum, in *Library Notes*, vol. 2 (1887), 97–100; H. Jenner, Movable presses in the British Museum, in *Library Chronicle*, vol. 4 (1887), 88–90; R. Garnett, The sliding press at the British Museum, in *The Library*, series 1, vol. 3 (1891), 414–20; R. Garnett, The sliding press at the British Museum, in *Library Journal*, vol. 17 (1892), 422–4; R. Garnett, On the provision of additional space in libraries, in *The Library*, series 1, vol. 7 (1895), 10.

15 Because of the absence of artificial lighting in the original Iron Library, large amounts of open space were left to allow daylight to reach the lower floors. Artificial lighting was not installed in the Iron Library until after 1900. (Esdaile, op.cit., 364).

16 The principal manuscript guides and records relating to placing are preserved in the Placer's office and are listed by R. C. Alston in his *Topical Index to Pressmarks in use in the British Museum Library (1823–1973) and the British Library (1973–1985)*. (1986.)

17 Report by H. H. Baber dated 12 May 1827, in BM Archives (Officers' Reports), CE 5/10, 2143 etc.

18 The final report of the BL Working Party on Classification and Indexing was published in 1975 as no. 5233 of the BL Research and Development Reports.

19 *Report of the Commissioners appointed to enquire into the constitution and government of the British Museum* (Parliamentary Papers, House of Commons, 1850, vol. XXXIV), question 4154.

20 Ibid., question 4241.

21 Ibid., qustions 4072, 4312.

22 Ibid., question 9500.

23 Ibid., question 9505; G. F. Barwick, *The Reading Room* (1929), 151.

24 *List of the Books of Reference in the Reading Room of the British Museum* (1859), preface by J. Winter Jones, xxi, xxix.

25 *Report of the Commissioners*, 1850 (*see above* note 19), questions 9483–4.

26 *Report from the Select Committee*, 1835 (*see above* note 11), question 473.

27 *Report of the Commissioners*, 1850 (*see above* note 19), questions 4051, 4304; R. Garnett, On the provision of additional space in libraries, in *The Library*, series 1, vol. 7 (1895), 10. *See above* note 14.

28 J. Winter Jones, Report from the Select Committee on Public Libraries, in *North British Review*, vol. 15 (1851), 177; R. Garnett, On shelving periodicals, in *Library Chronicle*, vol. 2 (1885), 56.

29 E. E. Thomas, Professor Dziatzko on the British Museum, in *Library Association Monthly Notes*, vol. 3 (1882), 10–15, 26–35, 46–53.

30 J. Winter Jones, op.cit. (*see* note 28), 177.

31 A. H. King, *Printed Music in the British Museum* (1979), 42, 48, 55–7.

32 A. H. King, The Hirsch Music Library, in *MLA Notes*, Sept. 1952, 381–7.

33 *Report of the Commissioners*, 1850 (*see above* note 19), questions 9182–92, 9757.

34 BM Archives (Trustees' Sub-committee on Printed Books and MSS minutes) CE 7/3, 1545–6; ibid., 1653–4; (Trustees' Committee minutes) CE 3/35, 13038.

35 BM Archives (Trustees' Committee minutes) CE 3/40, 1586–9; E. Miller, *That Noble Cabinet* (1973), 275–6.

36 BM Archives (Trustees' Sub-committee on Printed Books and MSS minutes) CE 7/5, 2541; (Trustees' Committee minutes) CE 3/50, 1223; *The Library*, series 1, vol. 7 (1895), 400.

37 BL Newspaper Library newsletter, no. 5 (1982).

38 BM Archives (Officers' Reports) CE 5/1, 109; CE 5/10, 2143 etc.

APPENDICES

A   PRINCIPAL PRIMARY SOURCES OF CLASSIFICATION

The main primary sources of classification are listed by R. C. Alston in his *Topical Index to Pressmarks* (1986), as follows:

1   Barnard's classed catalogue of the King's Library [1827?];
2   A placing guide to the presses up to 3000 [*c.*1840?];
3   A placing guide to the presses 3001–12991 [*c.*1877];
4   A placing guide to guard-books [*c.*1920];
5   A placing guide to case-books [*c.*1920];
6   An index to the pressmarks for Academies (Ac.);
7   A handlist for Academies (Ac.);
8   An index to the pressmarks for Periodical Publications (P.P.);
9   A handlist for Periodical Publications (P.P.);
10   A placing guide to the State Paper Room (4 vols.);
11   A placing guide to Official Gazettes;
12   Manuscript and typescript placing guides used in the Department of Oriental Manuscripts and Printed Books;
13   Alison Gould, *Named Special Collections* (1981);
14   The heading *Collection* in the General Catalogue.

B   CLASSIFICATION IN THE OLD LIBRARY

Comparison of samples from the first and second series of classification in the Old Library, indicating the greater detail in the second.

520, 521	Aristotle. Philosophy		
522–524	Politics, etc.	713	Politics and political economy
		714	Politics and trade
524–528	Moral philosophy		
529–530	Mathematics, etc.	715	Mathematics
		716	Mathematics and natural philosophy
		717	Chemistry and military art
		718–719	Occult sciences

[58]

535, 536	Natural philosophy	720	Philosophy
		721, 722	Essays and moral philosophy
537, 538	Mechanics		
		723, 724	Botany
		725	Botany and geology
		726	Geology and mineralogy
539–549	Medicine	727	Natural history and physiology
		728–730	Natural history
550–565	Art		
566–571	Geography		

C   COMPARISON BETWEEN THE CLASSIFICATIONS OF WATTS AND BRUNET

Brunet	*Watts*
Bible:	Bible and parts thereof:
Polyglott	Polyglott
Hebrew and Syriac	Hebrew
Greek	Greek
Latin	Latin
French	French, Italian, Spanish
Italian, Spanish and Portuguese	
German and Dutch	German
	Dutch and Scandinavian
Romansch	
English, Irish, and Gaelic	English
	Celtic Languages
Danish, Swedish, Finnish	
Slavonic and Esthonian	Slavonic
Arabic, Armenian, Turkish and Georgian	Oriental
Indian Dialects	
Chinese	
Malay	American, Polynesian, etc.
North American	
Books of the Old Testament	
New Testament and Separate Books	
	Concordances
	Commentaries

[59]

In Liturgies: Brunet begins with works on Liturgies, Watts places them at the end. In Philosophy and science: Brunet groups Occult philosophy, alchemy, etc., in an appendix, more logically than Watts who has the order Mathematics, astronomy, astrology, occult sciences, spiritualism, and then returns to physics, optics, etc.

These, and many more examples make it clear that Watts was familiar with Brunet's work and drew upon it, without adopting it *in toto* in compiling his own classification.

D   OUTLINE OF WATT'S 'ELASTIC SYSTEM' OF CLASSIFICATION

3005–3110	Bibles
3125–3268	Biblical commentaries
3355–3405	Liturgies, Latin
3406–3409	Liturgies, English
3425–3438	Hymns
3455–3457	Prayers
3474–3479	Liturgies (Appendix)
3504–3507	Catechisms
3553–3606	Religious series
3622–3805	Collected works of theologians
3832–3851	Mediaeval theology
3900–3943	Controversial theology
4014–4018	Christian evidence
4033–4092	Jews, Papacy, etc. (not historical)
4103–4184	Controversial theology, England and America
4192–4381	Miscellaneous theology
4397–4422	Christian practice. Religious fiction
4423–4499	Sermons
4503–4507	Non-Christian religions
4515–4786	Religious history
4804–4999	Religious biography
5005–5806	Law, ancient and foreign
6003–6786	Law, English and American
6825–6956	Military and international law
7001–7299	Natural history
7305–7689	Medicine
7700–7711	Archaeology
7742–7877	Art
7889–7900	Music
7904–7920	Games
7940–7960	Useful arts

8004–8181	Politics
8204–8207	Political economy
8218–8248	Trade and finance
8275–8289	Social science
8304–8385	Education
8403–8436	Ethical subjects
8458–8486	Philosophy
8503–8567	Mathematics
8610–8634	Occult science
8703–8777	Physical sciences
8803–8839	Naval and military science
8896–8913	Chemistry and photography
9004–9781	History
9902–9930	Genealogy
10001–10009	Geography
10024–10498	Topography
10600–10899	Biography
10902–10923	Letters
11304–11410	Greek and Latin texts
11420–11689	Poetry
11704–11806	Drama
11822–11868	Literary history and criticism
11898–11926	Bibliography
12199–12224	Series and encyclopaedias
12225–12299	Collected works
12301–12360	Speeches, proverbs, and essays
12403–12730	Fiction
12800–12832	Children's books
12901–12991	Philology

For the pressmarks used for books on the ground floor of the Reading Room and in the first gallery (2000–2410, BB, AA etc) *see* above pp.35–7.

Extracts from Watts's classification, as used until 1964, showing the varying degrees of geographical subdivision in different headings.

Education

General	8304–8313
S. Europe, Africa, India	8355–8356
N. Europe	8357–8359
England	8364–8369
America	8385

Theology

Controversial works. S. Europe	3900–3902
Reformers. Separate works	3905–3906
Controversial Works: Germany	3907–3914
Holland, Scandinavia	3925
Russia, Eastern Church	3926
R.C. Controversy in England	3932–3943

(Then a break for general works on Jews, Papacy,
Monasticism, and Jesuits.)

Controversial Works: Church of England	4103–4110
Nonconformists	4135–4140
Society of Friends	4151–4152
Scotland and Ireland	4165–4176
America	4182–4184

History

General	9004–9012
Ancient Greek	9025–9027
Ancient Roman	9039–9043
Asiatic (including 1939–45 War)	9055–9059
African	9060–9062
Europe: (early, mediaeval, general)	9071–9073
(to 1914, 18th and 19th cents)	9075–9080
(1914–1918 War)	09080–9088
(from 1919, including 1939–45 War)	9100–9102
Turkish Empire, modern Greece, Balkans	9134–9136
Italy	9150–9170
Spain, Portugal	9180–9196
France: (early and general)	9200–9220
(Revolution and modern)	9225–9232
Switzerland	9304–9305
Austria-Hungary	9314–9315
Germany: (early and general)	9325–9340
(from 1870)	9365–9386
Holland	9405–9406
Belgium	9414–9415
Scandinavia	9424–9435
Russia and Finland	9454–9456
Poland	9475–9476
England (early and general)	9501–9507
Ireland	9508
Scotland	9509–9510

England (modern), British Empire	9512–9525
America: (discovery and early)	9551
(French and English colonies, Canada)	9555
(USA)	9602–9617
(Central and Southern)	9770–9774
Australasia	9781

The division of English history into two by the intervention of Irish and Scottish history will be noted. Another instance of the same division occurs in Topography, where the subdivisions for America are: General and USA; Polar Regions (North and South); Canada; West Indies; Central and South America.

E   NEW CLASSIFICATION FOR PLACING, 1964

BOOKS

Class		
X.10	Religion	Covering subjects now in theology, church history, canon law
X.20	Law	No change
X.31	Natural history	Present subjects: natural history (general), botany, geology, zoology
X.32	Medicine	No change
X.41	Archaeology	No change
X.42	Visual arts	Present subjects: art (general), architecture, painting, sculpture, ceramics, etc.
X.43	Music	No change
X.44	Skills	Present subjects: useful arts, sport
X.51	Economics	Present subjects: trade, communications, industry
X.52	Human science	Present subjects: social science, education, ethics, philosophy, occult science
X.61	General Science	Present subjects: mathematics, astronomy, general science
X.62	Technology	No change
X.63	Naval and military	Present subjects: naval science, military science
X.70	History	Present subjects: history, genealogy, heraldry, politics
X.80	Local history	Present subjects: geography, ethnography, topography
X.90	Literature and language	Present subjects: literature, literary criticism, philology
X.97	General series	No change
X.98	Encyclopaedias	No change
X.99	Children's books	No change
Y.	South Bank books	No change

WORKS IN PROGRESS

As above, but insert figure 0 before class number, e.g. X. 0618/32

PERIODICALS

New classification

P. [0.]		Bibliographical periodicals
P.1	= Class X.10	
P.2	=	X.20
P.3	=	X.31, 32
P.4	=	X.41–44
P.5	=	X.51, 52
P.6	=	X.61–63
P.7	=	X.70
P.8	=	X.80
P.9	=	X.90
P.10	= Unclassifiable general periodicals	
P.11	= Children's periodicals	
P.12	= Directories	
P.13	= Ephemerides	
P.14	= Annual Reports (if necessary; preferably continue at A.R.)	
P.20	= NRLSI (South Bank)	

F   SPECIAL PRESSMARKS

Special pressmarks have from time to time been allocated to individual collections or categories of material when it was considered useful for them to be shelved as unities, e.g. because of historic ownership or formation, or subject significance. Those associated with a particular collector or previous owner are listed in Alison Gould's *Named Special Collections in the Department of Printed Books* (1981) and are not included here.

AA.   Reading Room reference books
Ac.   Academies. See p.39
A.N.   American novels
A.S.   Official Publications Library. (US official publications)
B.A., etc.   Official Publications Library. Case books
Bar.   Reading Room reference books
BB.   Reading Room bibliographies
Book jackets
Braille.   13007–13008
B.S.   Official Publications Library. British official publications

C.   Case books. See p.31
Car.   Comic and other illustrated booklets
CH.   Children's books
Circ.   Reading Room reference books
Crach. Tab.   Case books in the North Library. Formerly in Cracherode Room table cases
C.S.   Official Publications Library. (British Commonwealth official publications)
Cup.   Cupboard books. See p.31
D.A., etc.   Official Publications Library case books
Election Posters
H.   Paperback fiction
I.A., I.B., I.C.   Incunabula
I.C.S.   International Correspondence Schools
I.S., I.S.A., etc.   Official Publications Library. (Indian official publications)
K.   Map Library case books
K.C.   King's Library case books
King's Pamphlets.   King's Library case books
K.T.C.   Books formerly in King's Library table cases
L.   Large books
L.A.S.   Official Publications Library. (Latin American official publications)
L.C.C.   Official Publications Library. (London County Council publications)
L.R.   Large books. (Abbreviation of Large Room, precursor of the North Library, in which these books were shelved.)
Maps, Mar.   Map Library
Mic.   Microcopies
M.K.   Music Library case books
Mon.   Oriental Mss. and Printed Books. (Mongolian)
M.R.   Music Library. (Music Room)
N., NN., NNN.   Novels
N.L.   North Library
N.L.Case   N.L.Tab.   Case books, formerly in the North Library
N.   Tabs
Nov.   Novels
N.U.C.   National Union Catalog (of the United States). Reading Room reference shelves
O.G.   Official Publications Library. (Official Gazettes)
P., P.P.   Periodical publications
Parl. Papers   Official Publications Library. (Parliamentary papers)
Ref.   Reference books, in the Reading Room and staff workrooms
S., S.A., etc.   Official Publications Library
S.C.   Sale catalogues
S.P.R.   Official Publications Library. (Under its earlier name of State Paper Room)
S. Ref.   Official Publications Library reference books

T.   Tracts

Tab.   Table case

T.C.   Some case books in the North Library. (Formerly Table Case)

Th. Cts.   Theatrical newspaper cuttings

Thomason Tracts.   Photographic reproductions of the original set at pressmark E., which is listed by Gould

T.T.   Time tables

U-Burney.   A microfilm set of the Burney newspapers

U.N.   Official Publications Library. (United Nations publications)

Voting Registers.   Official Publications Library

W., W.E.   Woolwich Repository

W.P.   Works in progress

G   NEW PRESSMARKING SYSTEM FOR ST PANCRAS, FROM 1986

Pressmarks retained

1   Some Case and Cup. as used at present. There is no further separate provision
for locked-up books in the new system. A few special pressmarks, such as Cerv,
IA, IX have been retained.

2   All existing series and dumps, of all types of pressmark.

3   MIC – all microforms

4   SC – all sales catalogues

5   Nov – hardback copyright fiction. This will now include the date, e.g. Nov 1986/
742.

6   H – paperback copyright fiction

7   667 – bookbinding

8   2700 – bibliography, librarianship

New pressmarks

1   *Horizontal storage.* All books over 38 cm high or 36 cm deep will be placed
in the HS class.

Each of the following classes will be subdivided into three size categories:

2   *Rare books, i.e.:*

All non-locked-up books published up to 1870.

All later books over 23 cm deep (supersedes the L sequence).

Pressmark example: RB.23.a.1.

3   *Non-rare books, i.e.* all non-locked-up books published from 1871. (This class
will also incorporate the date. Supersedes X.200, etc.)

YA.   General non-copyright

YC.   General copyright

YH.   High use (copyright and non-copyright)

YK.   Low-use copyright

YL.   Low use non-copyright

YM. Music
YV. Visual arts
Pressmark example: YA. 1985.a.1.
For serials, the same categories are used, the prefix Z replacing Y.
4   *Periodicals and series* (Supersedes P., also X.0200, etc.)
ZA.9. General non-copyright.
And so on, following the pattern for non-rare books, above. Dates are not
included in this group of pressmarks.

H   CLASSIFICATION OF PERIODICALS, TO 1964

Outline of the classification scheme for shelving periodical publications to 1964.
It should be noted that many of the divisions are again subdivided, e.g. that for
Useful Arts, which has sixteen subheadings.

Religion	P.P. 1–1041	Statistics	3890–3895
Sociology	1046–1180	Travel and Geography	3900–4016
Education	1181–1234	Literature	4067–4881
Philosophy	1235–1260	Philology	4884–5126
Law	1263–1416	Theatre, Drama	5141–5204
Economics and Trade	1423–1424	Journalism	5264
Science and Technology	} 1425–1891	Reviews	5270–5939
Useful Arts		Children	5990–5993
Art, Archaeology	1898–1948	Magazines	5998–6018
Natural Science	1949–2361	Country Magazines	6019–6089
Almanacs, Directories	2374–2677	University and School	
Medicine	2681–3312	Magazines	6090–6153
History and Politics	3330–3803	Bibliography	6460–6527
Anthropology and		Annuals	6600–6758
Ethnography	3860–3868	Propaganda	7000, etc.
Genealogy and Heraldry	3869–3881		

For the classification of periodicals from 1964 *see* Appendix E.

I   ARRANGEMENT OF THE ACADEMY PRESSMARKS

1–1997   General academies arranged topographically.

Theology	1998–2095	Statistics	2401–2495
Law	2098–2196	Commerce	2498–2577
Sociology	2247–2294	Education	2592–2703
Economics	2300–2400	Philosophy	2705–2753

Natural Science	2799–3100	Industries	4401–4497
Geology	3101–3200	Fine Arts	4506–4732
Mineralogy	3204–3238	Architecture	4746–4901
Botany	3239–3323	Photography	5038–5064
Horticulture	3327–3381	Music	5125–5178
Agriculture	3382–3549	Chess	5186
Zoology	3550–3601	Archaeology	5198–5808
Entomology	3603–3694	Numismatics	5809–5899
Medicine	3695–3870	Genealogy	5901–5988
Veterinary Medicine	3871–3882	Geography	5996–6215
Chemistry	3890–3965	Anthropology	6220–6308
Meteorology	4036–4117	History	6430–8640
Astronomy	4121–4197	Oriental Studies	8796–8830
Mathematics	4205–4288	Literature	8836–9232
Engineering	4304–4327	Individual Authors	9384–9514
Military Science	4330–4362	Bibliography	9524–9745
Hydrography	4365–4400	Philology, Folklore	9756–9986

NB Included under 'Education' at Ac. 2592–2703 are the publications of the majority of universities (a few have been entered in the topographical series), and this section is in consequence very bulky.

J OFFICIAL PUBLICATIONS

The present classification of official publications has developed during the last century; it was greatly expanded since 1945, and then simplified from the 1970s.

B.S. British official publications. Subdivided numerically for government departments, and again for individual publications (e.g. B.S. 47/15).

B.L. British local government publications, subdivided by a further letter and numeration, with abundant intervals for additions. E.g. B.L. B. 1. Barking.

B. 5. Barnsley.

B.L. S. Scotland.

B.L. W. Wales.

This is used only for Registers of Electors, though it was hoped to include all local government publications. Those of the London County Council and the Greater London Council were, however, shelved together under the pressmark L.C.C.

C.S. British Commonwealth official publications. Subdivided geographically and again numerically

C.S. A. Europe (includes Channel Islands, Isle of Man, and Republic of Ireland

C.S. B.	Asia
C.S. C.	East and West Africa
C.S. D.	Central and South Africa
C.S. E.	Canada
C.S. F.	West Indies
C.S. G.	Australasia
C.S. H.	Was originally intended to cover Commonwealth organisations extending over two or more continents, but in practice the publications of such bodies as the Commonwealth Agriculture Bureaux and the Commonwealth Secretariat are placed at B.S. or in the General Library.
A.S.	United States official publications. Those of individual states are distinguished by abbreviations, e.g. A.S. A. Alabama, A.S. C. Connecticut. Where two or more states begin with the same letter each has a block of numbers allocated to it.
L.A.S.	Latin American official publications, with the exception of colonies in Latin America. Originally arranged in a simple numerical sequence, but the blocks allocated to individual states were far too small (e.g. L.A.S. 436–40 for the Dominican Republic). Now, countries are arranged alphabetically and each has a further distinguishing letter (not necessarily an initial) in the pressmark, e.g. L.A.S.A. Argentina, L.A.S.B. Brazil. Within these classes there are numerical sequences for provinces and government departments in alphabetical order.
I.S.	Indian official publications, with numerical subdivision for departments, and initials for provinces, e.g. I.S. M. Madras, I.S. MY. Mysore, and including I.S. BU. Burma. I.S. also includes I.S. BA. for Bangladesh and I.S. PA. for Pakistan.
S.	All other official publications. Subdivided geographically, S.A.-S.R. for European countries, arranged alphabetically except for a few groups (e.g. the Scandinavian and Slavonic countries): S.S. – S.Y. for non-European countries. Originally all official publications other than those from America and the Commonwealth were given shelfmarks beginning S, and followed by a block of numbers for each country. The block for Austria and Hungary is still currently used and added to, but a further alphabetical suffix has been used for all other countries. Some large series however, such as the Swedish parliamentary papers, have kept their old shelfmarks although they are shelved with other publications from the relevant country.

There are further subdivisions for component members of a federation (e.g. USSR) or province of a country (e.g. Italy S.H. 1–500: Kingdom of Naples S.H. 551–570).

Other subdivisions. Within the shelfmark allotted to each country, etc., further arrangement is by numeration, originally in alphabetical order of departments, but now in most cases following the arrangement of the General Catalogue, commencing with the Legislature and proceeding to Laws and Government Departments. Numbers are allocated in blocks, and very generous gaps left for future expansion.

After each number the individual publications from that department etc. are given their own number following a /, e.g. A.S. 285/30. More recently the first vacant number at the end of a country's block has been used to place new publications from all departments in order of accessioning.

U.N. Publications of all international bodies, other than those exclusive to the British Commonwealth. This pressmark has been commenced since the formation of the United Nations Organisation; previously, such publications were placed either with those of one of the countries concerned, or in the General Library (e.g. publications of the League of Nations, formerly at Ac. 2299.). The arrangement is:

U.N. A,B.	United Nations
U.N. D,E.	League of Nations
U.N. F–O	Large subsidiary bodies of the United Nations (e.g. International Labour Office)
U.N. Q.	Minor organisations affiliated to the United Nations (e.g. World Meteorological Organisation)
U.N. P.	International bodies not connected with the United Nations (e.g. Caribbean Commission; Conference summoned by the Holy Alliance, 1818–20; International Military Commands)
U.N. R–W.	Important subdivisions of the League of Nations, including International Courts (U.N. S.)

O.G. Official Gazettes, with subsidiary letters and blocks of figures allocated for all countries in the world, in alphabetical order. Sub-series and supplements indicated by additional numeration, using / and (). C.G. is used for some gazettes on permanent loan from the Foreign and Commonwealth Office.

S.P.R. Ref. Was originally used for the working collection of official indexes, bibliographies, etc., for use by staff and readers. This collection has now been dispersed.

B.S. Ref.   Those British State Papers most commonly required by readers,
            e.g. Censuses, Public General Acts, Sessional papers, etc.

Publications of dependent territories other than those of Great Britain, are
arranged within the general geographical classification at pressmark S., without
regard to the parent country.

Rare or valuable State Papers are kept in locked cases, formerly in the Arched
Room, and then in the former State Paper Room. All publications issued before
1700 are included in this category. There are two main divisions, for British and
foreign, distinguished by the letters B. and D. respectively. The British is
subdivided by sovereigns, distinguished by additional letters, from Edward IV, B.A.,
to William III, B.O., and further by regnal years within which items are shelved in
order of accession, e.g. for a publication of Charles II, B.L. 12/1. This provides a
complete conspectus of early official publications, in chronological order. The
foreign section is subdivided according to countries and provinces in alphabetical
order, e.g.

D.A.   Denmark
D.B.   France
D.C.   Germany
D.C.d.   Baden
D.C.n.   Danzig

A place is included for Scottish publications issued before the Act of Union.

K   MAPS

The classification for maps of R. H. Major. The main classes are:

The World; Europe; Great Britain, England and Wales, Scotland, Ireland, France,
Italy, Switzerland, Germany, Austria-Hungary, Netherlands, Prussia, Poland, Scandi-
navia (collectively and individual countries), Russia, Turkey in Europe and Balkans;
Asia; Africa; America; Pacific; Australia.

Under modern towns the sub-headings used are: Atlases, General Plans, Special
Plans, Collections of Views, Views, Harbour, Bay, Environs.

Pressmarks are allocated as follows:

5	Collections of Astronomical Charts, Celestial Atlases, etc.
10	Solar Systems. General Charts
15	Particular Charts
20	Celestial Planispheres and Charts of the Zodiac
23	Eclipses
24	Comets
45–64	Ancient Geography
65–449	Europe
450–589	Asia
590–689	Africa
690–734	Sacred Geography (12 subdivisions)
735–864	Ecclesiastical Geography
865–915	Geography of the Middle Ages
865	France in the time of Clovis.
870	Various maps of France in the Middle Ages.
875	Britain in the time of the Saxons.
879	Wales in its Ancient Divisions.
880	England in the time of the Saxons.
885	Flanders in the Middle Ages.
890	Friesland in the Middle Ages.
895	Parts of Europe in the Middle Ages.
896	Empire of Charlemagne.
899	Syria and Palestine in the time of the Crusades.
902	Spain during the occupation of the Moors.
903	Tables relating to the geography and history of the Middle Ages.
905–915	Charts of the Dépôt de la Marine.

916–98580   Modern Geography (by continents, countries, etc.)

A revised version of Major's schedules was produced in 1987 by R. C. Alston and J. D. Elliot. It is entitled *The British Library Map Library Geographic Classification Schedule,* 5 vols. The copy in the Map Library is placed at Maps 210.a.56.

L   ORIENTAL PRINTED BOOKS

Arrangement of Oriental printed books is by language.

First Pressmark	Last Pressmark	Language
753	756	Coptic/Syriac
757		Persian

1900	01985	Hebrew
11092	11102	Translations from Chinese and Japanese
11103		South East Asian
11110		Translations from Chinese and Japanese
14002	14102	Sanskrit
14104	14119	Urdu
14120	14164	North Indian
14165		Sinhalese
14169	14187	South Indian
14300	14304	South East Asian
14310		Tibetan
14400	14499	Turkish
14500	14599	Arabic
14620	14654	Indonesian/Malay
14701	14797	Persian
14807	14837	Persian
14889	14997	Kurdish
14990		Iranian
14999		Persian
15000	15018	Ref. books
15019	15234	Chinese
15236	15684	Chinese
16000	16310	Japanese
16500	16599	Korean
16602	16697	Vietnamese
17000		Coptic
17021	17089	Armenian
17100	17120	Yiddish
19951	19968	Manchu
19999		Tibetan
BUR. 1–		Burmese
C.49, C.049, C.50, C.50*		Hebrew Case Books
HP.1– (BOUND VOLS)		Hebrew Periodicals
HP.269 (NEWSPAPERS)		Hebrew
JAV.1–		Javanese
KAN.1–		Kannada
MAL.1–		Malayam
M.DRAV		Various
MON		Mongolian
MPC		Guard Book (Misc. Papers, Chinese)

MPJ	Guard Book (Misc. Papers, Japanese)
OP (BOUND VOLS)	Various
OP (NEWSPAPERS)	Various
OR.59, OR.64 – OR.65, OR.70 – OR.77, OR.80, OR.81	Select Books
OR.90	Indian Select Books
PIB	Proscribed Indian Books
SIAM	Siamese
TAM	Tamil
TEL	Telugu

2

THE MOVE OF PRINTED BOOKS FROM MONTAGU HOUSE, 1838–42

P. R. HARRIS

INTRODUCTION

When Antonio Panizzi became Keeper of Printed Books on 15 July 1837,[1] he was faced with difficult problems. He was short of staff, he lacked sufficient money for acquisitions, he had the enormous task of compiling a new general catalogue, his deputy H. F. Cary was furious at having failed to achieve the Keepership and was to submit his resignation in October and cease duty on 13 December[2] – but the problem requiring most immediate attention was that of moving the old library from Montagu House to the recently completed North Wing of the new British Museum building.

It was not of course the whole British Museum library which had to be moved. The collections of the Department of Manuscripts (except for the rolls and charters) had been moved to the Manuscripts Saloon to the south of the gallery intended for the library of George III in April 1827.[3] The Reading Rooms were also moved from Montagu House to the two southernmost rooms of the east wing (now called the Middle and South Rooms) in 1827[4] (Fig. 6). The move of George III's library from Kensington Palace to its new gallery (at first called the Royal Library and subsequently the King's Library) began on 23 June 1828 and was completed in less than six weeks.[5]

The transfer of the manuscripts had eased the problem of over-crowding in the old house but only for a short time. In December 1831 Henry Ellis, the Principal Librarian, reported to the Trustees that space for books in the old house was running out. The Trustees thereupon wrote to the Treasury saying that Montagu House would only hold normal accessions of books for two or three years; a bequest or purchase of 2,000 or 3,000 volumes could not be accommodated. Moreover the old house was a great fire risk because much combustible material had been used in its construction. For these reasons it was urgently necessary to commence building the North Wing of the new Museum in 1832 to provide space for the library and for the increasing number of readers.[6] Given the normal attitude of the Treasury the Trustees cannot however have been very surprised to be told at their meeting on 11 February 1832 that the necessary funds would not be forthcoming.[7]

Pressure on space was so great that Robert Smirke, the architect to the British Museum, was asked if anything could be done to cure the damp in the basement of Montagu House and thus make it suitable for the storage of books. He replied on 12 January 1832 that nothing effective could be done – the level of the floor was about four feet below the level of the courtyard, and the average level of the springs in the area was not more than three feet below the floors.[8] Despite this depressing report, Henry Baber, the Keeper of Printed Books, noted on 14 January 1833 that between 13,000 and 14,000 volumes of printed books were stored in this basement. This represented about ten per cent of the old library (i.e. excluding the King's Library of George III) because in March Baber informed Forshall, the secretary of the Museum, that he had had the books in the old library counted (including the Banks collection) and the total was 146,957.[9]

I · CONSTRUCTION OF THE NORTH WING

In January 1833 the Trustees renewed their request to the Treasury for funds to begin the construction of the North Wing. In March the Treasury agreed in principle but wanted an exact description of the proposed building and an estimate of the cost before authorising any expenditure. Smirke submitted to the General Meeting of the Trustees held on 18 March a report referring to the plans approved by the Treasury and the Trustees in July 1823. He estimated that the building would hold 200,000 volumes and cost £63,000. It would be 350 feet long, with the centre part forty-four feet wide and the two ends each forty-two feet wide; there would be a colonnade on the south front. The Trustees decided that they wanted a means of communication between the King's Library and the rooms holding books at the west end of the North Wing, which did not involve passing through the two Reading Rooms at the east end of the North Wing. They asked Smirke to prepare a new plan, abandoning the colonnade and bringing the edge of the building to the line of the proposed columns – thus creating the rooms which in due course held the Banksian and Cracherode libraries and extending the large central room southwards[10] (Fig. 7). On 26 March the General Meeting considered and approved the amended plans – the cost had risen to £70,000 and Smirke now thought that the building would hold 300,000 volumes and could be ready by 1836.[11] On 20 April the Trustees' Committee gave orders that Smirke should be sent details of Baber's requirements for the new building. He had already stated these in a document dated 25 March – officers should have studies, and dry rooms should be provided for storing large collections awaiting processing, for housing duplicates, for classifying the books, for sorting the great mass of newspapers received from the Stamp Office, and for storing catalogues and other works published by the Museum. Baber suggested that these workrooms and storerooms should form a low building to the north of the main structure.[12] Smirke replied to this document on 31 May. He said that Baber's suggestion of a low range of rooms to the north was not feasible because there

6 Montagu House, drawn by George Scharf in 1845 from the west side of the forecourt, looking north-east. The great gateway is on the right and the front of Montagu House on the left. Rising above the south-east corner of Montagu House is the south end of the east wing of Smirke's new building (BM Dept of Prints and Drawings, Scharf, book 3, p.8 (644)).

was not sufficient space between the North Wing and the boundary wall, but he added that the basement rooms of the main building could be used for storage. Because of the enlargement of the central part of the North Wing there would be no room for the studies requested by Baber – officers would have to use the recesses in the bookcases of that part of the building.[13]

The construction of the North Wing began in the latter part of 1833 and in March 1835 Smirke informed the Trustees that it should be ready to receive the books in 1837. By December (when the wing was ready for plastering and internal finishes) he had come to the conclusion that his estimate of 1833 that the North Wing would hold 300,000 volumes had been over-optimistic. He had based this estimate on a sample count in the King's Library where 17,200

7 The Large Room (later called the North Library) as it was in 1851 (*Illustrated London News*, 7 June 1851).

volumes occupied 1,640 feet (i.e. ten and a half volumes per foot). However, doorways and staircases reduced the amount of shelving in the North Wing, which Smirke now thought would amount to 25,285 feet, and at ten and a half volumes per foot this gave a total of about 266,000 volumes. To this figure should be added the 1,080 feet of shelving in the centre room of the basement which would hold another 11,340 volumes. In Smirke's opinion therefore the new building would accommodate about 280,000 volumes.[14]

Baber submitted some critical comments on these figures. In the first place he believed that only 7.61, not ten and a half, volumes could be accommodated in each foot of shelf space. In the second place, Smirke stated that there would be 26,365 feet of shelf space (including 1,080 feet in the basement) – but the library already occupied 22,570 feet, and 250 feet would be needed for books reserved by readers each day in the reading rooms, thus increasing the total to 22,820. So the expansion space would only be 3,545 feet which would hold about 27,000 volumes. If the library continued to grow at the rate of the preceding three years one third of the expansion space would be needed by the time of the move, and within four years more the building would be full. It must also be remembered that the 1,080 feet in the basement was not suitable for the permanent storage of books – so this reduced the expansion space from 27,000 volumes to 19,000.[15] When Baber's report was read to the Trustees' Sub-Committee on the Buildings on 22 December 1835, Forshall reminded them that it had always been intended to use part of the South Wing for book storage, when it was eventually built. There had also been mention of a building at the west end of the North Wing (the future Arch Room) to hold 100,000 volumes. Forshall also suggested a low building to the east of the King's Library (the Long Room, which was built in the mid-1840s) to hold 60,000 volumes of printed books, and provide unpacking and storage space for the Department of Manuscripts. The Trustees did not however feel inclined to pursue these possibilities at that stage; they thought that the first priority was to complete the ground floor of the North Wing so that the books could be removed from the fire risks inherent in Montagu House.[16]

II · BABER'S PLANS FOR THE MOVE

In December 1836 Smirke wrote to say that the North Wing would be ready for the move of the books by 1 September 1837, and that the Reading Rooms in the north-east corner would be ready for occupation by May.[17] Baber (Fig. 8) began to consider the detailed steps which would be involved in the transfer of approximately 163,000 volumes.[18] But then, in February 1837, as a result of the recommendations of the Select Committees of the House of Commons held in 1835 and 1836 to investigate the Museum, the Trustees introduced new regulations to govern the duties and remuneration of the staff. These included a provision that officers should hold no paid employment outside the Museum. So on 7 March 1837 Baber (who was also rector of Stretham in Cambridgeshire) wrote to Forshall saying that he could not accept the increased salary offered, because his existing commitments would prevent him carrying out the extra duties involved. Moreover, his health and strength would not permit him to undertake additional exertions. He hoped therefore

8 Henry Baber, Keeper of Printed Books, 1812–37 (BL Archives).

that during his few remaining months of service, after thirty-one years in the employment of the Trustees, he might be permitted to continue as before.[19]

The fact that he had decided to retire did not cause him to neglect his duties. On 8 April he reported that he had been spending part of his time making an inventory, class by class, of each press of books in the old library, to expedite their removal when the time came.[20] He also compiled a memorandum for the guidance of his successor detailing the way in which the move might be organized. This document is dated 24 June 1837, his last day of service after twenty-five years as Keeper, and he left copies of it with Ellis, the Principal Librarian, Cary, his Assistant Keeper, and Panizzi.[21]

He began by stating that the first object must be to place the books so that they occupied the least possible space without being too crowded, and to make the library agreeable to the eye by arranging the books according to size. To avoid difficulties for both readers and staff no more books should be removed at any one time than would be roughly sufficient to fill one press. When the books were in their new rooms they should be placed on temporary tables in rows, beginning with folios and working down to the smallest sized books, and then divided into shelf-lengths. Then each volume or set should have attached to it one of the tickets (measuring about one inch by four inches) which members of the staff had prepared, giving its pressmark in the old house, e.g.:

4 L b Pflaumern, H.a.
1669.

As soon as the book had been placed on the shelf its new mark was to be added in red ink to the ticket, e.g.:

4 L b Pflaumern, H.a.
1669.
350.a.

The ticket was then to be removed from the book and given to a copyist who would alter the pressmark in the interleaved copy of the catalogue kept in the Reading Rooms, and in the other copy kept in the library itself. The tickets, sorted into pressmark order, could then form the basis from which hand catalogues could be transcribed containing an inventory of every shelf in the library. Extra large books, such as atlases and books of plates, were to be laid aside and then placed in class order in the extra deep shelves provided.[22]

Baber was in favour of placing the books in classes so far as possible. He was of the opinion that the classified arrangement adopted by Samuel Harper (Keeper of Printed Books from 1765 to 1803) was not satisfactory; and in any case, because of lack of space, it had been less and less observed for many years past. He therefore recommended a new scheme based on the system of classification drawn up by T. H. Horne and printed for submission to the Trustees in 1825. This scheme should employ Horne's six principal classes (religion, jurisprudence, philosophy – intellectual, moral, political, natural and mathematical – arts and trades, history and literature), the sections of each class, and the primary divisions of each section; but to employ the subdivisions of each primary division would be too complicated.[23] To assemble the books in classes it would be necessary to examine the summary view drawn up by Baber of the contents of the presses in Montagu House, and then mark a copy of Horne's *Outlines for the Classification of a Library* showing where the books of each section were to be found in the old house.

Baber went on to advocate a good collection of reference books in the reading rooms. To his edition of Baber's document Richard Garnett added the following note: 'So far as I am aware this is the first suggestion extant for the formation of a library of reference for the use of visitors to a public reading room. Something of the kind must have existed in Montagu House, but Mr. Baber's observations plainly imply that it was exceedingly meagre and inadequate.'[24] This comment fails to take account of the fact that in the Reading Rooms at the south end of the East Wing (in use from 1827 to 1838) there were about 5,000 reference books.[25] Baber recommended an ample supply of dictionaries in every language, biographical and historical dictionaries, gazetteers, atlases and maps, encyclopaedias, dictionaries of science and the arts, the *Gentleman's Magazine* and other journals frequently used, collections of the classics, a few of the best classed catalogues, county histories and other topographical works, the *London Gazette,* Acts of Parliament, Parliamentary Sessional Papers and the Journals of the Lords and Commons.

The newspapers were to be placed in a room specially prepared for them. The Thomason Tracts must be kept together and so should the pamphlets from room XIII of Montagu House.[26] Periodical works such as the transactions of societies, journals and magazines should be placed in one or more rooms set aside for them, with room for expansion; as the space required was not easy to estimate they should be moved in the final phase. The Trustees would have to decide whether the Cracherode library and the collections of Sir Joseph Banks and Sir Richard Colt Hoare should be kept together or distributed to the appropriate classes throughout the library.[27]

Baber was of the opinion that the most useful form of pressmark would be a number to show the press in which a book was placed with a letter following it to indicate the shelf. He was not in favour of using a number following the letter to indicate the position of the book on the shelf, even though this had been done in the case of the King's Library. (In the event however Panizzi had such third marks affixed in the early 1840s.[28]) Garnett approved of this deviation from Baber's plan: 'to fasten books down by third marks is fatal to strict classification on the shelves, an object of great importance were it not eclipsed by the still more important object of meeting the requisitions of readers with the least possible delay'.[29] As the number of the last press in the King's Library was 304, Baber recommended that the first press in the North Wing should be numbered 305.

III · PANIZZI BECOMES KEEPER

Baber then made preparations for his departure to his rectory at Stretham, Cambridgeshire, and on 19 July Panizzi was officially informed that he had been appointed Keeper.[30] In September he obtained the permission of the Trustees to postpone his vacation until a future year since he had to prepare for the move of the library and supervise changes which he had made in the procedures of his department.[31] He submitted various proposals to the meeting of the Trustees held on 14 October, dealing with such important matters as the purchase policy which he intended to adopt, the condition of the catalogue, and the need to impose restrictions on the use of rare books – but above all he drew attention to the need for more staff to carry out the work involved.[32] Over two years earlier Baber had set Yeates, an Assistant, to work transcribing on tickets the names of the authors and the dates and pressmarks of all the books to be moved, but by the end of July 1837 about 50,000 items still remained to be dealt with. So Panizzi had to put five of his Attendants (out of the staff of eighteen) on to this essential preparatory work, and they were fully occupied on it until mid-September when the figure had been reduced to 5000–6000 and Yeates could be left to complete the task; this he did by October. The five Attendants were transferred to the work of adding pressmarks to the copy of the catalogue kept in the Reading Room, and Panizzi estimated that they would finish by mid-December, when they would be needed for the task of adding new pressmarks to the two copies of the catalogue (kept in the Reading Room and in the library itself) as the books were moved from Montagu House to their new locations.[33]

As Baber had explained in his memorandum the fact that all the books moved would have to be given new pressmarks considerably complicated the move, and rendered essential the tickets referred to above. It is obvious that the arrangement of the books in Montagu House had become very confused because of lack of space. In 1808 when the first edition of the *Synopsis of the Contents of the British Museum* was published the printed books were arranged in classes in twelve rooms on the first state storey (ground floor) of Montagu House, in room XIII in the basement and in room XIV in the upper part of the house.[34] By December 1810 Baber had to ask for another room in the basement, which was granted to him.[35] The arrival of the Hargrave collection in 1813 made the space problems worse, as did the somewhat increased intake of copyright deposit material after the Copyright Act of 1814 came into operation. In 1814 Planta, the Principal Librarian, reported that he had inspected the three rooms in the basement used for book storage; two were in reasonable condition but that in the north-east corner used for the Hargrave library was very damp and the books were becoming 'hoary'.[36] In June 1815 Baber drew attention to the urgent need for more space, particularly in view of the imminent arrival of the Von Moll collection from Germany. The Trustees gave orders that plans should be prepared for the construction of galleries in the rooms occupied by the Department of Printed Books, and in

July Baber reported that rooms IV to XI could accommodate such galleries, which would provide space for about 38,000 volumes; in addition extra presses could hold another 50,000 volumes. The construction work took place in 1815 and 1816 and a general rearrangement of the library followed.[37] In May 1817 Baber stated that about 24,000 volumes had been arranged in the galleries in classes according to the system adopted in the library.[38] By January 1820 space was again at a premium, and at Baber's request the Trustees ordered that the mezzanine floor above room III, which was empty, should be fitted up with shelves to hold more than 20,000 tracts (probably the French Revolutionary tracts purchased in 1817) which needed to be arranged and catalogued.[39] By 1825 the collection of printed books was still crammed into sixteen rooms,[40] but the move of the manuscripts to the new building in 1827 provided some relief – in particular it made it possible to bring the Banksian collection to the British Museum and house it in three rooms on the second state floor of Montagu House.[41] However, as has been stated above, by the early 1830s the space problem was serious, and eventually the Treasury agreed that extra accommodation must be built. By the end of 1837, on the eve of the move, the 163,363 volumes of the old library were in twenty rooms in Montagu House (including one room called rather ominously 'the dark room').[42] In a note dated 23 June 1838 Panizzi recorded that these consisted of 407 extra folios, 14,845 folios, 22,964 quartos and 125,147 octavos and smaller items.[43]

On 1 October 1837 Smirke wrote to say that the two new Reading Rooms in the north-east corner were ready apart from the casings round the heating coils. The large Centre Room and the south-east room (the Banksian Room) would be ready in a fortnight, and the two west rooms (the Supplementary Rooms) and the south-west room (for the Cracherode library) would be finished in three weeks. There was little to do in the basement; in the centre room there,[44] a specimen case for the newspapers had been constructed to Baber's specification. In a note dated 5 October Panizzi said that this case was well suited for the London newspapers in large folio; the small folio and quarto papers could be put in slightly different cases under the windows. On 18 November in response to a query from Forshall he wrote that he had no suggestions about fitting up the two rooms in the north-west corner of the basement for country newspapers, except that it would be desirable to cut through a door to connect the two rooms. On 6 October he had asked for extra shelves for the ground floor presses of the new rooms. These presses were eleven feet high and were normally only fitted with eight shelves; the presses in the King's Library (which were only three inches higher) had often been fitted with eight shelves, but sometimes with nine. In Panizzi's opinion the presses in the new rooms should each have two shelves extra. (The gallery

[85]

presses in both the King's Library and in the new library were eight feet six inches high; the King's Library presses normally had nine to ten shelves, but the seven shelves usually fitted to the new library presses would, Panizzi believed, be sufficient in the first instance.) By the following day he had a new idea – that the shelves in the new building should be lined with soft leather to preserve the bindings of the books. By 19 October he was asking for a first instalment of furniture for the new rooms, and that the presses of the south-west room should be glazed; he also wanted the presses of the south-east room fitted with wire grills (as the presses in the Reading Rooms were) if there was any possibility of the room being needed for reader accommodation. He also advocated leather falls for every shelf in the library to protect the books from dust to some extent.[45] On 25 October he wrote to Forshall recommending glazed leather for covering the shelves – it should be heavyweight for one third of the shelves, and less heavy for the remaining shelves which would hold the lighter books. Messrs. Taprell, Holland and Son of 19 Marylebone Street submitted an estimate on 8 November for padding the shelves with wadding and covering them with black patent leather at a cost of £1,559–14–11½ and fitting falls at a cost of £342–8–5; this was for a total shelf-run of 22,413 feet.[46] On 18 November the Sub-Committee agreed that falls should be attached to all the shelves, but they only approved the spending of £50 on covering the shelves with leather. They asked Smirke to prepare plans for fixing glazed doors to the furthest compartment of the north-west room (the Second Supplementary Room), but decided that wired doors should not be fitted to the cases in the south-east room (the Banksian Room). On 24 November Smirke estimated that the cost of fitting glazed doors to 26 cases in the Second Supplementary Room would be from £300 if the doors were of wainscot fitted with plate glass, to £770 if the doors were made of brass and fitted with crown glass. The Sub-Committee on the Department of Printed Books considered the matter the next day and deferred a decision – causing Panizzi to submit a report on 7 December deeply regretting that the work was not to proceed.[47]

IV · THE MOVE BEGINS

Panizzi laid before the meeting of the Trustees' Committee held on 16 December the plan which Baber had drawn up for the move, and reported that he proposed to act in accordance with this plan provided that the Trustees approved. The Reading Room should be kept open as usual while the transfer of books from Montagu House took place, but this would necessitate more help, both literary and manual, for the Department of Printed Books. The

Trustees decided that the move should begin while the Museum was closed from 1 to 7 January for one of its thrice-yearly cleaning weeks. On 20 December Ellis informed Forshall that Madden had agreed to allow Coxe and Richards (two of the three Assistants in the Department of Manuscripts) to assist with the move, but in the event this offer of help was withdrawn. In a letter to Forshall dated 28 December Panizzi accepted this philosophically, but pointed out the importance of constant rather than irregular help.[48] From 26 to 30 December the Assistant Yeates and the Attendants Bygrave senior, Bygrave junior, Schofield, Cowtan and Leach were engaged in last-minute corrections to the tickets which were to be used in the move, and in writing out tickets for books bought after the bulk of the tickets had been prepared. According to a note written by Panizzi on 11 January, after the move began on 1 January the number of people employed on it varied considerably from time to time. Forshall helped on 1 and 2 January, and three persons from the Department of Antiquities sometimes assisted. Jones (Assistant in Printed Books), Bach (appointed on 2 January to help Cates, the Superintendent of the Reading Room, but in fact always employed in the Department of Printed Books), Cates, Grabham and Osman of the Reading Room staff, Kemp and Scott (from Forshall's office) and all the Attendants of the Department of Printed Books who could be spared from the service of the Reading Room, were engaged in the move. After the Museum reopened to the public on Monday, 8 January, the Attendants, Phillips and Buckland, helped Panizzi arrange the books in their places on the new shelves when they were not required for the service of the Reading Room. The same applied to six of the Attendants who arranged the tickets for the books. Jones, Bach, Grabham, Kemp and Scott continued to help. Birch of the Department of Antiquities came in as often as he could be spared by Hawkins, the Keeper of his department. Butler the clerk in the Secretary's office had worked on the move from 1 to 6 January.[49]

Since the Trustees wanted a precise record kept of the amount of staff time occupied by the move, Panizzi asked Forshall on 22 January to obtain from the Stationery Office a suitable ruled book. This was supplied and the record was kept up day by day until October 1842. At a meeting of the Sub-Committee on the Department of Printed Books held on 11 January Panizzi was asked what extra help he needed and he requested three Assistants and two or three Attendants. The Sub-Committee recommended that these extra staff should be employed for the period of the move. The first of the Supernumerary Assistants to arrive was Thomas Watts who began work on 17 January and was soon to take over from Panizzi the bulk of the work of organizing the move (Fig. 9). He was joined by Bullen and Russell by the end of January.[50]

By 8 February the Cracherode collection had been moved, new pressmarks had been assigned to the volumes, and most of the new marks had been entered in the catalogues. The Colt Hoare collection had been moved, and nearly all re-pressmarked, and the Banksian collection was being moved. A month later all the Banksian books were in their new locations and had mostly been re-pressmarked. Works in the class religion were being moved.[51]

Panizzi was concerned about pamphlets in the Banksian collection and in the general library. About 700 or 800 volumes of pamphlets which formed part of the Banksian collection had been numbered without reference to their respective sizes. If they were arranged in this order in the new library they would detract from its appearance; but to alter the pressmarks in the volumes and in the catalogues would take up a great deal of time. The same applied to the large collection of pamphlets still in Room XIII in Montagu House. In Panizzi's opinion the best solution would be to place these pamphlets in the small basement room under the new west Reading Room, and open a communication between it and the large newspaper room in the basement. The unsightliness of the arrangement of the pamphlets would not matter in a strictly private room, and space would be available there for a large number of additions. The Banksian pamphlets would of course be kept separate from the others. This plan found favour with the Trustees and on 10 March the Sub-Committee on Buildings ordered that communication should be effected through the south wall of the Newspaper Room and the west wall of the room which was to contain the pamphlets.[52]

By the end of March Panizzi reported that the move was not proceeding as quickly as he had hoped, because Grabham had been withdrawn to attend more to the readers, and large arrears of cataloguing had accumulated and must be dealt with. He asked for an extra Assistant, and another Attendant, and the Trustees agreed that he could have these for the period of the move. They also granted the request which he made a month later to engage two more Attendants and to employ the Supernumerary Assistants (Watts, Bullen, Russell and Simons) for three extra hours each day from 1 May to 31 August. The Trustees also agreed to Panizzi's proposal to postpone his annual vacation until the move of the library was complete.[53]

Between April and June 1838 all the books on religion, on natural history and on jurisprudence were moved, as were the Thomason Tracts and the two collections of French Revolution tracts. The works on natural history filled up the room in which the Banksian collection had already been placed (the south-east room). The newspapers formerly kept in the Journal Room at the top of the old house were temporarily placed in rooms X and XI on the ground floor of Montagu House, and those hitherto housed in the gallery of the old Reading Rooms (the Middle and South Rooms) and in the gallery of the King's Library were moved to the new Reading Rooms (not yet in use) in the north-east

9 Thomas Watts, Keeper of Printed Books, 1866–69. He was Placer from *c.*1840 to 1857, and Superintendent of the Reading Room, 1857–66 (BL Archives).

corner, because the basement rooms of the North Wing designed for their use were not properly dried out.[54]

In a note dated 23 June 1838 Panizzi recorded that 92,251 books remained to be moved from Montagu House, while 71,112 had already been transferred, and of these 47,810 had been finally placed. So in a little less than six months about forty-four per cent of the books had been moved from one building to the other – a total of about 3,000 volumes per week – but only about thirty per cent had been finally arranged on the shelves. The 47,810 volumes which had been placed occupied 104 presses on the ground floor (at an average of 208.5 volumes per press) and 119 presses in the galleries (at an average of 219.5 volumes per press). As there was a total of 307 presses on the ground floor and 253 in the galleries they should house 119,559 volumes. There still remained to be placed a total of 115,553 volumes; of these 1790 volumes of newspapers and 2241 volumes of pamphlets would be housed in the basement, leaving 111,522 to be accommodated on the ground floor and in the galleries. This would leave expansion space for only 8037 volumes. Moreover this was on the assumption that every press would be completely filled; but the original plan provided that 153 presses on the ground floor and 109 on the gallery level were to be left partly empty for additions. Panizzi calculated that if this plan was adhered to there would at the end of the operation only be room for 138 volumes of accessions. He was never averse to making the flesh of the Trustees creep by prophesying disaster.[55]

His next task was to arrange the move of the Reading Rooms from the south-east to the north-east corner of the new building. He recommended that the work should be carried out during the week when the Museum was closed from 1 to 7 September, so that the new rooms would be ready to receive readers on 8 September. At their meeting on 28 July the Trustees approved this plan and gave instructions that the readers should enter the new rooms from Montague Place to the north of the Museum, rather than from the door leading from the King's Library. The work went smoothly and on 6 September Panizzi was able to report that the reference books from the old Reading Rooms (about 5000) had been transferred and a large number of items had been added to them. The new Reading Rooms opened as planned on 8 September 1838.[56]

In order to help the Attendants find their way round the new presses Panizzi arranged for 100 copies of a plan of the presses to be lithographed, and for twelve framed copies to be hung up in various parts of the North Wing.[57]

The new shelves filled steadily. In the second part of 1838 books on philosophy, literature, mineralogy and chemistry were moved. By November Panizzi was complaining that he was so short of Attendants that the move would be held up if he was not granted extra help. The Trustees instructed the Secretary to apply to the Principal Trustees for two or three Supernumerary Attendants to ease Panizzi's problems – three started work early in December.[58] On the 12th of that month Panizzi reported on the duties of his staff, who then numbered 38. The following persons were working on the move of the library: Bach (Assistant) found or wrote tickets for the books being moved; Watts (Assistant) selected in the old house the books to be moved, arranged them in classes, and placed them on their new shelves; Russell, Bullen and Simons (Supernumerary Assistants) found or wrote tickets for the books being moved – the two former put pressmarks in the books and on the relevant tickets when the items had been placed in their new locations. So far as the Attendants were concerned Leach, Cowtan and Schofield revised the new pressmarks put on the books and on the entries in the catalogue; Phillips assisted Watts and dealt with the mechanical parts of the move; Caston, on three days each week, helped to move the books from the old house; Yeates, Bygrave senior and Birchell put tickets or titles in order; and eight Supernumerary Attendants added the new pressmarks to the two interleaved copies of the catalogue, and to the copy of the King's Library catalogue showing which items in the King's Library were duplicated in the general library. About 2,500 such alterations were dealt with each week and entering all the new pressmarks would take about two years. Panizzi himself, amongst his other duties, directed which books were to be moved, looked them over when Watts had selected them, and also when they had been placed in their new presses. So at this time about half the staff of the Department of Printed Books were involved either full-time or part-time in the move.[59]

V · PROGRESS IN 1839

On 10 January 1839 Panizzi reported that journals and periodicals had been placed in the new library, as well as letters and part of the Latin and Greek poets. French and Italian poetry was just being moved. The books in the lower presses of the reading rooms had been pressmarked, as well as English poetry and drama and some of the novels lately added to the rest in the galleries of the reading rooms. In February and March works of literature, some journals, the works of polygraphers, a large collection of medical theses, the remainder of the classics, modern poetry, philology and miscellaneous writings were moved, as well as some books on the arts. Watts (who had been promoted from Supernumerary Assistant to permanent Assistant on 21 December 1838) continued to direct the removal of the books and their rearrangement. In March he recorded that he had been arranging polygraphic authors, medical theses, literary criticism and classical and modern poetry in the ninth recess of the Large Room, in the Second Supplementary Room, in the gallery of the Cracherode Room, in the last recess of the Second Supplementary Room and in the gallery above it.[60]

Although the move itself was going well, the consequential tasks of re-pressmarking the books, and altering the pressmarks in the catalogues was proving a considerable burden. So in April Panizzi decided that in the case of dissertations, theses and other works not much in demand, he would leave the addition of the new pressmarks to the catalogues until more staff could be made available for this work. In his report on the work of his department for the twelve months up to May 1839, he noted that whereas in May 1838 only the Cracherode, Banks and Colt Hoare collections and part of the class of divinity had been moved, the only books now remaining in Montagu House were medical and historical works, the transactions of learned societies, and works recently purchased. Most of the books had been re-pressmarked; between November 1838 and April 1839 new pressmarks had been written in both sets of the catalogue for 102,398 items.[61]

Even before the North Wing had been completed the Trustees were aware that they would soon need more space. They therefore asked Smirke to draw up plans for an additional building at the west end of the North Wing, and in March 1837 he submitted drawings for such a structure, showing how much land would have to be purchased from the Duke of Bedford before work could commence. Not until 1839 did the Treasury approve the grant of the necessary funds. In May the work of excavating the foundations began, and the Keepers whose collections would be housed in the new structure (Panizzi, König of Mineralogy, Children of Zoology and Josi of Prints and Drawings) were asked whether they wished any alterations to be made to the plans which Smirke had produced in 1837.[62] On 8 June the Sub-Committee on Buildings considered a letter from Smirke in which he said that he would prefer not to divide the new large room for the library (the Arch Room) into two floors, but to keep it the same height as the adjoining Supplementary Rooms and provide an extra gallery so that it would hold as many books as were provided for in the previous plan. This would ensure that the north front of the Museum (which would be visible to everyone passing along Montague Place) would present a uniform appearance. The Sub-Committee approved this proposal, but at their next meeting on 15 June they were presented with a letter from Panizzi saying that if the Trustees proposed to allot to the Department of Printed Books the two small rooms marked on the new plan as 'working rooms' he would be well content; but if this was not the case, the desperate need of his department for properly lighted work rooms rendered the new plan much less desirable than the old one. The Sub-Committee confirmed their decision that the new room should be as high as the Supplementary Rooms, but were of the opinion that the well lighted space for officers requested by Panizzi could be provided by enlarging the window at the west end. The Secretary put this to Smirke, and on 27 June he wrote to say that he would construct a very large window, ten feet wide and seventeen feet high, with the sill about thirty inches from the floor, and a semi-circular head similar to the openings in the walls within the room (Fig. 10). He confirmed that the superficial feet of bookshelves would be nearly the same as in the previous plan. The whole episode is an interesting example of planning a building with an eye to its exterior appearance rather than its internal convenience.[63]

On 11 May 1839 the Trustees gave Panizzi permission to employ the Supernumerary Assistants engaged on the move of the library for three extra hours each day until 1 September, as had been the case in 1838. His hope however that this would enable him to complete the move by September proved to be over-optimistic. By that time geography, topography, local histories, voyages and travels, the works presented by Lady Banks (hitherto in the gallery of room IV), some biography, some medicine, and some recent acquisitions had been transferred. All the books in the galleries of Montagu House had been transferred to the ground floor in preparation for the move. During the remainder of the year the historical works were moved.[64] Watts was of course very busy. In May he reported that he had been arranging on their new shelves, books on music, architecture, painting, sculpture and the arts in general. In October he wrote that he had been arranging geography and topography in the Second Supplementary Room, and directing the move of the historical works from Montagu House. He then turned his attention to arranging books of unusual size of all subjects in the fifth recess and in the tables of the second and ninth recesses, and to distributing a large number of books of all classes from room XIV of Montagu House.[65]

In the report which he made on 25 January 1840, giving an account of work done in the Department of Printed Books between June 1838 and December 1839, Panizzi recapitulated the stages of the move. It had begun on 1 January 1838 and of the approximately 165,000 volumes concerned, by the end of June, 47,000 volumes had been moved and placed, 24,000 were being dealt with, and 94,000 had not then been touched. To this figure of 118,000 volumes awaiting attention must be added the 10,000 volumes acquired between June 1838 and December 1839, making a grand total of 128,000 volumes. Of this figure, by December 1839 only about 12,000 volumes remained in Montagu House, while 5,000 more had been moved to the new building and awaited placing on the shelves. So between June 1838 and December 1839 more than 110,000 volumes had been moved and arranged on their new shelves. The Reading Rooms were kept open while this large scale operation took place, and on average only 8,000 volumes (five per cent of the whole) were unavailable at any one time.

Moving the books and arranging them in their new places was however only part of the task. The new pressmarks had to be entered, a) on the books, b) on the transfer tickets, c) on the catalogue kept in the library, and d) on the catalogue kept in the Reading Rooms. Between June 1838 and December 1839

10 The Arch Room, looking west towards the great window, photographed in 1953 (BL Archives).

the pressmarks for 93,000 items had been altered in these four places, while in the case of a further 10,000 items the pressmarks had been altered in the books and on the transfer tickets, and needed to be altered in the two catalogues. The total number of alterations thus made amounted to 392,000. It was Panizzi's intention in due course to add a third mark to individualise the place of each book on its shelf. The pressmarks on the titleslips which were being prepared for the compilation of the new catalogue also had to be altered. By the end of 1839 about 168,000 slips had been altered or the old pressmarks on them verified. In addition the titleslips for the books acquired in 1838 and 1839 (about 9,000–10,000) had been pressmarked.[66]

As has been stated above, in December 1838 about half the staff of the Department of Printed Books were working on the move. In the first half of 1839 the amount of staff-time involved increased slightly, but after that the numbers involved began to decline, so that by the end of the year the only Assistant involved was Watts, aided by one Attendant full-time and three part-time, and four Supernumerary Attendants part-time.[67]

VI · PROGRESS IN 1840

In January 1840 the books on heraldry and 3,000 medical works were transferred from Montagu House, and by mid-March Panizzi was able to report that the whole of the old library had been moved, except the Musgrave tracts and the Burney interleaved classics. He said that the final arrangement would take some weeks more, apart from the work of clearing up queries regarding the correctness of several thousand entries which had arisen during the course of the move. He recorded that the transfer of the library had been almost entirely carried out under Watts's control, with Panizzi supervising the operation. In the early stages about 20,000 volumes were moved and placed by Panizzi himself, but he could not have continued without neglecting his normal duties. He testified that Watts's work had been very satisfactory.[68]

In April Panizzi wrote that now that the books were in their new locations, it would be necessary to arrange them properly on the individual shelves before third marks could be added and the hand catalogues (i.e. shelf-lists) could be compiled. In his report on the previous twelve months' work dated 6 May 1840, he mentioned that the move of the library was complete, apart from a few hundred recently purchased volumes which were still in Montagu House. The number of books removed and placed since May 1839 was about 52,000. Most of the items moved had received new pressmarks and these new marks had been inserted in the two copies of the catalogues – about 160,000 pressmarks altogether. About 12,000 items still awaited new pressmarks.[69]

On 10 June 1840 Panizzi gave the Trustees details of the method used in adding third marks in the books and in the catalogues. He also submitted specimen sheets for the hand catalogues – these were about twelve and a half inches long and five inches wide, ruled into five columns in which could be inserted the pressmark, the author, the place of publication, the date of publication and the size of each item. He mentioned that the few thousand books still awaiting new pressmarks would be dealt with in the next four or five weeks; it would then be necessary to cope with the problems provided by the transfer tickets for works which had not been found.[70]

Before going on holiday Panizzi wrote a note to his deputy Garnett, dated 17 August, concerning the sheets for the hand catalogues which would soon arrive from the printer. Garnett was to pass these to the binder and tell him to bind 100 leaves in each volume. He was to prepare 120 such volumes which would contain 12,000 leaves which was about the number of shelves in the library (including both the old library and the King's Library).[71]

In October Panizzi issued detailed instructions about the way in which various special collections should be pressmarked. The tracts formerly in room XIII of Montagu House were to be marked T; the Banksian tracts from room XVII were to be marked B; the French Revolution tracts from rooms IV and XX were to be marked F; novels were to receive a progressive number as in the past but with the prefix N; the Musgrave tracts (from room XIII) and the Garrick collection were to be marked as hitherto, but in pencil; the English Revolution (Thomason) tracts from room XII were to be marked E; the 273 volumes of political tracts from presses A and B in room XII (which did not form part of the Thomason collection) were to be marked P.[72]

VII · THE COMPLETION OF THE MOVE

By the end of 1840 with the physical move of the library completed, Watts was able to concentrate on other activities, and the work of dealing with pressmarks and catalogue alterations was in the hands of J. H. Parry (a Supernumerary Assistant) with the part-time help of four Attendants and 10 Supernumerary Attendants. As 1841 went on the number of Attendants and Supernumerary Attendants employed on the consequential work of the move diminished, and during 1842 only Parry (part-time) and two Attendants (part-time) were involved.[73]

On 31 March 1841 Panizzi reported that several hundred volumes acquired in the previous year (which had been temporarily stored in Montagu House) had been moved to their proper places in the new library. However space was running short and it was essential to complete the new north-west building (the Arch Room) as soon as possible. By February 1842 some books must still have been temporarily stored in Montagu House because Panizzi wrote that if the old house was pulled down before the Arch Room was finished there would be nowhere to place the books which would have to be moved. By the beginning of October he was able to report with relief that the new room was open and almost complete, and by January 1843 books had already filled 100 presses in the Arch Room. As has so often been the case in the history of the library, the new accommodation was filled up far sooner than had been anticipated.[74]

In his report on the previous twelve months work, dated 28 January 1841, Panizzi recorded that the remaining books (about 18,000 volumes) had been moved from Montagu House, arranged on their new shelves, and given new pressmarks. In addition the books on about 1365 shelves in the general library had been given third marks (the books in the King's Library had of course been given third marks soon after they arrived at the Museum in 1828). About 30,700 pressmarks had been altered in one copy of the old catalogue, and 28,700 in the second copy. In volume 1 of the new printed catalogue (of which three copies were marked with pressmarks) about 2,600 entries had been altered. About 4,500 entries had been made in the hand catalogues. The work of adding third marks, compiling hand catalogues, and correcting pressmarks in the general catalogues went on steadily, until on 5 October 1842 Panizzi was able to report that every work and article in the library (except those in the Reading Rooms) had received a third mark, and items in volumes of tracts had received individual (fourth) marks.[75] The work of moving the library could be considered complete, and Panizzi therefore ceased making entries in the register of persons involved in the move which had been begun on the Trustees' orders at the beginning of 1838.[76]

To sum up the various stages of the move and the consequential work. The 163,000 volumes of the general library were moved between 1 January 1838 and May 1840.[77] The Reading Rooms were transferred to their new location between 1 and 7 September 1838. New pressmarks were assigned to the books which had been moved between early 1838 and July/August 1840. The bulk of the work of altering the pressmarks in the various copies of the catalogues was completed by the autumn of 1842, by which time work was in progress on the compilation of the hand catalogues. Panizzi was therefore justified in saying in October 1842 that the move could be considered complete. He was understandably proud of the fact that it had been accomplished without any significant harmful effects on the service to the readers.

NOTES

SOURCES

British Museum Archives
  CE 1 Minutes of the Trustees' General Meetings
  CE 3 Minutes of the Trustees' Committee
  CE 4 Original Papers
  CE 5 Officers' Reports
  CE 7 Minutes of the Trustees' Sub-Committees

British Library Archives.
  DH 1 Panizzi Papers

Some of these volumes, in both the British Museum Archives and in the British Library Archives, are foliated and some are paginated; in such cases the references are to folio or page. Where volumes have neither of these series of numbers, the reference is to the date of the appropriate document.

1   CE 5/21, 4977–8. Report by Madden dated 20 July 1837 asking for the apartments hitherto occupied by Baber, on the grounds that Madden was appointed an Assistant Keeper in 1828, while Panizzi only became an Assistant Keeper in 1831. In Madden's opinion this over-rode the fact that Panizzi's appointment as Keeper on 15 July 1837 antedated Madden's appointment as Keeper.
2   CE 5/21, 5013; CE 3/16, 4668.
3   CE 5/10, 2129, 2141. The minutes of the meeting of the Sub-Committee on Manuscripts and Printed Books held on 14 June 1828 record that by that date all the ancient rolls and charters had been moved from Montagu House to the new Reading Rooms (CE 7/1, 8).
4   Smirke wrote on 12 January 1827 that the workmen would be out of the new Reading Rooms by the end of the month (CE 3/10, 3000). On 12 May 1827 the Trustees agreed that another Attendant could be engaged temporarily for the new reading rooms (CE 3/11, 3020). On 12 July 1828 Ellis reported that on several occasions the new Reading Rooms had been completely full (CE 5/11, 2323).
5   Report by Baber dated 8 November 1828 (CE 5/11, 2342).
6   CE 1/6, 1405–8 (10 December 1831).
7   CE 3/12, 3449–50.
8   CE 4/10, 12 January 1832. This document is misplaced in the volume for 1833.
9   CE 4/10, 14 January 1833, 14 March 1833.
10 CE 3/12, 3546 (12 January 1833); CE 1/6 1425–6 (18 March 1833). The plan drawn up by Smirke in the 1820s, showing the North Wing with a colonnade on the southern front is reproduced as illustration 47 in J. M. Crook, *The British Museum* (1972).
11 CE 1/6, 1432–5; CE 4/10, 26 March 1833.
12 CE 3/12, 3583; CE 4/10, 25 March 1833.
13 CE 4/10, 31 May 1833.
14 CE 4/12, 13 March 1835; CE 4/13, 11 December 1835 (two documents bearing this date); CE 3/14, 4126–7.
15 CE 5/19, 4196–7 (report dated 19 December 1835).
16 CE 3/15, 4144–7.

17 CE 3/15, 4410 (10 December 1836).

18 In a note dated 13 June 1838 Panizzi calculated that there were about 163,000 volumes in the old library, about 65,000 in the King's Library, almost 5,000 volumes in the Reading Rooms and about 1,500 volumes awaiting processing – a total of almost 235,000 volumes. (DH 1/1, 198)

19 *Copies or Extracts of any Minutes made by the Trustees since 20 July 1836 with reference to the resolutions passed by the Select Committee* (Parliamentary Papers, House of Commons, 1837 (409) vol. xxxix, pp. 181–7). The individual document is paginated from p.1 to p.7. The Trustees' decision that members of the staff should not hold positions outside the British Museum appears on p.4 of the document. Baber's resignation is in CE 4/16, 7 March 1837.

20 CE 5/21, 4812.

21 CE 5/21, 5166–70. This document was printed by Richard Garnett in *The Library Chronicle*, vol. 2 (1885), pp.1–5; Garnett took the opportunity of paying tribute to Baber as a good administrative librarian, as well as a good scholar.

22 In 1835 Smirke gave details of the amount of shelving of different depths to be provided in the North Wing – it ranged from 7¼" to 3'4½" (CE 4/13, 11 December 1835). For further details regarding the hand catalogues, see pp.95–96.

23 The following is an example of the way in which Horne's classification scheme operated:
    Class I. Religion.
       Section II. Revealed religion.
          Primary Division V. Liturgies.
             Sub-division 3. Liturgy of the Latin Church.

24 *Library Chronicle*, vol.2, p.3.

25 DH 1/1, 198. This figure was doubled to about 10,000 reference books in the Reading Rooms which were in use from 1838 to 1857. (Robert Cowtan, *Memories of the British Museum* (1872), p.209.)

26 The tracts which are now pressmarked T. (Garnett, in *Library Chronicle*, vol.2, p.4.)

27 Garnett (*ibid.*) commented: 'it seems surprising that the idea of dispersing them should ever have been entertained'. But a marginal note by Panizzi on the copy of Baber's document which he sent to Forshall in December 1837 shows that he was generally in favour of dispersal: 'The Cracherode collection should be kept together but not the other two' (CE 5/21, 5170, 12 December 1837). The Trustees however did not approve of the plan to break up the Banks and Colt Hoare collections. (CE 3/16, 4668 (16 December 1837).)

28 See p.95.

29 When the 3,000 to 12,000 series of pressmarks was introduced at the end of the 1840s, third marks were omitted, but they were introduced again for new accessions from 1875, and in due course were added to nearly all the items which lacked them. (Garnett in *Library Chronicle*, vol.2, p.5.)

30 E. J. Miller, *That Noble Cabinet* (1973), p.149.

31 CE 5/21, 4985; CE 3/16, 4559.

32 CE 5/21, 5052–61.

33 CE 5/21, 5054–5, 5002.

34 *Synopsis of the Contents of the British Museum* (1808), p.xxiii; CE 5/1, 138–9; CE 5/2, 325–6.

35 CE 5/2, 331, 347.

36 CE 5/3, 696.

37 CE 5/3, 762–3; CE 3/9, 2605 (10 June 1815); CE 5/3, 775.

38 CE 5/4, 977.

39 CE 5/6, 1273; CE 3/10, 2744.

40 CE 5/8, 1949 (10 December 1825).

41 CE 5/10, 2195 (8 November 1827).

42 DH 1/1, 51. On 7 June 1836 Panizzi told the Select Committee of the House of Commons that the Department of Printed Books was allotted the ground floor of Montagu House, three rooms in the basement, and four on the first floor (Q. 4804).

43 DH 1/1, 198.

44 CE 4/17, 1 October 1837. This room was below the north end of the Large Centre Room.

45 CE 4/17, 5 October 1837, 18 November 1837, 6 October 1837, 7 October 1837, 19 October 1837. The furniture requested on 19 October consisted of 24 chairs, 8 deal tables, 24 step ladders like those in the King's Library, and 12 more of three steps each for the galleries. Falls were strips of leather about 3″ deep, attached to the shelves so that the leather extended below the tops of the books on the shelves below, and thus reduced the amount of dust settling on them.

46 CE 4/17, 25 October 1837, 8 November 1837.

47 CE 7/1, 84–5; CE 4/17, 24 November 1837; CE 7/1, 94 (25 November 1837); CE 5/21, 5137.

48 CE 3/16, 4666–8; CE 4/17, 20 December 1837, 28 December 1837.

49 CE 4/18, 11 January 1838.

50 CE 4/18, 22 January 1838; CE 7/1, 97; Register of Persons employed . . . in the removal of the library (BL Archives, Acc. 1).

51 CE 5/22, 5259, 5368.

52 CE 4/18, 21 February 1838; CE 7/1, 110.

53 CE 3/16, 4730 (31 March 1838); 4753–4 (25 April 1838); 4763 (12 May 1838).

54 CE 5/22, 5473 (10 May 1838); 5569 (7 June 1838).

55 DH 1/1, 198, 199.

56 CE 5/22, 5667 (27 July 1838); CE 3/16, 4830; DH 1/1, 198; CE 5/22, 5683, 5721.

57 CE 4/19, 27 July 1838, 29 August 1838; CE 3/16, 4836.

58 CE 5/22, 5626, 5683, 5807, 5887; CE 3/17, 4890 (10 November 1838), 4899 (1 December 1838), 4916 (15 December 1838).

59 CE 5/22, 5892–5.

60 CE 5/23, 5979, 6039, 6113, 5988, 6124.

61 CE 5/23, 6180, 6229.

62 CE 1/6, 1529 (11 March 1837); CE 3/17, 5061–2 (11 May 1839).

63 CE 7/1, 172–4, 177; CE 4/20, 27 June 1839.

64 CE 3/17, 5065; CE 5/23, 6237, 6297; CE 5/24, 6401, 6507, 6588.

65 CE 5/23, 6247; CE 5/24, 6520, 6657; CE 5/25, 6715.

66 CE 5/25, 6768–71.

67 Register of Persons employed . . . in the removal of the library (BL Archives, Acc. 1).

68 CE 5/25, 6822, 6907, 6908.

69 CE 5/25, 6972, 7050.

70 CE 5/26, 7152–6.

71 DH 1/3, 359–60. The printing bill for these sheets amounted to £47–2–4 (DH 1/4, 126).

72 DH 1/4, 59.

73 Register of Persons employed . . . in the removal of the library (BL Archives, Acc. 1).

74 CE 5/27, 7785; CE 5/29, 8370; CE 5/30, 8811; CE 5/31, 9026.

75 CE 5/27, 7645–6; CE 5/30, 8810. On 6 September 1843 Garnett reported that the last remaining books in Montagu House (mainly duplicates and odd volumes) had been moved to the ground floor of the new library (CE 5/32, 9492).

76 CE 5/30, 8810. The last entry in the Register of Persons employed ... in the removal of the library (BL Archives, Acc. 1) is dated 8 October 1842; it records that on that day Panizzi had been involved part-time, as had Leach (Attendant) and Hill (Supernumerary Attendant).

77 Between January and June 1838, 43½% (71,000 volumes) of the General Library was moved; between July 1838 and December 1839, 49% (80,000 volumes). The remaining 7½% (12,000 volumes) was moved between January and August 1840.

11 Richard Garnett, Keeper of Printed Books, 1890–99 (BL Archives).

3

THE ACQUISITIONS POLICIES AND FUNDING OF THE DEPARTMENT OF PRINTED BOOKS, 1837–1959

Ilse Sternberg

I · PANIZZI TO BULLEN, 1837–86

WITHIN A FEW months of his appointment on 19 July 1837 as Keeper of the Department of Printed Books, Panizzi wrote his first report to the Trustees on the subject of acquisitions, and it is the principles set down at that time which still in many ways guide the acquisition requirements of the British Library today.[1]

The main points he expressed were:

1. The attention of the Keeper of this emphatically *British* library ought to be directed most particularly to British works and to works relating to the British Empire . . . The rarer and more expensive a work of this description is, the more reasonable efforts ought to be made to secure it for the library.
2. The old and rare as well as the critical editions of ancient Classics ought never to be sought for in vain . . . nor ought good comments [*sic*] as also the best translations in the modern languages by wanting.
3. With respect to foreign literature, science and arts the library ought to possess the best editions of standard works . . .
The Public have moreover a right to expect finding in their national library heavy as well as expensive foreign works such as literary journals, transactions of learned Societies, large collections . . . , completed series of newspapers and collections of laws and their best interpreters, etc.

The policy thus defined was concisely expressed in the conclusion to the report prepared by Panizzi and his staff entitled, 'On the Collections of the Printed Books at the British Museum' and presented to the Trustees in 1845, where it was stated that the ideal was to form,

a public library . . . giving the necessary means of information on all branches of human learning, from all countries, in all languages, properly arranged, substantially and well bound, minutely and fully catalogued, easily accessible and yet safely preserved, capable, for some years to come, of keeping pace with the increase of human knowledge.[2]

Later it was still further refined by Thomas Watts[3] to a concept of the universal library. This he expressed in an article in *Knight's English Cyclopaedia* of 1859 and in a report to Panizzi of February 1861, when he summarised the common object of Keepers and Assistant Keepers, during almost a quarter of a century, as being to 'bring together . . . the useful, the elegant, and the curious literatures of every language; to unite with the best English Library in England, or the world, the best Russian library out of Russia, the best German out of Germany, the best Spanish out of Spain, and so with every language from Italian to Icelandic, from Polish to Portuguese'.[4]

John Winter Jones,[5] who followed Panizzi both as Keeper of the Department of Printed Books and as Principal Librarian, emphasised the importance of trying to collect the earliest evidence of printing wherever it occurred.

> If we give to the history of printing the importance it really possesses, and regard libraries like that of the British Museum as a depository of the evidences of its miraculous progress and effects – then a fragment of a Donatus, a Caxton, an early edition of a Bible, a first edition of a classic, or the first productions of the printing press in the United States, Mexico, California, Australia, or the Sandwich Islands, cease to be curiosities, and take their deservedly prominent place in the history of civilisation.[6]

But he was equally well aware that it was most economical to purchase current works regularly, as is evidenced by his memorandum to the Trustees of 1861 reporting the purchase of newspapers and gazettes from Australia and requesting more money for further purchases where he stated, 'the prices are already high and will certainly increase as the importance of these publications becomes more felt.'[7] Early in the following year he requested that the Trustees should relax their order 'directing that no bills shall be sent in for payment until the Estimates for the year . . . have passed the House of Commons' and allow him £1,000 for 'works in progress and . . . for books agreed to be purchased'. And he took exception to the Trustees' reminder that he should 'direct his attention to the acquisition of comparatively modern works rather than of rare or curious books' pointing out that from the grant for 1861–62 'he has expended upward of £8,000 in the purchase of works published in the course of the 18th and 19th century . . . the remaining £2,000 for the purchase of books published prior to 1700, for Maps and for such few rarities as had been acquired during the [past] twelve months'.[8] However, within a few months he was arguing again for the purchase of rare items when he told the Trustees:

> The importance of a public library cannot properly be estimated solely by the number of books it may contain. Works of general utility will necessarily demand and receive the first attention – but books which are of rare occurrence cannot well be neglected. Their high price generally places them beyond the means of the greater number of students who, if they cannot find them in the public library, may be debarred from the use of them all together.[9]

In 1863, while noting the extremely high rate of exchange in America which had interfered very greatly with the book trade in that country;[10] the lack of some intelligent and enterprising bookseller for Italian works; the still considerable outlay which it was necessary to expend on maps,[11] and the increasing numbers all over the world of periodical publications, which 'require a large sum to keep them perfectly represented in the National Library,' he reported that:

> In compliance with the wishes of the Trustees Mr. Jones has given very much of his attention to the purchase of books of small price – particularly to those published in the United Kingdom and still finds fresh purchases necessary in this direction. In so doing he has avoided purchasing rare books to any extent.[12]

The necessity of keeping up with the publication explosion, especially in the colonies, inspired Watts in his Estimates for 1867–68 to remark:

> The large increase in the number of publications in the English language on various points of the globe not only in America, but in India and Eastern Asia, in South Africa and Australia seems to render it every year more desirable that care should be taken to bring together the scattered parts of so glorious a whole in one great repository... It is proposed to continue the same plan to fill up deficiencies and endeavour to attain an equal degree of completeness with regard to the literary production of Canada, South Africa and India...

It was not only the publications of the English colonies and ex-colonies which concerned Watts. He drew the Trustees attention also to the fact that

> A much more vigorous and promising literature than is generally supposed has risen and is making progress in the American countries which were formerly colonies of Spain and Portugal... The literature of Holland has lately been remarkably rich in publications on the history and geography of its Indian possessions and that of Russia in information on its dominions in Asia and the contiguous countries.

He went on to stress the necessity of bringing together 'in the English metropolis an ample provision of the vast amount of floating information' of use 'not only to the student but to the merchant and the statesman whose purpose the student may affectually [sic] assist when the materials are ready to his hand'. He noted that this observation 'will apply to the past as well as the present literature of all these countries.'[13] Again, in the Estimates submitted for the following year, Watts stated, 'The field of acceptable literature is becoming every year more extensive', and he went on to reiterate the importance of collecting contemporary works whilst not ignoring retrospective collecting to fill gaps.[14]

In a memorandum sent to Winter Jones in 1869 he stressed that

> It has always seemed to me one of the first objects the Museum should propose to itself [is] to have a complete library of all books worth reading or referring to in the English language whether [printed?] in Europe or America, Asia or Australia.

In the Estimates for 1869–70 he noted the increasing success of the efforts 'to bring under one roof the leading works of the literature of every nation in the world without exception.'[15]

The officers of the Department of Printed Books were aware also of the benefits for the acquisitions programme which would be derived from the printing and distribution of catalogues of the collections. Rye in his report to the Trustees of 12 February 1874, concerning the offer of Trübner, a main agent for Oriental and Latin American materials, to turn printer-publisher for the purpose of producing the catalogue of Sanskrit books in the British Museum, observed that publishing the catalogue

> would afford considerable assistance in filling up those deficiencies which may still exist. It has been found by experience that in respect to the printed Hebrew catalogue its dissemination made known the Museum's deficiencies to persons who were able to supply them.'[16]

He noted that should the Trustees accept this offer (which they did) Trübner intended at a future date to submit plans for printing the Arabic, Persian, Turkish, etc., catalogues.

For the next decade purchases continued at a steady pace with the emphasis generally on the purchase of 'new foreign books . . . appearing not only on the Continent but in America, in the East, in fact throughout the world'.[17] Periodicals took a large share of the grant and 'in order to remedy the deficiencies in modern foreign works which have arisen from the inadequate amount of the grant previous to 1844, a systematic examination of various bibliographies is being carried out'. Numerous efforts were made also to acquire Indian and Colonial publications with the help of the India Office and the Colonial Office because, although the Museum officials felt that under the provisions of the Copyright Act 5 & 6 Vic. C.45 Sect. VI.18 the Museum was clearly entitled to all books published in India and the Colonies, they were aware that there were 'no doubt many which are not in the Museum and which it would be desirable to have'. Should they be required to purchase all these works the amount 'to be deducted from the annual allowance' would be considerable and the Keeper would 'grudge such an expenditure'.[19] Prices generally were rising. The Keeper sometimes had to report that the original sum requested for purchases at a sale was insufficient because of the high prices fetched and to request an additional sum if desirable early works were to be purchased.[20]

By 1883 a 'recommendation... for a general system of exchange of publications with independent Governments, ... India and the Colonies'[21] provided the Museum with another means of adding to the collections without increasing the demands on the purchase grant. This was fortunate as 'unusual expenditure' had 'rendered it necessary to hold over until 1883 a considerable number of bills properly belonging to 1882', and, in fact, the sum spent on continuations (£1,752) and new books and periodicals (£3,350) only just exceeded the amount spent on old books (£4,768) in that year.[22]

II · THE FIRST REDUCTION OF THE BOOK FUND, 1886–1900

It was also fortunate that at this time the deposit of works from the colonies and the receipt of publications by international exchange were becoming viable means of augmenting the purchase grant, because in 1886 Lord Randolph Churchill was appointed Chancellor of the Exchequer and, although his term in office lasted only a few months, the substantial reductions in government spending which he proposed had full Treasury approval. His successor, the more liberal-minded Goschen[23] was left no option but to enforce these economies, although less stringently than Churchill had intended. The British Museum as a whole was required to reduce its expenditure by £10,000 for the financial year 1887–88 and it was proposed that the acquisitions grant for the Department of Printed Books should be reduced by thirty-nine per cent from £10,000 to £6,000 to cover the purchase of books, although an additional £200 was allowed for maps.[24]

The Keeper's reaction was immediate. On 6 January 1887 Bullen addressed the Trustees 'on the subject of the reduction required by the Lords Commissioners of the Treasury... and on the scheme for distributing the reduction over the Estimates of the several Departments... prepared by the Principal Librarian'. Although he was not objecting to the justice of the apportionment (he could hardly do that when Bond[25], the Principal Librarian, had proposed a forty per cent reduction of the grant for his former Department of Manuscripts from £2,500 to £1,500), he felt it:

his duty to point out that the action of the Treasury will fall with special severity upon the Department of Printed Books, inasmuch as a large proportion of the annual grant is spent in the acquisition of current literature other than that published in the United Kingdom.

He went on to predict that the 'withdrawal of so large an amount ... would be most disastrous for the Library' and would arrest its proper development for a long time if not for all time. He pointed out that of the annual grant of £10,000, half was spent on current literature and at least £200 was for the purchase of maps and charts necessary to maintain the utility of the Library and that if its function as a national collection worthy of the country was to continue it was 'imperatively necessary that the acquisition of the current representative literature of the world should not be neglected or delayed'. It was also important to continue the efforts to remedy the defects known to exist especially by acquiring 'those books which can only be obtained on rare occasions and even then only at a considerable cost' because if they are not to be found in the Museum 'scholars and literary workers cannot get access to them elsewhere'.[26] However, the reductions were enforced and the Principal Librarian felt it necessary to recommend that 'purchases be as much as possible confined to current literature'.[27]

The Keeper took every opportunity to remind the Trustees of the devastating effects of the reduction of the purchase vote. In November 1887 he pointed out the injuries inflicted, noting that there were serious deficiencies in '1. Privately printed books ... 2. Books with ms. notes ... 3. Music, other than modern ... 4. Provincial literature ... 5. Colonial publications ... 6. Books published in Eastern Europe ... 7. English periodicals ...' as well as 'loss of connection with booksellers' which had in the past enabled the Museum to secure valuable acquisitions. He added that there were 'missed opportunities of buying important books at sales etc. at low rates'.[28] He also pressed strongly for the Trustees to remind the colonies of the Museum's claim under the Act 5 and 6 Victoria of 1842 even though the International Copyright Act of 1886 (clauses 8 and 9)[29] expressly exempted colonies from deposit in the mother country. In consequence the Trustees ordered that the purchase of colonial works required should be continued and that the Secretary of State for the Colonies was to be asked 'to press for consideration of [the] Museum claim in future colonial legislation'.[30]

In October 1889 Richard Garnett (Fig 11)[31], in the absence of Bullen whom he was soon to succeed, presented the Estimates for the coming financial year. He noted the success which the Trustees had the previous year in pressing the Treasury for more money (the acquisitions grant of the Department was increased from £8,000 to £9,000). However, he still insisted that the sum of

£10,000 was necessary for an efficient acquisitions programme since a large proportion of the grant was spent on periodicals and works in progress which could not be discontinued without destroying the value of the sets. Furthermore he reminded the Trustees of what he had reported to them the previous May, that 'the annual cost of French and German periodicals had nearly trebled, and that of American and Belgian more than doubled since 1872'. He especially regretted the reduction of the grant without any inquiry as to the manner in which it would affect the Museum.[32] In his first Estimates as Keeper (1891–92) he repeated his application of the previous year for the restoration of the grant to its former figure, noting that 'since this unfortunate interference, the Lords of the Treasury, deferring to the repeated representations of the Trustees, have gradually augmented the grant to within £500 of the original amount of £10,000'. He trusted that their Lordships would now return the grant to the sum which the Trustees had represented as essential to the proper administration of the Department of Printed Books.

Garnett continued to press the Trustees reminding them annually that he had 'lost no opportunity of urging the restoration of the grant for purchases . . . without which . . . the Printed Books Department cannot be administered on the scale, or with the spirit, befitting a great national library'. (This was in spite of the fact that his Department was no longer responsible for Oriental language works after the formation of the Department of Oriental Printed Books and Manuscripts in May 1892.)[33] He even asked for (but did not receive) £11,000 in the Estimates for 1893 when he knew of the forthcoming Heredia Library sale of Spanish literature. The Trustees allowed him to purchase important works from this sale but as a result of that expenditure many desirable purchases had to be declined, discouraged, or postponed so that, in Garnett's words, he had 'rather to avoid than to seek opportunities for enriching the Library'. Furthermore 'were any important sale to occur now, the Museum would be helpless, unless by anticipating next year's grant, or by an official application to the Treasury'. He also complained that 'no reason . . . has ever been given why . . . the Museum can be administered, as regards its purchases, on a more contracted sum than was formerly thought requisite' pointing out that 'on the contrary, causes are perpetually at work tending gradually to the augmentation of necessary expenses'. These causes were 'the increased literary activity of almost all sections' but more especially of periodical literature; the continual establishment of new learned societies with their new journals which although acquired very selectively were often absolutely requisite and constituted 'an annually recurring additional expense for an indefinite period' while seldom could the discontinuance of any periodical already taken be justified. The development of fine printing and book illustration was another cause of increased expenditure as was the increased use of secondhand booksellers' catalogues which accounted for more expenditure than the 'costly and splendid acquisitions ... laid before the Trustees' and mentioned in the annual reports. Finally he noted the competition from American libraries. These he divided into those libraries which previously had concentrated on American literature but which were beginning to enter the European book market; the many new American libraries recently founded; and the Library of Congress whose new building gave it added space to allow for the further growth of its collections. All of these were in direct competition with the Museum for antiquarian purchases and had these factors prevailed at the time of the Heredia sale the Museum 'would have lost many books'.[34]

Garnett repeatedly pleaded that the Department of Printed Books differed from the other Museum Departments and needed special consideration as a large proportion of its expenditure was inevitably pledged beforehand. Since 'nearly a moiety of the grant' was devoted to periodicals and works in progress the Department had much less 'elasticity' in the administration of its grant which led either 'to the absolute loss of valuable opportunities of enriching the Library, or to a most undesirable accumulation of arrears by the postponement of accounts'. He was especially anxious at that time because of 'the great probability that a library rich in the rarest early English books will shortly be in the market' and although the Museum might have the opportunity to acquire some of 'this unique collection by private contract' he could not successfully negotiate for it 'without the command of considerable funds'. Should the negotiations fail, he threatened, the books would either be 'acquired in the mass by a private purchaser, in which case they may be lost to the country altogether, or submitted at auction' which would mean that not only would the Museum lose many items through competition from other purchasers but the prices it would pay for the items it did acquire would be higher.[35]

In November 1895 he presented the Trustees with an eloquent statement of the 'reasons against restricting the purchase of Books for the British Museum, especially in foreign literatures' to which he received the reply:

> that in the selection of current foreign books, only such as can be recognized as works of permanent value in the literature of any particular country should, as a rule, be chosen; and that the discretion should be most carefully exercised in acquiring such works of second rate importance as may be deemed, for any special reason, essential to the Library.[36]

The Trustees went on to ask that 'current foreign books' should if possible be 'submitted on approval before being purchased' and that these same principles should apply to 'old books' except those with special bibliographical interest. Further they approved of the practice of 'employing Assistants, who have special knowledge of the literature of particular countries, to select for purchase from the current literature of those countries' and they felt that the practice could 'be advantageously carried further' and the Assistants be encouraged 'to perfect [their] knowledge'.

In spite of all efforts to achieve the opposite, the grant was decreased, and from 1897–98 until well into the twentieth century it was a mere £6,000. However, from that year onward grants for individual Departments of the Museum were no longer specified in the printed Civil Estimates so the Trustees were undoubtedly allowed a greater latitude in deciding how to divide their money between the needs of the various Departments as presented by the Keepers;[37] also they were able to alter the allocations during the year, or to provide extra funds from the Museum's reserve fund. Sometimes a Keeper borrowed money from another Department, but he had then to repay it in the following year.

In his final request to the Trustees for funds before he retired, Garnett again stressed:

> the necessity of a liberal grant for purchases if the Library is to maintain the position which it now holds at the head of all libraries of the world ... as that library which has made most progress towards the ideal of a universal library in every department of literature and information ...

The efficacy of the acquisitions policy was, he claimed, borne out by the fact that readers continually reported that 'when there is a demand for information respecting some exceptional subject, the resources of the Museum are usually found adequate'.[38]

III · THE NEW CENTURY, 1900–19

With the retirement of Richard Garnett in 1899, the direct link with Panizzi was broken. Although the aim of universality was still paid lip-service, the new Keeper, Fortescue,[39] in his annual requests for the purchase grant, showed a more pragmatic attitude to the continuous lack of an adequate book fund. In 1900 there was even threat of a possible further deduction of nine per cent[40] from the already low grant of £6,000. However, in March 1901 the Trustees gave the Keeper the authority 'to make purchases of current books and continuations to an amount not exceeding £200' beyond the sum allotted to the Department.[41] Fortescue continued to find the grant sufficient to cover ordinary purchases so long as he was allowed to draw upon the reserve fund for unusual expenditure or for the replacement of books in constant use such as those in the Reading Room.[42] In 1905–06 the Trustees warned that although they had allocated £6,300 for purchases 'a vote has been taken on account, which has been less than usual' and the Keeper should therefore 'take care not to spend more than two-fifths before the end of July'.[43]

In 1908 Fortescue finally complained that he had:

> consistently endeavoured to keep the expenditure on purchases within the sum allotted . . ., but the experience of the last eight years . . . proves that the expenditure has as a rule, exceeded the ordinary grant by not less than £500 . . . He therefore ventures to ask the Trustees for . . . £6,500[44]

in the hope that in future he would not need to ask for sums from the reserve except for special purchases. So he went on, always finding the 'sum is sufficient for normal purchases',[45] but still hoping to be 'permitted to ask for a grant from the Reserve Fund' and sometimes asking booksellers if he could postpone payment[46] until the grant for the next year was available. He even told the Trustees how much better off his Department was than the Bibliothè-que Nationale:

	BM	DPB	Bib. Nat.
Salaries	£60,557	£20,583	£17,800 (incl. MSS, Prints and Drawings and Coins, as well as Printed Books)
Purchases	£22,000	£7,000	£3,508
Binding	£10,821	£8,000	£1,532

Fortescue retired in October 1912 after forty-two years in the Department and his successor Miller[48] immediately complained of rising prices and the urgent need for more money for new books and periodicals. Although he was Keeper for two years only, he pressed hard to have the grant increased to £7,000, noting the unsatisfactory situation of the past five years and that:

> In addition to the steady rise in prices which affects old books . . . the Department . . . has been confronted of late years with an equally marked increase in the number of important new foreign books and more particu-larly of works containing facsimiles or elaborate illustrations of other kinds and issued at high prices.[49]

He went on to remind the Trustees of the increasing numbers of important foreign periodicals and that when 'additional facilities are granted for consult-ing these' with the opening of the 'new Large Room (i.e. what is now called the North Library), a demand will arise for some which are not at present bought'. In April 1912, according to normal practice, Miller had been told that the 'vote' was taken on account and that only 'one-third' was then available.[50] But these were troubled times;[51] in his Annual Report of January 1913 on the work of the Department during the previous year Miller complained that the number of old books acquired had been unusually small and that increasingly large sums were necessary to keep abreast of the growing output of modern books.[52] Nevertheless, for a meeting on 8 March of the Standing Committee, the Department was asked to report 'all liabilities... for which payment will be required to 31 March 1913' and Miller was told: It is very important that your report should include every such liability. The Trustees require to deal with any savings it may be possible to effect... and they will regard your statement as final.'[53]

He did, however, get his grant of £7,000 plus £500 from the Reserve for 1913–14,[54] and his successor, Barwick,[55] asked that it should 'be maintained... in order that if peace be restored the Museum may be in a position to make good the arrears now accumulating'.[56] But, in his annual report of 2 February 1915 on the work of the Department during 1914 Barwick had to report that although:

> the usual purchases of current literature of foreign countries was maintained up to August, and since then to the utmost that circumstances would permit... owing to [the] depletion of the staff the work of the Department is reduced to maintaining its current service, and nearly everything else is at a standstill... The Department has incurred no liabilities beyond the usual understanding to maintain subscriptions for periodicals and other works in progress published in neutral countries. The amount for the year 1915–16 may be roughly estimated at £500.[57]

The government was looking for ways to cut expenditure and in December the Director and Principal Librarian, Sir Frederic Kenyon,[58] warned Barwick that in the interests of economy 'the Treasury have officially intimated their desire that the national collections should be closed for the period of the war'.[59] The importance of the Museum Library as a source of information for Government Departments (over 4,000 books and maps were lent to them),[60] as well as the need to deal with copyright deposit receipts,[61] precluded this drastic measure and throughout the period of hostilities the Reading Room remained open until dusk,[62] while other parts of the Museum were closed to the public. The war years were inevitably trying. Many activities were suspended but the continued pressures of increased world publication and the lack of space caused problems.[63]

When the war ended, Barwick, in a review of the state of the Department of Printed Books, wrote that 'the policy inaugurated by Mr Fortescue of using the greater part of the grant available for old books upon the books of a particular country or period has great advantages'; however, since for twenty years books printed in the fifteenth century and English books printed from 1501–1640 had been given a deliberate preference (and in the case of English books that preference really began with the preparation of the special catalogue in 1883) the Museum was 'now extraordinarily rich' in these works. As the prices for them were then very high he proposed to transfer the emphasis to French and Spanish books of the sixteenth century, works in which the Museum was not nearly so rich as in those of Germany and Italy, and to English books published during the sixty years following 1640. Furthermore he added, 'It is to facilitate purchases in these special fields that the preparation of short-title lists of books already mentioned is mainly desirable.'[64]

IV · CO-OPERATION OR ISOLATION, 1920–21

The next Keeper, Pollard,[65] described by Edward Miller as 'one of the most distinguished scholars the Department has ever possessed'[66] was quick to make his presence felt. He reorganised the Department on the lines suggested by Barwick in his report of April 1919 to give 'more responsibility to Senior Assistants with greater recognition of any expert knowledge they have acquired in foreign languages and literatures and better training to the younger men'. The selection of foreign books was linked to the revision of the catalogue and the Assistants were 'formed into a permanent Committee on Cataloguing and Book selection'.[67]

However, the long continuing battle with a penurious Treasury in the face of ever increasing world literary output, the increased competition from other libraries, and rising prices were having their effect. In April 1919 Barwick, immediately after compiling his special report, had written to Sir Arthur Evans[68] asking that the 'Trustees should come to see [the] chaos for themselves'.[69] The grant requested of £7,000 was 'found quite sufficient for the present year' (1919–20) because the 'depreciation of the Mark, Lira and Franc' counteracted the 'appreciation of [the] moneys of Switzerland, Scandinavia, Holland, Spain and [the] United States and [the] increased price of books', but there was the probability that 'measures will be taken to bring all foreign exchanges nearer par, which the increased prices of books are not likely to lessen'.[70] Nevertheless Pollard was happy to report in March 1920:

the fact that the state of the Foreign Exchange during the past year has so multiplied the value of the purchase grant that the acquisition of the books now recommended will still leave a probable balance of nearly £1,000 available for the Common Fund.[71]

He noted in his Estimates for the following year that the 'exchanges (on balance) continue to counteract the increase in the prices of foreign books'.[72]

These moments of good fortune were quite rightly not allowed to lull the Museum officers into a false sense of security and Pollard, in his annual report on the work of his Department for 1920, asked the Trustees to consider:

> As regards the purchase of Modern books and Periodicals in certain special subjects, notably Law, Medicine and Technology ... whether the Museum is not buying either too many foreign books and periodicals or too few; too many in comparison with the actual use made of them in the Reading Room and too few if the Trustees consider it essential that the Museum should be as strong in the subjects for which specialist libraries exist in London, as it is in others for which the Museum stands almost alone.

He went on to request that they 'sanction his getting in touch with the librarians of the specialist libraries (taking one group at a time!) with a view to being able to report to them with a better knowledge, on the facts of the case'. And he asked the Trustees for a general instruction:

> (i) to disregard the existence of the libraries of the Royal College of Surgeons and Royal Society of Medicine, and make the Museum collection representatively complete in itself;
> or (ii) to rely on these libraries as supplying the more highly specialised needs ... and so save money for other subjects;
> or (iii) to enter into understanding with these libraries with a view to taking a share in the more complete covering of the ground with less duplication.

He feared that the position of the Museum would again become untenable as soon as the 'foreign exchanges cease to neutralise the increased cost of books'.[73] To this plea the Trustees replied cautiously instructing the Keeper 'to correspond with other chief specialist libraries in London to determine how far duplication – especially of periodicals – is desirable'.

In the following year Pollard took the opportunity to remind the Trustees of this when he asked for two assistants to work on the *World List of Scientific Periodical Literature* commenced by Barwick and Wyndham Hulme, Librarian of the Patent Office.[74] He urged that the Museum should head co-operative library work and he hoped that the scientific union list would be followed by a similar one for the arts.[75]

V · THE GEDDES AXE, 1922, AND ITS AFTERMATH

Pollard's fears were not without substance but it was not an adverse exchange rate which was to lead to reduced purchasing power. The war had been expensive and prices had risen to nearly three times what they had been before 1914. National expenditure was out of hand. In 1921 Lloyd George appointed Sir Eric Geddes Chairman of the Committee on National Expenditure with the following terms of reference:

> To make recommendations to the Chancellor of the Exchequer for effecting forthwith all possible reductions in the National Expenditure on Supply Services, having regard especially to the present and prospective position of the Revenue . . . to review . . . expenditure and to indicate . . . economies[76]

This committee, which was intended to save the Government £1,000,000,000, presented three reports between December 1921 and February 1922.[77]

The first Report examined 'the Fighting Services', 'Social Services' and 'Pensions' and recommended reductions of £70,300,000 'over and above the £75,000,000 reductions which the Departments themselves have proposed'.[78] The second Report dealt with among other matters 'Civil Service Estimates'. But it was the third Report and more especially 'Part XIII. Art and Science. Chapter I. Museums and Galleries'[79] which most concerned the Museum officials. This noted that expenditure on staff accounted for over eighty per cent of the Museum's costs. The committee made no recommendations for reduction of higher and semi-technical staff but felt that economies might be produced by a close investigation of the warding staff especially in the British Museum and Natural History Museum 'where a reduction of the number of expensive Regular Police and their substitution by ex-soldier warders would effect a saving'. Purchase grants which formed a mere ten per cent of Museum expenditure were not to be reduced owing to 'special opportunities which now occur for making purchases for the Nation as the result of the breaking-up of many continental and private Collections, owing to the war'. The Committee was also informed that 'the suspension of reduction of the National Purchase Grants discourages gifts or bequests of private benefactors'.[80] The item of expenditure which the Committee criticised most heavily in the Estimates of the British Museum was the

> greatly increased cost of bookbinding. The item, which in 1913–14 cost £11,900, is estimated in 1921–22 at £26,500 and in 1922–23 at £22,000. We suggest that, in the present circumstances, this item should be reduced by £3,000.

The Keeper was of necessity influenced by the political and economic situation. When in 1920 he presented the Estimates for 1921–22 he emphasised that there were reductions in the wages for the staff of the firm which printed the catalogues and a proposed reduction in the wages of the binding staff of two and a half per cent, as well as savings occasioned by reduced costs of materials, and economies of staff, extra labour and materials used in binding. Although the exchange rates continued to favour the Museum's purchases Pollard warned again that with the enhanced prices of foreign books and increasing numbers of desirable works 'if exchanges become less favourable . . . [the] grant would become seriously inadequate'. To mitigate the worst effects of this he told the Trustees that the cutting down of orders had already begun.

The necessity to cut the binding budget (which was at this period three times larger than the amount of the allocation for the purchase of books) caused Pollard great concern because of the large number of valuable works requiring binding. In an attempt to diminish the pressure on this fund he proposed among other changes that the gift from the Colonial Institute of 300 Colonial newspapers should be reduced by at least one half in consultation with the Librarian of the Institute.

In order to deal with the worst effects of the requirements of the Geddes Committee, the Standing Committee of the Trustees appointed a sub-committee on 10 March 1923 with the following terms of reference:

> to consider:
> (a) the principles which should guide the purchases . . ., having regard to the desirability of conserving the resources of the Trustees for the acquisition of objects of the first importance and to the improbability of any building extensions for many years to come;
> (b) the method in which recommendations for purchase should be made to the Standing Committee; and to report thereon.[81]

This sub-committee which consisted of Viscount Dillon, Viscount Ullswater and Mr Bentink[82] was given the power in the interval pending their report, if they deemed it necessary, to 'examine proposals for purchases, and recommend such as they approve to the Standing Committee'. However, after five meetings at which 'objects proposed to be purchased' were submitted (this is most unlikely to have applied to purchases of *new* books by the Library), the sub-committee concluded that as in only '2 or 3 cases have any of the purchases proposed been negatived' they were not spending their time to the best advantage. They decided that the influence of the Trustees was best exerted through informal visits by individual Trustees to Departments in which they were interested. These visits they noted were welcomed by the officers. Given that the necessities of public finance required the strictest economy, the sub-committee recommended that the Standing Committee should lay down certain principles to guide the Keepers of the different departments in their purchases. Furthermore they were of the opinion that the situation was likely to continue for some years (perhaps ten or fifteen), during which time no money would be available for increased accommodation for the Museum, or for increased staff. This meant that purchases had to be made within the strictest limits and that 'quality should be the first aim; quantity only when it is essential for the adequate presentation of the evidence on a particular subject'. Given these constraints the principles which they recommended in purchasing were that:

no object should be purchased unless
(a) it is required to fill a gap in the collections.
(b) it has some genuine antiquarian, historical or artistic importance.
(c) that it will not involve any appreciable increased expenditure in its exhibition, care or maintenance.

They went on to specify:

three more principles which should be closely adhered to
(i) that no purchase of a portion of a collection or even of a single object of a collection should be recommended which may lead on to the purchase of the whole without the special attention of the Standing Committee being called to the circumstances.
(ii) that no gift should be accepted, the acceptance of which might compel the Standing Committee from a sense of courtesy or honour to purchase the remainder of the collection or set of which the initial gift formed a part.
(iii) that no purchase should be made in a new field of discovery, art or antiquarian interest without calling the special attention of the Standing Committee to the new departure.[83]

Finally they stated the desirability of building up a strong reserve so that they should be able to sanction the purchase of important but high-priced objects or collections as they became available. In order to do this they recommended that 'the annual Parliamentary grant... be divided in the proportion of approximately 2 to 1, instead of 3 to 1 (as now), between the Keepers of Departments and the Reserve Fund'.[84]

Before retiring, Pollard wrote a report to the Trustees pointing out that in his forty-one years service the stock had increased from nearly a million to not quite three millions, and that over a mile of new shelving was needed every year.[85] Thus, when in 1924 R. F. Sharp[86] succeeded Pollard (who recommended him to the Trustees as a 'man of literary tastes' with 'ample knowledge both of old books and of the needs of readers using them to guide policy as regards purchases and publications')[87] he, Sharp, had to contend not only with insufficient funds but also with rapidly decreasing storage space. In his Estimates he complained annually of the inadequate grant which was only just sufficient to maintain a very moderate standard of completeness; of the need when maintaining current purchases to encroach upon the grant for antiquarian books and of the necessity of carrying over an indebtedness into the following year.[88] At the same time he warned of the effects of ever increasing congestion and emphasised that delay in providing additional storage space must end in having a disastrous effect on the care and arrangement of the collections.[89] In view of these problems it is not surprising that he 'rationed'[90] the ordering of books and warned selectors to bear in mind the guiding principle, 'If in doubt about a book, don't order it.'[91]

In his annual report on the Department for the year 1927–28 Sharp emphasised the economies made as a result of cancelling subscriptions to 107 German, French, Dutch, Scandinavian, Italian and Spanish medical periodicals which were little used in the Museum and available elsewhere in London. The £165 thus released was to be spent on foreign literature for which the funds available during the past two years had been insufficient to keep the collections as representative as was desirable.[92] In the following year he stated in a letter of 24 April to the Secretary of the Royal Commission on Museums and Galleries that he had in recent years drastically reduced the Museum's collection of German technical and special periodicals.[93]

In his final year as keeper, in desperation, he requested £10,000 (£7,000 for new books and £3,000 for old). This request was turned down, but the Trustees' Sub-Committee on the Departments of Antiquities in an effort to assist the Keeper of Printed Books in his untenable position (or because they feared his inefficiency) 'considered favourably a proposal that the Keepers of Departments should assist the Keeper of Printed Books in the selection of books to be purchased for the General Library'. It was felt that their special knowledge of the literature of their respective subjects would ensure that books of real importance were not overlooked but that at the same time they would make savings as they would not need to purchase for their Departments books which they knew would be available in the General Library. If the system was to work the recommendations would have to be regular and systematic.[94]

VI · THE DEPRESSION AND AFTER, 1927–38

In 1927 a Royal Commission under Viscount D'Abernon[95] had been set up to investigate the affairs of museums and art galleries. The main problem to which it addressed itself at the British Museum was the overcrowding in the Library and in the Department of Ethnography. A fourth storey had been added to the South-East Quadrant of the Iron Library in 1923 and this (combined with the increasing use of 'sliding' presses) had the result that, as well as increasing the fire risk, the structure became 'extremely dangerous' and plans to add fourth storeys to the other three quadrants had to be abandoned.[96] It must have been a great relief to the new Keeper, W. A. Marsden (Fig. 12),[97] to be informed that the Trustees were seeking legislation arising from the Report of the Royal Commission which would allow them to extend their powers to refuse certain categories of printed matter sent in under legal deposit regulations and to discard unwanted material already here.[98] In 1931 there was a 'presentation in Parliament by members interested in the Museum, with a view to emphasising the importance of the Museum as one of the chief instruments of public education, and obtaining for it more adequate recognition and financial support'.[99] This support was timely because of the world-wide economic crisis which resulted in the 'Great Depression' of the early 1930s. Instead of reducing the Museum's funds the Treasury took notice of the plea in the Royal Commission Report and increased the purchase grant sufficiently to allow the sum for the purchase of books to be increased to £9,000.[100] Thus the Committee set up by the Trustees 'in response to a request for the stringent pruning of expenditure in view of the serious financial situation' was able to inform the Keepers:

> The purchase of books, both for the general Library and for the Departmental Libraries is not to be reduced, since these are the working tools of the Museum, and, in the case of the General Library, concern the whole nation, not merely the Museum staff . . . As regards the purchase of antiquities of all kinds (including old books or MSS. which are the subject of antiquarian research rather than the instrument thereof) it is expected that, while all legal or moral commitments for next year must be honoured, no further purchases should for the present be made. This does not apply to the grant for the current year; it is proposed to issue that grant in full; but it is expected that, both in the current year and next year, apart from commitments, only objects of outstanding importance should be purchased, and any balance remaining should be placed to reserve. These retrenchments will probably reduce the purchase grant for next year . . .'[101]

Unfortunately, on 21 September 1931, it was necessary for Parliament to suspend the Gold Standard and the consequent devaluation of the pound and the rise in price of foreign books and periodicals more than cancelled out the gain.[102] Marsden, again in his Estimates for 1932–33, requested £9,000 because 'although orders will be restricted' the same amount was likely to be required.[103]

An unexpected effect of the financial crisis was a large decrease in the number of volumes used by readers in spite of the fact that there was little difference in the number of attendances. This curious decline the Keeper attributed to the absence of a number of students from America who in recent years had made large demands on the collections.[104]

The Royal Commission of 1927 had also considered the relationship between the various libraries responsible for supplying the nation, especially the British Museum Library and the Science Museum Library. In Part I of their final report the Commissioners urged co-operation and 'expressed the opinion that "mutual collaboration" would be of particular benefit in the matter of the purchase of expensive foreign books and periodicals'.[105] However, this suggestion did not imply any change in the function of the British Museum as the 'universal reference library'. In Part II of their Report the Commissioners made it clear that the British Museum library should be kept intact. A suggestion that British scientific periodicals and books received under the Copyright Act might in future be deposited in the Science Museum Library instead of in the British Museum was thought after careful considera-tion to be neither efficient nor economic. The Science Museum Library had a lending as well as a reference function and the student whether British or foreign expected to find the material he required immediately at his disposal when using the British Museum. Furthermore the *World List of Scientific Periodical Literature* which might be used to decide whether or not any individual title should be considered a scientific journal contained many works which were equally important to the study of the humanities and when monographs were considered the distinction would be even more difficult. The Report concluded that the Commissioners were 'opposed to the principle of any disintegration of the supreme National Library' and they added:

> Any defects in present arrangements as between the British Museum and the other great National Libraries can, in our view, be remedied by the scheme of methodical co-ordination which we have already recommended in Part I of our Final Report . . .[106]

The integrity of the collections was to be maintained but the cost to the Library was perhaps more severe in terms of the balanced collection of materials than

12 W. A. Marsden, Keeper of Printed Books, 1930–43 (BL Archives).

has even today been assessed. In a 'Memorandum on the Report of the Advisory Council of the Science Museum on the Science Library' Marsden restated the Panizzian interpretation of the responsibilities of the Trustees as custodians of the National Library:

> (a) to ensure the delivery of a copy of every printed book falling within the scope of the Copyright Act;
> (b) to acquire, as far as possible, a copy of every English book falling outside that scope by reason either of date or manner of publication;
> (c) to build up the completest library of the literature of each foreign country outside that country; and
> (d) to make the whole accessible to students.

In direct conflict with these aims was the principle that the National Library was to be viewed as the holder of the printed records of the nation – 'the primary object is to conserve'. Lending could only be considered for the purpose of exhibition. Therefore, co-operation could only be by means of sharing the obligation to purchase, but, as ideally 'the National Library ought to contain all the elements of research', duplication was acceptable if expense permitted. But expense did not permit and an understanding had worked on general lines for many years between the British Museum, the Science Library, the Patent Office and the Library of the Victoria and Albert Museum that 'the British Museum buys, of foreign scientific books and periodicals only those of a general nature', and not those 'on scientific and technical subjects which are written for the expert and the specialist'.[107]

Even this departure from the comprehensive collecting policy was not sufficient to suit the economic conditions of the time. Competition among buyers temporarily disappeared, but the Keeper had to make a special request to the Trustees for money from the Reserve Fund for antiquarian purchases. In his annual report of 1932 Marsden told the Trustees that no important purchases were being considered nor would be, so long as economies were demanded. A 'highly priced book of solely bibliographical interest' would in future be acquired only by 'exchange or sale of superfluous and alienable duplicates'.[108]

The Director, Hill,[109] who had been appointed at the height of the financial crisis reminded the Keepers of the privileged position of certain Museums as set out in the Finance Acts of 1921 and 1930 when purchasing objects exempted from death duties. The Act of 1921 directed that 'duty shall not become chargeable on the sale ... of any property in respect of which exemption has been allowed' if the sale was 'to the National Gallery, British Museum', etc.[110] This provision was retained and elaborated in the Act of 1930 which stated that 'objects exempted from duty... shall not be taken into account for the purpose of estimating the principal value of the estate... or the rate at which estate duty is chargeable thereon' while in the possession of the heirs, but in the event of the sale of such objects 'duties shall become chargeable at the rate appropriate' except when 'the sale is to the National Gallery, British Museum or any other similar' institution.[111] Hill urged that the Keepers 'should be careful to point out that, if the Museum buys it, the vendor will not have to pay duty on the sum received, nor will that sum be reckoned in calculating the principal value of the estate'. A factor which could have the effect of 'bringing the whole estate down into a class on which a lower rate of duty is leviable'.[112]

In an attempt to reduce government expenditure the Treasury issued a circular directing that administrative costs should be reviewed with the idea of a 'slow down, suspension, or abolition of work or services'.[113] Hill sent this circular to his Keepers and Marsden replied that no further action was possible as economies had already been instituted.[114] In October he wrote to Hill sending him some remarks on the adequacy of the Department's Purchase Grant which if approved and required could be used in any attempt to obtain more funding. While conceding that 'the existing grant suffices, in the case of *modern foreign books*,' and if used cautiously might even cover the attempt 'to make good deficiencies due to the inadequacy of the grant in recent years'; it was different in the case of '*current foreign periodicals*'. The grant was not adequate to allow for extensive purchases and students were constantly pointing out periodicals to which the library was unable to subscribe. This was particularly regrettable 'now that so much original work makes its first and often its only appearance in periodicals and learned journals'. The category which most embarrassed the Department was, however, the restrictions on the purchases of old books, that is books from the fifteenth to the nineteenth centuries. The market was very favourable and the Museum could have been benefiting from exceptionally favourable offers which dealers were being forced by circumstances to make. He continued that if the restrictions were observed literally, about £1,000 would be handed back to the reserve at the end of the financial year a saving which he concluded was being made at the expense of his duty towards the collections.[115]

In spite of these constraints the Museum was holding its own. Marsden, in reply to a worried letter from Strickland Gibson, Sub-Librarian of the Bodleian Library, enquiring about methods which the Museum was using to maintain its foreign purchases, revealed that the increase in the annual purchase grant had made things easier and that the Museum was still able to keep pace fairly well, even with the expensive foreign books. The 'Swagger' foreign books such as elaborate and costly works produced for collectors were seldom purchased and books dealing with special branches of the fine arts were left to the Victoria and Albert Museum unless specially requested by the 'Print Room' (i.e. the Department of Prints and Drawings). If it was felt that a book was really important and likely to be asked for at the Museum it was purchased regardless of its price. To the suggestion that the purchase of some books might be deferred and that they should be put on a waiting list, Marsden replied that he found such a system too risky and that in his experience it did not work.[116]

Marsden's apparent complacency was not shared, however, by the Principal Librarian, Hill, described by Edward Miller as 'already a comparatively elderly man . . . regarded as something of a stop-gap . . . [who] nevertheless proved to be a capable Director'.[117] When attempting to pursue some research he had found gaps in the collections which were not in his own 'obscure subject' (numismatics) but were 'important books on Civil Law in general'. In August 1933 he wrote, with Marsden's approval, to his predecessor Sir Frederic Kenyon, asking for the assistance of the British Academy[118] on a regular basis in the selection of works on 'Ancient History, Medieval and Modern History, Biblical Studies, Philology (all branches), Philosophy, Law, Economics' and suggesting that the Academy Council might 'be willing to ask the various sections to appoint small sub-committees to draw up annual lists of the most important foreign publications on their particular subject'. These sub-committees need not meet but could work by correspondence, present their lists at the spring sectional meetings and send them on to the Museum. He anticipated the response that 'in most of the subjects printed bibliographies . . . appear from time to time' by pointing out that these 'usually aim at complete-ness rather than critical selection' which was what the Museum required.[119] Kenyon replied following the meeting of the Council in October that there was some doubt as to whether the Academy would perform this service efficiently but it had agreed to refer the matter to the several Sections, adding that the provost of Oriel had mentioned that the Bodleian was assisted by 'a committee nominated by the Boards of Faculties' and that he thought that some form of co-operation could be arranged.[120]

The report of the Sections was forwarded by Kenyon to Hill in May 1934 but seemed 'rather unsatisfactory' so Hill suggested to Marsden that they 'adopt the other plan' which was to ask the Bodleian and Cambridge University Library to let the Museum 'see their desiderata lists as prepared, not merely the list of books they decide to purchase'. Hill wrote to H. H. E. Craster, Bodley's Librarian,[121] and contacted A. F. Scholfield, Librarian to Cambridge University[122] with a request for their assistance. Craster replied that they were willing to send lists which were 'prepared by the Library staff from the reviews, prospectuses', etc. and sometimes 'amplified by suggestions from members of the Committee'. The lists were produced for 'Law, English Language and Literature, Modern History and Theology . . . Lit. Hum. subjects (Philosophy, Ancient History, Classical Languages and Literature) Social Studies (Political Philosophy and Economics) and Oriental Languages and Literature' but not at present for 'Fine arts, Archaeology, Modern Languages and Literature and the Physical Sciences'. Scholfield wrote that the 'meeting of the "Recommendations Subsyndicate" was over' but that he could send copies when they reconvened in October of the 'List of Recommendations' which would 'bear indications of what we buy and what we reject'. In thanking Craster for his helpful offer Hill concluded, 'We shall continue to trust to our own judgement and to what Cambridge can tell us for scientific books.'[123] I have found no copies of any such lists in the archives of the Department of Printed Books.

Marsden in his Estimates asked for £9,300 in 1933–34 and £9,500 in 1935–36 to meet the cost of additional purchases of periodicals.[124] The adverse exchange rate for France, Belgium, the Netherlands, Germany, Switzerland and Italy was not balanced by the slightly improved rate for the USA, Spain, Norway, Sweden and Denmark and consequently the value of the grant in 1934 was 'reduced by 40 per cent' so that instead of spending £2,385 on foreign purchases the Museum had to spend £3,425.[125]

In an effort to preserve a balanced acquisitions programme various proposals were considered, such as an exchange of duplicates with the Bibliothèque Nationale[126] and selection from the Library of Congress catalogue cards which (contrary to the expectations of the Museum officers) were 'not found . . . [to] largely represent books of merely local American interest . . . since the Library of Congress, unlike the Museum and the Bibliothèque Nationale, has and exercises the right to select from the copyright deposit and also buys largely'.[127]

From 1936 to 1938 the grant remained at £9,500 p.a. The problems of the revision of the catalogue and the enormous arrears of binding, especially at Colindale, greatly overshadowed those of the inadequate purchase grant. Sanctions against Italy in 1936 resulted in the setting up of the Anglo-Italian Clearing Office and the Museum applied for 'permission . . . as a Government Department, to clear books and periodicals from Italy (and other restricted countries) without filling up the usual forms' on the grounds that a similar concession had been granted to the Department of Printed Books during the 1914–18 war and that it would save time and extra work.[128]

The agreement in 1937 to purchase the Ashley Library for £66,000, by making an initial payment of £6,000 and further payments of £10,000 on the 6 April for the following six years, decreased further the funds available to the Department.[129] The unexpended portion (about £900) of the grant for antiquarian books was to be put towards the initial payment, and £1,500 of the annual grant for purchase of books was to be the Department's contribution towards the cost of the Ashley library over the next six years.[130] With so much of the fund for antiquarian purchases already committed, the staff of the Library was left no choice, over the next few years, but to exchange desirable duplicates, including incunabula, in order to obtain antiquarian desiderata.[131]

In 1938 an Inter-Office Committee on the Science Museum Library looked at the British Museum policy on 'Acquisition and Service'. It concluded that the 'British Museum's collection may be considered complete... as far as English works are concerned', but in the field of 'foreign literature... the ... Museum has for many years past pursued a policy of collaboration with other libraries'. As well as the 'understanding' with the other 'national' libraries 'the stock of the libraries, of the various learned Societies are taken into account when purchases are being considered'.[132]

VII · THE SECOND WORLD WAR, 1939–45

Meanwhile the threat of another war was increasing. Along with other government departments, the Museum drew up plans for the deployment of the staff and the security of the collections in the event of air raids.[133] Marsden complained to the Director, Sir John Forsdyke,[134] that in view of the increasing responsibilities of the Department 'the number of higher posts is inadequate to our needs'.[135]

The war, which was declared on 3 September, affected the Estimates for 1940–41 presented in October 1939. Marsden stated that they made 'provision only for works essential to the life of the library and to the service of the public using it and its catalogues'. The grant requested was reduced by £2,000 to £7,500 (i.e. £6,000 plus £1,500 for the Ashley Library) as account was taken of a probable reduction in the number of books to be printed. Nearly fifty per cent of this sum was for subscriptions to periodicals but in the case of German works it would be seventy-five per cent.[136] This was not, however, a sufficient reduction in the eyes of Treasury officials who suggested that payments for the Ashley Library should be suspended or spread over a longer period and that the Grant-in-Aid, which had been £30,000 in 1938 and had been reduced to £24,000 for 1939, should be further reduced to £10,000, being the amount normally needed for the purchase of current books for the main and departmental libraries.[137] F. N. Tribe of the Treasury,[138] in a letter to Forsdyke urging the reduction, noted that 'the output of published books ... will be greatly curtailed'. He went on to cite the Trustees' willingness to make great sacrifices in times of crisis, reminding Forsdyke that 'the normal grant [to the Museum] of £25,000 was reduced to £2,000 in 1915, to £3,500 in 1916, to £3,000 in 1917 and 1918 and to £15,000 for the years 1932–35' and urging him to make greater use of the reserve.[139]

In his Report to the Sub-Committee on Printed Books of June 1940 Marsden remarked that the progressive depletion of the staff due to the war was slowing down the machinery but in spite of this all the activities of the Department were still being carried out and none of its responsibilities had lapsed. The Department's 'real character as the National Library, with statutory obligations under the Copyright Act and duties to the public at home and throughout the civilised world' was emphasised.[140] The purchase grant requested by the Department for 1941–42 was only £4,500 which was to include £1,500 for the Ashley Library. This represented a reduction in the amount of money for the purchase of new books from £5,500 to £3,000. Both the Ashley Library grant and the £3,000 for the purchase of current publications were allowed.[141]

By July 1941, with the staff of the Museum almost halved (ninety-five were serving in the Armed Forces and sixty-six had been transferred to other Departments),[142] the Department was counting the cost to the collections of the more than 250,000 volumes which had been lost as a result of enemy action.[143] No normal work was possible. Everyone available helped in the salvage work under the direction of A. F. Johnson the Placer of books.[144] Marsden indicated to the Trustees that 'a special State Grant' might be needed as well as the help of 'private owners and the Friends of the National Libraries' to make good the losses.[145] In the Director's words:

> The Library is in fact part of the machinery of government, and when in consequence of air raid damage its use has been temporarily withdrawn from the general public, it has hitherto been possible to meet the needs of other Government Departments, the armed forces and the various Allied headquarters and Embassies.[146]

However, the Reading Room had to close on 23 September 1940, following damage by a high explosive bomb. It reopened in the North Library on Monday 10 November, from 9am to 4pm daily. Then again it had to be closed following the damage inflicted by incendiary bombs on 10 May 1941 while the whole of what remained of the staff worked in 'shirt sleeves . . . in order to put things tolerably straight . . . for a rather impatient public'.[147]

No special purchases were made during 1941. A mere seven donations were reported to the Trustees and two of these were declined. In the report on the principal acquisitions for 1941, Marsden listed only the following:

... 600 books mostly English poetry and books on Italian art and architecture from the library to F. T. Palgrave

... 200 modern books mostly French, German and Russian on art, music and the theatre library of Sam Kallin A facsimile reproduction presented by the Spanish government.[148]

The Library was under constant pressure. Forsdyke wrote to the Treasury that 'the Library or at least the Department of Printed Books is a unique establishment ... It only belongs by accident to the British Museum and its functions do not in any way resemble those of museums or galleries.' While the Museum Departments had ceased work entirely the Library 'conditioned by the constant inflow of books' and 'the public use of them' had by necessity continued to operate.[149] Marsden fought to resist further depletions of his staff and wrote to Forsdyke:

> It must be understood and repeated that (1) what we are engaged upon is of national, not to say international, importance; (2) that the Reading Room Service is steadily increasing; (3) that any further decrease in the Departments intake of publications is hardly to be expected.
> Therefore, what we are committed to will not allow the release of any more men; and I beg you to press for an unlimited 'period of deferment' for those at present retained.[150]

Books were again being loaned for use by the Government in some numbers although not so many as in the previous war because the Royal Institute of International Affairs, which was doing the work of some of the government departments, had its own extensive library.[151] Nevertheless, loans went to several bodies at this period: among them there was the Treasury, the War Cabinet, the Admiralty, the War Office, the Ministry of Agriculture and Food, the Ministry of Labour, the Allied Governments, and to A. J. Toynbee whose Foreign Research and Press Service of the R.I.I.A. was operating from Balliol College, Oxford and was unable to find the books it required in Oxford.[152]

For the next two years the grant requested remained at £4,500 (i.e. £3,000 for current purchases plus £1,500 for the Ashley Library).[153] The Reading Room service was continued from the North Library which was crowded daily; and books were lent at the discretion of the Keeper to British and Allied Government Offices. The replacement of the destroyed books or at least those of the 'first importance' had started.[154] An index of '160,000 books lost' was compiled on cards. Marsden, on the Trustees' instructions, was devoting the whole of his purchase grant not required for new books to the replacement of destroyed books.[155]

As part of the war effort people were asked for unwanted books. The Library Association, worried by the destruction of libraries in the bombing, set up a

'Committee of Allocation for Salvage Books . . . to distribute those which have been sent for pulping, but would be useful in libraries . . . in this country or elsewhere'.[156] C. B. Oldman,[157] represented the British Museum on the Committee. Cambridge University Library had been thinking of disposing of some 'definitely second-rate' journals but the Librarian, Scholfield, wrote to Marsden offering them to the Museum, in case any were required to make up losses at the Colindale Newspaper Library.[158]

In spite of protests, the younger members of staff were called up.[159] Longer hours had to be worked and staff aged fifty-nine years or over were encouraged not to retire. The number of staff in the Department was reduced to eighty-six but the 'ripe experience' of the senior members allowed Marsden to report that the Department was holding its ground.[160] In January 1943 Marsden was forced to suspend the printing of the revised version of the General Catalogue because the Department had 'reached such a state of depletion that no individual member of the Staff can any longer be allotted exclusively to one particular task'. The effort to keep the Department going, or the disappointment of having to suspend the work which had been his main occupation for the last fourteen years, proved too much for Marsden and in March 1943 he retired leaving the Department in the capable hands of Dr Henry Thomas,[161] who, although himself nearly sixty-five, was much more energetic in pushing for the future development of the Library.

In his first report to the Sub-Committee on the Department, Thomas was able to state that 6,500 important books had been bought 'in replacement of those destroyed in the air-raid of May 11, 1941' and that many more were being acquired as gifts from war salvage.[162] Later in the year replacements were offered by many libraries: the Board of Trade via HMSO, the Guildhall, the Law Society, the Science Museum, the Victoria and Albert Museum, and from the Allied Ministers of Education there came books in the languages of their countries.[163]

The most important question raised immediately by the Keeper in view of the cramped accommodation (less than thirty years growth space) was the possible removal of the Library from the Museum. As a first step 'the separation of Library and Museum finances and establishments in the Parliamentary Estimates' would give 'general recognition of the Library as a unique National Institution' and allow it a better chance to fight for 'adequate provision for its accommodation, material and staff'. The Standing Committee accepted this view, but regarded it as essential that the Library remain in London. They decided to refer the matter to the Library Sub-Committee for further discussion and report and directed that in the meanwhile the Treasury be approached on 'the separate statement [in the Estimates] of library finance and establishment'.[164]

In 1944 and 1945 the affairs of the Department were at their lowest ebb. The Printed Books staff (well under half strength) were, in 1944, 'reduced to the lowest limit compatible with effective public service'. The Museum case for the urgent return of staff seconded to the war effort was given low priority. There was inadequate accommodation, no proper working rooms for the acquisitions staff, and insufficient equipment. There was only limited use of the Newspaper Library. The main Reading Room, with its leaking roof, was unusable. Readers used the North Library and had to demonstrate that they were engaged on research of public importance.[165]

At the end of May 1945 A. G. Crawley, who for thirty-four years was 'in charge of the selection (in part) and the ordering of foreign books and of English and American books not claimable under the provision of the Copyright Act' and who had compiled the register of books lost through war damage, retired. Thomas used the occasion as an opportunity to push for adequate organisation and staffing of this important section.[166] Then, in July, Duval,[167] Crawley's principal assistant for nearly a quarter of a century, died unexpectedly.[168] Another member of the Department, F. D. Cooper, who like Crawley had completed fifty years service and who was not in good health, was due to retire in November. Cooper had dealt with the acquisition and processing of colonial copyright material since 1900 and had been for the last few years in charge of the State Paper Room. In reporting Cooper's impending retirement on 25 September, Thomas recommended (and the Trustees agreed) that, in view of the extreme congestion and continued lack of staff, Cooper should remain on a temporary basis.[169]

In spite of these and many other problems Thomas had, in 1944, reminded the Sub-Committee on the Department of Printed Books that 'the time has in fact arrived for an expansion of the National Library parallel to that of a hundred years ago'.[170] In the Estimates for 1946–47 his request that the book fund for the purchase of foreign books be doubled to £10,000 'to buy books missed in the last five years, to replace losses and to meet increased prices' due to adverse foreign exchange rates was approved, even though grants could not be allocated to other departments and their Keepers had to draw on the General Reserve for essential purchases.[171]

The Department returned slowly to more normal working conditions. Thomas became Sir Henry in the 1946 Birthday Honours list and was appointed the first Principal Keeper in February 1947. A. I. Ellis[172] and C. B. Oldman were appointed Keepers; all three appointments were back-dated to 1 January 1946. Ten members of the Department, including Thomas, were over the age of fifty-nine but in view of the shortage of staff[173] the departmental Sub-Committee recommended the retention of all except two who wished to retire. The senior staff were only fifty-nine per cent and the junior staff sixty-nine per cent of those in post in 1939 before the war. Salaries improved[174] and the number of staff gradually began to increase.

In a 'War Report', written anonymously for the American *Library Journal*, Thomas pointed out that 'the lost books were for the most part ordinary books published between 1857 and 1941 on the following subjects: archaeology, architecture, art, costume, dancing (including ballet), domestic science (including cookery and household management), games . . ., handicrafts, law, medicine, . . . books about music . . ., numismatics, printing . . . sport . . . [and] journals [on] medicine, bibliography, philology, poetry, drama and literature.' He went on to state that the post-war obligations of the Library were threefold: to purchase current books, to fill gaps caused by the inability to acquire some books during the war, and to replace books destroyed in the air raids.[175] Gifts of books flooded into the Library. Connection was re-established with agents in foreign countries cut off by the war and books (except those from Germany and Austria) were again purchased in the usual manner. The Foreign Office had set up a Committee to arrange for the acquisition of German and Austrian books missed by English institutions during the war years. HMSO acted as collector for the Museum which was given priority over other libraries. Dr Liebstaedter (trading as Asher & Co.) the Museum's agent for German and Central European books was technical adviser to the Committee.[176]

Museum officials began cautiously to look towards the future and to consider what role (if any) the Library should play in national and in international library affairs. In May Thomas attended the Library Association annual conference which was devoted to 'The Public Library service, its post-war reorganisation and development' and reported to the Trustees that, although none of the proposals directly affected the Museum, the 'discussions were highly instructive and that the presence of a Museum representative was much appreciated'.[177] In October 1946 Sir Henry, who had been encouraged by the Trustees to remain another year,[178] was appointed to represent the Museum on the National Co-operating Body for Libraries. This was the United Kingdom organisation through which institutions interested in education, science and culture could be associated with the work of UNESCO. He also accompanied the Director to America to inspect library developments there. While in the US they met representatives of the Rockefeller Foundation who encouraged them to apply for a complete technical installation for the conversion of newspapers to microfilm.[179] In December 1947 with the books which had been removed for safe-keeping back on the shelves, an inventory of the stock well advanced, the book fund (after sixty years) finally restored

13 C. B. Oldman, Principal Keeper of Printed Books, 1948–59 (BL Archives).

to £10,000[180] and the immediate post-war planning well under way, Sir Henry, now sixty-nine years old, retired and was succeeded by C. B. Oldman (Fig. 13).

The book fund did rise, if only slowly from £10,000 in 1946–47 to £53,000 in 1959–60[181] but, as P. R. Harris[182] in a recent article notes, by 1950–51 domestic prices had risen by 124 per cent so that £18,000 was worth only just over £8,000 in terms of 1935–6 prices. It was only because a large share of the grant was devoted to the relatively cheap replacements of war-destroyed books that the rate of acquisitions increased. Oldman in his Estimates

[134]

continually reminded the Trustees of steeply rising prices. In 1954 he requested an increase to £30,000 (the existing grant being £23,000 plus £5,000 from the Reserve) because as well as the increased cost of books there was the necessity to purchase more from such countries as India, Pakistan, West and East Africa, the West Indies and the Philippines. From many of these countries the British Museum had formerly received books free of cost under colonial copyright deposit regulations, while others were countries which were being opened up.[183]

In 1955 Oldman produced as an appendix to his June Report to the Sub-Committee[184] a full account of 'The Acquisition of Foreign and Antiquarian Books' giving details of departmental practices, and the strengths and weaknesses of the system. Following Treasury investigations, the familiar panacea for insufficient funding in the face of increased commitments (a reorganisation of the Acquisitions Section) had been undertaken. Foreign books, as today, were purchased by language. 'The general aim is to allot responsibility for ordering books in each of the main languages of the world to individual Assistant Keepers.' Suggestions also were received from staff in the Department, users of the Library, subject experts, and others. Experience showed that 'a skilled selector, who keeps up-to-date with current reviews, covers the field with a high degree of success'. Even so, subject advice on particular groups of books was, from time to time, welcome. Normal practice, as now, was for a selector to read through current national lists of publications as soon as they were issued. Orders were then despatched and a card index record of the orders kept. The main languages and the main publications (trade or national bibliography) used for selection were listed. Only Albania, Esthonia, Latvia and Lithuania had no selection tools available. New map publications were selected by Map Room staff, music was purchased from agents; but lack of staff time made it impossible to undertake systematic searching for State Papers.

The areas which were covered only in the most cursory fashion included South America, Africa, and the Near, Middle and Far East. The main emphasis was placed on subjects which could be broadly characterised as humanistic, but even so some categories were poorly covered. Those fields considered by the selectors to be insufficiently provided for were: publications of local academies and antiquarian societies; many important series; archaeology and art; illustrated and fine editions; law; sociology; theology; travel and topography; facsimiles of important manuscripts and early books; volumes published on the occasion of centenaries; illustrated histories of institutions and catalogues of collections; American books (the purchase grant was not sufficient to keep up with the publishers which ceased to distribute in the UK and thus to deposit their works in the Copyright Receipt Office); books published in the Commonwealth, and English language books published in Asia. Books judged to be of outstanding historical importance in any subject or which dealt with the history of a subject were, however, purchased. The subjects not covered or covered only imperfectly included mathematics, applied science and technology and medicine.

The main problems were the difficulty of finding satisfactory booksellers; the booksellers' natural inclination was to accumulate orders whereas the Department preferred a speedy service of smaller parcels; the problem of maintaining a correct balance between books and periodicals; and the frequent necessity to hold over invoices from one year to the next, which resulted in a considerable portion of the year's purchasing being swallowed up in paying for orders from the previous year. In addition a major difficulty for the Department was to provide adequate coverage of periodicals and State Papers.

So far as antiquarian material was concerned, although attempts had been made to cover all fields in the usual manner, the Library would benefit from a planned policy. Areas which needed attention were eighteenth-century publishing; important English authors; and subjects where the collections were haphazard and unrepresentative. The Music Division had compiled a list of important works not held. It was in the production of surveys of this kind that special subject consultants would be of great value.

Oldman went on to say that the specialists in various languages were expected to keep the collections under constant review and to make recommendations for the purchase of antiquarian books to fill serious gaps. The burden of routine duties prevented the really systematic performance of this task. The selectors had to confine themselves to recommending individual purchases as they happened to come up in the second-hand book market. More encouragement could be given to Assistant Keepers to develop this side of their work if a sum could be allotted for antiquarian purchases.

A striking development during the post-war period had been the growth of the system of barter exchanges. Academic institutions with large publishing activities, now bartered their publications instead of presenting them as they used to do. Moreover, experience had shown that the only satisfactory way of acquiring publications from Eastern Europe was by exchanging them. These arrangements were now on such a scale that it was no longer possible to fulfil the Department of Printed Books side of the transaction by sending only British Museum publications; thus current British books had to be bought and despatched to Eastern Europe. The system generally was very 'prodigal of staff-time' and, in the long-run, an uneconomic method of acquiring publications. It also had the disadvantage that staff were 'chary of refusing any of the proposals for exchange in case the source of supply should become difficult or dry up altogether'. These were, in part, the reasons why the expenditure on Russian books had tended to be larger in proportion to that on books from other countries. The Department was, however, confident that the collection of current material from there and from other Iron Curtain countries was representative and justified the amount being spent on it. Unfortunately, disproportionate expenditure in this area could only be at the expense of purchases elsewhere.

Oldman summed up by saying that the allocation of funds (even including an increased Grant for 1955–56) was quite inadequate to maintain a level of purchases which would conform to the needs of the Museum. The reputation of the Museum had suffered seriously as a result of the inadequacy of its collections of modern books and periodicals. Also, it was failing to build up and exploit its collection of older books.

During the year under review, funds available for purchase fell short by about £10,000 of what was needed. Still more money was required for making good gaps in the collections and for acquiring important series and periodicals which were not bought in the past. The increase of £4,000 which had been granted still left a shortfall of £6,000. In addition an extra £5,000 was necessary, 'as a first step', to extend the area of purchase of foreign books and to make a beginning in filling past gaps. Future expenditure must be planned with the object of extending this operation still further in order to provide the reference materials which the Museum ought to possess and which could not be looked for in any other library in this country.

This impassioned plea gained Oldman a grant of £33,000 for 1955–56. The allocation for purchases increased year by year but the severe shortage of appropriate staff to make use of the increased resources continued to plague the Department. (In 1953 the Government had declared a policy of reducing the size of the Civil Service and any requests for an increase of staff were subjected to an exacting scrutiny.)[185] In his Report for 1957, Oldman recorded a modest increase in staff but bemoaned the demise of the recently devised 'five-year' plan for regular increases which had evidently been consigned to oblivion. He acknowledged that he must be grateful for small mercies, but he had to sound a warning note. If an increase in the higher grades (Assistant Keepers and Executive Officers) was postponed indefinitely, the staff of the Library would become more and more out of balance, and the cataloguing and acquisitions work which was largely done by members of these grades would necessarily fall behind.[186]

With Oldman's retirement from the post of Principal Keeper in 1959, this account of the acquisitions policy and funding of the Department of Printed Books comes to an end. He had worked hard to improve the financial resources available for acquisitions but he knew that his successors would have a struggle to keep up the momentum. Apart from adequate money the Department urgently needed more space to house the rapidly increasing collections. This had been, from its earliest days, a continual problem for the Library. It is one which can never be completely solved in an institution which, for the sake of posterity, rarely and only very selectively disposes of material. On the other hand the Department of Printed Books has been fortunate – it has had a knowledgeable and dedicated staff to work on the selection, evaluation, cataloguing and preservation of its collections. Money and space for acquisitions are essential, but they count for little unless a library has a skilled staff to exploit its resources properly.

NOTES

1   It should be noted that this article deals mainly with purchased acquisitions, and to some extent with exchanges and colonial copyright legal deposit. It does not deal with the question of the legal deposit of UK publications.

2   DH1/1 :11–13, 12 October 1837; Weimerskirch, Philip John. *Antonio Panizzi's acquisitions policies for the Library of the British Museum*. DLS Columbia University, 1977; Royal Commission 1847–49, para 8975 (Panizzi was Keeper, 1837–56; Principal Librarian, 1856–66); *On the Collections*, p.74.

3   Keeper, 1866–69.

4   BM CE4/69, 23 February 1861. A letter of 20 February 1861 from Watts to Panizzi requesting consideration for promotion to Keeper and DH2/124 :259 pp.1–17. Report on 'The purchasing Policy of the Library' by R. A. Wilson 7 October 1959 which notes the anonymous article by Watts in *The English Cyclopaedia of Arts and Sciences;* conducted by Charles Knight. Vol.2, pt.VI. 1859. Column 385.

5   Keeper 1856–66; Principal Librarian, 1866–78.

6   'Public libraries' (by J. Winter Jones) in *North British Review,* Vol.XV p.173 (May–August, 1851); Weimerskirch p.93.

7   DH2/6, 6 November 1861. Jones to the Trustees.

8   DH2/6, 19 March 1862. Jones to the Trustees.

9   DH2/6, 7 May 1862. Jones to the Trustees.

10   A result of the American Civil War, 1861–65, during which the North imposed a blockade on the South.

11   A considerable number of maps from the Humboldt Library were purchased in February/March 1862.

12   DH2/6, 10 November 1863. Jones to the Trustees. Estimates to 31 March 1865.

13   DH2/8, 22 October 1866. Watts to the Trustees. Estimates to 31 March 1869.

14   DH2/8, 9 October 1867. Watts to the Trustees. Estimates to 31 March 1869.

15   DH2/10, 15 July 1869. Watts to Jones.

16   DH2/15, 12 February 1874. Rye to the Trustees. William Brenchley Rye, Keeper, 1869–75.

17   DH2/8, 11 October 1876. Porter to the Trustees. George William Porter, Assistant Keeper, 1870–88.

18   An Act to Amend the Law of Copyright. 5 & 6 Vict. c.45. 1842.

19   DH2/18 :50 and 54. 10 October and November 1877. Bullen to the Trustees. George Bullen, Keeper, 1875–90.

20 DH2/24 Sect. I :8. and Sect. III :8. 9 & 10 July 1880. Bullen to the Trustees concerning the Ramirez Sale (principally books printed in Mexico).

21 DH2/30 Sect. I, 10 February 1883. Minute of the Trustees concerning a Treasury letter of 25 January transmitting a report of a committee on the exchange of official publications.

22 DH2/33 Vol. II, Sect. II. Misc. letters. 5 January and 20 February 1884.

23 George Joachim Goschen, Chancellor of the Exchequer, 1887–92.

24 DH2/37 :20. 30 December 1886. Bond to the Keepers.

25 Sir Edward Augustus Bond, Keeper, Dept. of MSS., 1866–78; Principal Librarian, 1878–88.

26 DH2/38 Sect. IV. Misc. Reports (Important). 6 January 1887.

27 DH2/38 Sect. I. Minutes relating to the acquisition of books. 12 March 1887.

28 DH2/38 :106, 9 November presented 12 November 1887. Bullen to the Trustees.

29 *An Act to Amend the Law Respecting International and Colonial Copyright.* 49 & 50 Vict. c.33. 1886.

30 DH2/40 Sect. I :24, 12 May 1888. Trustees' Minutes commenting on a report of Bullen, and Sect. III :21 9 May 1888.

31 Keeper, 1890–99.

32 DH2/42 Sect. IV. Misc. Reports :40, October 1889. Garnett in the absence of Mr. Bullen.

33 DH2/48 Sect. IV :13, 23 September 1892. Estimates. *See also* DH2/50 Sect. IV :4. 9 October 1893; DH2/52 Sect. IV :7. October 1894; DH2/54 :267. 5 October 1895.

34 DH2/48 Sect. IV :13, 23 September 1892.

35 DH2/50, 9 October 1893 & DH2/52, October 1894. The Isham books purchased 'last July for upwards of £1,100' thanks to 'the addition of £250 to the grant for the present year'.

36 DH2/54 :38. Minutes of Meetings of [the] Sub Committee on Printed Books ... 18 November & 6 December as reported to the Standing Committee on 14 December 1895.

37 DH2/99 :229, 20 June 1934. Marsden to Dingwall explaining that the Treasury had for many years left the allocation of the 'block' grant entirely to the Trustees.

38 DH2/60 Sect. IV. Misc. Reports. Important. 30 September 1898.

39 George Knottesford Fortescue, Keeper, 1899–1912.

40 DH2/64 :214. Estimates, 1900–01.

41 DH2/65 :27, 5 March 1901.

42 DH2/65 :197, 2 March 1901 and DH2/67 :162, 29 September 1903.

43 DH2/69 :140, 13 April 1905.

44 DH2/72 :137, September 1908.

45 DH2/77 :156, September 1912.

46 DH2/75 :98, 1 April 1912.

47 DH2/75 :171, 1912. Rough reckoning ... in 1910.

48 Arthur William Kaye Miller, Keeper, 1912–14.

49 DH2/77 :205–6, October 1913.

50 DH2/77 :209, 2 April 1912. Bound in vol. for 1913.

51 As well as marked inflation, there were numerous strikes, problems in Ulster with Home Rule, and internationally the shifting alliances and ententes with their secret clauses, unrest in the Balkans and the growing threat of an increasingly armed Germany.

52 DH2/78 :215–226, January 1913.

53 DH2/78 :211, 17 February 1913.

54 DH2/78 :2, 7 March and :192, 10 January 1914.
55 George Frederick Barwick, Keeper, 1914–19.
56 DH2/78 :194, 29 September 1914.
57 DH2/79 :115–118, 2 February 1915.
58 Sir Frederic George Kenyon, Director and Principal Librarian, 1909–30. The designation Director had been added in 1898.
59 DH2/79, 30 December 1915. Unfoliated minute following :148.
60 DH2/85 7, 14 February and :204, 10 February 1920.
61 DH2/80 :111, 3 January 1916. Barwick to Kenyon.
62 DH2/80 :113, 24 January 1916. Kenyon to Barwick.
63 DH2/79 :139, 1915. Annual report.
64 DH2/83 :163–66, 4 April 1919. Barwick on 'the present state of the Dept. of Printed Books in respect of the restoration of normal conditions'. The special catalogue was the *Catalogue of Books in the Library of the British Museum printed in England, Scotland and Ireland, . . . to the year 1640,* compiled by G. Bullen and G. Eccles. 1884.
65 Alfred William Pollard, Keeper, 1919–24.
66 Miller, Edward. *That Noble Cabinet.* London, 1973. p.324. Footnote.
67 DH2/85 :208, 1920. Pollard to the Trustees. Annual report.
68 Sir Arthur Evans, 1851–1941, as President of the Society of Antiquaries, 1914–19, was a Trustee of the British Museum.
69 DH2/83 :179, 8 April 1919.
70 DH2/83 :171, 1919. Estimates for 1920/21.
71 DH2/85 :133–4, 6 March 1920. Report respecting offers of purchase.
72 DH2/85 :225, 23 October 1920. Estimates for 1921/22.
73 DH2/85 :208–211, 1920. Annual report(?)
74 Edward Wyndham Hulme, Librarian, Patent Office Library, 1894–1919.
75 DH2/86 :96, 23 July 1921. Catalogue of scientific serials.
76 Committee on National Expenditure. First interim report. Cmd. 1581, 1922. p.1.
77 2nd interim report, 28 June 1922. Cmd. 1582; 3rd report, 21 February 1922. Cmd. 1589.
78 First interim report. p.171–72.
79 Third Report. p.373.
80 Third Report. p.374.
81 DH2/88 :193–95, 20 October 1923. Sub-Committee to the Standing Committee of the Trustees.
82 Harold Arthur Lee Dillon, 17th Viscount Dillon, 1844–1932, an elected Trustee of the British Museum, 1905–32; James William Lowther, 1st Viscount Ullswater, 1855–1949, Principal Trustee (as Speaker of the House of Commons), 1905–21 and elected Trustee, 1922–31; Frederick Cavendish Bentick, 1856–1948, Harley Family Trustee, 1909–48 and member of the Standing Committee of the British Museum.
83 DH2/88 :194–95, 20 October 1923.
84 DH2/88 :195, 20 October 1923.
85 DH2/89 :172, 30 January 1924. Pollard to the Trustees.
86 Robert Farquharson Sharp, Keeper, 1924–29.
87 DH2/89 :148, 1 June 1924. Pollard to the Trustees.
88 DH2/89 :194.; DH2/90 :151.; DH2/91 :180.; DH2/92 :197.; DH2/93 :216, 1924–28. Estimates.
89 DH2/91 :169–71, February 1926. Sharp to the Trustees. Annual report.
90 DH2/94 :167, 25 March 1929. Memo by Sharp. 'Ordering of Foreign Books'.
91 DH2/124 :259. op.cit.

92   DH2/93 :192–94, 1 February 1928. Sharp to the Trustees. Annual report.
93   DH2/124 :259. op.cit.
94   DH2/94 :182, 30 September 1929. Memo from Kenyon.
95   Sir Edgar Vincent, 16th baronet, Viscount D'Abernon, 1857–1941, Chairman of the Royal Commission on the National Museums and Public Galleries and subsequently of the Standing Commission.
96   Miller. op.cit., p.325–26; Royal Commission, p.97.
97   Wilfred Alexander Marsdcn, Keeper, 1930–43.
98   DH2/95. Unfoliated following :102, 18 February 1930. Report of Sub-Committee on legislation arising out of report of Royal Commission. Sect. III. 6. Extension of powers to refuse certain categories of printed matter.
99   DH2/96 :95–96, 14 March 1931. Department of Printed Books.
100 DH2/124 :259. op.cit.
101 DH2/96 :119, 10 October 1931. At a Committee.
102 DH2/124 :259, op.cit.
103 DH2/96 :323, 6 October 1931. Estimates.
104 DH2/94 :151, 4 January 1928. Annual Report.
105 DH2/124 :259, and Royal Commission, para 11(1).
106 DH2/124 :259, and Royal Commission, para 10.
107 DH2/98 :92–94, 1933. 'Trustees approved – circulated in full to General Board'.
108 DH2/97 :136, October and :242, February 1932.
109 Sir George Francis Hill, Director and Principal Librarian, 1931–36.
110 DH2/97 :243–44, 6 February 1932. Purchases of Objects Exempted from Death Duties and Finance Acts 1921 Sect. 44, and 1930 Sect. 40.
111 DH2/97 :243, ibid.
112 DH2/97 :243, ibid.
113 DH2/97 :329, Treasury Circular No.12/32 E.27871, 15 July 1932.
114 DH2/97 :330, September 1932. Treasury Circular E.27871.
115 DH2/97 :354, 11 October 1932. Marsden to Hill.
116 DH2/97 :359, 27 October 1932. Marsden to Gibson. Strickland Gibson, Sub-Librarian of the Bodleian Library, 1931–45.
117 Miller. op.cit. p.331.
118 Kenyon was Secretary of the British Academy, 1930–50.
119 DH2/98 :314, 29 August 1933. Hill to Kenyon.
120 DH2/98 :316–17, 24 October 1933. Kenyon to Hill, and Hill to Marsden pointing out that 'Kenyon suggests that London University might be a better source; advice could be sought through the Senate'.
121 Sir Herbert Henry Edmund Craster. Bodley's Librarian, 1931–45.
122 Alwyn Faber Scholfield, Librarian to the University of Cambridge, 1923–49.
123 DH2/99 :222, 5 and 7 June 1934. Correspondence between Hill and Craster.
124 DH2/98 :321, 2 October 1933 and DH2/99 :251, 3 October 1934. Estimates.
125 DH2/99 :251. op.cit.
126 DH2/99 :262, 24 September 1934. Hill to Professor C. K. Webster. Sir Charles Kingsley Webster, Stevenson Professor of International History, London School of Economics, 1932–53.
127 DH2/99 :273, 13 November 1933. Donald Coney, Supervisor of Technical Processes, The Newberry Library, Chicago to Esdaile, Secretary, British Museum.
128 DH2/101 :256, 2 September 1936. Thomas to Controller, Anglo-Italian Clearing Office.

129   DH2/102 :18, 9 October 1937. The Ashley Library of books, manuscripts and autograph letters of English (mainly Romantic) poets was collected by Thomas James Wise over a period of more than forty years. He had hoped to bequeath it, but economic vicissitudes forced his estate to offer it, on very favourable terms, to the British Museum, Esdaile, *The British Museum Library*, pp.199–201. P. R. Harris in his article 'Acquisitions in the Department of Printed Books, 1935–50 . . ., (*British Library Journal* vol.12 no.2, 1986) described it as 'one of the most important collections which the Department has ever acquired'.

130   DH2/102 :247, 18 October 1937. Estimates 1938–39.

131   DH2/103 :1, 8 January 1938. Exchange recommended.

132   DH2/103 :263, 1938. Acquisitions and Service.

133   DH2/103, 1938. Sect. VII. AIR RAID PRECAUTIONS. :264, 20 January 1938.

134   Sir (Edgar) John Forsdyke, Director and Principal Librarian, 1936–50.

135   DH2/104 :200, 17 July 1939. Marsden to Forsdyke.

136   DH2/104 :237, October 1939. Estimates.

137   DH2/105 :56, 10 February 1940. Grant-in-aid, 1940–41.

138   Frank Newton (later Sir Frank) Tribe, Principal Assistant Secretary, H.M. Treasury, 1938–40.

139   DH2/105 :138, 8 January 1940. Tribe to Forsdyke.

140   DH2/105 :172, June 1940. Annual report.

141   DH2/105 :196, 10 October 1940; DH2/106 :114, 7 February and :127, 29 May 1941.

142   DH2/106 :30, 12 July 1941. Staff transferred or on service with H.M. Forces.

143   DH2/106 :59, 12 July 1941. Losses caused by air raid damage. Also Miller. Chapt. 13 especially p.335.

144   DH2/106 :127, 29 May and :128, June 1941. Allocation and annual report. Alfred Forbes Johnson, Assistant Keeper, 1922–49, re-engaged, 1949–51, Special Assistant (part-time) 1952.

145   DH2/106 :59. op.cit.

146   DH2/106 :137, 17 July 1941. Director. The British Museum and the National Library.

147   DH2/106 :66, 8 November 1941. Reading Room: reopening, and :128, June 1941. Annual report.

148   DH2/106 :69, 1941. Sect. IV. Principal acquisitions during . . . 1941.

149   DH2/106 :115, 24 February 1941. Forsdyke to L. Lionel H. Thompson (Sir (Louis) Lionel (Harry) Thompson, Assistant Principal, Treasury, 1919–29; Principal, 1929–40; Assistant Secretary, 1940–47; Under Secretary, 1947–50; Deputy Master and Comptroller of the Royal Mint, 1950–57.)

150   DH2/106 :119, 29 March 1941. Marsden to Forsdyke.

151   DH2/108 :149, 7 July 1943. Thomas to the Trustees.

152   DH2/106 :126, 17–21 May 1941. Marsden-Toynbee correspondence.

153   DH2/106 :155, 6 October 1941. Estimates for 1942/43; DH2/107 :136, 6 October 1942. Estimates 1943/44.

154   DH2/106 :128. ibid.

155   DH2/107 :59, 12 December 1942. Library Association: Committee of Allocation for Book Salvage.

156   DH2/107 :59. ibid.

157   Cecil Bernard Oldman, Keeper, 1946–48, Principal Keeper, 1948–1959.

158   DH2/107 :114, 13 March 1942. Scholfield to Marsden.

159   DH2/107 :116, :122, :123, May–June 1942. Correspondence and memos regarding working hours and holidays.

160 DH2/107 :118, June 1942. Annual report.
161 Dr (later Sir) Henry Thomas, Keeper, 1943–45, Principal Keeper, 1946–48.
162 DH2/108 :64, 10 July 1943. Minutes of the Sub-Committee on Printed Books, etc.
163 DH2/108 :5; :79; :6; :81; :7; :77; :80; :8; :83; :11; :86; :70, October–December 1943. Reports of gifts.
164 DH2/108 :64.
165 DH2/109 :78, 1944 and DH2/110 :42, 13 October and :75, 14 July 1945.
166 DH2/110 :73, 14 July and :90, 30 January 1945. Ellis in the absence of Dr Thomas. Alfred George Crawley, Assistant Keeper, 1921–45.
167 William Milton Duval, Higher Clerical Officer, 1934–45.
168 DH2/110 :109, 2 August 1945. Thomas to the Trustees.
169 DH2/110 :42, 13 October, :75, 14 July and :113, 25 September 1945. Retirement of F. D. Cooper (i.e. Frederick Daniel Cooper, Assistant Keeper, 1931–45, retained temporarily to 1948).
170 DH2/109 :78, 1 July 1944. Thomas to the Trustees.
171 DH2/111 :71, 13 April 1946. Forsdyke to Thomas.
172 Arthur Isaac Ellis, Keeper, 1946–48.
173 DH2/111 :75, 13 July 1946. Minutes of the Sub-Committee on Printed Books, etc.
174 DH2/111 :202, October 1946. Treasury letter to Forsdyke. Salary revision-scale.
175 DH2/112 :161, and *Library Journal* vol. 72, August 1947, pp.1085–87, 'B.M. library removes war's traces'.
176 DH2/111 :181, 6 June 1946. Annual report.
177 DH2/111 :73, 13 July 1946. Library Association: annual conference.
178 DH2/111 :50, 12 October 1946. Retention of services: Sir Henry Thomas.
179 DH2/112 :183. Estimates.
180 DH2/110 :164, 2 November 1945. Estimates.
181 DH2/111, 1946 to DH2/124, 1959. Estimates.
182 P. R. Harris, *British Library Journal*, vol. 12, no. 2.
183 DH2/119 :114, 10 July 1954. Estimates.
184 DH2/120 :142, June 1955. Department of Printed Books Report to Sub-Committee of Trustees. Appendix on the Acquisition of Foreign and Antiquarian Books by the Department.
185 DH2/118 :116, p.3, 11 July 1953. Annual report.
186 DH2/122 :148, 13 July 1957. Annual report.

4

THE BOOK WOLF BITES A BOHN: PANIZZI, HENRY BOHN, AND LEGAL DEPOSIT, 1850–53

K. A. MANLEY

The practice of reminding men of their civil duties through a police court
is not a very English proceeding, and it reminds the publishers that the
gentleman who pursues it with such zest is not an Englishman.

'The Book Wolf', *The Leader*, 10 July 1852.

THE LIBRARY OF the British Museum was always intended to be a national library,
inheriting as it did the mantle and privileges of the former Royal Library. The
difficulty in transferring concept into practice revolved around the question
of ways and means; to be a true repository of the country's literature, statutory
provision was needed. Hence the misleadingly entitled 'Copyright' Acts which
required of publishers the compulsory deposit of all their publications in
certain specified libraries. When Panizzi (Fig. 14) was at the height of his
power, the relevant legislation was the Copyright Act of 1842 which granted
legal deposit to the British Museum, the Bodleian, Cambridge University
Library, the Advocates' Library, Edinburgh, and Trinity College, Dublin. Publishers were obliged to deposit books in the British Museum, subject to a
penalty not exceeding five pounds as well as the cost of the books; the other
libraries had to claim their copies within twelve months. The libraries could
also claim works published anywhere in the British Empire, but this was quite
unenforceable. When the Act was debated in Parliament, only authors' rights
were discussed. The topic of legal deposit had already been aired at great
length in 1836 during the passage of that year's Copyright Act, when James
Silk Buckingham attempted to persuade the Commons to bring an end to this
privilege. He failed, although the number of deposit libraries was reduced
from eleven to the five mentioned above.[1]

The legal deposit libraries had only spasmodically tried to enforce their
rights. In 1812 Cambridge University Library had successfully prosecuted
Henry Bryer for non-compliance in a case significant only because of its rarity.
Bryer was a minnow amongst publishers and was chosen because Cambridge
was afraid to tackle one of the big fry. The university legal deposit libraries
suffered under a greater burden because they found it more difficult to justify
their need to acquire every single publication, regardless of merit.[2] They
aggravated the situation by actively discarding material felt to be worthless, a
practice begun by Sir Thomas Bodley himself who held strong feelings against
Shakespeare and his ilk: 'Happely some plaies may be worthy the keeping',
he wrote to Thomas James in 1612, 'but hardly one in fortie'. Bodley was
horrified at the thought of 'the harme that the scandal will bring vnto the
Librarie, when it shalbe giuen out, that we stuffe it full of baggage bookes'.[3]

As is well known, many publishers did their best to evade their liability. The story of how Panizzi increased the volume of accessions by prosecuting recalcitrant publishers has been oft repeated, but the details of the resulting court cases have not been published before. Edward Miller's biography of Panizzi refers to the trial of 'a Mr. Bohn' and comments that the latter was fined a mere shilling, which suggests that the subject was treated leniently, if not frivolously, by the courts.[4] In truth Bohn was fined one shilling for each transgression, plus costs. Although the total was less than £12, an important principle had been upheld, and publicly so. The case became a *cause célèbre* because of the surrounding harmful publicity. Panizzi was portrayed as the British Museum's tyrannical servant, and a foreigner to boot. No matter that his goal was to ensure that the Museum really did become a national library. Panizzi's prosecutions are not of solely academic interest. As the British Library moves into the 1990s, a policy of deliberately declining to accept certain classes of literature deposited under the current Copyright Act is seriously being considered. The result may well be to turn the clock back until before even Panizzi's time. How to decide what should be declined? It is interesting to observe that in about 1836, according to Arundell Esdaile, the Trustees instructed their Copyright Receipt Officer not to claim publications of 'a socialistic or sceptical tendency'.[5]

During 1850 Panizzi must have felt under siege. There was constant public criticism of the inadequacies of the British Museum's catalogue, and the scandal of the Libri affair, in which Panizzi had supported the unworthy count. Pressure from books and readers was forcing Panizzi to think of expansion and ultimately towards the design of the circular Reading Room, opened in 1857. The rising number of accessions meant more space was required, but Panizzi was aware that the number of acquisitions should be even greater. In May 1850 Panizzi was granted power of attorney to enforce the Copyright Act. His chosen mode of procedure was to use an agent, not a member of the Museum staff, to purchase an undeposited book from the shop of the non-compliant publisher, and then take the proofs of purchase and non-receipt before a magistrate.[6]

Panizzi opened his campaign by issuing warning letters to thirteen known recalcitrant publishers in London. Five responded with abject apologies, but in November 1850 Panizzi instructed the Museum's solicitors, Bray, Warren, and Harding, to institute legal action against the remainder. The first incredulous victim was the firm of Spettigue and Farrance of Chancery Lane, who were summonsed to appear at the Guildhall on 5 December. Panizzi was pleased to report to the Trustees that, 'having begged for mercy, [the firm] brought a much larger number of books than it was known to have published, and promised to obey the law in future'.[7] Less compliant was James Gilbert, summonsed on the same occasion for non-delivery of a map. Though dated

14 Antonio Panizzi, Keeper of Printed Books, 1837–56; Principal Librarian, 1856–66. Photograph of the bust by Baron Marochetti, 1856, which stands above the entrance to the Reading Room and was paid for by subscriptions from members of the staff of the Department of Printed Books.

1850, Gilbert claimed the map had been engraved more than seven years earlier, i.e. before the Copyright Act of 1842, and was exempt. He complained of Panizzi's actions as 'robbery', but was fined ten shillings plus costs.[8] Panizzi later commented to the Trustees that 'altho' some publishers so far forget themselves as to designate by the term *robbery* the inforcing of an act of parliament, they never forget to charge in their estimates for publishing a work the five copies which they are bound but omit to deliver'.[9] Gilbert was fined a further fifty shillings and £2 costs on 20 February 1851 for a fresh non-compliance over a pamphlet on the late papal aggression. His defence was that he had intended to send a better copy.[10] At about the same time James Burns was prosecuted,[11] while John Chapman appeared at Bow Street on 7 August and was fined a nominal one shilling and £3.13s. in costs.[12]

These few successes were merely preliminary skirmishes. During 1852 no less than twenty-one summonses were issued against London publishers, while the field of combat was extended to the rest of the United Kingdom. Amongst London publishers to be dragged through the courts were Routledge, H. G. Collins, Cassell, Day and son, James Darling, and Bradbury and Evans. Most apologised, promised to be more careful, and were fined a nominal sum. J. Saunders was more defiant. He appeared at Bow Street on 20 March 1852 and was fined £2 after a rebuke from the magistrate because of his behaviour. Panizzi promised a further summons against him for another offence.[13] On the same day George Sowerby was 'summoned to the felons' bar', as the *Literary Gazette* put it, for not sending a fascicule of his *Thesaurus conchyliorum*. He complained about his treatment to Panizzi, who offered to prosecute him on two other offences. Panizzi's view was that Sowerby had deliberately defrauded the Trustees on previous occasions. He had, for instance, failed to provide his *Mineral conchology* under the previous Act. An incomplete copy had come with the bequest of General Hardwicke; nine parts of the *Conchology* were lacking for which Panizzi had had to shell out money in 1850 to Sowerby because he could not claim under the old Act: 'Mr. Sowerby was paid £1.16s. by the Trustees, beside having been paid for what he had sold to General Hardwicke; a reward for his infringement of the law'. The *Literary Gazette* reported Sowerby's prosecution by way of a warning to others and added inconsequentially: 'No wonder that Mr. Panizzi has been so many years getting over letter A in the new Catalogue, when he has to resort to such oppressive measures to get the books in'.[14]

Sowerby was not the only focus of discontent. John Chapman, already once prosecuted by Panizzi, was plotting revenge. Famous to posterity as the lover of George Eliot and less so as an author himself (he wrote books on diarrhoea and sea-sickness), Chapman had become the proprietor of the *Westminster Review*. In the issue of April 1852 he published an attack on the 'forced "benevolences" ' which publishers had to make to the five copyright libraries, urging that the 'tyranny of *compelling* the publisher *himself* to *deliver* the copies demanded might at least be dispensed with'. If manufacturers had to donate five copies of every product, he opined, this would be an interesting use for the new Crystal Palace.[15] Panizzi would not let that pass. In May Chapman was summonsed for failing to send the January number of the *Westminster Review* and was fined £2 despite protestations of innocence. Chapman complained to the Trustees that Panizzi was being vindictive: 'I presume such a motive will not bear the scrutiny of Englishmen, and therefore I write to enquire whether Mr. Panizzi's frequent practice of issuing a summons without the courtesy of a previous notice meets with the approval of the Trustees of the British Museum'.[16] The Trustees did approve. The *Literary Gazette* pursued its own vendetta: 'Our exposure of this oppressive system of police fines had not, it seems, been agreeable to the government functionary. For the present venial oversight Mr. Chapman was mulct in the sum of 47s.. We think if Mr. Panizzi could get to work upon letter B of the Museum Catalogue, his services would be of far more advantage to the country than in manifesting these petty ebullitions of private pique to the country's shame'.[17]

The successful prosecution of Bradbury and Evans in July 1852 provoked more press criticism, including a notable piece entitled 'The Book Wolf':

> The practice of reminding men of their civil duties through a police court is not a very English proceeding, and it reminds the publishers that the gentleman who pursues it with such zest is not an Englishman. The affrighted publisher feels like the industrious ants, conscious of dreadful Formica Leo or Ant Lion, lying in ambush for him to snap him up if he stumble into the pit; and he regards that devouring insect with the more horror since it is an outlandish species – a sort of crawling Machiavel, whose pit is the British Museum, and whose slaves are policemen. "We should not see this morbid appetite for booksellers", they say, "if the Librarian were an *Englishman*".[18]

Shrugging off his critics (though deeply wounded), Panizzi decided to move against publishers outside London. He travelled to Scotland on 26 July 1852 where he took legal advice on the best way of proceeding, and also discovered a clerk in the Advocates' Library, Edinburgh, who was prepared to send him quarterly lists of new books. During 1853 several reluctant Scottish publishers received admonitory circulars from Panizzi, and all complied with a minimum of fuss.[19] September 1852 found Panizzi in Ireland, visiting Dublin and Cork. He claimed that he was hoping to remain incognito, but was soon recognised.

This was hardly surprising since he took as his travelling companion the bookseller Henry Stevens. It is scarcely conceivable that the tall, striking Italian and the well-built self-styled 'Green Mountain Boy of Vermont' could have long remained inconspicuous, even in Dublin. He did not visit Belfast, since a chance acquaintance in Glasgow had promised to provide information about publishers in the former city. As in Scotland Panizzi's foray produced immediate gains.[20] *En route* they passed through north Wales, with encouraging results. Stevens recalled how he had drawn from an unsuspecting bookseller in Caernarvon the admission that, though he published large numbers of books, he sent none to the British Museum.[21]

A further half-dozen London publishers were prosecuted on 6 November 1852, including H. G. Bohn, William Dickinson, and J. Russell Smith. The latter pair, according to Panizzi, 'pleaded ignorance of the law, which Mr. Panizzi thought was by this time well known'. Day of Lincoln's Inn Fields,

> an old offender, . . . was summoned for the non-delivery of Wyatt's *Mosaics of the middle ages*. He pleaded among other things that the work was published in 1848; which if true would be an aggravation of the offence: the fact is that he omitted delivering the book when originally published in 1848, and he also omitted to deliver a re-issue of it which is now taking place. The book has no date. He also pleaded his great punctuality in delivering books, however expensive: one of which, he said, delivered since his last conviction, was worth six guineas. The book in question he was, however, obliged to admit, had been delivered about an hour before this statement was made by him.[22]

George Bell was summonsed for a book 'printed and published for' Macmillan's, then of Cambridge, but with Bell's name on the fly-leaf, which was sufficient evidence for Panizzi. On the day of the hearing Macmillan's ('habitual offenders') wrote to Panizzi in mitigation of Bell. Panizzi offered to drop the prosecution, but Bell refused the offer and was fined only a nominal shilling.[23] Macmillan's themselves claimed to be eager defenders of the Act but pointed out that their name was often put on pamphlets, especially poetry, without their knowledge. They were sure, they added, their authors would be proud to be in the British Museum: 'We daresay they wd. also gladly pay all the expenses of your lawyer at the Guildhall for the fame it wd. give them to have it reported in *The Times*'. After the case, the British Museum's solicitors sent to Macmillan's their usual letter declining, on Panizzi's behalf, to send them a list of further undeposited books; that was the publishers' responsibility, they maintained. Macmillan's continued to protest their innocence of failing to supply all their publications: 'But if it cannot be helped we shall not vex ourselves, nor get in a rage with you, nor call you ugly names, nor in any way disturb our equanimity about the matter'.[24]

And so to Bohn. The publisher Henry G. Bohn (Fig. 15), well known for his series of cheap reprints,[25] was first prosecuted on 6 November 1852 at Bow Street for not supplying Andrew Fuller's *Works*. Panizzi's agent, a solicitor's clerk, had purchased a copy from Bohn for five shillings. Bohn had disputed this in court, producing a copy priced at 3/6d. (Panizzi later told the Trustees this only meant that Bohn kept two copies at different prices: 'Of the respectability of such a way of doing business the Trustees will judge'.) Bohn's shop register was produced in court to show that the book could not have been sold for 5/-, but no transaction was recorded. Bohn pleaded his great punctuality in sending books; 'as they all do', commented Panizzi to the Trustees, adding: 'He [Bohn] gravely stated that he sent waggon-loads of books to the Trustees, which waggon-loads he went on to say were worth many hundred pounds. During the present year Mr. Bohn has delivered 29 books worth £4.10s. altogether at the very utmost. As to punctuality Mr. Panizzi told Mr. Bohn then, what can now be proved, that he owes more than a dozen books'. To complicate the matter Bohn brought up the question of the Museum catalogue's alleged deficiencies, claiming that books deposited by him six months earlier had not yet been catalogued, an accusation denied 'with a not unnatural degree of warmth' by Panizzi.[26]

Following the court case Bohn wrote to Panizzi: 'As you threatened me last week, in the Police Court, with at least a dozen summonses, in revenge for my having stated that the new books sent to the British Museum were often inaccessible to the public six months after their delivery, from being in the cataloguing room, I have thought it prudent to turn my immediate attention to possible liabilities in the matter'. As Panizzi's lawyer commented in the ensuing court case: 'Mr. Panizzi, of course, is in a position not to have his temper ruffled, or his mind in any way disturbed, by a letter of this description'. Since the British Museum declined to send to Bohn any lists of undelivered books, and since Bohn still disputed what had or had not been deposited, the Bohn saga continued. On 27 January 1853 Bohn was arraigned before the same Bow Street magistrate, David Jardine, on summonses relating to no less than thirteen works.[27]

The British Museum was represented by William Bodkin, and Bohn by William Ballantine. The latter immediately opened the proceedings by questioning the court's competence in the matter. Ballantine's ingenious argument was that the 1842 Copyright Act related to the deposit of books in certain public libraries, but that the British Museum was not defined therein as a public library: 'If I can shew that the clause under which these informations are laid has reference to certain public libraries – the British Museum being

15 Henry G. Bohn, publisher. From an album of photographs collected by Robert Cowtan (BM Dept of Prints and Drawings, 210* b 11 – 1943–11–15–1).

no longer classified therewith as a Library – then I submit that my friend is not entitled to sue for the recovery of penalties'. The Act specified that books had to be delivered between 10a.m. and 4p.m. to an approved officer of the Museum, who was to issue a receipt. The penalties for non-compliance could only be invoked by the public libraries after a due demand for books had been ignored, contended the barrister, and could not be claimed by the British Museum. The word 'library' was not in the Act in connection with the British Museum, 'so that Mr. Panizzi is a mere cipher in the matter – as any other officer of the establishment might be authorized to receive them – the word 'librarian' being never once mentioned or thought of . . . I say that Mr. Panizzi, who is the informer here to-day, is not the "officer of the library" entitled to proceed for the penalty.'

Bodkin leapt to the defence of the national library: 'you are asked to believe', he addressed the magistrate, 'that a Building, containing the largest collection of books in the world, – or, at least, in this Kingdom – and secured to the nation by legislative measures designed it may be said to provide literary food for the people – is not to be considered as a Library, because the legislature has called it the British Museum, and has passed stringent enactments to give it certain advantages in favor of which, as my friend remarks, a more stringent enactment is inserted, not only as to the manner of delivery, but also in respect to what is to be delivered; which constitutes the important difference between the Library of the Museum, and the Bodleian, or other libraries enumerated . . .'. The magistrate did not need convincing and pointed out that the original British Museum Act of 1753 had catered not only for the Sloane collection, but the Cottonian, Harleian, and other libraries, and their additions, as well as for the appointment of a librarian. Clearly the intention was to provide a public library, and so the 1842 Act was applicable.

The Museum's lawyer informed the court of what had happened since Bohn's last appearance. Further books had not been sent, which the Museum had now purchased, and the expense of which they had claimed from Bohn during January. Bohn's porter had delivered several books, but because it was almost closing time the Copyright Receiver, John Knight, would not issue receipts. Bohn's porter believed the clerk to be the great Panizzi himself. When Panizzi realized on the next day they had been sent by Bohn, he declined to accept them on the grounds that Bohn had acted clandestinely, and that the solicitors had claimed the value of the books, not the books themselves. For this reason the matter had come to the court: 'it is just these omissions that cause the whole grievance', remarked Bodkin. 'And a little ill-feeling in the matter also', commented Jardine. 'And possibly, as you say, a little ill-feeling also', admitted Panizzi's lawyer. The first book, Jules Michelet's *History of the French revolution*, part 2, was admitted by Bohn to have been forgotten by oversight, for which he pleaded guilty. The second, Vasari's *Lives of painters*, vol. 1, was one of those delivered but turned away by Panizzi. 'I may say', added Ballantine, 'that the porter had always taken the gentleman who received them for Mr. Panizzi, but it turns out it was Mr. Knight. It was a mere mistake on the part of the porter, who did not know, as we know, that public officers generally depute somebody else to do their duties'. They pleaded guilty to that count.

For the next book, Luigi Lanzi's *History of painting in Italy* (three vols),

a clerk employed by William Pickering, the publisher, testified that he had
purchased the work on Panizzi's behalf at Bohn's shop. Panizzi took the stand
and confirmed that the work had not previously been deposited.

'How do you know that?', queried Ballantine.

'Because I have ascertained', replied Panizzi.

'Am I to understand that you undertake to swear that no copies of that
work are in the British Museum?'

'None of that edition.'

'But how do you ascertain this?'

'Because I have looked for them, and cannot find any.'

'Looked where? You do not mean to say that you have a Catalogue of all
the books in the British Museum!' cried Ballantine in incredulity.

'Yes we have – up to within two months.'

'What? A catalogue representing every book in the Museum, and accessible by the public?'

'Yes, certainly.'

'And you have looked there for this work?'

'Yes I have. I looked for it a quarter of an hour before I came here.'

'And you will swear this work is not in the Museum?'

'Yes, to the best of my belief. There are plenty of other editions.'

'What editions?'

'Several. They are here.'

'What editions are they?'

'I don't know. There are those here who can tell you, and who have also
looked for this edition.'

'Let us see them.' The volumes were produced.

'How many editions of this same work are there in the Museum?',
continued Ballantine.

'I don't know. You can ascertain.'

'I *want* to ascertain, and please to remember that you are not at the Library
of the British Museum now, but in the witness box of a Police Court. Now
how many copies of this work are there at the Museum?'

'I cannot tell.'

'Then what are you at the British Museum if you cannot tell? Are there a
dozen copies, or more?'

'I do not know. I know there are duplicates, but I cannot say how many.
The Catalogue is here. And there are others here – other gentlemen who
have looked and can tell you.'

'Have you ascertained what difference, if any, there is between this and
the editions already in the Library?'

'No I have not.'

'I believe you stated in this Court, when you were last here, that you would
be revenged on Mr. Bohn.'

'I did not say anything of the kind, and I am sure the worthy magistrate will bear me out in that assertion.'

'Certainly nothing of the sort was said here, in my hearing', affirmed Jardine, and Panizzi was allowed to leave the stand.

John Knight gave evidence that the work had not been received under the Act, and Bohn pleaded guilty.

The next work, William Roscoe's *Life of Leo X,* was an abridgement of an edition already in the British Museum and, urged Ballantine, should not be regarded as a new edition under the terms of the Act; this proves the court action was vexatious, he added. He continued that Bohn would take advice on this matter from the magistrate and not from the librarian of the British Museum, and he wished that Bodkin or Jardine was at the head of the Museum. Ballantine argued that the Act specified that a 'new' edition had to have 'additions and alterations'. Since an abridgement contained omissions rather than additions, the Act could not apply, Ballantine continued:

> The object of the legislature was, doubtless, to give the public an opportunity of reading all that could be said upon the subject, and not merely to enable them to gratify themselves by looking at the possible varieties in the binding, or other exterior peculiarities of such works ... For myself I must protest against these unnecessary and vexatious demands for works which can only be required for the sake of giving annoyance to publishers, and augmenting the useless heap of duplicates already crowding the floors of the British Museum.

One of the planks supporting Ballantine's case was that the other deposit libraries were not so demanding; it was clearly a question of personality:

> Mr. Bohn has resided a great many years in England, having intercourse with all classes of men; and he knows the sort of spirit in which men of business like to deal with each other. At the British Museum however he had not been treated with that English spirit which is understood here. Mr. Bohn, and a vast many others in Mr. Bohn's position, have felt that a degree of persecution has been practised towards them which they would never have met with from a countryman of their own ... I say when I look at these things I cannot help thinking how different a result might have been brought about by a single word of kindness – a single act of courtesy and civility. But no. Mr. Panizzi prefers to wrap himself up in an artificial importance, and to say "You are bound to do this by Act of Parliament – so do it!!"

Panizzi, so he accused, was only trying to conceal his own negligence: 'It is a fact, notorious to the public, that the shelves are already over-crowded – all the available space is occupied – and the cry is that there is no room for more'.

'How do you know that?' interjected Bodkin. 'I am sure Mr. Panizzi has not said so'.

'It is notorious that the library is crowded to excess with rubbish – mere trash', replied Ballantine.

'No, no', shouted Bodkin.

'Besides', intervened the magistrate, 'they must take in the trash, as well as the useful publications.'

Ballantine insisted that even though Bohn admitted omissions over the past few years, the whole matter could have been settled amicably had it not been for Panizzi's desire for revenge. Jardine disagreed: 'I have known Mr. Panizzi a great many years, and I must say that I do not believe there is anything malignant in his heart'. As Ballantine now admitted Bohn's guilt over a further three books, Jardine was able to be even-handed: 'I have known Mr. Bohn also a good many years as a very good neighbour, and every one must admit that the public is much indebted to him for his services to literature'. Jardine rejected Ballantine's arguments and had no doubts over Bohn's guilt, but agreed that it was unfortunate that personalities should have arisen over such a matter.

They moved on to another work, Lord Kingsborough's *Antiquities of Mexico*. This was a curious case. Only a handful of copies had been printed over twenty years earlier but because of a legal dispute had remained in Chancery until five years previously, when Bohn had been appointed to sell them. Panizzi's agent bought the book from Bohn, and the Museum now demanded twelve guineas in recompense. Bohn argued that the trade price was only £9, which he would have charged the Museum; the remainder had been paid to the agent as his fee, which Ballantine argued was a waste of public money. Jardine agreed that the book had not been published in the normal sense, and ruled that Bohn need only pay £9. In a spirit of forgiveness Bodkin dropped the remaining charges, which all concerned reprints made by Bohn from the original publishers' stereotypes. Bohn was found guilty on all counts, but Jardine, sharing the spirit of reconciliation, only fined him a nominal shilling in each case, in addition to the costs of the summonses and the prices of the books purchased by the Museum. The total was £11.16s.6d. He refused to award against Bohn the costs of the Museum's counsel. Jardine wound up the proceedings by hoping that there would be no further cases; he suggested that Bohn be more liberal, and Panizzi less severe.

The affair did not quite end there. The court case was reported in *The Times* on the next day.[28] On 2 February Panizzi wrote at great length in that newspaper, setting out the terms of the 1842 Act and emphasizing that he had not been acting in a draconian way. The Act allowed him to mount a prosecution without prior notice, he pointed out, yet he had sent circulars to all publishers in 1851 reminding them of their obligations. This was an act of courtesy, because:

> 'I have no right to impair the privileges of the Trustees by volunteering to do what the Legislature has especially exempted them from doing; and because if, in any one single instance, I were to claim any one single book, I should be bound, in fairness, to claim every book from every publisher in the British dominions before taking legal steps; the consequence of which would be, that no book would be delivered till claimed'.

He was impelled solely by a sense of duty, he insisted: 'All I get is blame. If the books are not in the Library I am found fault with, and I am found fault with if I use the only means I now have of procuring them'. He added that the number of new accessions had increased from 9,871 in 1851 to 13,934 in 1852.

An editorial in the same issue of *The Times* pointed out that Panizzi had not mentioned the name of Bohn, the immediate object of Panizzi's wrath. With imperious impartiality The Thunderer suggested that both sides were behaving in a petty fashion, and that it was really up to their respective clerks to settle an essentially administrative problem. Panizzi replied on the next day, explaining how Bohn had failed to obey the Act and complaining that Bohn's lawyer abused him for being a foreigner. He revealed that on the day before the hearing Bohn's lawyer had demanded that Panizzi produce 364 books in court to demonstrate the amount of duplication in the Museum. Bohn wrote to give his side of the affair and explained that his comment about 'waggon-loads of books' referred not to books sent to the Museum but to the numbers of free copies of his works which he distributed.[29]

A much longer letter by Bohn was declined by *The Times* and printed in the *Morning Advertiser* instead. Bohn's main contention was that Panizzi should have sent him a detailed list of books claimed by the Museum, instead of merely issuing a general circular to all publishers:

> Mr. Panizzi says he took the 'lenient course' of summoning me for only one book (published at 3s. 6d.), and that had I applied to him in the *proper* manner (with my best bow, I suppose), the information would have been withdrawn. But this never once occurred to me, and as the summons was issued I thought only of answering it. I pleaded 'not guilty', because it is absurd to call the trifling oversight of a servant the guilt of a principal, and

because I felt that the public ought to be made aware of the vicious and un-English operation of an Act which makes one particular class of tradesmen accountable, without the least notice, for the oversights of their servants, and even the *laches* of their predecessors, for all time, there being no literary statute of limitation.[30]

And here the Bohn affair expired, after a veritable hurricane of wind had been exhausted on the subject. Panizzi retired to lick his wounds, particularly the jibes over being a foreigner. Throughout the entire case, no one had thought fit to mention Bohn's German parentage and his lack of English blood. There had been a precedent for the whole affair when Henry Baber, a previous Keeper of Printed Books, had summonsed John Murray. Baber, like Panizzi, had subsequently summonsed the publisher for a further non-compliance without prior notice: 'The Act did not require it', said Baber, 'and by his former incivility, he had forfeited it'.[31] Panizzi told the Trustees that Bohn had only been prosecuted at Bodkin's insistence; Panizzi and his solicitor had only wanted to proceed against the most flagrant culprits. Panizzi was also angry over the magistrate, who 'considered the Act . . . a "strong" Act and its enactments harsh, and said so openly in Court to the great surprise of Mr. Panizzi who thought that the duty of the magistrate was to administer the law and not to criticize it'.[32]

Discouraged by the constant sniping, Panizzi had in November 1852 unsuccessfully tried to persuade the Trustees to revoke his legal powers, so that he did not have to initiate prosecutions himself. The enforcement of legal deposit was an onerous and thankless task, and Panizzi was not the only person to be affected. While the Bohn case was taking place, the Trustees declined to raise the salary of John Collyer Knight, the Museum's Copyright Receiver, and yet he carried out the arduous clerical work involved in discovering what had been published and delivered. Knight, author of *Pentateuchal narrative vindicated from the absurdities charged against it by the Bishop of Natal* and similar titles, was eventually promoted in 1854 to work on the new catalogue. The new Receiver was Robert Cowtan, whose father, Mawer Cowtan, had been Knight's predecessor. Referring to Mawer Cowtan, Henry Baber had informed the 1836 Commission on the British Museum: 'With respect to the number of articles that are entered at Stationers' Hall, taking the year 1835, there were 931 articles entered at the Hall, and 2,263 which they would have cheated us of, if we had not had a collector to obtain them'.[33]

The Bohn dispute generated bad publicity for Panizzi, but helped to turn the tide. No publisher could now claim ignorance of the law. In May 1853 Panizzi was pleased to inform the Trustees that a provincial publisher who had never previously obeyed the Act had, after receiving a threat of legal action, sent almost 180 works.[34] Summonses against three London publishers were issued in 1853, including one against Smith and Elder, and no less than twenty during 1854. In December 1853 the publisher, John Russell Smith, a previous victim of Panizzi, complained to *The Times* that Panizzi was demanding an expensive book on architecture, published abroad but with Smith's name on the titlepage; he claimed that to avoid this iniquitous tax, he would reprint the titlepage with his name omitted.[35] Panizzi's actions were strongly supported by Serjeant Parry, who wrote:

> It has been said that the mode of enforcing compliance has been harsh and severe, looking to the trifle value of the books claimed. The proceedings themselves, however, show that this charge is not well founded; every defaulter has been warned before being summoned, most of those summoned have been defaulters of long standing, and to a very considerable extent. And as to the question of value, Mr. Panizzi and the solicitors to the Trustees have repeatedly stated at the hearings before the magistrates, that books of small price have been purposely selected as the subjects of informations, in order that the penalties might fall as lightly as possible on the offenders. It is hardly fair that considerations of this kind should be misconstrued into oppression.[36]

By 1855 the publishers had received the message that Panizzi would not be cowed by their opposition. The number of prosecutions fell significantly in that year, when there were only six. Although they rose to fourteen in 1859, there were none at all in 1862–63, 1866–67, and 1869. Between 1850 and 1874, thirty-two London publishers were convicted and fined, while 131 settled out of court after receiving solicitors' letters. No prosecutions were brought between 1879 and 1918. In the latter year six publishers were prosecuted at Bow Street, including Herbert Jenkins.[37] Francis Griffiths was summonsed in 1932, but no prosecutions have occurred since then. Panizzi's example was eventually followed by the other deposit libraries who in the 1860s appointed a joint agent to co-ordinate their claims against publishers.[38] The problem of non-compliance may not have been absolutely eradicated, but future generations of British Museum (and British Library) users have good reason to be thankful for Panizzi's persistence.

NOTES

1   R. C. B. Partridge, *The History of the Legal Deposit of Books* (London, 1938) explains the various Acts.

2   The Bryer case and its background is studied in D. McKitterick, *Cambridge University Library: a history* (Cambridge, 1986), chap. 10.

3   G. W. Wheeler, (ed.), *Letters of Sir Thomas Bodley to Thomas James* (Oxford, 1926), pp.219, 222.

4   Edward Miller, *Prince of Librarians* (London, 1967; repr. 1988), pp.205–6.

5   *Library Association Record* vol.28 (1926), p.222.

6   Miller, pp.201–7, briefly describes Panizzi's enforcement of the Copyright Acts.

7   British Library Archives (hereafter BLA), DH 1/11, 19 December 1850, Panizzi to the Trustees. The author is grateful to the Board of the British Library for permission to quote from the Archives, and particularly to P. R. Harris for his assistance in making them available.

8   Ibid.

9   BLA, DH 1/12, 20 April 1852, Panizzi to the Trustees.

10 Reported in *The Critic* vol. 10 (15 March 1851), p.142.

11 The names of those prosecuted are drawn from two sets of papers in BLA: *Papers relating to prosecutions, 1850–72,* and *Copyright prosecutions, 1850–   : London publishers.*

12 Gordon S. Haight, (ed.), *George Eliot and John Chapman* 2nd edn (Hamden, Conn., 1969), p.198.

13 *See* note 9.

14 *Literary Gazette* (20 March 1852), p.280.

15 *Westminster Review* new ser. vol. 1 (April 1852), p.524.

16 BLA, DH 1/12, 15 May 1852, Chapman to the Trustees; 2 June 1852, Panizzi to the Trustees.

17 *Literary Gazette* (22 May 1852), p.436.

18 *The Leader* (10 July 1852), p.661.

19 BLA, *Decisions of the Law Officers of the Crown, 1852–8,* 30 August 1852, Legal opinion; BLA, DH 1/12, 13 August 1852 & DH 1/13 18 July 1853, Panizzi to the Trustees; many other papers are in BLA, *Letters, prosecutions, and other documents relating to cases under the Copyright Acts, 1829–70.*

20 BLA, DH 1/12, 9 October 1852, Panizzi to the Trustees.

21 Wyman W. Parker, *Henry Stevens of Vermont* (Amsterdam, 1963), pp.155–6.

22 BLA, DH 1/12, 9 November 1852, Panizzi to the Trustees.

23 Ibid.

24 BLA, *Letters, prosecutions, etc.,* 6 & 10 November 1852, Macmillan's to Panizzi.

25 For a general account of Bohn's career, see: A. Lister, 'Henry George Bohn (1796–1884)', *Antiquarian Book Monthly Review* vol. 15 (1988), pp.54–61.

26 BLA, DH 1/12, 9 November 1852, Panizzi to the Trustees.

27 This account of the Bohn case, including all the quotations, is taken from a transcript of the trial proceedings in BLA, *Letters, prosecutions, etc.,* 27 January 1853.

28 *The Times* (28 January 1853).

29 *The Times* (8 February 1853).

30 *Morning Advertiser* (7 February 1853).

31   Quoted in: *Quarterly Review* vol. 21 (1819), p.209.
32   BLA, DH 1/13, 3 February 1853, Panizzi to the Trustees.
33   Robert Cowtan, *Memories of the British Museum* (London, 1872), pp.166–7, 175.
34   BLA, DH 1/13, 5 May 1853, Panizzi to the Trustees.
35   *The Times* (6 December 1853).
36   Quoted in: Cowtan, p.180.
37   *The Times* (19 September 1918).
38   Sir Edmund Craster, *History of the Bodleian Library, 1845–1945* (Oxford, 1952), pp.62–3.
39   BLA, *Decisions of the Law Officers of the Crown, 1852–8*, 23 March 1853, 24 August 1854, 25 May 1855.

APPENDIX: THE OPINION OF THE ATTORNEY-GENERAL

On 23 March 1853 the Trustees of the British Museum sought the opinion of the Attorney-General and the Solicitor-General over the interpretation of certain aspects of the Copyright Act. Further queries were made on 24 August 1854.[39] The Questions and Answers are summarized below:

Q. A book is printed and sold in Dresden; on the titlepage the bookseller adds: 'Agent in London J. French 13 Paternoster Row'. Is French bound to deliver a copy?

A. We think not.

Q. A book printed at New York has 'J. Tallis London and New York' in it. Should Tallis comply? Whom to sue?

A. Tallis must comply, and only he can be sued.

Q. A book is published at Paris; a London bookseller strikes out the French titlepage and substitutes one with his name and address. Is he liable?

A. Yes.

Q. Does the mere name of a publisher at the foot of the titlepage imply he is the publisher, e.g. 'London. J. Murray'?

A. Yes, but it is open to the defendant to rebut the presumption.

Q. Who is the publisher if the titlepage says: 'London 100 Oxford St.', or 'at the Religious Tract Society', or 'at the Office of the Imperial Cyclopaedia'?

A. Anyone trading as a bookseller or publisher at those addresses.

Q. A book is published in Leeds; the titlepage adds: 'sold by John Mason in London: Leeds. J. H. Walker'. Who are the publishers?

A. Both.

Q. Who is the publisher of 'London, to be had of any Bookseller'?

A. The person who actually publishes it.

Q. 'London printed and published for the Author; sold by J. Murray, Wm. Pickering &c.'. Do all these booksellers publish this book?

A. Yes.

Q. When several publishers are named on a titlepage, are they all bound to deliver?

A. Yes, but compliance by one discharges the others.

Q. J. Smith prints a book but fails to comply; he sells his stock to another publisher. Are they both liable?

A. Yes.

Q. Are bird's-eye views or panoramas, e.g. Sebastopol, construed as publications under the Act?

A. No, they are engravings of pictures.

Q. Can engravings constitute a book?

A. A collection of engravings with a mere titlepage could not be regarded as a book, unless the plates contained letterpress which conveyed information independent of the engravings.

Q. If the publisher's name is not apparent, can any vendor of the book be liable?

A. Only the real publisher is liable, but if no name is given, the seller must prove he is not the publisher.

5

THE TRADITIONAL MAINTENANCE OF THE GENERAL CATALOGUE OF PRINTED BOOKS

Alec Hyatt King

APPENDIX: Guide to the Arrangement of Headings and Entries in the General Catalogue.

INTRODUCTION

FROM THE LATER part of the eighteenth century onwards, the production and maintenance of its General Catalogue were the cardinal function and preoccupation of the Department of Printed Books. The present essay is not concerned in detail with the complex history of this catalogue (though some reference to it is necessary), nor with the evolving rules and the practices derived from them.[1] It deals, rather, with the intellectual and physical methods by which the General Catalogue, as it stood well over half a century ago, was kept up to date with accessions and regularly corrected wherever required. This was an elaborate and demanding process, based on the co-ordination of the very varied skills of four groups of staff, two within the department itself and two others which were non-departmental but attached to it. The nature of these groups, their names and functions will be explained in the course of this essay.

The initial time to which it refers is the early winter of 1934, when the present writer entered the department. By then, the publication of the second, revised edition of the General Catalogue (always known for convenience as GK II)[2] had been in progress for some three years, involving a third group of departmental staff. This task went on simultaneously with the work of current cataloguing already mentioned and converged with it at several points. GK II gave rise to new techniques which imposed their own fairly sophisticated discipline, and differed in many ways from the rapid production of the first revision of the catalogue (known as 'GK I')[3] which, as described briefly below, had been completed in twenty-four years, with its supplements, by 1905. The work of current cataloguing, on the other hand, proceeded along lines which had probably changed little in essentials since the turn of the century, and included certain fundamental practices which had first been adopted some fifty years before that, and were still in use because of their proven reliability.

I · CURRENT CATALOGUING (GK I)

The first stage was to bring the material together, which was done in the Keeper's Ante-Room.[4] Books received under copyright deposit had already been stamped with a blue stamp in the Copyright Receipt Office (Fig. 16) and were delivered to the Ante-Room basement. There they were joined by books, mostly foreign, acquired by purchase: these also were stamped in the basement with a red stamp bearing the date at which the invoice was passed for payment. Donations, stamped at that time with a yellow stamp[5] bearing the date of the Trustees' meeting at which they were accepted, were usually stored on shelves round the upper Ante-Room. All else was stored in the basement, copyright books in order of their date stamp and purchased in sequence of their invoice dates.

Each cataloguer received, on request, a barrow-load of books, comprising about sixty per cent copyright, thirty per cent purchased, and the remainder donations. (Copyright was generally given priority.) The clerk in charge kept a register in which the name of the recipient and the relevant dates of each batch of the several categories were entered. Because the wooden staircase from the upper Ante-Room to the basement was steep and rather dangerous, all books from the latter were sent up on a hoist operated by a rope, a type then used elsewhere in the library. The sideless barrows were of a Victorian four-wheeled design, with two large wheels at the rear and two smaller ones at the front. The latter were mounted on a swivel, so that the barrow could be guided smoothly through the narrow doorways of the department. Each full barrow-load could take, on average, about a hundred books, tightly packed in three rows.

The Catalogue Room (Fig. 17), to which the loaded barrows were delivered, was rebuilt and refitted in 1932–3. All round its walls ran four tall steel shelves in two banks divided by a projecting desk-top. Here stood the interleaved folio volumes of the working copy of the General Catalogue. The run of catalogues was broken at the south door leading into the King's Library, at which point the shelves on the inner side of the entrance passage were used for a large quantity of dictionaries and other essential reference books. On receiving his full barrow, the cataloguer picked half a dozen or so books at a time and, having put them into alphabetical order by author, took them to the catalogue desks, along the vertical edges of which were secured at frequent intervals little boxes holding oblong white slips. As the cataloguer checked each book against the appropriate author – or other heading in the catalogue – he took a white slip on which he wrote, in pencil, various data. If the author of the new book was already in the catalogue, the cataloguer copied out on to this slip the full heading, with style, all christian names, etc., putting a 'K' on the slip, and if the book had appeared in a previous edition or editions, he also wrote down the pressmark of the most recent one. If the author were not in the catalogue at all, he put an 'O' on the slip, and would later search for the christian name or names (if not on the titlepage) in works of reference. The same procedure was followed for editors, collaborators, translators, etc., named on the titlepage, in the preface, or elsewhere in the book. The cataloguer also had to write on his white slip any relevant information about translations, with the title of the original, and about the extent of completeness of any

16 The Copyright Receipt Office on the sub-ground floor of the King Edward VII Building, photographed in 1966 (BL Archives).

17 The Catalogue Room in 1936, after it had been rebuilt (BL Archives).
Assistant Keepers: 1 R. A. Skelton, 2 A. H. Chaplin, 3 F. C. Francis, 4 F. L. Kent, 5 R. A. Wilson, 6 W. C. Smith, 7 C. B. Oldman. *Assistant Cataloguers*: 8 G. L. Clutton, 9 D. Barrett, 10 A. H. King, 11 G. H. Spinney. *Attendant*: 12 C. A. Norris.

selections or extracts. If a volume of the catalogue were unavailable for any reason (*see below*, 'II · Incorporation'), the cataloguer had to put the book on one side to wait until the volume reappeared: it was strictly forbidden to take any uncatalogued new book into the Reading Room.

The languages represented by foreign publications – at least for a cataloguer of some experience – were fairly wide. He was expected to have competence, if not more, in Latin, French and German, whatever the field of his degree. He was also encouraged to acquire some knowledge of the Iberian languages and Italian. Books in modern Greek were dealt with by a classic. Specialists in Scandinavian catalogued works in those three tongues, just as the great range of Slavonic publications went separately to other specialists. The average cataloguer who knew German fairly well was expected to try his hand at Dutch and Afrikaans. For the complexities of name forms and the like in English-language books issued in oriental countries the cataloguer often had to consult a colleague in the Department of Oriental Printed Books and Manuscripts, where books printed entirely or largely in those languages were handled. Older books, acquired mainly by purchase, were not generally dealt with by the cataloguer but were sent to a language specialist, either a reviser, or someone working on GK II. The cataloguer did, however, receive parts of English and foreign serials. Besides making entries for new publications, he received all continuations of old ones whenever a change of title or publishing body occurred.

Taking his pile of books, with the white slips inserted, back to his table, the cataloguer then began to write the entry or entries for each. He used oblong slips of plain blue paper each of which, from the time of their first use in the early 19th century, measured about four inches high by ten inches wide. These slips, which were of the highest possible durability, were known as 'title-slips', a phrase which in turn was generally abbreviated to 'titles'. The all-important spacing and layout on these titles followed a conventional form. At the top in the centre the cataloguer wrote the author's name or other appropriate heading. A little lower, and to the left, followed the transcription of the titlepage, from which the author's name was omitted and represented, if necessary, by three dots. Editors' names were transcribed and for each the appropriate cross-reference was written on a separate title. Any supplementary, or corrective, information was given in square brackets, while round brackets were used for any words taken from the body of the book. Close after these details came the pagination, the number of plates and the like, with the imprint, date and size (expressed as octavo, quarto etc.) written lower down on a new line. The top left and right corners were always left blank.

If the cataloguer had found additional information about the author's names, sources of the text, and the like, he added these details neatly in pencil on one of the blank lower spaces on the title. Near the left-hand edge he wrote the day, month and year, exactly as stamped, in whatever colour, on the book itself, and the method of acquisition. Sometimes the process of cataloguing a new book produced new or corrective information relating to a previous entry in the catalogue. In such cases the cataloguer sent for the title for this entry from the Title Room (about which more will be said later), added the information in red ink and initialled it in pencil.[6] He then put this title, together with the new ones he had written, into the book and gave this and all the others he had catalogued to his reviser. The time actually spent in writing the titles was relatively small. What took up a good two-thirds of the cataloguer's time was checking the new books against the catalogue and making sure that he collected all the information needed to make the new entries as complete and accurate as possible, and to relate the new book to any previous editions of it. At the end of each day he made an entry in his official diary, summarising what he had done and giving the number of new titles written and old ones altered. A good average was thirty to forty titles (representing some twenty-five to thirty books) in a full day which consisted of six and a quarter working hours, plus forty-five minutes for lunch but no intervals for coffee or tea. The Saturday working hours were 9.30a.m. to 1.00p.m. At the end of each month all diaries were collected and submitted to the Keeper, who initialled them after scrutiny, and interviewed any cataloguer if lapses in his work had been reported to him and were borne out by the diary.

At this point the reviser, who was usually an Assistant Keeper of some seniority, took up the thread of work. (Normally one reviser looked after two or three cataloguers, and was probably also intermittently engaged in proof-reading, perhaps did some book selection, and from time to time joined a small committee responsible for considering modifications in the rules and practices of cataloguing.) First he checked the accuracy of the transcription. Then he might add new information as to form of name, or other details, where the cataloguer's search had drawn blank. He would point out any errors, and, if the handwriting or layout tended to idiosyncrasy, suggested ways in which these could be modified, without loss of character, to help the printer. Finally, the reviser added an *imprimatur* – his initials and the date on the main title, on all others his initials only, in the bottom left-hand corner of each title. Then any old, altered title was taken away from the rest and delivered to the incorporator (whose work will be described below), and the batch of books, with all the revised titles securely held in each by the pressure of the pages, went to the placing section. Here the volumes were allocated to the shelves according to category and size, the pressmark being added in pencil to the blank upper left-hand corner of the titles, which were accumulated for fairly quick return to the Catalogue Room.

Here the accumulation was held by the Incorporator's assistant until it amounted to between 4,000 and 5,000. He then sorted the titles into three groups, one for copyright books, the second for purchases and donations, and a third comprising 'supplementary' titles (marked 'supp.' in the upper right centre):[7] those which (as will, again, be described later) had been newly written relating to books already in the catalogue, or which, as already mentioned, had been altered by hand and needed to be reprinted. When the titles had been put into strict alphabetical order within each group, the Incorporator's assistant numbered the whole accumulation, using a rotating, partly fixed, numbering machine. This device, called a 'serial numerator' stamped, in the empty top right-hand corner of each title, the number of the 'Accessions Part' followed by the *numerus currens* for each title-slip. This machine could be manipulated to stamp up to seven digits.

The primary reason for this elaborate procedure was a simple precaution. After the numbering was complete, the slips were packed in parcels of 600 or so each, which were labelled and numbered on the outside for sequence. The parcels were then collected by a van sent from Messrs William Clowes & Sons, the printers, for ultimate despatch to their printing works at Beccles in Suffolk. This firm had printed for the department since 1880 (and earlier for the Museum in general) and possessed the great range of sorts (individual characters in type, sometimes non-Roman) required. The parcels were distributed among several compositors, who knew the style of the department's work very well. But it was always possible that a parcel might become loose in transit, or the titles run out of order at a compositor's desk. Against such hazards numbering was an essential precaution.

So expert were Clowes's compositors and readers that they soon became familiar with the vagaries of the cataloguers' hands, and their proof-readers often raised points of possible error or uncertainty on the master proof. They were usually right. The proofs, first in galley, then re-imposed in two columns, were distributed to various revisers via the Ante Room, where a clerk noted all dates of receipt and return. Such was the monthly procedure for assembling each Accessions Part and converting it from manuscript titles into definitive printed form. An almost exactly similar process governed the production of accessions in Slavonic languages, which yielded one part, or occasionally two, a year. The only difference was that because of the complexity of those titles which were in Cyrillic, the slips were mostly arranged in order by one of the officers who had done the cataloguing. (It may also be mentioned here that the Map Room and the Music Room produced a single Accessions Part about once a year, on a roughly similar pattern.) Once the monthly part was returned in its final form from Clowes, it was ready for the processes preliminary to 'incorporation'.[8] But before all this can be explained, something must be said about the evolution of the general catalogue, into the latest form of which the new entries were to be inserted.

The earliest edition appeared in 1787, in two volumes folio, with the title *Librorum impressorum qui in Museo Britannico adservantur catalogus*. It had generous margins on which the pressmark for each book was gradually added by hand.[9] The titles for accessions were accumulated separately for nearly twenty years, intercalated alphabetically with the earlier titles from March 1807 to November 1810, and the whole was sent to the printer as the second edition which appeared, in seven volumes octavo, at the rate of one a year, from 1813 to 1819. In due course a copy was inlaid on large folio sheets and similarly interleaved, for the use of readers, so that the pressmarks could again be added by hand, and – what was more important – entries for new accessions, with pressmarks, written on both the wide margins of the inlaid sheets and on the blank interleaves. Even before this process ceased, in 1849 – by when this catalogue amounted to 109 volumes[10] – the somewhat haphazard manner of alphabetisation, in addition to the mixture of print and manuscript, must have made the catalogue very difficult indeed for readers to use. Radical change was essential.

It was, apparently, in 1849 that two men, E. A. Roy (a transcriber on the staff) and John Wilson Croker (man of letters and famous collector of the huge quantity of French Revolution tracts which were eventually acquired by the British Museum) conceived independently the idea of a catalogue consisting of narrow, oblong movable slips of thin paper, which could be produced in quadruplicate by a device called the 'Wedgwood Manifold Writer'.[11] These slips, after being backed on stronger paper, were lightly pasted, along the top edge and the bottom only, on to folio sheets bound to make up substantial volumes. In order to maintain strict alphabetical order when entries for accessions were made, these slips could easily be lifted, rearranged as needed, and pasted down again. Instead of having only two copies of the catalogue, there were now four – one for the staff, one for readers, and a spare copy used to keep the readers' copy complete when any volumes were removed for updating. The 'fourth copy' comprised the entire catalogue arranged not in alphabetical order, but by numerical sequence of pressmarks corresponding exactly to that of the books on the shelves.[12]

When first placed in the Reading Room in 1851, this 'transcribed' catalogue, as it was called, amounted to 150 volumes. But by 1875 the rapid growth of the library had swollen it to 2,000, and it was expected to grow very quickly to 9,000, because each of the expanding volumes had to be broken up and rebound in three. The only way to save space was to use print, which would also facilitate publication, and this solution (which had been considered earlier but rejected) was put into effect in 1879. Printing of accessions began first and in 1881 work commenced on the entire catalogue which was finished in 1900, excluding supplements. The format was folio, with two numbered columns to each page. (Accessions were printed in the same format.) In order to adapt the published volumes for the use of readers and staff, several copies were printed on one side of the sheet only, the sheets were cut vertically down the line dividing the columns and each separate column was pasted down on the left-hand half of a sheet of stout paper.[13] The right-hand half of the sheet was kept blank, and the quires of sheets, with guards inserted on to which new single sheets could be edged with paste, were bound into substantial half-leather volumes, all the lower edges of both covers being cased in brass shoes.

This 'laying down' was at first done 'one in one', later generally 'one in three',[14] so that as the volume lay open each printed column was followed by three equivalent blank spaces. On these spaces there were edged down with paste, as in the 'transcribed' catalogue, the accessions cut up singly from each

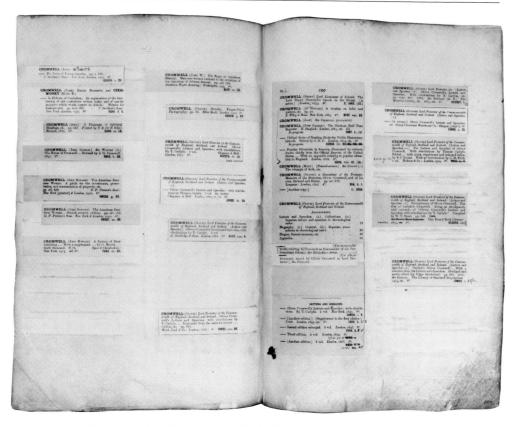

18 An opening from one of the laid-down volumes of the General Catalogue, showing the column of entries from the original printing of 1880–1900, with the slips for accessions added later.

successive part (Fig. 18). Now, however, at a single opening of the catalogue fifty or more entries, in the sharp definition of print, could easily be seen at a glance, several times the maximum number of the rather faint transcribed slips. The three copies of the catalogue were bound in the traditional distinctive colours – green for the staff copy, blue for that placed in the Reading Room, and red for the one used to replace any volume removed from it. A fourth copy of the accessions sheets printed on one side only was cut up into single entries, each one of which was pasted on a card of its own width, and almost half the width of the 'titles' and intercalated into the shelf list.[15] When in due course the first edition of this 'General Catalogue'

[174]

(GK I) was replaced by the second (GK II), which began to appear in 1931, the processes used to produce the working copies from the published volumes remained essentially unchanged. Such was the physical nature of the working copies of the catalogue into which the Accession Parts prepared by GK I were to be inserted, by the process known as 'incorporation'.

II · INCORPORATION

Central to the working of the department, this complex process had evolved a technical language of its own, and controlled tightly the many currents of work which flowed into it and out again in many directions. The incorporation needed the support of the Catalogue Shop and of the Bindery (whence the Catalogue Shop staff was drawn), and also worked closely with the Title Room. Full details of these three important staff groups will be given as their duties arise in the course of this narrative. The total effect was one of continual circular activity demanding endless vigilance and avoidance of errors. The overall complexity was such that the incorporation, more perhaps than any other area of the department's work, needed continuity, a quality which was probably most effective in the late 1920s and 1930s.

Because, after training, most cataloguers moved on to other places, and because revisers likewise came and went, GK I seemed generally to be in a state of flux. The one point round which it gravitated was the Incorporator himself and his assistant who together formed a close, remarkable partnership. As an exception to the otherwise impersonal nature of this essay, this partnership warrants an attempt to draw a verbal portrait of the two men concerned.

The Incorporator was George Dean Raffles Tucker,[16] who had joined the department in 1900 from Magdalene College, Cambridge (the third name, by which he was known domestically, was believed to have been given him after the colonial governor, Sir Thomas Stamford Raffles.) He graduated in classics, later specialised in Old High German, and was a good all-round linguist. Besides winning a half blue at billiards, he was a competent violinist who played in quartets at the Oxford and Cambridge Music Club (not far from the Museum). Early in his service an illness seriously impaired the vision in one eye, but his remaining sight was sharp enough to allow him to climb regularly all over the Alps, and later to become an enthusiastic amateur astronomer specialising in the observation of variable stars. A keen croquet player, he represented England in tournaments at Roehampton, and in 1937 published a small volume of witty, clever verses on the subject. The defect in Tucker's sight gave him a misleadingly bland appearance behind his gold-rimmed spectacles: though deliberate in his work, he was extremely shrewd and keen of mind. He had a slight stammer, which he could cleverly exaggerate at will, if, for instance, he wished to give vent to an affected explosion of rage at a colleague's carelessness, or whenever he need to gain time during an argument about some complex point of arrangement or the like. Tucker was in fact the embodiment of amiable Edwardian eccentricity. Towards the end of his career, the Trustees were told that for many years he had been a very jealous guardian of the principles of arrangement.[17]

H. A. ('Jack') Richbell, Tucker's permanent assistant, had secured gradual promotion in the Bindery and Catalogue Shop to the rank of 'first copy man' (of which more in what follows), and was seconded to work with the incorporator at some time in 1931. Stocky, fresh-faced and cheerful, with a puckish smile, Richbell combined a natural intelligence and much common sense with an unfailing passion for accuracy and a remarkable grasp of all the ramifications of the catalogue.[18] By observation and enquiry, he became thoroughly familiar with the principles of arrangement of both English and foreign titles. As will become clear shortly, his duties were multifarious and demanding, and he spared no pains to get things right. His loyalty and helpfulness were held in high regard by all who knew him and especially by every incorporator, until his long service ended in 1954.

This then was the binary system round which there revolved in elliptical orbits a number of satellite activities, not the least of which was the Catalogue Shop, on whose preliminary and subsequent work the incorporation was entirely dependent. (The Catalogue Shop was a branch of the British Museum bindery which had been managed under contract by His Majesty's Stationery Office since 1927, in succession to Messrs. Eyre & Spottiswoode.)

A number of copies of every Accessions Part were printed on one side of the sheet only. Three such copies were delivered to the Catalogue Shop, as the raw material for incorporation. There, three sheets at a time were superimposed with great precision on a large metal plate. The first single cut was made vertically down the central line separating the two columns. The second stage of cutting was horizontal, exactly along the thin rules printed above and below each entry. Using a straight edge to guide his knife, a skilful cutter could eliminate almost all sight of these rules, and produce a perfectly rectangular slip, leaving the margin untrimmed. Each cut sheet produced about 30 separate slips, which were carefully picked up, still in triplicate, and eased into shallow cardboard boxes, each some two feet long and only half an inch or so wider than the slips. Their accumulating sequence in the box corresponded exactly to that on the intact sheets. When cut up, each Accessions Part usually amounted to between two or two and a half boxes of slips. The Part number was written on the lid of each box, which was secured at each end with tape, before being conveyed by hand to Richbell, usually near the end of the month.

The ritual of incorporation could then begin. On a large table across which he faced Tucker, Richbell kept both the boxes containing the cut-up slips and the much bigger boxes containing all the titles from which they had been printed. He also had in another box the accumulated older titles which bore alterations made in the work of GK I, GK II, and elsewhere. First, he began to interfile the slips from the three sections of the Accessions Part which had been kept separate during the cutting-up process. Then on the first day of each month, or as near to it as possible, Richbell started his routine. He removed from the catalogue shelves the first dozen or so volumes of letter A, and inserted into each those slips and such altered titles as fell within the range of the catch-letters on its spine. Leaving the slips and titles protruding an inch or so from the top of each volume and all securely held at the inner margin by the pressure of the leaves, Richbell took the prepared volumes round to the large stool on Tucker's left, on which he laid them one on top of the other, with the wide spines and narrower foredges in alternation, so that they could not fall off.

Tucker's first task was to examine the printed slips (still neatly adhering in repeated triplicate) and find the right opening in the volume for the first in the alphabetical sequence. He checked its heading against those in the column or those already on the blank spaces opposite to it. If the author of the older book were the same as that represented on the new entry, Tucker laid the latter visually under the former, to check for identity. This process, known as 'apposition', sometimes revealed discrepancies, either in the names, the epithet or title (e.g. 'Poet', 'Bishop of Winchester'), or subheading. If the error were minor, Tucker corrected it by hand himself. In the case of a major error or some fundamental, puzzling discrepancy, Tucker would first ask Richbell for the title slip in the boxes before him. Then failing an explanatory pencil note on that slip, he fastened the three printed slips to it with a paper-clip and sent them back, via Richbell, to the cataloguer with a polite request for a prompt explanation, or sometimes took them himself. The volume, flagged at the opening with the delinquent's name, was retained until the slips came back, and a white marker was placed in the title-box at the place of extraction.

But such errors were relatively few, and generally 'marking in' was done quickly. If (as was then still often the case in the early GK II volumes), the opening was blank, Tucker wrote in pencil the figure '1' on the page, and '2' on the verso of the lowest of the three slips. A second entry falling within the same column sequence was marked '3', and so on. But if the pages already bore previous accessions, the procedure was different. A sequence of, say, four new slips would rarely follow one older one uninterruptedly. So Tucker wrote '1' on the margin of the old slip, '2' as before on the new slips then '3' on another old slip, '4' and '5' on two more new slips, all to secure a correct new alphabetical order. A large number of new slips to be inserted on an already crowded page might cause considerable difficulties in renumbering old slips, some of which might need to be lifted and perhaps pen alterations of small details added. The delicate process of lifting old slips involved use of the 'excorporator' – a small ivory paper-knife[19] ground down to a round point at one end. By inserting this point at the open end of a slip, Tucker could run it right along the lightly pasted upper edge until the slip was loose and attached to the page by its lower edge. This could then easily be detached by hand.

Great care had to be exercised because if a slip was torn in lifting, the entry might have to be reprinted, a costly business if done too often. In many cases, however, a damaged slip could be replaced by a duplicate taken from the series of original Accessions Parts, of which a fairly complete set was preserved in the Catalogue Shop, stored in numerical order and by years, in parcels. Renumbering part of a large, complicated heading was a slow business. Tucker often had to take out all the necessary old slips and intercalate them with the new ones, using the space on his desk to lay out and unify them in trial order before proceeding to the renumbering. This also involved rubbing out any previous numbers on the old slips, in order not to confuse the Catalogue Shop. When the renumbering at one opening reached the figure '99', as it well could when, for example, there had been catalogued a large quantity of government documents, a new sequence had to be begun because of the difficulties that might arise by exceeding two digits. Such large sequences did not often occur, but when they did, they slowed up the pace of incorporation considerably. On the average, a volume could be dealt with in ten minutes or so, including manuscript alterations arising from the old titles inserted in the volume as mentioned above.

When Tucker finished each volume, with all marked slips firmly inserted into the inner margin of the relevant openings, and the top inch or so protruding, he put it on the stool on the right of the table, which stood next to the gangway of the Catalogue Room. When a score or so of volumes had accumulated, Richbell went to the telephone (the only one in the entire room), made a quick call to the Catalogue Shop, and a porter came down to collect them on a large, deep barrow. This routine continued daily, the aim being to incorporate each Accessions Part within the month. If unexpected pressures built up and delays occurred, accuracy could not however be jeopardised, and Tucker became worried, as he was a deliberate and meticulous worker. At that time, salaries were paid about the 20th of each month, and if letter 'P' in the alphabet was not reached by pay-day, the Part might well not be finished before the end of that month. In such an event, Tucker usually asked the Keeper for an extra pair of hands which, from March 1936 onwards, were often those of the present writer.

The responsibilities of the Incorporator's job were considerable. This was the last point at which current errors could systematically be detected. They might ultimately be picked up by GK II, assuming its continuance (and indeed in the later 1930s its progress gave cause for optimism).[20] Otherwise detection was a matter of chance. Errors could lie not only within the entries themselves, but also in their arrangement. Even small headings are likely to become large in due course, and all too easily one error begets another. Vigilance and benign suspicion were therefore the incorporator's watchwords in dealing with a large number of colleagues, some of whom would be ready to admit their errors, while others would not. He had also to acquire a thorough grasp of the principles of arrangement (which could vary in detail between one large heading and another), and understand the reasons for the single and correct place for each entry in headings which included works of commentary, controversy and the like. In Tucker's case, though he had not done cataloguing for quite a long time, he had to be aware of changes in its rules and practice which might affect the arrangement. He was an active member of a small committee concerned with compiling a pamphlet on this subject, the famous 'ROSE' list, which, after long deliberations, was ultimately printed in 1940 as *Guide to the Arrangement of Headings and Entries in the General Catalogue of Printed Books in the British Museum* (*see* Appendix).

Above all, he had to think about the repercussions of current cataloguing on headings elsewhere in the catalogue which cataloguer and reviser did not always have time to anticipate. To round off his manifold duties, the Incorporator himself had to write what were called 'index slips' which were essential to maintain very large headings, such as those for countries and towns, and facilitate the readers' use of them. These small white slips (the same as those used by cataloguers when first checking their new books) bore the titles of all important new headings or subheadings for official or unofficial bodies of many kinds, for new liturgical works, titles of significant official publications, and the like. Besides the title, these slips carried the column or accession page number of these large headings. In the course of a year, such slips amounted to a thousand or more. After numbering by Richbell, they went to the printer, who set them in small type. When the incorporator had read the proofs, these too were cut up in triplicate and duly incorporated as a separate task.

III · THE CATALOGUE SHOP

The Catalogue Shop (Fig. 19) was the embodiment of careful, orderly method based on a high degree of manual skill. Its job was to follow exactly the incorporator's markings and other instructions in order to achieve the maximum clarity and consistency on the open page. The staff, controlled by a foreman, F. Gillman, comprised three grades – first copy hands who worked on the green copy of the catalogue, and second and third copy hands who worked on the red and blue copies respectively. After the senior first copy hand had laid out the marked slips at any one opening, his experience told him whether or not they could be easily inserted in the space available or, if not, how many old slips he would need to remove to make room for the new ones. There were two essential skills in this work – edging the slips with paste, and aligning them vertically and horizontally. Each was turned on its printed side, and the paste applied, by use of a masking plate, at its top and bottom, to a depth of less than a sixteenth of an inch or so. This was about the maximum needed for the slip to adhere firmly to the sheet, and it was also thin enough for the slip to be lifted whenever necessary, without tearing.

When laying the pasted slip down, the copy hand had to ensure that the left-hand line of the heading (which was printed in Clarendon capitals) fell exactly under the imaginary straight line formed by the headings of all the other entries in that half of the sheet. (He ignored the blank, untrimmed margin of the slip.) Again, the slip had to lie parallel to all the other slips, and precisely at right angles to the edges of the sheet. These visual, geometrical niceties gave great help to the eye of a reader scanning the page. Even with the aid of squares and other implements, such tasks needed care and judgement. As each green volume was finished, the inner margin of every opening was checked in case any slips had slid down from the top in transit and lurked unseen. Each opening where slips had been pasted in was flagged with a piece of thin white paper, as a ready guide to the second copy hand who then worked on the corresponding red-bound volume. On completion, a batch of these was taken to the Reading Room (Fig. 20) to replace its blue-bound copies which in turn were treated so that they followed exactly the alignment and spacing of the insertions made in the green copy. This copy, which contained scattered pencil notes in a number of complex headings for staff guidance, was never used in the Reading Room. Gradually, the green volumes were all sent back to the Catalogue Room, and the cycle began anew each month. At any stage of all this work, a sharp-eyed copy hand might detect an error in marking the sequence made by Tucker or his assistant. If Gillman confirmed this, he himself took the volume down in triumph to Richbell, who

19 The Catalogue Shop, photographed in 1966 (BL Archives).

showed it to Tucker. Such a detection was always a feather in the cap of the Catalogue Shop!

This remarkable group of men, who took much pride in their work, had other duties as well. Besides the preservation of former Accessions Parts, and extraction of entries from them they could soak up, cut up as required and mount, on fresh margined paper, any sections of the old printed columns. (The Incorporator might request this when a move to a new heading was necessary.) They could also use small, neat, hand-printing sets to supply headings in triplicate to slips that needed to be remounted when replacements could not be found. They inserted new leaves on to the existing guards, at the Incorporator's request, so that the entries in an overcrowded heading could be spaced out, and when this was done, added the new pencil foliation to these leaves in all copies. These and similar skills were all essential to keeping the catalogue neat, tidy and consistent. There were however some tasks in this field which were the responsibility of the Bindery. If any one catalogue volume became too stout and had to be split, it was pulled there, resewn and rebound in two, and relettered according to the Incorporator's instructions. (This was not undertaken lightly, partly because of the high cost and because all succeeding volumes in the same letter had to have the labels indicating the

20 Placing a laid-down volume of the General Catalogue in the Reading Room in 1971. The volume being placed on the shelf by L. Blackmur (Supervisor of the Catalogue Shop) is the last volume of the photolithographic reprint of 1959–66 (known as GK III). On the left is F. Fletcher, the last person to hold the post of Incorporator.

numerical sequence soaked off and replaced. Another job assigned to the Bindery was to cut up the fourth copy of each Accessions Part printed, as mentioned, on one side only, mount each entry on a card four and three quarters by four inches, and send the completed cards each month to the Title Room, a cardinal point of the department's work, to which we may now turn.

IV · THE TITLE ROOM

Self-evidently, the Title Room was the place where there were kept the title-slips from which the catalogue was printed. But its functions went far beyond the routine of accumulation. Though the work was unspectacular, it was always mentioned with much warmth in any report to the Trustees, and rightly so because it was central to the smooth running of everything to do with the catalogue. The origins of the Title Room are obscure, and its early location seems to be unrecorded. The need to preserve title-slips must go back to the first days of systematic cataloguing, in the 1760s, and some method of looking after the older slips, while interfiling the ever-growing mass of new ones,[15] probably dates from Panizzi's Keepership (1837–56) and the concomitant growth of the collections of printed books. After the introduction of the 'Wedgwood' process already mentioned to provide the 'fourth copy' of the catalogue, the work of the 'Title Room' (probably then not named as such) doubled at once. For it then became, as it were, the mirror image of the catalogue in two complementary physical forms, both of which expanded as the work on it grew in ways unimagined by those who produced the earliest one in 1787.

The chief source of work flowing into the Title Room must always have come from current cataloguing. In the 1930s the entire numerical sequence of the titles in each Accessions Part was checked by Richbell after their incorporation. The places of any titles removed from it had been flagged and the number and destination of each noted: he, backed by the incorporator if need be, recovered as many as he could, and passed a note of any outstanding to the Title Room to which the boxes were conveyed. The staff then began the perpetual task of intercalating the new titles into the 'main set'. The titles were filed under the headings and sub-headings as given in the catalogue, but within these divisions they were filed chronologically not alphabetically, as this was a simpler procedure. The same applied to headings consisting partly or wholly of titles in non-roman alphabets. The reasons for preserving these titles – even then amounting to some six million – were both practical and historical. Whenever a manuscript alteration was required in the catalogue – and there were many such small enough not to call for reprinting the whole entry – this had to be written in red ink on the title-slip first, and initialled. After the incorporator had done the entry in the green copy, a member of the Title Room staff would then take a batch of such titles and attend to the red and green copies. Thus the three copies tallied, and the source of the correction was kept in the Title Room.

The titles also bore in pencil a wealth of other information: the source of obscure names in the heading; evidence for attribution of anonymous or pseudonymous books; the source of the identification of initials; notes about the scope of editorial work of various kinds; notes of the pressmarks of any earlier editions as a possible help to the placing section; reasons for changing the date, or the name or place in an imprint, and so on. Above all, the title bore in its upper left-hand corner all the pressmarks ever given to the book, each successive one being neatly crossed through in pencil, never erased. This showed the history of the book in the collections, and was also invaluable if, as sometimes happened, in course of time and shelf-wear, the book lost its fly-leaf or titlepage bearing these particulars. Titles for older books have also proved invaluable for the details added about provenance.

The second source of the Title Room's work came from the 'fourth copies', which comprised the easier part of it. As with the monthly despatch of title-slips from the current Accessions Part, so, though in batches at intervals and not all at once, the fourth copies were sent to the Title Room from the bindery where all the entries on the one-sided sheets had been cut up and mounted on cards, as already mentioned. They merely had to be sorted into pressmark order, and then interfiled with the second 'main set'. Probably from its very origin in 1849, this process served two ends. The principal one was to provide the basis for a subject catalogue of the books in the library, which theoretically was possible because the classification devised, in two stages, by Thomas Watts (the first in 1838, the second in the late 1840s) was very sound for its time.

Though the preparation and possible publication of such a catalogue was discussed more than once during the mid-nineteenth century, nothing came of it, and the value of the fourth copies remained primarily as a check on any books which were lost or temporarily misplaced. In addition, as the catalogue grew in size and complexity, the fourth copies could also be used by cataloguers to discover exactly how many entries and of what kind had been made for each book. If any title-slip were missing, that too would be revealed. While this system was defective for older books acquired by the library before 1849, it was extremely useful thereafter, and as the library grew rapidly its value increased. It was also an essential part of the Title Room's work to add by hand on to the fourth copies all corrections and additions made in manuscript on the title-slips.[21] As in the Catalogue Shop, so too the Title Room's routine work, in this case interfiling done by experienced men, could show up inconsistencies of various kinds – in headings, pressmarks and the like – which had escaped the notice of those engaged in earlier stages of routine, and errors so found were gratefully accepted by the incorporator or by one of the revisers. The methods used in the Title Room were part of a well-established process dating back to the inception of GK I in 1881 and even earlier. The greatest test of its skills was to come when the second revision of the general catalogue (GK II) began in 1931 and gathered pace some years later.

V · GK II

The supply of the raw material was simplicity itself. On a large table near the centre of the working area was kept the volume of GK I under current revision. This was always the green copy, pulled into sections and cased loosely in the old covers. Beside it, in long boxes, lay the corresponding run of titles, supplied by the Title Room. These volumes naturally varied in bulk, but the quantity of titles available was generally between 7,000 and 9,000. A large folio card, ruled in three columns, lay beside the boxes. When a cataloguer took a batch of 'copy', usually amounting to 500 or 600 titles, he wrote the heading of the first and last titles in the first column on the card, added the date in the second, and signed his name in the third. It was desirable for a batch of copy, whenever practicable, not to begin or end in the middle of a heading. With few exceptions each cataloguer took whatever was the next batch of titles in a box and revised them all. Those for Slavonic books and for incunabula he sent to specialists, and did the same for any rarer languages such as Basque, Gaelic and Icelandic. Specialists would also take complex historical headings in their entirety and at one time the heading 'Bible' was under revision by a small group who generally did nothing else. But otherwise the cataloguer had to be prepared, with occasional advice from colleagues and by using the ample supply of language dictionaries, bibliographies and other reference books, to deal with books in every language, printed from 1 January 1501 onwards.

Having taken a batch of copy, the cataloguer's first task was to check the titles against the printed entries. If a missing title could not be found, he copied the entry in the catalogue on to a 'temporary title', marking it clearly as such. Then he examined the titles, taking fifty or so at a time, and decided which books he had to send for in order to supply pagination, complete the imprint and check other points that appeared defective or suspicious. (It was not until the post-war period of GK II that all books were sent for and examined.) He made a list of the pressmarks, fixed to the foot of it a gummed slip printed with his name, dated it, and left it in a box on a large table manned by three attendants. One of them wrote the cataloguer's name on a shelf-board, added the date and pressmark,[22] and procured the books from the stacks. In due course the cataloguer received the books on a barrow arranged in the sequence on his slip. After adding the particulars given above, verifying names in the headings (especially for early books) and looking for previously unnoticed relationships between successive editions, a translation and an original, and so on, the cataloguer proceeded to 'edit' the completed titles. With the use of a blue pencil and several kinds of rubber stamp, the long titles of successive editions, issues and the like could be drastically shortened, to save space without loss of essentials. Similarly in all headings which exceeded one title, the names at the top of the second title and all subsequent ones were struck through with a blue pencil. Words such as 'Appendix' were also supplied after the heading with a stamp. During this process the cataloguer also wrote any 'supplementary' titles – such as cross-references, references of form, entries for contributory editorial work not previously noticed – and left these in his completed batch of 'copy'.

Then the reviser took over. His work was similar to that of his counterpart in GK I, but on a far more complex scale. In the case of large, complicated headings he had probably discussed the layout and arrangement in advance with the cataloguer. Even so, many pitfalls remained, not least because the sheer scale of GK II was continually creating new precedents of many kinds and modifications to the rules – topics beyond the scope of this essay. During revision, any supplementary titles written or old ones altered, were abstracted and either sent to Richbell for the appropriate treatment or, in the case of titles from later letters in the alphabet and bearing non-urgent corrections, were stamped with an 'R', and sent to the Title Room for refiling in the main set. (The extra burden on the Title Room due to this and other work on GK II was quite heavy.) When the reviser had finished a batch of work, he signed his name on the big card beside that of the cataloguer and added the date. The titles then went to a collecting point where the entire sequence of the broken-up volume was gradually reassembled. When a sufficiently large continuum was ready, it was stamped with a numbering machine by a man from the Catalogue Shop, who carefully used only the space in the top right corner of each slip, beneath the original Accessions Part number. The titles were then parcelled up in numbered batches, and sent to Clowes, the dates of their despatch and return being recorded in the Ante-Room. The battered sections of the broken-up volume were retained, in their casing, for reference at all points in this and the subsequent processes.

The first proof came back in galley, and was read by one of the revisers.

Inevitably, a good many errors came to light, because however careful the preparation – and in some difficult headings the slips had been laid out in sequence on a table for comparative scrutiny – corrections and changes in arrangement had to be made at this stage. Transfers, too, from one galley to another, were often unavoidable in large headings. It was crucial to get such transfers right because they proved very awkward, if not impossible in the final page-proof, which embodied all the galley corrections. Only at this stage, when all the pages were available in numbered columns, could the very important indexes of titles and sub-headings be compiled as required, in the same type as used for the very large headings already mentioned in connection with GK I.

The size of the finished volume depended on the run of the headings and the need to avoid breaks in them, if possible: the average number of entries was about 18,000. Work on a volume was by no means finished, however, when it was laid before the Trustees and then distributed to subscribers. Three unbound copies in sheets, printed on one side only, were sent to the bindery where the pages were cut down the line separating the two columns, and each column was pasted down on the left-hand side of a sheet of cartridge paper, all exactly as had been done with GK I. One printed volume yielded five or six such laid-down, newly-bound volumes, each foliated and ruled in pencil down the centre of the blanks, and then bound in the three distinctive colours. (The blue used pre-war for the Reading Room copy was later changed to buff.) Fitted with brass shoes, even stronger than those used for GK I, to withstand shelf wear, with heavy straps on the upper spine for ease of handling, lettered with catch-words, and labelled in numerical sequence, these great leather-bound folio books went resplendently to their three departmental places.

For the Title Room, too, still more work remained. Another set of the one-sided sheets of each finished volume was prepared in the Bindery in the manner of an Accessions Part, as a fourth copy. But there was an additional complication. Whereas in the Part, each entry was complete with full heading, in the volume repeated headings had been omitted, as already explained, to save space. When therefore each batch of cards, mounted in strict column order, arrived from the Bindery in the Title Room, the first thing the staff of the latter had to do was to add the headings to numerous entries. This they did, with a volume of the catalogue to hand, by using printed stamps for any longish run of cards, and, for just a few, by writing the names in ink. Once the headings were completed, interfiling into the main set could be done. Here yet another stage of checking was necessary, because all the old, transcribed, full-width fourth copies had to be compared for completeness against the new half-width printed ones before the former could finally be thrown away and the bulk in the drawers substantially reduced.

GK II and GK I clearly formed a closely interwoven structure which was continually expanding, the former naturally retrospective, the latter concerned with the present. As an intellectual entity, both were constructed within the British Museum's library of printed books, yet the very existence of both depended on an external foundation – the invaluable work of the printer, Messrs William Clowes and Sons. They have already been mentioned briefly, but since the firm became a true cornerstone of the whole enterprise, it is fitting that a little more should be said here of their contribution to it. Clowes's reputation as a printer of catalogues had been enhanced by the excellent quality of their work on the original GK I, and their capacity to meet its rigorous schedules from 1881 to 1905. After its conclusion, they continued to produce all the department's Accessions Parts, with neatness and style. It was natural that when GK II began, the contract should be given to Clowes, who had, of course, also to produce simultaneously the current Accessions Parts which grew in size as the cataloguing staff increased.

Clowes responded to this challenge with a resourceful collaboration which went far beyond purely commercial considerations. The pressure on the printers (and on the cataloguers and revisers) can be gauged from the following GK I schedule of 1937:

> numbered titles delivered 10 days before the end of the month
> proofs started within a week
> proofs completed by the 6th of the month
> corrected proofs back to Clowes by the 16th of the month.[23]

The then Keeper of Printed Books, W. A. Marsden, was in continual touch, by letter, telephone and personal meetings, with Maurice Clowes, the partner in charge of all the department's printing programmes. The demands of GK II in particular became so great that in 1934 Clowes prepared, for internal use, a detailed directive about layout, style, use of types, proof-corrections, understanding of title slips and a host of other matters.[25] When in March 1935 Marsden was able to report to the Trustees that he confidently expected eight volumes of GK II to be produced a year (cf. footnote 20), he knew that only Clowes's total reliability and flawless craftsmanship could make this possible.

The simultaneous production, revision and maintenance of a very large catalogue in volume form, comprising books printed in all European languages from the earliest times up to the present, was clearly a task of immense, perhaps unparalleled, complexity. Many people, with an extraordinarily diverse range of skills and knowledge, contributed to its success. At every level, both in GK I and in GK II, the work generated a sustained sense of loyalty, co-operation and dedication born of an individual responsibility keenly felt within a corporate unity. The underlying aim was to combine practical use with scholarly excellence and bibliographical quality in the widest sense, although the catalogue itself made no claim to be a bibliography. No catalogue that has ever existed has been free from error, and none ever will be, whatever the method of production. The system devised for the British Museum's General Catalogue of Printed Books was intended to keep errors to the minimum by a process of continuous control, checking and counter-checking, which also enabled errors, when detected, to be put right as smoothly and as consistently as possible. Such accuracy could only be achieved when everyone concerned matched care and thought with the highest degree of discipline compatible with a living, steadily expanding organism. These were the ideals underlying the finely printed pages of the revised edition of the *General Catalogue of Printed Books in the British Museum*. As its fifty-one volumes appeared from 1931 to 1954, they commanded world-wide respect, and it is a thousand pities that the effects of the Second World War combined later with other factors[25] to bring a unique enterprise of such high standards to a premature end.

VI · A NOTE ON LOCATIONS

The foregoing narrative has mentioned various rooms and other areas within the territory of the Department of Printed Books or adjacent to it, where its diverse work took place. It may be useful, with the help of the plan on p.xii, to make these locations clear and give something of the historical background.

When the rebuilding of the British Museum on the site of Montagu House was put in hand from 1823 onwards,[26] the first phase produced the King's Library which was completed in 1826. The second phase comprised part of the West Wing, and the North Wing, which abutted on the north end of the King's Library, and ran due east and west. Most of this huge structure, some 350 feet long, was finished in 1838,[27] The Arch Room was added between 1839 and 1842. The whole of its ground floor, and some of the basement rooms as well, were allocated to the Department of Printed Books. It comprised five sections, as the plan shows, the two easternmost rooms being separated from the two nearer the west by the Large Room. This stood on the southern part of the site occupied by the present North Library, and combined book storage round its walls and bays (the ground floor presses being enclosed with grilles) and occasionally was used as a public gallery for exhibitions.

The easternmost room of all served as one of the two reading rooms from

1838 to 1857, after which it became the Catalogue Room, and its use by staff engaged on the work of cataloguing continued uninterruptedly for almost a century. It was conveniently near to the Ante Room, which formed part of a building[28] constructed between 1846 and 1850 outside the eastern wall of the King's Library. The door covered with dummy book backs which gave access to the Ante Room through the book cases of the King's Library lay barely ten yards from that into the Catalogue Room. The room adjoining the latter to the west was also originally a Reading Room and remained in use until the new domed room in the centre of the 'Iron Library'[29] was completed in 1857. It was probably in the 1860s that this old reading room became the Music Room; it remained in use as such until 1920. The three rooms beyond the Large Room were all used for book storage. The entire ground floor of the North Wing had very high ceilings, above which lay the new galleries and offices allocated to various antiquities and natural history departments.

Apart from the expansion of the Large Room to form the North Library while the King Edward VII Building was being built from 1907 to 1914, the North Wing seems to have remained almost unchanged until the later 1920s, when the Trustees undertook a gradual rebuilding programme to provide more space for staff and books.[30] The great height of the ceilings enabled a mezzanine floor to be inserted in the whole of the eastern part of the North Wing. The Catalogue Room was closed in October 1932 and the staff (i.e. GK I) moved to the Old Newspaper Room in the White Wing near the south-east corner of the Museum. Barely a year later, from 28 September to 6 October 1933, they completed the move back to the rebuilt and entirely refurnished Catalogue Room, immediately above which was the much-needed new Title Room (Fig. 21). (This had previously been housed, in cramped, dingy surroundings, in the basement of the South-West Quadrant[31] of the 'Iron Library'.) The next phase of reconstruction followed in the spring of 1934, and included the Old Music Room and the Banksian Room. Those of the staff who had been working there on GK II took over the vacant Old Newspaper Room mentioned above, and it was in a wide lobby (now part of the Department of Manuscripts) just outside this that the North Library readers and staff moved while that area also was being rebuilt.

This phase took longer, and the whole set of new mezzanine rooms was not occupied until the autumn of 1937. Then GK II returned to fill both the Banksian mezzanine and Room A2, above the old Music Room, and at the same time much-needed space had been created for the Catalogue Shop above the Banksian mezzanine. This had been achieved by lowering the floor of the latter some six feet. The Catalogue Shop was previously housed within the Bindery[32] which had been built about 1898 at ground level outside the Museum itself, a few yards north of the western part of the North Wing. All

21 The Title Room, as it was after the rebuilding of the 1930s (BL Archives).

this activity lasted almost ten years from first plans to completion. During this period only one departmental area, other than the Ante Room, of all those relevant to GK I and GK II stood quite unchanged. This was the Copyright Receipt Office, which occupied the eastern part of the ground floor of the King Edward VII Building. It had one entrance in the east side of the north entrance and another, for trade delivery purposes, from the roadway of the so-called North Gate (more accurately the North-East Gate) at the extreme eastern corner.

NOTES

1   These topics form the subject of a detailed study by A. H. Chaplin, *GK: 150 Years of the General Catalogue of Printed Books in the British Museum*, Scolar Press, 1987.

2   The 'K' is derived from the first letter of Κατάλογος (the Greek word for catalogue). From the early 1840s, perhaps even before, the letter 'K' was written in pencil beneath the word or words on the titlepage of all books, to show that it had been catalogued and to indicate its heading in the catalogue. (This practice was discontinued soon after 1960.) The terms 'GK I' and 'GK II' were also used from the 1930s onwards to denote the groups of staff working on each.

3   GK I was published in parts. Their sequence and dates are fully listed in *The Catalogues of the British Museum I. Printed Books*, by F. C. Francis (London, 1952), pp. 15–21, and p.22 lists the volumes of GK II issued up to 1947. Those issued subsequently, up to its cessation in 1954, are listed in the reports of the Keeper to the Trustees.

4   The location and date of construction (or reconstruction) of this and all other relevant rooms and offices are given on pp.189–91 and on the plan, p.xii.

5   From the Department's very first donations, in the early 1760s, onwards, the stamp used was yellow: the change to green was made in about 1946.

6   Up until about 1920, no member of the department was allowed to make any alteration on a title until he had completed some five years' service.

7   Richard Garnett, *Essays in Librarianship and Bibliography* (London, 1899), pp. 77–8 and p.94, makes brief mention of the process of incorporation as it was during the early 1880s.

8   The British Museum Trustees generously gave free copies of all Accession Parts to many libraries in the United Kingdom and abroad.

9   Several copies of the 1787 catalogue survive, one (Cup.407.e.7) has pressmarks added; another (L.R.419.bb.3) is interleaved and has pressmarks and some accessions added.

10   The sole surviving copy is at L.R.419.b.1.

11   This machine is illustrated in the *Post Office London Directory* for 1857, p.2622. It is described in William Bryce Proudfoot's *The Origin of Stencil Duplicating* (London, 1972), pp. 24–6. Its practical use is outlined in some detail by Thomas Winter Jones in his excellent anonymous article on the whole working of the British Museum library in the *North British Review*, 1851, pp. 178–9. *See also* Alec Hyatt King, *Printed Music in the British Museum* (London, 1979), p.172.

12   The idea of preparing from the fourth copies a subject catalogue, possibly for publication, is discussed by Garnett, op.cit., pp. 222–3.

13   Garnett, op.cit., p.79, says the Reading Room copy was 'on a strong vellum paper'. Later, cartridge paper was used for all three copies.

14   'One in one' means that at a single opening there were two printed columns, one on the left-hand side of each sheet, occupying only half of it. 'One in three' means that a single opening showed only one printed column, the half sheet next to it and the whole of the opposite sheet being left blank. This latter scheme was apparently originated by Garnett (*see* his op.cit., p.91, note).

15   The steel drawers which housed the fourth copies and titles in the Title Room dated from its reconstruction in 1931, and replaced old wooden boxes, which had originally been pasteboard (Garnett, op.cit., p.223). In the drawers containing the fourth copies, the old, full-width transcribed titles lay at the back, with the cards of printed ones in two rows in front of them.

16 Tucker probably became Incorporator in the mid-1920s but the exact date cannot now be ascertained because the allocation of the post was a matter for the Keeper and was not reported to the Trustees. Richbell's predecessor was W. T. Nichols, who worked from 1908 to 1930. (Information kindly supplied by Frank Fletcher from the records of G.K. copy sent to the printer.)

17 Marsden's report, DH 2/102, 1937, f.159.

18 Richbell had in his charge a volume of specimen titles, compiled about 1937 by the present writer in order to record for posterity the hand-writings of members of the staff back to about the 1880s, the earlier ones being identified by senior colleagues who had entered the department before 1900. This volume is now in the departmental archives.

19 The use of an ordinary steel paper-knife was discouraged because the sharp tip could easily cut or damage the edge of the strip.

20 The then Keeper, W. A. Marsden (a realistic man), remained optimistic. He reported to the Trustees in 1935 (DH 2/100, f.205 (2)) that he predicted GK II would reach eight volumes a year, perhaps more, and again in 1938 (DH 2/103, f.168) he said that the volume of work achieved had probably never been 'exceeded in any year of the Department's history', and referred especially to GK II. This points to the probability that, but for the war, its conclusion would have been assured.

21 Pressmarks were printed solely on catalogue entries which bore a date, and therefore never to references of form, as these could easily have confused readers. Pressmarks were written on such titles but ringed off as a conventional instruction to the printer to ignore them. Nevertheless, it was imperative for the Title Room staff to copy them by hand on to the corresponding fourth copies.

22 Originally the Attendant supplied the officer's name and the date by hand: later rubber stamps were used for both.

23 DH 2/102, 1937, f.207.

24 A copy is preserved with the Reports of 1934, DH 2/99, f.201. It consists of four sheets of galley proof which reveal, among a wealth of technical information, that the man in charge of the large case of rare sorts, accents, diacritical marks and the like, was called the 'catalogue clicker'.

25 *See* an article by A. H. Chaplin, 'The General Catalogue of Printed Books, 1881–1981', *British Library Journal* Autumn 1981, vol. 7, no. 2, pp. 109–19, where Marsden's optimistic reports are not mentioned.

26 J. Mordaunt Crook, *The British Museum*, London, 1972, p.128.

27 A scale-plan of the North Wing was engraved *c*.1838, and includes the location of the book presses. A copy is preserved in the Map Library, Maps. C.26.f.7, f.50.

28 Arundell Esdaile, *The British Museum Library*, London, 1946, p.88; he says this building was begun at the north end and was half completed by 1848.

29 This comprised the bookstacks which, together with the round Reading Room, were built from 1853 to 1857 within the still empty rectangle formed by the Museum's galleries. The floors of these bookstacks were formed of iron gratings, so designed to allow daylight to filter down from the glass roof through all these floors to the basement. (Electric lighting was not introduced until the twentieth century). Hence the name 'Iron Library'.

30 The dates of all moves, reconstruction, and reoccupation are found in the Keeper's reports and other papers for these years, DH 2/94 (1929) onwards.

31 Reports DH 2/94, 1929, f.161. Barry Johnson, *Lost in the Alps*, London 1985, p.4, states that at one time the Title Room was in the White Wing.

32 DH 2/100, 1935, f.218.

APPENDIX

GUIDE TO THE ARRANGEMENT OF HEADINGS AND ENTRIES IN THE GENERAL CATALOGUE (THE 'ROSE LIST')

Section   I.—ARRANGEMENT OF HEADINGS IN RELATION TO EACH OTHER.

Section   II.—ORDER OF SUBHEADINGS AND ENTRIES UNDER THE NAME OF AN AUTHOR.

Section III.—ORDER OF SUBHEADINGS AND ENTRIES UNDER THE NAMES OF COUNTRIES AND PLACES.

Section   I.—ARRANGEMENT OF HEADINGS IN RELATION TO EACH OTHER

The following list illustrates the system adopted. The word ROSE has been chosen for the purpose of convenience, and most of the examples are imaginary.

Not as proper noun.

ROSE (flower, tool etc.).

Entries under such a word as ROSE, with its variety of meanings, are arranged alphabetically in one group, irrespective of language, except that in the case of words identical in form but etymologically distinct, e.g. BUT (English) and BUT (French), LOVE (English) and LOVE (Danish), the heading is repeated and entries are grouped separately.

Place.

ROSE (without epithet).
ROSE, *House of.*
ROSE, John, *Count of.* (Place unascertained, or a character in fiction.)
ROSE, *Italy.*

cf. London; Cambridge.
cf. Anjou, *House of.*

cf. London, *Ontario;* Cambridge, *Mass.*

ROSE, *Italy, Diocese of.*
ROSE, *Italy*, Henry, *Bishop of.*
ROSÉ, *Spain.*

The accent does not affect the arrangement.

ROSÉ, *Spain, Diocese of.*
ROSÉ, *Spain*, Carlos, *Bishop of.*
ROSE, *U.S.A.*

[194]

ROSE, *U.S.A., Diocese of.*
ROSE, *U.S.A.*, William, *Bishop of.*

Personal name.	ROSE. ROSE, *Abbot.* ROSE [da Pietro], called *the Gramarian.*	The epithet determines the order.
	ROSE, *pseud.* ROSE, *Saint.* ROSE, *Ship.*	
Compounds, other than compound surnames, arranged, irrespective of meaning, in alphabetical sequence.	ROSE AMELIA, *Queen.* ROSE AND COMPANY. ROSE AND CROWN. ROSE AND CROWN, *Diocese of.* ROSE BROTHERS. ROSE COMMEMORATION FUND. ROSE CULTIVATION MANUALS. ROSE GARDEN. ROSE GARDEN JONES FUND. ROSE GARDENERS CLUB. ROSE GAZETTE. ROSE JONES HOSTEL. ROSE-JONES INSTITUTE. ROSE LIMITED. ROSE-ON-SEA. ROSE RIVER COLONY. ROSE 7689. ROSE UNIVERSITY COLLEGE. ROSE WILHELMINA, *Queen.* ROSE, WILSON AND COMPANY.	e.g. an inn or the title of a periodical. cf. Bath and Wells. Rose, Christian name : Jones, surname. Rose-Jones, surname.
Possessives.	ROSE'S INSTITUTE.	
Body of persons so named.	ROSE, *Clan of.* ROSE, *Family of.* ROSE, *Messrs.*	
Surnames, plus round brackets	ROSE (J.) *Artist.* ROSE (J. de) ROSE (J. Albert) ROSE (John) ROSE, afterwards SMITH (John) ROSE (John) AND SONS. ROSE (John) *Agent.* ROSE (John) *2nd Earl.* ROSE (John) *Musician.* ROSE (*Sir* John) ROSE (*Sir* John) AND SONS. ROSE (John de) ROSE (John von) ROSE (John Daniel) ROSE (John D'Arcy) ROSE (John de Lancey)	

ROSEBERY.
ROSEBUD.
ROSE-JONES (John)   Compound surname read as
ROSEMARY.   [one word.

Section II.—ORDER OF SUBHEADINGS AND ENTRIES UNDER THE NAME OF AN AUTHOR

A. WITH SUBHEADINGS.

(a) *Works.*—Arranged by language. (See note 10.) Entries within each language group arranged in the chronological order of publication.

(b) *Two or more Works* or *Smaller Collections.*—Limited to editions of two or more works which have been previously published separately. Arranged as (a) above.

(c) *Letters.*—Correspondence proper, not pamphlets described as letters. Two or more letters precede single letters, each of these two groups being arranged in the same way as (a) and (b) above.

(d) *Single Works.*—Arranged alphabetically according to the title of the original, each single work being followed by translations (see note 10), extracts, arranged as (a) above, and indented entries for criticisms, replies, etc. (See note 9.)

(e) *Works written in collaboration.*—Cross-references to entries for works in which the author's name does not occur first on the titlepage, followed by entries for works in which his name does occur first. The latter are arranged on the same principles as the works of a single author.

(f) *Selections.*—Limited to excerpts from two or more single works, and arranged in the same way as (a) and (b) above.

(g) *Works edited, translated, or with prefaces by . . .*—Limited to cross-references. (N.B. In this Guide the term "cross-reference" is used to indicate an entry in which the reference precedes the title of the work.)

(h) *Doubtful or Supposititious Works.*—Arranged on the same principles as the genuine works.

(i) *Appendix.*—Subdivided where necessary according to subject, and grouped in the alphabetical order of the subheadings adopted, with the subheading "Miscellaneous" at the end. Within each group cross-references precede main entries. (N.B. In this Guide the term "main entry" covers, besides main titles proper, all entries in which the title of the work precedes a reference.)

Where desirable, the entries are preceded by a key to the arrangement of the main divisions set out in the order in which they occur, and are followed by an index of subheadings or an index of titles, or both.

The above list, while furnishing a general statement of the system followed, does not include the whole range of subheadings in use in the Museum Catalogue.

[196]

Many headings have special needs in the matter of subheadings and it is impracticable to give a complete list.

B. WITHOUT SUBHEADINGS.

The principles of arrangement are the same as those in Section II. A. except in the treatment of cross-references. The general scheme is as follows :—

I. General references to alternative headings.

II. Cross-references.

III. Main entries.

Section III.—ORDER OF SUBHEADINGS AND ENTRIES UNDER THE NAMES OF COUNTRIES AND PLACES

(*a*) *Constitutions.*—Collections first, arranged according to date of publication, followed by separate constitutions arranged according to date of promulgation.

(*b*) *Laws.*

I. *General Collections*, arranged according to date of publication.

II. *Collections of Laws on Special Subjects*, arranged alphabetically in order of subject, and within each group according to date of publication.

III. *Codes*, arranged as II.

IV. *Separate Laws*, arranged according to date of promulgation. Entries in which the year only is stated precede in alphabetical order all more precisely dated entries. The same principle is followed where the month but not the day of the month is stated.

(*c*) *Treaties.*—Collections first, arranged according to date of publication, followed by separate treaties, arranged according to date of signature.

(*d*) *Miscellaneous Public Documents* (Royal and Presidential Messages, Letters, Warrants, etc.).—Collections first, arranged according to date of publication, followed by separate documents, arranged according to official date of document.

(*e*) *Miscellaneous Official Publications.*—Collections first, arranged according to date of publication, followed by separate publications, arranged alphabetically.

(*f*) *Legislative Bodies.*—Generally arranged in their historical order. Under each body collections of proceedings first, arranged according to date of publication, followed by separate proceedings, arranged in chronological order of sittings.

(*g*) *Departments of State and Public Institutions.*—Subheadings arranged in alphabetical order. Entries under each subheading generally arranged in alphabetical order.

(*h*) *Miscellaneous Institutions, Societies, etc.*—Subheadings arranged in alphabetical order. Under each subheading constitutions, bye-laws, annual reports, calendars, lists of members, bulletins, journals, proceedings, transactions, etc., are placed first. The remaining entries follow in alphabetical order.

(*i*) *Appendix.*—Subdivided if necessary, as in Section II. A. (*i*).

The same arrangement, so far as applicable, is followed in the case of smaller territorial divisions, cities, etc., but in headings not provided with the subheadings "Official Documents" and "Appendix" (for anonymous works); official documents are, as usual, placed first and are followed by the anonymous entries. Any necessary subheadings for institutions, societies, etc., then follow in alphabetical order.

As in the case of author headings a key to the arrangement, and indexes, may be provided.

NOTES

(1) A title is treated as a sequence of words, and not as a single sequence of letters, e.g. "World without End" precedes "Worlds to Conquer"; also "Crime. Psychological studies" precedes "Crime and Punishment."

(2) The definite or indefinite article at the beginning of a title is ignored, except when it occurs in an oblique case in a form differing from the nominative.

(3) Archaic and variant spellings are treated as if they were in the standard form.

(4) Numerals are read as words in the language of the title.

(5) Contracted forms are treated as if written in full, except where the full form is not in general use, e.g. *Mr.*, *Mrs.*

(6) The author's name appearing in the possessive case at the beginning of a title is generally ignored in the arrangement.

(7) Entries consisting of descriptions supplied by the cataloguer and enclosed within square brackets are placed in chronological order before the alphabetical series, unless it is made clear by the wording that another place is appropriate.

(8) The order of the Slavonic alphabets is followed in exclusively Slavonic headings. In headings containing both entries in a Slavonic language and entries in a language using the Latin alphabet the Slavonic entries may be treated as if transliterated, or the entries may be grouped in two alphabetical series. In all cases translations follow their originals according to rule.

The same treatment is adopted in the case of Greek.

(9) Entries for criticisms, adaptations, etc., of a particular work, whether cross-references to another heading or main titles (for anonymous works), are indented under the work referred to.

(10) Polyglot editions of a work (either editions of the original text together with one or more translations, or translations into more than one language) are placed immediately after editions in the original language alone. Then follow translations into single languages, English standing first and other translations following in the alphabetical order of the languages.

[198]

Exceptions.

i. The complete Bible and the Old Testament, where the order of the translations is Greek, Latin, English, other languages in alphabetical order.

ii. The New Testament and the Greek Classics, in which the order of the translations is Latin, English, etc. This also applies to translations of the Kuran and certain Arabic classics.

In cases where the name of the original is not known, translations are placed at the end of the "Single Works," arranged by languages in the order just stated, and chronologically within each language group.

It is to be noted that in groups of works arranged chronologically according to date of publication, polyglot editions and translations are placed together after all works in the original language.

6

THE PRIVATE CASE: A HISTORY

Paul James Cross

APPENDICES

INTRODUCTION

THE HISTORY OF the Private Case, which has been veiled in mystery and distorted by rumour, has for the most part remained unwritten. Some important details have not been recorded but, even so, a great deal of information has come down to us along with the various scandal-mongering, and semi-fictitious accounts of the history and contents of the Private Case.

The most important unanswered question regarding the collection is the date of its inception. When was it created? In recent times two authors have presented theories on this. Peter Fryer, author of *Private Case, Public Scandal*, London, 1966, says that he does not know 'the exact date when the Private Case was established', but does 'not think that it can have been before 1856', because, he claims, he has 'never seen a book, now or formerly catalogued in the private case, bearing a BM accession stamp earlier than 1856'.[1]

Fryer goes on to argue that John Winter Jones (1805–81), Keeper of Printed Books from 1856–66, and then Principal Librarian of the British Museum, created the Private Case 'off his own bat about the year 1857', thus implementing 'a long cherished reform'.[2]

The second author, Gershon Legman, in his introduction to *The Private Case*, 1981, by Patrick J. Kearney, states that 'the Private Case was fully instituted between the years 1866 and 1870, and that the first cases were numbered P.C. 19 and 20'.[3] He adds that 'the creation of the Private Case probably dates from the receipt in 1866 of the "phallicism" collection of the antiquarian George Witt'.[4] (Only two items from the Witt Collection are today still in the Private Case.) Both these theories are contradicted by the findings laid out here.

Misconceptions about the birth of the collection have led to misconceptions about the collection itself, the major one being that the Private Case was created as an 'erotica collection'. It was not. It is obviously true that most of the works in the collection could be considered erotic but they were not given P.C. pressmarks because they were erotic but because they were considered by society, by the Trustees, and primarily by the Keeper concerned, to be obscene. Works such as *The German Prisoner* by James Hanley, London, 1935, or *The Naked Lunch* by William S. Burroughs, Paris, 1959 are definitely not erotic (in the general sense of the word, at least); neither are the works of de Sade, which were written as philosophical treatises and vicious polemics against French society and could not normally be considered to be erotically stimulating. But all these works are frank and brutal and many would indeed consider them to be very obscene.

The purpose of the present work is to present a historical account of the Private Case. This has only been achieved by a thorough examination of items in the archives of the British Library and British Museum as well as of published works.

I · THE NINETEENTH CENTURY

It is unfortunate that the exact date of the inception of the Private Case will, perhaps, always remain a mystery. There is no record, either in the Minutes of the BM Trustees' meetings, or elsewhere, of when a decision was made to segregate books on the basis of obscenity from the rest of the collections of the Department of Printed Books and to restrict their availability to all but a very few readers.

The reason why the Trustees' Minutes contain so few references to the Private Case is unknown but it is probably due to the nature of the material concerned, i.e. bawdy books, which were not only condemned by society in the nineteenth century (publicly at least), but which it was also illegal to publish and to sell. With this in mind, it is not surprising that the Keepers did not go out of their way to draw the attention of the Trustees to the Museum's holdings of obscene literature, especially as much of it had been purchased with taxpayers' money.[5]

The earliest recorded information about the Private Case comes from a manuscript catalogue contained in a folio guard volume entitled 'Catalogue of Books in Private Case' (*see* Appendix A, no. 5). This catalogue is the single most important document relevant to the beginnings of the collection.

All books that went into the Private Case were stamped, catalogued, and pressmarked in the same manner as other books. The only difference was that the title slips (manuscript catalogue entries) and fourth copy cards (which formed the shelf list) were filed on their own (probably in the Keeper's office), and the material was not recorded in the General Catalogue. It was the norm in the nineteenth century for newly-acquired books to be processed fairly swiftly (i.e. within a matter of weeks or months of being received). Backlogs did occur but these usually applied to large single deposits of material which, naturally, could not be dealt with immediately.

The earliest recorded item I have discovered, which was placed in the Private Case, is *Paradise Lost; or The Great Dragon Cast Out* by 'Lucian, Redivivus', published in London by John Brooks, Oxford Street, in 1838. This book, like the majority of the other early P.C. items, was purchased. It bears an accession date of 31 March 1841 and was catalogued in May of that year.

This book was possibly the first, and certainly one of the first, to be deposited in the Private Case. On its title slip the barely visible words 'Private Case' are written in pencil. This is the earliest indication of where the book was placed. It is not strictly speaking a 'pressmark' – as it includes no press, or shelf number. It was simply an indication of where the book was accommodated. The Private Case was originally a cupboard in the office of the Keeper of Printed Books. From 1837 until 1856 the Keeper was Antonio Panizzi (1797–1879), who if not instrumental in creating the collection must, at least, have known of its existence. As the collection was so small a proper pressmark was deemed unnecessary. Since none of the entries in the 'Catalogue of Books in Private Case' have pressmarks this catalogue must therefore contain the original nucleus of the collection which was kept in the Keeper's office and perhaps stored alphabetically by author or title.

The latest item in this P.C. Catalogue was catalogued in September 1864[6] and was presumably deposited in the Private Case soon after. It is probable that about this date, when the collection consisted of seventy-eight books, it had become too large for the Keeper's office and was transferred from the cupboard in that office to a new location. The most likely place was the Ante-Room basement in the East Wing, an area very close to the Keeper's office and the place in which the suppressed books (the 'S.S.' collection) would later be stored.[7] When this transfer was made, pressmarks were added to the words 'Private Case' on the title slips and in the actual books concerned. The earliest items were placed at P.C.20, 21, and 22,[8] and the pressmarks were written in the form 'Private Case. 20.a.', etc. The series did not begin 'Private Case 1' as would seem logical. Possibly this was because the cases, or cupboards, in the Ante-Room basement numbered from 20 to 22 were either empty, or were cleared, for the P.C. books. (These cupboards were destroyed when the Ante-Room was refurbished in 1976–77).

After about 1864, when the books were moved to their new location, new accessions, or items transferred to the Private Case, had the pressmark or prefix abbreviated either to 'Priv. Case', 'Priv. C.' or, in the majority of cases, to 'P.C.'. Eventually all Private Case pressmarks were standardised with a 'P.C.' prefix (*see* Appendix C). It was only after 1875, with the introduction of third marks (the number at the end of the pressmark, following the shelf letter, that denotes the number of a book on a particular shelf) that the full P.C. pressmark which is used to this day was finally created. Therefore, by checking the first item on the shelf at each Private Case press, one can ascertain when that pressmark came into existence (*see* Appendix D). (For the material that was placed in the P.C. before 1875 this is not so reliable as it does not allow for the fact that before this date third marks were not used.)

During the nineteenth century the Private Case collection grew from approximately twenty-seven books in 1850,[9] to approximately sixty by 1860,[10] seventy-eight by 1864,[11] and many hundreds by 1900.[12]

On 5 November 1890 Richard Garnett, the Keeper of Printed Books, reported to the Trustees that a letter from Wilfrid Ignatius Wilberforce, nephew of Samuel Wilberforce, Bishop of Winchester, a former Junior Assistant in the Department of Printed Books,[13] had been addressed to the Archbishop of Canterbury (one of the Principal Trustees of the British Museum). The letter complained about 'the expenditure of the funds of the Printed Books department in the purchase of immoral books'. Garnett submitted a few observations about the nature of these books, stating that many occupied a 'significant place in literature', or else were useful to students of philosophy, archaeology, or manners: 'similar instances cover the great majority of cases'.[14] He also explained the British Museum's policy towards readers applying for Private Case books. The books 'are locked up [and] they are excluded from the catalogue and anyone wishing to consult any of them must undergo a cross-examination calculated to deter all but really honest and legitimate research'. (This policy was enforced until the 1960s.) Garnett stated that 'the number of books now in the Museum is comparatively small filling some dozen cupboards of small size'.[15] It appears that he was trying to play down the incident somewhat, and to restrict the Trustees' knowledge of the true nature of many of the Private Case books and of the size of the collection.

The earliest items to be desegregated (i.e. transferred out of the Private Case), appear to be thirty-five French works which were moved during the late nineteenth century. (Five of these works are now placed at 1071.d.44–48). Nine of the pressmarks that these thirty-five works formerly occupied have since been re-used. (This is unusual as former pressmarks of P.C. items that have been desegregated are usually not re-used.) They include P.C.17.a.1 (accession stamp dated 7 April 1875) which was replaced by a work stamped with the accession date of 14 April 1891 (which was catalogued during November 1891). This obviously indicates that these works were transferred before or during 1891. The item on the shelf at 1071.d.43 (i.e. the last item on the shelf before the desegregated works were placed) was accessioned in 1860; the first item placed after these items (i.e. at 1071.d.49) was from the Ashbee Collection which was presented to the British Museum in 1900.

The Department of Oriental Printed Books and Manuscripts (later renamed the Department of Oriental Manuscripts and Printed Books, and now known as Oriental Collections) was created in May 1892 and works which were placed in the Private Case that came within its field were transferred to the new department and reshelved at the Or.P.C.59.e. pressmark (*see* Appendix F). This is the Private Case of the Oriental department. This collection was, and is, very small (albeit very fine) and at its greatest extent it contained fifty-two items; it now contains only thirty-three books. Some illustrated 'Pillow books' – with no text at all – were transferred to the British Museum Department of Oriental Antiquities in July 1973, when the British Library came into existence. Works in the Or.P.C.59.e. collection include *The Old Man Young Again* (Paris, 1898–9), as well as editions of the *Kama Sutra, Ananga-Ranga*, and *Le Jardin Parfumé*. There are also some items in this collection from the Ashbee bequest (with his manuscript notes) which were originally shelved at 14055.i. and were never placed in the Department of Printed Books Private Case.[16]

II · THE ASHBEE COLLECTION

Henry Spencer Ashbee, FSA, who was born in 1834, died on 29 July 1900. He amassed a large collection of books, including one of the world's major collections of erotica. On 6 August 1900 Ashbee's solicitors, Kennedy, Hughes, and Ponsonby, wrote to the Secretary of the British Museum offering Ashbee's collection of books, engravings, and other artefacts. The books were delivered to the British Museum on 28 September and filled about twenty cases. G. K. Fortescue, then Keeper of Printed Books, reported this to the Sub-Committee on Printed Books, Manuscripts, etc. on 13 October. Fortescue and the Keepers of the other departments concerned were instructed by the Director to examine the various parts of this collection and to report their findings to the Trustees. On 27 October Fortescue reported that he had carried out a thorough inspection and the collection consisted of 8,764 works in 15,299 volumes, including many books by, or about, Cervantes (384 editions of *Don Quixote* alone), and about '1,000 books in 1,600 volumes of an erotic or obscene character'.[17] He recommended that 'books of this class be placed in "Private Cases" where their inspection by readers may be subject to the same rigorous restrictions as the other books thus treated'. An inspection of the erotica collection revealed 'many works by Sade, Andrea de Nerciat, Mirabeau, Cleland, and Johann [*sic*] Meursius' (i.e. Nicolas Chorier). Fortescue added that 'the collection of obscene books' had been inspected and duplicates had been packed in six boxes. He asked the Trustees' permission to destroy them.[18] A. W. K. Miller, Keeper, reported to the Trustees on 2 February 1914 that some duplicates of Ashbee's erotica had recently been discovered. He reminded the Trustees that in 1900 most of the duplicates had been destroyed as authorised and he recommended that these recently discovered items be dealt with in the same way. On 13 March, however, G. F. Barwick (who was to succeed Miller as Keeper on the latter's sudden death in May 1914) urged that about 'a hundred duplicates of some value' should be 'presented to the Bodleian Library for preservation in the Private Case Collection there' (i.e. the Phi Collection).[19] This was the course of action followed. Two hundred and sixty-seven volumes and parts were received by the Bodleian Library on 23 September 1914.

Also in the Ashbee collection were two items which were bequeathed to the British Museum Department of Prints and Drawings and retained by them. Although they were of 'an erotic character' they were considered by Sidney Colvin, the Keeper of the department, to be 'of sufficient artistic value and interest to be worth preserving'. These were a volume of eighteenth-century French drawings entitled *Histoire Universelle* and six etched plates by Thomas Rowlandson.[20] Many of the engravings and artefacts from the Ashbee bequest were rejected by the departments concerned and passed to the Victoria and Albert Museum during January 1901, and to Sotheby's for auction during April 1901. The duplicates of the non-erotic books were distributed to other libraries, including the Bodleian and Cambridge University Library between February and May 1902.

In his will Ashbee requested that his bequest should be called the 'Ashbee Bequest', that a label bearing these two words should be attached to the spines, and that his bookplate was to be pasted into the front of all the books bequeathed except those which were to be 'withheld from the Public' (i.e. those for the Private Case). In point of fact nearly all the books bequeathed by Ashbee, including the obscene ones, were treated thus. Today only 109 books in the Private Case are identifiable as coming from this bequest.[21] All these books bear a yellow (bequest or donation) accession stamp with the date 10 November 1900. Most of them, as mentioned above, also bear his bookplate. Many of these works were catalogued and pressmarked fairly swiftly but (as in the case of the French Revolutionary tracts in the previous century) the sheer number of books involved prevented the whole collection from being processed rapidly. Many items were stored until they were catalogued during 1906–07[22] and another large portion of the collection was dealt with between November 1913 and May 1914.[23] The erotic books are now all shelved at Presses P.C.22, 30, and 31.

The Ashbee bequest was by far the largest single deposit of books during the nineteenth and twentieth century which was placed on the shelves of the Private Case. It greatly enhanced the collection, not only in size, but in the wealth of its rarities and in the diversity of its material. The bequest included, apart from the works by the authors mentioned by Fortescue, such items as *Histoire de Mademoiselle Brion*, Toulon, *c.*1856, Baron Dominique Vivant Denon, *Le Point de Lendemain*, Paris (Brussels), 1867, *Le Parnasse Satyrique*, Brussels, 1866, *Gyneocracy*, London, 1893, by the pseudonymous Julian

Robinson, and a number of fine editions of the more libertine verses of Alexis Piron.

The Ashbee bequest included the three volumes of Ashbee's own erotic bibliography: *Index Librorum Prohibitorum*, London, 1877, *Centuria Librorum Absconditorum*, London, 1879, and *Catena Librorum Tacendorum*, London, 1885 (*see* Appendix A, nos. 1, 2 and 3). (The BL also has copyright deposit copies of these works, received just after publication.) The first two volumes of the bequeathed set are annotated by the author and have extra leaves, and plates, inserted. The third volume is not annotated and has no extra leaves or plates. It is still held by the staff of the Reading Room Information Service (*see* Appendix A, no. 3), as were the two earlier works until 1965.

Legman states that Ashbee's three-volume bibliography is not the catalogue of his own collection as not all the books listed were in the 1900 Ashbee bequest to the British Museum.[24] However about 1900 the British Museum purchased a large collection of erotica (approximately 200 works). Nearly all of these had formerly belonged to H. S. Ashbee. These included books from the library of the French collector Louis Constantin which Ashbee had purchased from Paul Daffis of the Bibliothèque Elzevirienne, 7 Rue Guenegaud, Paris, in 1877. Constantin was an avid collector of anything erotic and possessed not only books but illustrations, sculptures and other objects.[25]

The full catalogue of the Constantin collection was published in 1867. His library contained mainly eighteenth- and nineteenth-century French works – for example *Pièces Echappées du Feu*, A N ... (*c*.1750), *Satan et Ève*, A Damnopolis, Paris, *c*.1832, and *Les Cinq jouissances amoureuses de Clindor et Cephise*, A Paphos, Paris, 1759. These works and most of the others in the *Bibliothèque Constantin* are of extreme rarity. Many had been catalogued by James Campbell [Reddie] in his manuscript 'Bibliographical Notes on Books'. Some books from Campbell's own collection[26] were included in this purchase. Among them were *L'Aretine François* by François Felix Nogaret, Londres, 1787, and a few editions of the *Elegantiae Latini sermonis* of Nicholas Chorier. These too were part of Ashbee's collection.

Also included in this purchase made by the British Museum about 1900 were four important manuscripts, all formerly in Ashbee's possession. Three of them were bibliographies: 'Catalogue de Dessins, Manuscrits et Livres' by Auguste Berard; 'Bibliographical Notes on Books' by James Campbell [Reddie], which is acknowledged by Ashbee as being one of the foundation stones of his own bibliography of erotic literature; and the 'Bibliographie' of Edouard Tricotel. The fourth was a poem, 'The Betuliad' by George Coleman. This work is generally known as *The Rodiad*. (Two editions bearing this latter title are in the British Library; the earlier of the two with the imprint Cadell & Murray,

1810, [J. C. Hotten *c.*1870?] was, until 28 March 1946, in the Private Case.[27]) The 'Betuliad' is bound in red morocco, with very curious gold tooling, and although unsigned this binding was perhaps produced by Trautz-Bauzonnet of Paris. It is almost certain that this work was formerly in the collection of the erotomaniac Frederick Hankey, who presented it to his friend Ashbee before the death of the former in 1882. Another item possibly from the Hankey collection and bound by Hardy of Paris was placed at P.C.31.h.38. Also from the Ashbee collection were a group of books all bound in full cherry morocco, with gilt tooling by Lortic, placed at P.C.30.f.1,5–8,10–18. Works in fine bindings from other collections can be found at P.C.30.i.17 (Trautz-Bauzonnet), P.C.30.K.27 (Van Roosbrock), and P.C.31.f.7 (A. Chatclis). An examination reveals that many more of the items in Ashbee's bibliography were actually in his possession, than at first would seem evident. With the exception of the four above mentioned manuscripts (which were transferred to the British Museum Department of Manuscripts in February 1914) none of these purchased items bears either Ashbee's bookplate or an 'Ashbee Collection' label. (All the manuscripts bear both, except for the 'Betuliad', which lacks the bookplate.) All the items, without exception are stamped with a red (purchase) stamp, which is undated. Yet works such as *The Romance of Lust*, London, 1873–76, *Letters from a Friend in Paris*, London, 1874, *Don Leon*, London, 1866, and *An Essay on Woman*, Aberdeen, 1788; which were not in the Ashbee bequest were a part of the Ashbee Collection. (Many of the less-literary items amongst his erotic books and all the erotic sale catalogues were not retained and were possibly destroyed in 1900, not for being duplicates but because they were considered to be of no value.[28]

New pressmarks were created to house this large influx of material. It was probably between 1900 and 1914 that the Private Case material was moved from the Ante Room basement to the Arch Room. This is the room in which the Library's incunabula collections, together with other rare materials, are housed. The collection had once more outgrown its shell.[29]

III · THE EARLY TWENTIETH CENTURY

Meanwhile, several Private Case works were desegregated during 1901 and 1902; these were eighteen translations of works by Emile Zola, who had scandalized the Victorians with his naturalist fiction – works such as *The Soil, How Jolly Life is* and *Nana*, many of which were published by Henry Vizetelly, who was prosecuted for obscene libel in October 1888 and May 1889. These works had formerly been placed at P.C.28.a.2–18, and P.C.29.b.49.

On 7 July 1913 *The Intermediate Sex* by Edward Carpenter, London, 1908, was desegregated. The furore surrounding this work and the works of Havelock Ellis prompted the first public disclosure that the British Museum had a collection of books, of an obscene character, that was generally unavailable to readers. It came in the pages of *The English Review*, in 1913, in an article written by E. S. P. Haynes entitled 'The Taboos of the British Museum Library'. This disclosure was neither official nor would it have been welcomed by the Museum.

Haynes wished to draw attention to something that, he thought, was 'perhaps not generally realised', namely: 'that there are numerous books belonging to the British Museum library ... which are absolutely not mentioned ... in the General Catalogue, and are practically inaccessible to the public'. These books were, he said, 'buried ... in the Private Case'.[30] The criteria for deciding what was to be buried, according to Haynes, were works subversive of the throne, of religion, or of propriety. In fact only the improper books were 'buried' in the Private Case. The other 'subversive' books were not placed in the Private Case but were simply sealed up and kept in the Keeper's cupboard until the pressmark 'S.S.' (Suppressed Safe) was added to such books in the early years of the twentieth century.[31] These books were moved to the Ante-Room basement (where the P.C. books had formerly been stored) where they were stored in seven safes until 1976–77 when they were transferred to a secure area of the bookstacks. Books in the S.S. are, because of legal complications, still omitted from the General Catalogue and under no circumstances are they made available to readers. Haynes also mentioned the Museum's refusal to make either Havelock Ellis's *The Psychology of Sex*, or *Κρυπτάδια*, a highly important work on erotic folk-lore, available to readers. The *English Review* article is useful because it provides an indication of intellectual opposition to the idea of Private Case material being unavailable. However, in many ways the article is misleading. Haynes supposed that the Museum's Trustees were 'probably quite ignorant'[32] of the suppression of books from the General Catalogue, and that works considered to be blasphemous or guilty of *lèse-majesté* were exiled to the Private Case. Both these suppositions were incorrect.

The main reason for writing and publishing such an article was, as Haynes admitted, to highlight the British Museum's censorship and to break the taboo. The article failed on the second count because the general climate of opinion was against it, although it did force the Museum authorities to relax their grip slightly: between 9 February and 31 March 1914 forty-two works were desegregated[33] and reshelved in the general library.

A. W. Pollard, Keeper of Printed Books, received a letter on 10 February 1920, through another member of staff, from the secretary to the Chancellor of the Duchy of Lancaster, the 27th Earl of Crawford (one of the Museum Trustees) offering a box of 'about 200 books' of 'the kind which are kept in the Private Case'. On 14 February Pollard reported to the Standing Committee of the Trustees that the books on offer formed part of 'an intestate estate devolving on the Duchy' and that the books were to be 'preserved or destroyed at the discretion of the Trustees'. The books were accepted on these conditions. Pollard reported to the Trustees on 30 March that they had been examined: 'they are mostly bad reprints of works of a very offensive character and few have any literary or bibliographical value'.[34] Twenty-four of the books were duplicates of works already in the Private Case and another twenty-nine were 'of no interest or value'. These Pollard recommended should be destroyed, leaving only nine books to be added to the Private Case Collection. The report only dealt with a total of sixty-two books. What happened to the remainder of the 200 items offered (if they ever existed and were not simply the result of a wild guess) is a mystery.[35] On 10 April the Trustees authorised the destruction of these fifty-three 'worthless' books.

In the same month seventeen books were removed from the Private Case and were transferred to the general library. These seventeen items are listed in the copy of the 'Catalogue of Private Case Books' known as 'Copy A' (*see* Appendix A, no. 6). This copy was kept in the Keeper's office and was used by him for reference purposes and for dealing with enquiries by readers.

A record of the contents of the Private Case as it stood in the early 1930s is provided by the *Registrum Librorum Eroticorum* by 'Rolf S. Reade' (*see* Appendix A, no. 15) the anagrammatical pseudonym of Alfred Rose (1876–1936), a rich collector, who about 1934 was given permission to copy, in full, the 'Catalogue of Private Case Books' as it then stood. Why this was allowed is not known but permission was probably granted by W. A. Marsden, the Keeper from 1930–43. The Rose *Registrum* is not a proper bibliography. It is in fact little more than a checklist of titles (albeit 5,061 of them – it was Rose's aim to list the titles of all the erotica ever written!). The printing of this work (which also contained the titles and pressmarks of the works in the Phi Collection at the Bodleian, and of the erotica in the Cambridge University Library, Guildhall Library, the *Enfer* Collection of the Bibliothèque Nationale, and the Biblioteca Apostolica Vaticana) was handled (very badly) by W. J. Stanislas. Rose had died by the time the book went to press and the proofs were not properly read. Many of the pressmarks of the P.C. books are incorrect, as are some titles, and some other bibliographical information.[36]

Rose donated, or bequeathed, seven erotic works from his collection to the BM and these were all placed in the Private Case – *The Bride's Confession*, 1917, *Cythera's Hymnal*, 1870, *Harlequin Prince Cherrytop*, [London], 1905, *The Dialogues of Luisa Sigea*, 1890, the *Polunbi Katalog*, 1926–9, *The Festival of the Passions*, London, 1863, and *The Index Expurgatorius of Martialis*, London, 1868; all are of exceptional interest.[37] He also donated an important typescript update of items that had been placed in the Bibliothèque Nationale's erotica collection, the *Enfer*, from 1913 (when the catalogue of the collection was published) until 1934. Rose also gave many works of a pro-Nazi character to the Museum during 1933 and 1934.

The official and most reliable record of the contents of the Private Case in the 1930s is 'Copy C' of the 'Catalogue of Private Case Books' which is complete up to *c*.1939. It contains 2,001 entries, including at least five books with Or.P.C.59.e. pressmarks. The latest entry in this catalogue appears to be Henry Miller, *Tropic of Capricorn*, Obelisk Press, Paris, 1939, which was catalogued on 10 June 1939.[38] This book has since been desegregated.

The Private Case engaged public attention again in 1937. The protagonist on this occasion was Alec Craig, who like Haynes was a liberal-minded man. He was also one of the founders of the Progressive League. In his work *The Banned Books of England*, London, 1937, Craig stated that in the British Museum certain books were 'removed from the public catalogue'. In fact the majority of Private Case books were not 'removed from the General Catalogue'; they were simply never entered in it. In the bibliography of the work mentioned above Craig included the pressmarks of two Private Case books – *L'Enfer de la Bibliothèque Nationale*, Paris, 1913, and Rose's *Registrum*.[39]

In *Above all Liberties*, his other account of, and attack on, literary censorship Craig stated that 'the British Museum's practice of excluding certain books from the General Catalogue is a serious matter'. He also quoted extensively from E. S. P. Haynes's article, and included the Private Case pressmarks of the *Bibliotheca Arcana* by Speculator Morum (i.e. William Laird Clowes), and of the three volumes of the Ashbee bibliography. Craig actually donated two erotic books to the Museum; a French translation of the *Memoirs of a Woman of Pleasure* (commonly known as *Fanny Hill*) by John Cleland, Paris, 1933, and an edition of *L'Oeuvre du Comte du Mirabeau*, Paris, 1921. Both were published by the *Frères* Briffaut in their *Bibliothèque des Curieux* series. Both were shelved in the Private Case and were therefore, ironically, suppressed from general availability.

Three works from the Ashley Library collected by the famous bibliophile Thomas James Wise (1859–1937) were also placed in the Private Case. All three are in one way or another connected with the poet Algernon Charles Swinburne, of whose works Wise had an almost complete collection. The three works were *The Whippingham Papers*, London, 1888, which contained contributions from the pen of Swinburne, *Opus Sadicum*, Paris, 1889, an English translation by Isidore Liseux of *Justine* by the Marquis de Sade, which Swinburne praised (as he praised all Sade's other works). (A letter from the poet to Theodore Watts-Dutton was formerly in this book but has since been removed to the Department of Manuscripts.) The third work was *Flossie, a Venus of fifteen*, London & Melbourne, 1904, which has been erronously ascribed to Swinburne on the strength of the Vienna *édition de luxe* which bore his name on the title page. Sadly *Flossie* was reported missing by C. B. Oldman, the Principal Keeper, on 25 February 1948. These works were all given Ashley pressmarks which they shared with their P.C. ones.[40] Erotic works from the collections of George III and Paul Hirsch were also given double pressmarks (see 52.k.22(2)/P.C.22.C.(2) and Hirsch.IV.1480a.(1–2)/ P.C.22.c.3(1–2).

The Edward Phelips collection of erotica was transferred from the Guildhall Library (where it had been when Rose was compiling his *Registrum Librorum Eroticorum* about 1934) to the British Museum in 1950. These works mostly bear the accession stamp dates of 2 May, 20 May, and 22 July 1950 (some others are undated). C. B. Oldman reported to the Trustees about this transfer of material (not all of which was erotic) on 13 July 1950.

The Trustees formally accepted the gift on 22 July. Seventeen items have since been transferred to other pressmarks so that today sixteen works from the Phelips collection remain in the Private Case. These works are all in French, with the exception of one in Italian, and another in English. They include two works by Henri d'Argis; *Sodome*, Paris, 1888, and *Gomorrhe*, Paris, 1889; also *Odor di Femina*, Paris, 1919, by the enigmatic Edmond Dumoulin and a French translation of extracts from *My Secret Life – Ma Vie Secrète*, Paris, 1923.

As a direct result of the publication of the first non-clandestine edition of John Wilmot, Earl of Rochester's complete works, in 1952, six editions were removed from the Private Case on 29 October, two on 16 December, and three on 17 December 1952. In fact the Department of Printed Books had been considering adopting a more liberal attitude towards the Private Case collection for many years when on 13 April 1953[41] F. C. Francis (later Sir Frank), one of the Keepers of Printed Books (1948–59), and from 1959–68 Director of the British Museum, suggested that works in the Private Case by important authors should be entered in the General Catalogue but in place of the pressmark, the word 'Reserve' printed. He continued: 'it might further be considered whether such books (i.e. those by 'important authors') should continue to be placed in the P.C.'.

IV · DR E. J. DINGWALL AND C. R. DAWES

Gershon Legman made the second recorded copy of the Private Case catalogue by a non-member of staff (Rose having made the first) in 1954. In

1945 he had also managed to obtain a copy of the 'S.S' Catalogue from H. Thomas, Keeper of Printed Books.[42] Mr Legman knew and was apparently much liked by Dr Eric John Dingwall (1890–1986)[43] (Fig. 22) who joined the British Museum as a Voluntary Assistant on 13 April 1946 and was granted the rank of honorary Assistant Keeper in the Department of Printed Books. Dingwall was more important than anyone else in building up the Private Case collection. Using his own money he purchased much material which he donated to the BM. The first erotic work which he presented was an English translation of *Un Été à la Campagne* (accession stamp dated 14 October 1939). On 13 December 1947 Dr Dingwall donated forty-four erotic books, the majority of which were in German. These included *Meine grausame süsse Reitpeitsche* by Durt Rombach, Pressburg, [c.1904], *Das Flagellantenschloss*, n.p., n.d., by Carlo Antonio [i.e. Konrad Schaumburg], and some extremely valuable typewritten and carbon-copied material produced by German flagellation clubs in 1927. All of these works were placed in the Private Case at P.C.15.a.28, and 29, P.C.15.aa.1–22, and P.C.15.c.3–22, although a number have since been desegregated.

In 1948 Dingwall had bought the Girard Collection of forty-six rare French and English works. This collection was donated in the following year (accession stamps dated 9 April 1949). Forty-four of these were placed in the Private Case soon after and were shelved at P.C.15. Two items were retained by Dingwall and bequeathed to the British Library in 1986. Included in the Girard Collection were such beautifully produced items as *Le Verger des Amours* by Guillaume Apollinaire [*et al.*], Monaco [Paris], 1924, and *Trois Filles de leur Mère* by 'P.L.' [i.e. Pierre Louÿs], *Aux dépens d'un amateur et pour ses amis* [Paris], 1926.

On 6 October 1951 Dingwall donated sixteen erotic, and sexological, works including three pederastic works which he had managed to acquire from the collection of the infamous Reverend Alfred Reginald Thorold Winckley. (Only one of these, *Men and Boys,* is still in the Private Case.) Over the next four years Dingwall donated another twenty-two erotic and sexological works including *Frank und Ich* by Georges Grassal (one of three erotic works donated on 9 February 1952), and *Nini à Lesbos* by Jacques des Linettes, Paris, 1950, donated on 2 October 1953 together with twelve other erotic works.

On Tuesday, 17 November 1953, Dingwall purchased a small bundle of books at Sotheby's.[44] The works, all in French, were from the Bad Reichenhall, and Moriz Boehm collections from Germany. All these works are very rare and all but one are placed in the Private Case. The one item which was not – the first volume of *Le Théâtre gaillard*, Galveston & Co., 1801 – was placed on the market when Dingwall died and is now in the possession of the present author.

22 Dr E. J. Dingwall (on the left) and Dr A. C. Kinsey, 1954 (BL Archives).

Of all the works acquired for the British Museum by Dingwall undoubtedly the most famous, and important, was *Memoirs of a Woman of Pleasure* by John Cleland. Dingwall had purchased two editions through John Carter in 1953[45] and presented them to the British Museum through the Friends of the National Libraries on 29 December 1955 (accession stamps dated 30 December 1955). The first of these two[46] was a copy of what is now generally accepted to be the first edition of this work. The title page reads: MEMOIRS / OF / A / WOMAN / OF / PLEASURE. / [rule] / VOL.I / [rule] / [Device] / [rule] / [rule] / LONDON: Printed for G. FENTON in the Strand/M.DCCXLIX. The second of these two editions is also dated 1749 but is thought to have been published about 1760. Both are of exceptional rarity and historical importance.

During July and August 1954 a great deal of material was placed in the Private Case, mainly at P.C.15. It appears that a large backlog had accumulated over a period of about three years and that the Placer had decided to deal with it *en masse* (*see* Index to Cases and Cups, Appendix A, 12).

A large and important collection of typescript leaflets and periodicals produced by the 'National Society for the Retention of Corporal Punishment in Schools' and the 'Corpun Educational Association' is also placed in the Private Case. All this material was produced by Eric Arthur Wildman of Walthamstow, London. The earliest items appeared in 1948 and arrived at the British Museum under the deposit provisions of the Copyright Act. Wildman was prosecuted in a London Court for publishing obscene libel and destruction orders were made in respect of some of his works. In May 1956 Dingwall discovered that the British Museum had received nothing from Wildman since June 1954. (None of the works had then been placed in the Private Case. Instead they had been shelved at Cup. pressmarks.) He set about acquiring these missing items. Eventually he obtained virtually everything that Wildman ever published and in September 1956 all 165 items were placed in the Private Case. P. J. Kearney, for some reason, did not catalogue in detail this remarkable collection in his work on the Private Case (*see The Private Case. An annotated bibliography* (entry number 1887)) even though two very detailed and complete manuscript lists already existed, both compiled by Dingwall; one in the 'Private Case Shelf index' (*see* Appendix A, no.8) and the other (which is more easily accessible) on index cards, placed with the Wildman Collection which is shelved at P.C.15.i.2a–119.[47]

Another collection acquired by Dingwall and donated to the British Museum was that formerly belonging to a mysterious *amateur* from Munich named H. H. Pinkus. This collection became the property of the British Museum on 31 December 1959. It is smaller than the Girard Collection (only twenty-four works), but is still of importance. It contains mainly late nineteenth-century German works, many of which are now virtually unobtainable. There are also a few English items in the collection such as *Forbidden Fruit,* London [Paris], 1898, and *Gyneocracy*, Paris & Rotterdam, 1883 [c.1899]. This collection is now shelved at P.C.17, and P.C.30.

Dingwall began to build up within the Private Case his own collection of ephemera and reference materials known as P.C.Ref. This included microfilms, bibliographies, publishers' prospectuses and other advertising material, and photograph albums. During the late 1960s and late 1970s the P.C.Ref. pressmark was abolished when the materials were given to the Museum and were then placed either in the Private Case, or elsewhere in the Museum's collections. Thus, for example, the fascinating collection of prospectuses and catalogues was re-pressmarked on 19 November 1962 (but continued to grow until c.1970). It was eventually catalogued fully in February 1976 (P.C.16.m.8). Other P.C.Ref. items can be found at P.C.16.h.3 and P.C.31.m.2.

Dingwall continued to acquire erotica for the British Museum. Among the items which he obtained were *Manuel de Civilité pour les petites filles* by

Pierre Louÿs, Londres [Nice], 1948, with eleven beautifully executed plates [by Peter Schemm], donated on behalf of an anonymous collector on 7 June 1957; *Whipsdom* by Greta X, Paris, 1962, (donated 1 March 1963); the *Pearl Christmas Annual 1881*, Atlanta, 1967, and *Françon Duclos* (an extract from *The 120 Days of Sodom* by de Sade), Los Angeles, 1967, both donated on 17 October 1969.

When Dingwall died his will provided that the British Library should have the choice of what it wanted from his collection. The items chosen (accession dated 31 October 1986) include many erotic works such as *Le Roman de Violette*, Lisbonne, 1870, and *La Philosophie dans le boudoir* as well as many bibliographies of erotica, such as those by Ashbee, Stern-Szana, and an extra annotated copy of the *Registrum Librorum Eroticorum* (*see* Appendix A, no.15). He also encouraged the (Kinsey) Institute for Sex Research of Indiana University, in the mid-1950s, to donate duplicates of erotic works in their collections to the British Museum. The first item which the Institute donated is the *Contes Saugrenus* by Pierre Sylvain Marechal, Paris, 1927 (accession stamp dated 31 May 1956), a reprint of an eighteenth-century erotic 'classic'.

The Obscene Publications Act of 1959 brought great changes, not just for publishers, but for society in general. The Act was followed in 1960 by the trial and eventual acquittal of Penguin Books on a charge of publishing an obscene libel in the form of *Lady Chatterley's Lover* by D. H. Lawrence (first published by Giovanni Orioli at Florence in 1928).

On 7 July 1960 A. H. Chaplin, one of the two Keepers of Printed Books, suggested that 'serious scientific and historical works should be excluded from the P.C. altogether'. In July 1960 a new pressmark – Cup.1000 – was instituted in a response to the new legalised availability of literature, especially novels, dealing openly with sexual matters. Cup.1000 was used for the first time about June 1961. It was to contain '(i) copyright material of the kind normally placed in the Private Case, and (ii) non-copyright books of the same description if it is desirable that entries for them should appear in the General Catalogue'. The books at this pressmark were kept in the Arch Room, in presses alongside the Private Case books. Even though Cup.1000 (and later Cup.1001) books were entered in the General Catalogue readers still had to 'apply to the Principal Keeper in writing, stating their reasons for wishing to see them'. Cup.1000 and 1001 eventually became the home of a large number of fairly innocuous pocket-sized 'girlie magazines', Obelisk Press novels from the 1930s, and some milder works that were transferred from the Private Case. Works by authors such as James Hanley, D. H. Lawrence, and William S. Burroughs were also placed at these pressmarks. But despite transfers to the general library the Private Case still contained about 2,160 books by the end of December 1962.[48]

Fifteen works which the courts had judged obscene and ordered to be destroyed, and had therefore been shelved in the S.S., were on 4 December 1961 transferred to the Private Case. These works included *The Rainbow* by D. H. Lawrence (condemned in 1915), and a few novels by Hank Janson (i.e. Geoffrey Pardoe)[49] which had been prosecuted in Sir David Maxwell-Fyfe's drive against pornography in 1954. Other works transferred from S.S. to P.C. included Potocki of Montalk's *Here lies John Penis,* 1932 and *The Sexual Impulse,* 1935 by Edward Charles [i.e. Charles Edward Hempstead]. The S.S. Collection therefore saved many books from the flames. Books adjudged to be obscene libels from about 1961 onwards were placed in the P.C. as a matter of course. The most famous were the Mayflower Books edition of *Fanny Hill,* London, 1963, *Last Exit to Brooklyn,* London, 1966, and *Oz, number 28,* London, 1970.

In the summer of 1963 in the wake of the Profumo affair, two men, who were friends of Stephen Ward, decided that it would be unwise to retain their collections of erotica any longer. The first was David Mountbatten (1919–70), third Marquess of Milford Haven, who donated the small erotica collection which he had inherited from his father, George Mountbatten (1892–1838) the second Marquess, to the British Museum in May. The second donor, Beecher Moore, an expatriate American, who lived in London, had already suffered the indignity of a police seizure of his collection. He offered the Museum his collection consisting of printed books, typescripts and manuscripts, also small paintings, prints and photographs covering 'every phase of the subject'. The collection was delivered to the Museum on 17 September 1963. The manuscripts were offered to the Department of Manuscripts, who declined them, and these together with the typescripts and illustrated materials were passed to the Sex Research Institute at Bloomington, Indiana, where they were received on 2 July 1964. (The amount of material delivered filled four packing cases and weighed twelve hundredweight.) The photographs were returned to Moore and a set of erotic playing cards was transferred to the British Museum Department of Prints and Drawings. The books were generally of poor quality, many were printed by English-language publishers in Paris in the 1950s such as the Olympia Press, and Patrick Garnot. Most of this collection is placed in the Private Case, at P.C.14.a, e-h, with a few other works at P.C.22, 25, and 30.

Legman also donated P.C. type material in 1963; it consisted of low-calibre French language pornography. His books as well as Moore's and one book from the Milford-Haven donation (*Sins of the cities of the plains,* London and New York [Paris] [*c.*1891]) bear the accession stamp date of 31 January 1964 and are all listed (together with their pressmarks, in a manuscript paste-up catalogue (*see* Appendix A, no.16). This catalogue contains entries for 238 items, 199 of which were shelved in the Private Case.

On 29 June 1965 Dingwall wrote to R. A. Wilson, the Principal Keeper, offering more material for the Private Case from Moore, which he described as 'mainly hard-core duplicated stuff'. Wilson refused the offer, 'because we are the Department of Printed Books and . . . not an institute of sexual research'.

On 17 April 1964 the British Museum received a great bequest of erotica; a bequest which many scholars now consider to be of more importance than the Ashbee erotica collection. The books had been selected by the Museum from the famous collection of Charles Reginald Dawes (1879–1964) author of *Restif de la Bretonne*, 1946, *The Marquis de Sade: His Life and Works*, London, 1927, and the unpublished *A Study of Erotic Literature in England*, Cheltenham, 1943. Most of the erotica from this bequest was placed in the Private Case, at a new pressmark (P.C.13) created especially to house the huge amount of material which arrived from Dawes's home, Willow Cottage, at Gotheringt on in Gloucestershire. A number of other erotic works from the 'Dawes Bequest' (with the odd exception all of his books, bequeathed to the British Museum, bear these two words on a fawn-coloured leather label attached to the front paste-down) have been placed at C.115., and Or. P.C.59.e. Some of the books placed in the Private Case have since been desegregated (for example *Boy* by James Hanley, London, 1931. Today 228 of Dawes books still remain in the Private Case;[50] most of these are bound in brightly coloured morocco or calf to the collector's specification. The Dawes collection included forty works by Alphonse Momus, published under some of his various pseudonyms; he has been described as 'the *pisse-copie* of French turn-of-the-century erotica and flagellantiana'.[51]

Dawes had been in contact with Dingwall since 17 November 1932, when Dawes first wrote to him with a query about the Beggars Benison Society of Anstruther, Fife[52] (*see* Louis C. Jones *The Clubs of the Georgian Rakes* New York, 1942, pp.174–201). Together they made legal arrangements for those items in the collection that the Museum did not possess to be passed to it on Dawes's death. By far the most important work in the Dawes bequest was the very rare *My Secret Life*, Amsterdam, Not for Publication, [*c*.1889] a huge eleven volume work. This autobiography is now considered by many to be one of the most important sociological documents of the nineteenth century. Another important work, a copy of the first edition of *Justine, ou les Malheurs de la vertu* by de Sade, which Dingwall described as the finest copy in existence, did not go to the Museum, but was instead auctioned at Sotheby's (where it raised £240) because the Museum already had a copy (albeit in not such pristine condition). Many of Dawes's other books were also later sold at auction at Sotheby's; these items had been bequeathed to his niece, Mrs Daphne Iles.[53]

[219]

V · INCREASED AVAILABILITY OF THE COLLECTIONS

The British Museum's policy of excluding from the General Catalogue the material in the Private Case came under increasing pressure from the intellectual community in the liberal atmosphere of the early 1960s. The whole question of obscenity and literary freedom was very much in the air and since the review of Alec Craig's *Banned Books of England and other Countries*, London, 1963, in *The Times Literary Supplement* of 4 January 1963, the debate had been continuing. The question of the efficiency of cataloguing in the Department of Printed Books was also debated. Christopher Deakin, compiler of *Catalogi Librorum Eroticorum*, London, 1964, then an undergraduate at Oxford, raised the matter in a letter to the Editor of *The TLS* (issue of 26 April 1963). Deakin's letter was the first in this series of letters to mention the Private Case. He voiced his concern about various aspects of the Museum's system which he thought were 'grossly unsatisfactory'. But his especial criticism was reserved for the 'Museum's practice of suppressing from the [General] Catalogue the call-marks of all books in the "Private Case" of subversive and erotic literature'.[54] In the next issue of *The TLS* two letters were printed in reply to Deakin's. One to counter his complaints, the other to support them. The supportive letter came from Peter Fryer, who gave examples of works in the Private Case which, he claimed, should not be there. He stated that the British Museum's policy was a 'fetter on scholarship and free enquiry'. R. A. Wilson (Principal Keeper of Printed Books) replied to Deakin's general complaints. With regard to the criticisms concerning the suppression of Private Case books Wilson wrote that the labour of transferring P.C. items into the General Catalogue 'would require resources which the Museum does not at present possess'.[55] In the issue of 10 May Deakin volunteered to undertake the job of desegregation himself![56] The last letter with direct reference to the Private Case came from the President (Josephine M. Newcombe) and members of the Oxford University Humanist Group was also complained about the Museum's policy towards its own collections.[57]

Peter Fryer was, like Craig and Haynes before him, in the forefront of the battle to end the secrecy surrounding the Private Case, especially that surrounding the titles and pressmarks. In his book *Private Case, Public Scandal*, published in 1966, he also complained about the difficulty of obtaining access to P.C. books. This book remains the most easily accessible and certainly one of the most entertaining on the subject (although the chapter entitled 'A Short History of the Private Case' needs expansion and correction). Its importance in publicising the collection and in accelerating the process of desuppression and desegregation, cannot be exaggerated including, as it did, details of many sexological works, amongst others, that he believed should

never have been shelved in the Private Case.[58] (Most of them have subsequently been removed.)

In August 1963 the Trustees decided to review the question of restricting
access to pornography and instructed R. A. Wilson to produce a report on the
subject for them. This paper was presented to the Trustees at the Sub-
Committee meeting on 13 May 1964. On 17 November 1964 they decided to
accept his main proposals and to have Private Case books entered in the
General Catalogue.[59] This historic decision was, on 22 December, confirmed
by the Standing Committee of the Trustees who stated that 'books entered in
the Private Case catalogue should, over a period of years, be entered in the
General Catalogue', starting with 'the more important authors already in the
General Catalogue'. One point suggested by the Sub-Committee and agreed
upon by the Standing Committee was that 'it would be undesirable to draw
attention to this change of practice by any public announcement'. The Trustees
also decided that 'no change in the procedure for the issue of such books to
readers was contemplated', although 'the department should, at its discretion,
remove [those] works from the Private Case category [that] no longer merited
so severe a restriction'.[60]

Both Fryer and Deakin underestimated the complexities involved in this
mammoth task. The work was exceedingly difficult and time-consuming.
Moreover it was carried out during a period when the number of copyright
deposits, not counting other accessions, was increasing at a substantial rate
(276,016 items in 1960, 284,820 in 1965, and 291,272 in 1970).[61] Consequently the work took from 1966 until 1983 to complete,[62] although a few
Private Case books have still not been entered in the General Catalogue. While
the titles of some Private Case books were beginning to be entered in the
General Catalogue many hundreds of others were being desegregated. This
process began in earnest in 1965 (although obviously many works had been
removed from the Private Case before this date) and mainly concerned works
of literary or scientific value, milder galante novels, and bibliographies that
were no longer considered to be obscene, or that had been recently published
legally for the first time. (A number of editions of *Lady Chatterley's Lover* were
transferred from the P.C. in November 1960.)[63]

Even in the late 1960s as desegregation and desuppression were proceeding, a written application to consult Private Case books was still required by
the Principal Keeper. The reader concerned had to be the holder of a long-
term readers' pass. The official catalogues of the Private Case were still, in the
majority of cases, withheld from readers because it was traditional and thought
prudent to do so, but primarily because the copies in the possession of the
Placer and of the Principal Keeper were being 'cannibalised' (entries were
being removed as books were either desegregated, or desuppressed) so that

today neither of these two copies contain many entries and their value as bibliographies is severely limited (*see* Appendix A, no.6).

On 28 April 1967[64] the Museum received a donation of certain materials which while definitely pornographic were not in the usual sense of the term 'printed' books. This donation consisted of thirty volumes of what are commonly known as 'Soho-typescripts' (now placed at P.C. 13.h.20–30., and P.C. 14.i. 6–24.). One of these works, *Madwomen* by James Pikes, had been prosecuted on 29 November 1966 at the Tribunal Correctionnel de la Seine, Paris 17[e]. The collection came from Dr Dingwall who had acquired them from a police official in Sussex, who had obtained them after a police raid on a local shop selling pornography.[65] All the books seized should have been destroyed, but these few copies survived. There is nothing literary, or even literate, about them and they are certainly not scientific. They are generally speaking poorly produced xerox copies of typewritten texts on extremely poor quality paper. Some have indecent photographs inserted. They are interesting only as 'a product peculiar to a particular era of the English erotica market.'[66]

A small collection of English- and French-language erotica was received in 1968 (later placed at P.C.26.c.2–15, 17 and 18). These sixteen volumes were donated to the Museum anonymously. All were published between 1898 and 1938 and consist of works related to 'la vice anglais' (flagellation). Examples are *Baby douce fille,* Paris, 1933, and *Petite Dactylo,* Paris, 1933, both by the French novelist Pierre Dumarchey. All the works in this collection bear the same accession stamp date – 30 June 1968. Some Scandinavian pornography published during the 1960s was purchased from 1966 onwards. The books were all typical hedonistic late-1960s poor-quality pornography – such as *Det Skönaste På Jordan* by Bengt Martin, Malmo, 1967, and Stellan Wiks *En Sjöman till sängs,* [Stockholm], 1967. This material is now shelved at P.C.15.df.10–18, and at P.C.27.a.62–65, while two other items are placed at P.C.15.df.20. and P.C.25.a.79.

On 4 January 1968 the *Daily Mirror* published a short article, as part of its 'Inside Page' feature. It was dramatically entitled 'Behind locked doors . . . The bluest room in Britain'. It referred to the Private Case as 'the unholy of unholies' and stated that 'From the controversies that have surrounded these shelves since the 1850s had grown a myth of a pit of iniquity bathed in blue light'. The article was also accompanied by the first photograph ever published of the Private Case, showing seven of the eleven glass-fronted presses that line the alcove in the Arch Room in which the collection was then kept (Fig. 23). This picture, the article stated, 'makes history. It is the first ever taken of the British Museum's Private Case', taken 'with the blessing of the Museum authorities.'[67] The photograph, taken by Tom King, is interesting, as many of the books are clearly visible and it also shows the shelf-layout at the time. The chair and table used by Dingwall are visible in the foreground. This is evidence of the Museum's more liberal policy.

In 1968 the Museum was bequeathed the erotica collection of 'Mr. E.', an Englishman with a penchant for works on corporal punishment. The collection consisted of forty-seven books, seventeen of which were given Private Case pressmarks.[68] The most notable items in the collection are the *J. B. Series* of pamphlets, published at London in 1937, publications by Jean Fort, and some prospectuses for the *Libraries Artistique et Éditions Parisiennes Réunies* of the 1920s.

Starting with a copy of Patsy Southgate's English translation of *L'Image* by Jean de Berg [pseudonym of Alain Robbe-Grillet?] which was donated in June 1971, the Library began receiving many items from Jeffrey Bruce Rund, of New York, a collector, bookseller, and publisher. Most of the material that Rund has donated is what can best be described as 'bizarre' – mainly modern works on bondage, fetishism, and sado-masochistic practices, with some older works as well. All of these books bear Rund's very unusual book plate.

Patrick J. Kearney began work around 1972 on compiling a catalogue of the Private Case collection. This huge undertaking took him seven years to complete in his spare time. The result was the publication, in 1981, of a satisfactory catalogue (*see* Appendix A, no.13) of almost the entire collection as it stood *c.*1972–77. This work remains the only reliable catalogue of the collection, although it does have many major drawbacks.[69] It is complemented by *Smut in the British Library* by Thomas Liebenzell, Hamburg, 1986 (*see* Appendix A, no.14).

In 1973 a collection, numbering fifty-one volumes, of English-language pornography mostly produced in the United States during the late 1960s and early 1970s, by such publishers as Tiburon House, Pendulum Books, and Brandon House, was presented anonymously to the British Library. All these books were date-stamped 30 April 1973 and include such works as *Her Brothers Two,* Sausolito, 1970, by Carl Van Marcus, and *Soldier's Bride* by Winston McElroy, Sausolito, 1969. This gift greatly enhanced the Library's holdings of recently-published erotic material.

From the late 1970s onwards very few books have been placed at Private Case pressmarks. As the climate of opinion concerning this type of literature had changed so dramatically, most erotica and pornography is now placed at such pressmarks as Cup.351–366, and Cup.800–822, which previously were reserved for suggestive novels or works dealing with sexology. Books which were placed in the Private Case in the past had always bordered on, or were definitely, legally impermissible. As large amounts of 'soft-core' pornography are now quite openly available the existence of, and continued use of, the

23 The Presses accommodating the Private Case Collection in the Arch Room (photographed in 1968), with David Rodger, one of the Assistant Keepers of the Department of Printed Books (*Daily Mirror*, 4 January 1968).

Private Case has come to seem rather antiquated and reactionary.

Today only a trickle of material is being assigned to the Private Case; from 1987 to 1989 only 8 items were placed there (*see* Appendix E; nos 7, 13, 17, 31, 35, 36, 37, 40). The eighteen items (mainly U.S. publications of the late 1960s) from the extremely unusual zoöphilia/bestiality collection of D. W. Boydell, donated in February 1989, will by their very nature almost certainly be shelved in the Private Case.

During 1976 and 1977, as a result of complaints by readers, the British Library sought legal advice concerning the procedure whereby written applications were required before Private Case and Cup.1000 and 1001, books were issued to readers. In March 1977[70] this was replaced by a system where the reader used a normal application ticket but also had to fill in a new 'Application for a Private Case Book' form, which states that the reader agrees that any material copied from a Private Case book 'will not be reproduced without written permission from the British Library Board'.[71] This form had to be countersigned by either the Head of Public Services, his deputy, or a Keeper, or Assistant Keeper. This countersigning policy ceased in February 1981.[72] Today any reader who wishes to apply for a Private Case book can therefore do so by simply filling in two forms. Such books must, however, be consulted on the front table of the North Library.

The Private Case books, together with those at Cup.1000 and 1001, were moved from the Arch Room to a security pen in the main bookstacks on 7 November 1984.[73] These new surroundings are aesthetically much-less attractive but are far more secure. The books are now housed in a specially constructed sheet-steel covered cage as opposed to Victorian wood-lined glass-fronted cases; security is a much more important issue here than aesthetics. On 22 March 1986 the security pen where the P.C. books are housed was penetrated by rainwater. Unfortunately 121 P.C. books, and eighteen from Cup.1000 and 1001, were affected by water but they were soon dried out and repaired by the British Library's preservation team. None of these books suffered any serious permanent damage.[74]

Today 2,143 works remain in the Private Case. Kearney's bibliography lists 1,939 items;[75] 883 books have been desegregated, and 79 works have been 'mislaid'.[76] This indicates that at one time, or another, 3,105 books were considered by the British Museum to be so shocking or so harmful that their very titles were suppressed from the public (in some cases since the 1840s). A dubious honour of sorts, but one that reflected the various mores of the times.

The Private Case constitutes the greatest collection of its kind in existence in the world. Only the *Enfer* of the Bibliothèque Nationale, in Paris, comes close. Yet this contains only about 1,500 works (of which 108 are in English),[77] and these cannot rival the diversity of the material in the Private Case – from the important works of authors such as Chorier, Andréa de Nerciat, Apollinaire, Mirabeau, Aretino, Baffo, and Piron, to 1960s contact magazines, from the crudest of Soho-type productions and Olympia Press novels to American cartoon fetishist magazines of the 1950s, as well as the beautiful *Venus wagen* series published at Berlin, and such historically important works as *L'École des Filles, An Essay on Woman, Memoirs of a Woman of Pleasure, Sodom*, and works from the collections of such notable persons as King George III, William H. Crawford, Michael Sadleir, Montague Shearman, Edward Vernon Utterson and William Alfred Eddy (*see* Liebenzell, Appendix A, item 14). The Private Case is a truly great collection. Scholars owe a debt of gratitude to those like Dingwall who considered that such works have played an important part in the history of European culture, and should be preserved for posterity as part of the collections of the national library.

NOTES

1   Fryer, Peter, *Private Case Public Scandal*, 1966, pp.40–1.
2   Ibid., pp.41–2.
3   Legman, Gershon, Introduction to *The Private Case* by Patrick J. Kearney (*see* Appendix A, no.13) p.20.
4   Ibid.
5   Invoices for purchases of books in the BL Archives: DH 5/1–.
6   *See* Appendix C, no.78.
7   Information from P. R. Harris.
8   As shown by the title slips, fourth copies and accession dates.
9   'Catalogue of Books in Private Case' (*see* Appendix A, no.5).
10 Ibid.
11 Ibid.
12 Transcribed fourth copies. (As printed fourth Copies were introduced with the printing of GK I, 1880–1905, manuscript fourth copies were phased out. Final figures indicate that there were at least 498 items in the P.C. during this period.)
13 Reports to Trustees, 1890 BL Archives DH 2/44.
14 Ibid.
15 Ibid.
16 For example *Kama-Shastra* (n.p., n.d.), Or.P.C.59.e.12, and *Les Kama Sutra*, Paris, 1885, Or.P.C.59.e.22.
17 Reports to Trustees, 1900, BL archives DH 2/64.
18 Ibid.
19 Report to Trustees, 1914. BL Archives DH 2/78.
20 Reports to Trustees, 1900. BL Archives DH 2/64.
21 Liebenzell, Thomas, *Smut in the British Library*, 1986.
22 As shown by the title slips.
23 Ibid.
24 G. Legman's introduction to P. J. Kearney *The Private Case*, p.29.
25 *Catalogue des Tableaux, Livres, Dessins composant le Cabinet de M. L.C.*, 1876. BL Pressmark: 11899.cc.24.
26 Dingwall, E. J., Private Case shelf catalogue (Appendix A, no.8).
27 'Missing board' on shelf.
28 Hankey was well-known for his love of unusual and fetishistic bindings (information from J. L. Moule). In a letter in the BL Archives, E. J. Dingwall refers to the destruction of the erotic sale catalogues.
29 Theory by the present author that the move took place between 1890 and 1920. The most obvious date for this is the arrival of the large quantity of Ashbee material.
30 *The English Review*, vol.16, December 1913, p.123.
31 Earliest pressmarking appears to have occurred around 1914. For example *Letters to my father* by Lord Alfred Douglas, London, 1914. SS.A. 34.
32 *The English Review*, vol.16, p.134.
33 Transfer boards.
34 Reports to Trustees, 1920. BL Archives DH 2/85.
35 Ibid.
36 *The Times Literary Supplement*, no. 1872, 18 December 1937, p.968.
37 P.C.15.a.11., P.C.15.a.14., P.C.15.a.13., P.C.15.a.12., P.C.15.a.15., P.C.27.b.20., P.C.31.f.18.

38   'Catalogue of Private Case Books' (*see* Appendix A, no.6).

39   Craig, Alec, *The Banned Books of England*, London, 1937, p.166.

40   P.C.27.a.35. *(Ashley 4395*), P.C.30.l.3. (Ashley 4464), P.C.17.a.16. (Ashley 2008).

41   BL Archives C.R. *File.

42   S.S. Catalogue. Dingwall bequest (Harry Price Library, London University Library) D.F.154.

43   Dingwall-Legman correspondence (*see* Appendix A, no.3) and Dingwall bequest (Harry Price Library). File C.A.

44   Sotheby's & Co. (London). Monday, 17 November 1953 Lot 243 (Lots 232–252 are all either erotic or galante works).

45   Fanny Hill File. Dingwall bequest (Harry Price Library) A.Z.

46   P.C.27.a.44.

47   Kearney lists this Pressmark as P.C.15.i.3. – 119. There is a third version of the list in the University of London Library (Harry Price collection).

48   'Index to Cases and Cups.363–367, 801–804' (*see* Appendix A, no.12).

49   It was proved at the trial of Stephen Daniel Francis, the supposed author of the Hank Janson novels, that he was not in fact the person who had written them (*The Times*, 12 February 1954). They were written by various persons. It has since been discovered that the works prosecuted were by Geoffrey Pardoe.

50   Liebenzell, Thomas, *Smut in the British Library*, p.xxxvii-xxxviii.

51   Legman, Gershon, introduction to P. J. Kearney, *The Private Case*, p.41.

52   Dingwall bequest (Harry Price Library) J.33–36.

53   Sotheby's & Co. (London). Monday, 12 April 1965 (Lots 1–59), Monday, 23 January 1967 (Lots 242–314), and Monday, 18 April 1988 (Lots 659, 706, 724).

54   *The Times Literary Supplement*, 26 April 1963, No.3,191, p.295.

55   *TLS* 3 May 1963, no.3,192, p.323.

56   *TLS* 10 May 1963, No.3,193, p.341.

57   *TLS* 17 May 1963, No.3,194, p.357. (Other letters and articles in the *TLS* refering to the obscenity/literary freedom debate can be found in the issues of 4 January, 15 February, 22 February, 29 March, 5 April, 12 April, 17 May, 31 May, and 14 June 1963. There were also letters concerning the Private Case in the *TLS* of 14 October, 21 October, 4 November 1965, and 27 January 1966 and in the *New Statesman* of 30 April, 5 May, and 15 October 1965.)

58   Fryer, Peter, Op.cit., pp.57–69. *See also Encounter* vol.xxvii, no.4, October 1966, pp.68–77.

59   Reports to Trustees, 1964. BL Archives DH 2/129.

60   Ibid.

61   *Department of Printed Books: Statistical Report* 1960, 1965, and 1970.

62   *A Directory of rare book and special collections in the UK and the Republic of Ireland*, edited by Moelwyn I. Williams, London, 1985, pp.119–20. (Note: the article on the Private Case should be treated with caution.)

63   'Index to cases and Cups.363–367, 801–804' (*see* Appendix A, no.12).

64   Receipts of works donated by Dr E. J. Dingwall.

65   Information from J. L. Wood.

66   Kearney, Patrick J., Op.cit., p.67.

67   Article by D. Miller. Dingwall bequest (Harry Price Library), C.O. 185.

68   'E' collection: *A Man and 3 Maids*, P.C.25.a.74.; *Dolly Morton*, P.C.25.a.82.; *Dorothy*, P.C.27.a.70.; *Droits du Seigneurs*, P.C.31.d.41.; *En Russie Rouge*, P.C.31.d.38.; *Fêtes barbares*, P.C.31.d.43.; *Fouetteurs et Fouettes*, P.C.31.d.40.; *J.B. Series*, P.C.27.a.57.; *Lovely*

Lisette, P.C.25.a.80.; *Love's Enyclopaedia*, P.C.27.a.56.; *Margot the birching beauty*, P.C.31.d.42.; *Nuits de Messaline*, P.C.31.d.39.; *Painful pleasures*, P.C.15.df.9.; *Petite Dactylo*, P.C.20.b.30.; *Princesses de Cythère*, P.C.25.a.73.; *Prospectuses*, P.C.27.a.55.; *Straps*, P.C.25.a.76.

69　Edwards, A. S. G., 'The Private Case laid bare?', *The Book Collector*, London, Winter 1983, pp.439–48.

70　D. W. G. Clements, Minute to 'All Keepers & Deputy Keepers' 16 March 1977.

71　Ibid.

72　K. L. Gibson, BL Reference Division, Staff notice 2/81, February 1981.

73　Information from R. S. McFarlane.

74　Information from R. W. Hill.

75　In the Kearney catalogue are 1920 entries, of which 6 are empty entries (numbers missed out, etc) = 1914, plus 25 items at entry 463 = 1939 works.

76　Cross, Paul J. and Brown, Paul. 'Shelf check of Private Case', January 1989. Copy with North Library issue desk.

77　Cross, Paul J. *English-Language Erotica. A List, in press-mark order, of English Language books in the ENFER erotica collection at the Bibliothèque Nationale* (London, 1988). Copies deposited with the BL, the Bodleian Library and the Cambridge University Library.

APPENDICES

A   A BIBLIOGRAPHY OF IMPORTANT MATERIALS RELATING TO THE
PRIVATE CASE COLLECTION

1   FRAXI (Pisanus), *pseud.* [i.e. Henry Spencer Ashbee] *Index Librorum Prohibi-torum: being notes bio-biblio-icono-graphical, and critical, on curious and uncommon books.* (London; privately printed, 1877). 4°., pp. lxxvi. 542.
Two copies in the Private Case:
          (1) P.C. 14.de.3.
          (2) P.C. 18.b.9.
The first copy is Ashbee's own annotated copy (*see The Private Case* by P. J. Kearney, entry no.148). This copy was formerly kept in the Principal Keeper's office. Another uncatalogued copy is with the staff of the Reading Room Information Service; it is unstamped and has been rebound.

2   *Centuria Librorum Absconditorum.*
(London: privately printed, 1879). 4°., pp. ×. 593.
Two copies in the Private Case:
          (1) P.C. 14.de.4
          (2) P.C. 18.b.9*.
First copy is as copy 1) of *Index Librorum Prohibitorum* (*see* Kearney, op.cit., entry no.150). An uncatalogued copy is with the staff of the Reading Room Enquiry Service. It is unstamped and has been rebound.

3   *Catena Librorum Tacendorum.*
(London: Privately Printed, 1885). 4°., pp. lvii, 596. One copy in Private Case at P.C. 18.b.9**. Another copy is with the Reading Room Enquiry Service; it is uncatalogued and bears an accession stamp dated 10 November 1900 and includes the prospectus for it together with several communications between Dr E. J. Dingwall and Mr G. Legman, concerning the Private Case. These were written between 1953 and 1959.

4   'Books belonging to Ashbee. Books known to have belonged to H. Ashbee and placed in the Private Case or a cupboard' (Typescript, *c.*1970). 4°. ff. 6. Typed on the rectos only. Compiled by Mr J. L. Wood. This work is far from complete but is still of some use. A copy is kept with the Reading Room Enquiry Service.

5   'CATALOGUE of Books in Private Case', fol., ff.52. Guard volume, containing 78 main entries, which was formerly kept in the Principal Keeper's office. The entry slips are carbon copies of manuscript catalogue entries. This catalogue contains a complete list of the contents of the Private Case when the collection was housed in the Keeper's office (i.e. *c.*1841–1864). It is at present in the British Library archives but is unnumbered (*see* Appendix B).

[229]

6 'CATALOGUE of Private Case books', two volumes (Vol.1: A–L, Vol.2: M–Z), fol., ff.100,100. There are three copies of this catalogue (collation is the same for all three):

'Copy A' (Principal Keeper's copy; kept in his office): manuscript notes by J. L. Wood and R. S. Pine-Coffin. Most entries were removed during desegregation/desuppression, 1966–83. A note states that in August 1933 this catalogue contained 793 cross-references and 1,360 main-title entries. 'Copy B' (Placer's copy, kept in Placer's office): manuscript notes by H. G. Whitehead, P. A. H. Brown, and R. S. Pine-Coffin. Again most entries have been removed.

'Copy C' (Ante-Room Copy, kept in strong room in Ante-Room basement): complete up to c.1939. No entries have been removed from this copy. Volume one contains 1,053 entries, and volume two 2,948 entries, i.e. a total of 4,001 entries (inclusive of cross-reference).

Copies A, B, and C all bear a type-written note by P. R. Harris giving brief details of their history and use. They are now kept in the Placer's Archives.

7 DAWES (Charles Reginald) 'Catalogue of the Erotica Collection of C. R. Dawes', fol. pp.498. Xerox copy of Dawes's own manuscript. Second of two volumes (volume one listing Dawes's non-erotic collection). Kept by the Reading Room Enquiry Service.

8 DINGWALL (Eric John) Private Case shelf catalogue. Manuscript in oblong 4° loose-leaf binder originally compiled 1951 to 8 August 1953, with more recent acquisitions added later. This index contains an abundance of very useful information, specially relating to donors of, and illustrations in, Private Case books.

9 Cup.1000/1001 shelf index. Manuscript in oblong 4° loose-leaf binder. Compiled c.1961 onwards.

Items 8 and 9 are uncatalogued and unstamped. They are kept in the security pen with P.C. and Cup.1000, and Cup.1001 books.

10 EROTICA File. 'East-light' box file containing prospectuses, xerox copies of bibliographies, letters from members of the public concerning erotica, reviews of books, lists of illustrators and pseudonyms, and other such material. Kept with the Reading Room Enquiry service.

11 FOURTH Copy Cards, for books placed at Private Case and Cup.1000, and Cup.1001 pressmarks. These are filed in press-mark order and kept in the Title Room. (Discontinued c.1976).

12 INDEX to Cases and Cups.363–367, 801–804. Fol. Alphabetically indexed. This is a complete catalogue of books placed at Case, Cup., and P.C. pressmarks from 15 November 1947 to 31 December 1962. Between 153 and 159 items were placed in the Private Case during this period.

From 1963 to 1977 a complete record of works placed at these pressmarks was recorded on 5″ × 3″ cards. Both versions of this index are stored in the Placer's Archive.

13 KEARNEY (Patrick John) *The Private Case. An Annotated Bibliography of the*

introduction by G. Legman. (London, Jay Landesman Limited, 1981.) 4°. pp.354. Two copies in the British Library:

> (1) P.C. 30.1.19
> (2) N.L. 4.c.

14   LIEBENZELL (Thomas) *Smut in the British Library. Index zu Kearneys Private Case.* (Hamburg, C. Bell Verlag, 1986.), 4°. pp.88. A very useful work (but one which must be used with caution) containing lists of authors, titles, collectors (donors), publishers, and languages of works in Patrick Kearney's P.C. catalogue. Two copies in the British Library:

> (1) N.L. 4.c.
> (2) 2725.g.1065.

15   READE (Rolf S.) *pseud* [i.e. Alfred Rose] *Registrum Librorum Eroticorum vel (sub hac specie) dubiorum: opus bibliographicum et praecipue bibliothecariis destinatum.* (London, Privately printed for subscribers, 1936.) 4°. Two volumes; pp.xi.398 (continuous pagination). Limited edition of 150 numbered copies. Two copies in the British Library:

> (1) Cup.504.g.18.

> (2) An interleaved copy, with annotations and additions by Dr E. J. Dingwall. Bequeathed by him to the B.L. in October 1986; Cup.504.f.17. (Pressmarked 21 March 1989).

16   [THIRTIETH January 1964 Catalogue.] Large 4°. manuscript catalogue of B. Moore, G. Legman, and Milford Haven (1 book) donations. All items were stamped 30 January 1964. 238 items in total, 199 placed in the P.C. A note by the present writer has been inserted into this catalogue. Kept in the British Library Archives (unnumbered).

17   TITLE-Slips of authors/anonymous works placed in the Private Case. Filed alphabetically, and interfiled with title-slips for non-obscene works. These were formerly kept in separate boxes. In August 1988 the present writer discovered approximately 300 title slips of P.C. items in the B.L. Archives, still awaiting inter-filing. Title slips are kept in the Title Room.

B   A SHORT-TITLE LIST OF BOOKS IN THE PRIVATE CASE
FROM *c.* 1841–*c.*1864

Taken from the earliest surviving version of the Private Case catalogue, to which has been added dates of cataloguing, where known. Listed under original catalogue headings

ANTONIA
1   *The Crafty Whore* 1658.
2   [Another copy.]
AROUET DE VOLTAIRE (François Marie)

3   *La Pucelle, or the Maid of Orleans.* 1785–6.
4   *La Pucelle, or the Maid of Orleans.* 1796–7.
5   AUSTRIAN
    L'Autrichienne en goguettes. 1789.
6   AUVERGNE (Martial d')
    Aresta amorum LII. 1566.
    Catalogued (cat'd) October 1852.
7   BARTHOLD (Friedrich Wilhelm)
    Die geschichtlichen Persönlichkeiten. 1846.
8   BOUVIER (J. B.) *Bishop of Mans*
    Dissertatio in sextum Decalogi. 1843.
9   BUNYAN (John)
    A Few Sighs from Hell. 1658.
    CASANOVA DI SEINGALT (Giacomo Girolamo)
10 *Memoirs.* 1826–38.
    Cat'd January 1845.
11 *Memoires.* 1843.
12 CASSANDRA, *pseud.*
    A Letter to the Bishop of London. [1781?]
    Cat'd September 1853.
13 CEREMONIES
    Matrimonial Ceremonies display'd. 1748.
14 CHARLOT
    Les Amours de Charlot et Toinette. 1789.
15 CIBBER (Colley)
    A Letter from Mr Cibber to Mr Pope [1742?]
    Re-cat'd, no information.
16 CLITORIDES (Philogynes)
    The Natural History of the Frutex Vulvaria. 1741.
17 COLLECTION
    C'est ce qui manquoit à la collection. 1789.
18 CUCKOLD
    The Cuckold's Chronicle. 1793.
    Cat'd April 1852.
    CULVERWELL (Robert James)
19 *Lecture to Young Men on Chastity* [1847?]
20 *On Single and Married life* [1847?]
21 *Porneiapathology* [1855.]
22 *The Solitarian* 1849.
23 CURLL (Edmund)
    Curlicism display'd. 1718.
    Formerly at another press-mark.
24 DEMAUNDES
    Delectable demaundes. [1566.]
    Re-cat'd, no information.

25 DIDEROT (Denis)
La Religieuse. [1797.]

26 DU MOULIN (Antoine)
La Deploration de Venus. 1561.
Cat'd October 1852.

27 FAMIN (Cesar)
Musée Royal de Naples. Peintures, bronzes, et statues érotiques. 1857.

28 FERRAND (Antoine)
Pièces libres. 1760.
Cat'd October 1852.

29 FIEDLER (Franz)
Antike erotische Bildwerke. 1839.
Cat'd November 1842.

30 FITZROY (Augustus Henry), *Duke of Grafton*
Intrigues à-la-mode. 1811.
Cat'd September 1853.

31 FRANK (Edward)
Barefaced Adultery. 1825.
Cat'd September 1853.

32 GARLAND
Ane Pleasant Garland of sweet scented flowers. 1835.
Cat'd 18 February 1858.

33 GODMICHÉ
Le Godmiché royal. 1789.

34 GRAHAM (James), *MD.*
The Guardian Goddess of Health [1785?]
Cat'd May 1846.

35 GREECE
Un point curieux des moeurs privées de la Grèce. 1861.

36 HACKABOUT (Moll)
The Harlot's Progress. 1740.
Cat'd April 1856.
HAMILTON (Thomas)

37 *Select Poems on several occasions.* 1824.
Cat'd January 1844.

38 [Another copy.]

39 JOHNSON (Abraham), *pseud.* [i.e. Sir John Hill, MD].
Lucina sine Concubitu. 1750.

40 JOLYOT DE CRÉBILLON (Claude Prosper)
The Sopha. 1801.
Cat'd December 1849.

41 L***, M. C**** de
Dangerous Connections. 1784.

42   LA FONTAINE (Jean de)
     Contes et nouvelles en vers. 1762.
     Re-cat'd, no information.
43   LE GRAND (Marc Antoine)
     Le Luxurieux. 1760.
44   LEWIS (Matthew Gregory)
     The Monk. [1820?]
45   LUCIAN, *Redivivus*
     Paradise Lost. 1838.
     Cat'd May 1841.
46   MANNINGHAM (Sir Richard)
     An Extract see Sharp, J. *The English Rogue.* 1776.
     MOODIE (John)
47   *A Medical Treatise.* 1848.
48   [Another copy.]
49   MOORE (A.)
     The Annals of Gallantry. 1814.
50   PALACE MISCELLANY.
     The Palace Miscellany. 1733.
     Cat'd November 1850.
51   PENANCOËT DE KÉROUAILLE (Louise Renée de)
     The Duchess of Portsmouth's Garland. 1837.
     PERIODICAL PUBLICATIONS. – London
52   *Harris's List of Covent Garden Ladies.* 1788–90, 93.
53   *The Night Walker.* 1696.
     Cat'd April 1856.
54   *The Rambler's Magazine.* 1824–25.
55   PHARMACOPOLA
     Nobilis Pharmacopola Historia, si non vera, etc. 1693.
     Cat'd December 1850.
     PHEUQUEWELL (Roger) *pseud.* [i.e. Thomas Stretzer?]
56   *A New Description of Merryland.* 1741.
     Formerly at another press-mark.
57   *Merryland display'd.* 1741.
     Re-cat'd, no information.
58   PHILO-BRITANNIAE, *pseud.*
     The Potent Ally. 1741.
     Formerly at another press-mark.
59   PHILO-PUTTANUS, *pseud.*
     The Whores Rhetorick. 1683.
     Cat'd July 1853.
60   POPE (Alexander)
     Eloisa in dishabille. 1822.
     Cat'd April 1856.

61 RAKE
The Rake's Progress. 1753.
Cat'd April 1856.

62 RELATION
Relation curieuse de différens pays. 1741.
Formerly at another press-mark.

63 RELIGION
Physical, Sexual and Natural Religion. 1855.

64 ROE (Richard)
A Letter to Dr Abraham Johnson. 1750.
Formerly at another press-mark.

65 ROWE (Nicholas)
The Story of Pandora, see Philo-Britanniae, *pseud., The Potent Ally.* 1741.

66 SAETTLER (Joannes Caspar)
Joannis Caspari Saettler in sextum decalogi praeceptum. 1840.
Cat'd February 1845.

67 SAPHO, *Mademoiselle*
Anandria. 1789.

68 SHARP (Jeremy)
The English Rogue. 1776.

69 STRONG-COCK (Paddy), *pseud.*
Teague–root display'd. 1746.

70 THÉOPHILE [De Viau], *Sieur.*
Le Parnasse satyrique du Sieur Théophile. 1660.
Cat'd September 1852.

71 TOUCHET (Mervin) *Earl of Castlehaven.*
The Case of Sodomy. 1708.
Formerly at another press-mark.

72 TRAITÉ.
Traicté de la dissolution du mariage. 1851.
Cat'd October 1848.

73 TRIPON (J. B.)
Historique monumental. 1837.
Cat'd June 1841.

74 V***, *Monsieur de*
La Pucelle d'Orleans. 1755.

75 VESTINA (Hebe) *pseud.*
Il convito amoroso! 1782.

76 WHET-STONE
The Whet-Stone or the Spawn of Puzzle. 1745.
Cat'd January 1846.

77 *The Edge taken off.* 1745.
Cat'd January 1846.

78 WILSON (Harriet)
Memoirs. 1825
Cat'd September 1864.

C   A SUMMARISED HISTORY OF THE PRIVATE CASE PRESS-MARK

Private Case	Used *c*.1841 to *c*.1864 when books were stored in a cupboard in the Principal Keeper's office.
Private Case. 20.a.	Usually items from the above period with press-number and shelf-letter added after transferral to new location around 1864.
Priv.C. 20.a. Priv. Case. 20.a. P.C. 20.a.	Items placed in the Private Case after 1864.
P.C. 20.a.1.	The above with a third-mark added to pressmarks from 1875 to 1911.

D   DATES OF PLACING AT P.C. PRESSMARKS

Pressmark	Accession Stamp Date	Date of Cataloguing
P.C.13.a.1.	13 June 1964	Sept. 1965[1]
P.C.13.b.1.	13 June 1964	Sept. 1965[2]
P.C.14.a.1.	30 Jan. 1964	(No information)

(Shelves P.C.14.b; and c were never used. Work at P.C.14.d.1. was transferred from the S.S. on 20 Nov. 1964).

P.C.15.a.1.	8 Jan. 1938	Feb. 1938
P.C.15.b.1.	12 April 1947	(No information)
P.C.16.a.1.		

(Book at P.C.16.a.1. was on loan. It was returned to its owner on 13 May 1965. Shelves b, c, and d were kept clear in anticipation of other material being loaned to the P.C.; these shelves were never used. The next item at this pressmark is P.C.16.e.1.; accession date, 1865.)

P.C.17.a.1.	7 April 1875	(No information[3])
P.C.17.b.1.	24 April 1879	(No information)
P.C.18.a.1.	10 Oct. 1871	(No information)
P.C.18.b.1.	(Formerly at Private Case.20.b.)	June 1868
P.C.19.a.1.	2 May 1876	May 1876
P.C.19.b.1.	7 June 1866	(No information)
P.C.20.a.1.	29 July 1909	May 1910
P.C.20.b.1–3.	(No information)	Oct. 1875
P.C.21.a.1.	5 May 1845	April 1846
P.C.21.b.1.	No information	Nov. 1842
P.C.22.a.1.	10 Nov. 1900	April 1906
P.C.22.b.1.	(No information)	April 1849
P.C.23.a.1.	(No information)	Sept. 1875
P.C.23.b.1.	7 Dec. 1871	March 1872

P.C.24.a.1.	23 July 1873	Nov. 1873
P.C.24.b.1.	10 May 1882	(No information)
P.C.25.a.1.	8 Nov. 1882	Jan. 1883
P.C.25.b.1.	(No information)	(No information)
P.C.26.a.1.	10 April 1884	Oct. 1884
P.C.26.b.1.	10 Sept. 1892	(No information)
P.C.27.a.1.	3 Nov. 1885	(No information)
P.C.27.b.1.	(No information)	(No information)
P.C.28.a.1.	(Formerly at P.C.29.a.14.)	(No information)
P.C.28.b.1.	31 May 1889	(No information)
P.C.29.a.1.	3 March 1891	(No information)
P.C.29.b.1.	(No information)	(No information)
P.C.30.a.1.	10 Nov. 1900	Dec. 1913
P.C.30.b.1.	(No information)	(No information)
P.C.31.a.1.	10 Nov. 1900	Dec. 1913
P.C.31.b.1.	10 Nov. 1900	Dec. 1913
P.C.32.a.1.	(created 2 Aug. 1989)	
Or.P.C.59.e.1.	(used c.1892 onwards)	
Cup.1000.a.1.	30 May 1961	(No information)
Cup.1001.a.1.	(Book formerly in P.C.)	(No information)

Both Cup.1000, and Cup.1001 pressmarks were first used in 1961.

1 Placed at pressmark on 6 October 1965.
2 Placed at pressmark on 29 October 1964.
3 Since replaced by another work with an accession date of 14 April 1891 (which was formerly at another pressmark). It was catalogued in November 1891.

E A SHORT-TITLE LIST OF WORKS WHICH ARE IN THE PRIVATE CASE
BUT WHICH ARE NOT INCLUDED IN P. J. KEARNEY'S
THE PRIVATE CASE

1 ANDRÉA DE NERCIAT (André Robert) *The Devil in the Flesh.* 1970.
P.C.24.a.37.
2 APOLLINAIRE (Guillaume) *Les Exploits d'un jeune Don Juan.* 1949.
P.C.32.a.11.
3   *The Debauched Hospodar.* 1969. P.C.24.a.36.
4 [BARRIN (Jean)] *Venus in the Cloister, or the Nun in her smock.* 1725.
P.C.25.a.93.
5 BARTH (Caspar von) *Incogniti Scriptoris Nova Poemata.* 1634. P.C.30.k.34.
6   [Another edition. A facsimile of the 1624 edition.] 1972. P.C.30.k.33.
7 [BELOT (Adolphe)] *L'Éducation d'une demi-vierge.* 1903. P.C.30.k.35.

8 [CLELAND (John)] *Memoirs of F**** H****. 1779.   P.C.24.a.43.

9 DART. *Dart*, no.1, *etc.* [1974– .]   P.C.30.l.16.

10 DRIALYS, *Lord, pseud. Les Belles flagellantes de New-York*. 1907. P.C.32.a.7.

11 FARREL (Joseph) *Parfums de souffrance. Painful Flavours*. 1978. P.C.31.m.3.

12 FLOGGER (A. W.) *Poker de dames*. 1929.   P.C.32.a.9.

13 FURRYA (Sophia) *Les Geôles de dentelles*. [c.1960.] P.C.32.a.6.

14 GERVAISE DE LATOUCHE (Jacques Charles) *Dom B., the lascivious monk*. 1970.   P.C.24.a.41.

15 GRAND. *Grand Théâtre des petites passions de société*. [c.1840?] P.C.31.m.6.

16 HERVEZ (Jean) *pseud.* [i.e. Raoul Vèze.] *La Régence galante*. 1909. P.C.32.a.8.

17 HISTOIRE. *Histoire d'O: No. 2*. 1988.   P.C.30.l.20.

18 HORN BOOK. *The Horn Book*. 1899.   P.C.24.a.39.

19 IBELS (André) *La Bourgeoise pervertie*. 1930. P.C.32.a.10.

20 JANSON (Hank) *pseud.* [i.e. Geoffrey Pardoe.] *Auctioned*. 1952. P.C.21.aa.9.

21 JAVELIN. *Javelin*. [1977– .]   P.C.30.l.17.

22 KEARNEY (Patrick John) *The Private Case*. 1981. P.C.30.l.19.

23 LENGEL (Frances) *pseud.* [i.e. Alexander Trocchi.] *The Carnel Days of Helen Seferis*. 1954. [Soho-type forgery. Printed c.1959.] P.C.31.d.47.

24 LUSTFUL TURK. *The Lustful Turk*. 1967. P.C.24.a.42.

25 MASQUE. *Masque*. no.1, 2, 4. [c.1958.] P.C.18.b.48.

26 MELTZER (David) *The Martyr*. [1969.] P.C.24.a.40.

27 [PHOTOGRAPH ALBUMS.]   P.C.31.m.2.

28 PICHARD (Georges) *Marie-Gabrielle de Saint-Eutrope*. 1978. P.C.31.m.4.

29 PIETRO, *Aretino. Genuine and Remarkable Amours of the celebrated author Peter Aretin*. MDCCLXCVI [*sic*, not before 1799.] P.C.25.a.94.

30 PORNOGRAFI. *Pornografi* [af] Karen Borgnakke [and others]. 1974.   P.C.15.d.19.

31 RÉAGE (Pauline) *pseud.* [i.e. Anne Declos.] *Histoire d'O*. 1954. P.C.25.b.25.

32   *Story of O*. 1978.   P.C.30.l.18.

33   *Retour à Roissy*. 1969.   P.C.28.b.36.

34 ROBINSON (Julian) *pseud. Confessions of Georgina*. 1968. P.C.24.a.38.

35 SADE (Donatien Alphonse François) *Marquis de. Histoire de Juliette*. 6 vol. 1797 [c.1860].   P.C.30.k.36.

36   *Histoire de Justine*. 4 vol. 1797 [c.1860]. P.C.30.k.37.

37   *Les 120 Journées de Sodome*. 3 vol. 1931–5. [With a fourth volume of plates.]   P.C.30.l.21.

38 SOURCES. *Sources de plaisir*. [c.1830?] P.C.31.m.5.

39 SUBMISSION. *Submission . . . Plus . . . bizarre and unusual drawings by 'Taco'*. [1958.]   P.C.19.a.43.

40 VIENNA.-*Institut für Sexualforschung in Wien. Bilder-Lexikon*. [Edited by Leo [Vol. 1–3 only; lacking vol.4.] P.C.15.l.15.

F   A SHORT-TITLE LIST OF WORKS IN THE ORIENTAL COLLECTIONS PRIVATE CASE (Or.59.3.)

1   'ABD AL ḤAKK, *Efendi. Le Livre de volupté.* Erzeroum [Brussels, 1879.]
Or.59.e.36.

2   [Another copy.]   Or.59.e.36*.

3   AL-SUYŪTĪ, (Jalāl al-Dīn 'Abd al-Rahmān ibn Abi Bakr) *Marriage – Love and Women amongst the Arabs.* Paris, 1896.   Or.59.e.42.

4   BĀHNĀME. *Bāhnāme.* [A work on sexual intercourse.] n.p., n.d.   Or.59.e.8.

5   FENG-YÜEH CHU-JEN, *pseud. Feng-liu te-i t'u.* [Erotic illustrations with poetic captions.]   n.p. [c.1840?]   Or.59.e.9.

6   FLEUR. *La Fleur lascive orientale.* Oxford [Brussels?], 1882.   Or.59.e.39.

7   *Oriental Stories.* [Translated from the French version entitled 'La Fleur lascive orientale'. The English translator's preface signed: Neaniskos, pseud. of Leonard C. Smithers.] Athens, 1893.   Or.59.e.40.

8   GULIK (Robert Hans van) *Sexual Life in Ancient China.* Leiden, 1961.
Or.59.e.34.

9   IBN KAMĀL PĀSHĀ, (Aḥmad ibn Sulaimān) called Kamāl-Pāshā-Zādah *The Old Man Young again.* Paris, 1898–9.   Or.59.e.38.

10   JIN PING MEI *The Arcanum of the Golden Lotus.* n.p., n.d.   Or.59.e.50.

11   KALȲNA-MALLA Ananga-ranga . . . translated . . . by A. F. F. and B. F. R. [F. F. Arbuthnot and Sir Richard Burton.] Reprint. Cosmopoli, 1885.   Or.59.e.1.

12   [Another copy.]   Or.59.e.1*.

13   [Another issue. This differs typographically from the one at Or.59.e.1.] Cosmopoli, 1885.   Or.59.e.14.

14   [Another copy.]   Or.59.e.15.

15   *Ananga-ranga . . . Traduit sur la première version anglaise (Cosmopoli, 1885) par Isidore Lisieux.* Paris, 1886.   Or.59.e.13.

16   *Kama-Shastra . . . Translated . . . by A. F. F. and B. F. R.* [F. F. Arbuthnot and Sir Richard Burton]. n.p., n.d.   Or.59.e.12.

17   PILLOW BOOKS. [Album of erotic illustrations.] ff.6. 23 × 16 cm. n.p., n.d.
Or.59.e.11.

18   [Album of erotic illustrations] ff.12. 22 × 30 cm. n.p., n.d.   Or.59.e.7.

19   [Album of erotic illustrations.] ff.12. 24 × 18 cm. n.p., n.d.   Or.59.e.10.

20   'UMAR IBN MUḤAMMAD, *al-Nafzāwī. Cheikh Nefzaoui. (Le Parterre parfumé.)* [Algiers,] 1850. At the end is the date 1877.   Or.59.e.26.

21   *Ouvrage du Cheikh . . . Sidi Mohammed al-Nefzaoui.* Algiers, 1850. At the end is the date 1877.   Or.59.e.37.

22   *Le Jardin parfumé.* Paris, 1886.   Or.59.e.30.

23   *The Perfumed Garden . . . Translated from the French version of the Arabian MS.* Cosmopoli [London], 1886.   Or.59.e.2.

24   *The Perfumed Garden . . . Revised and corrected translation.* Cosmopoli [London], 1886.   Or.59.e.29.

25   *The Perfumed Garden.* London, [1934.]   Or.59.e.5.

26 VĀTSYĀYANA, called Mallanāga. *The Kama Sutra . . . Translated [by Sir Richard Burton and F. F. Arbuthnot] from the Sanscrit.* Benares, 1883.   Or.59.e.23.

27   [Another copy.]   Or.59.e.3.

28   [Another issue. Reprint of the Benares edition.] Cosmopoli, 1883.
                                                                    Or.59.e.16.

29   [Another copy.]   Or.59.e.16*.

30   [Another issue. Decorated title, different from Or.59.e.16, and type apparently reset.] Cosmopoli, 1883.   Or.59.e.4.

31   *Les Kama Sutra . . . Traduit sur la première version anglaise [Bénarès, 1883) par Isidore Lisieux.* Paris, 1885.   Or.59.e.22.

32 WU SHAN SHENG, *pseud. Érotologie de la Chine.* Paris, 1963.   Or.59.e.35.

33   *Die Erotik in China.* Basel, 1966.   Or.59.e.41.

7

QUODLIBET: SOME MEMOIRS OF THE BRITISH MUSEUM AND ITS MUSIC ROOM, 1934–76

ALEC HYATT KING

I · THE BRITISH MUSEUM IN THE 1930s

'WHY DID YOU go into the British Museum?'. Quite a lot of people have asked me that question, during my early years, and since. There were several reasons, not the least important being the fact that in 1933 there were some two and a half million unemployed, a far higher proportion of the working population than at any time since. There was also a tiny number of places for post-graduate research in the humanities available, even to those with proven gifts, and I was not one of them. On the other hand, many who like myself had spent eleven years or so taking an intensive sequence of competitive exams were heartily sick of them, and could not face the prospect of yet more work to reach a standard possibly equal to the demands of the most testing of all – that for the Higher Civil Service. School-mastering had no appeal. So unless one had family business connections, the choice was very limited indeed. I had heard, however, that the stiff entrance exam for the British Museum had recently been abolished, and replaced by a competitive interview. I had hoped for a vacancy in the Department of Greek and Roman Antiquities, but there was none. (Perhaps this was just as well in view of the scandal of the mis-cleaned Elgin Marbles which rocked the Department a few years later.)

I thought, rather vaguely, of the library, and learned that though the current financial crisis had caused the Treasury to suspend all established (i.e. pensionable) posts, there were others, to the ultimate total of twenty, about to be advertised, called 'Temporary Assistant Cataloguers'. My step-grandfather had some indirect acquaintance with the Museum's secretary Arundell Esdaile, and it was arranged for me to have an informal interview to learn a little more about the work. So, if memory serves, it was early in October 1933 that I was ushered in to the office of Sir George Hill, the Director and Principal Librarian, whose name I had known from various essential textbooks on Greek epigraphy. A quietly spoken man, he explained that he was the titular head of the library, asked about my qualifications, and then said: 'I will pass you on to Marsden'. He asked for a number – there was no dialling then: 'I have Mr King for you', and my escorting Messenger appeared. Hill added, 'I hope we shall meet at the interview'.

The walk along the gallery with its classical busts, across the Front Hall and down the King's Library seemed a very long one, and when the Messenger rang the bell beside a false door in the bookcases at the far end, it was like the end of a pilgrimage. I suppose that by that time I was in a fairly nervous state, and perhaps because of that I was receptive to the occasion. Whatever the reason, I recall it as vividly as if it were only yesterday. The Keeper's room, which lies at the north end of a narrow apartment, built about 1846 and known as the 'Ante-Room', is gloomy, perhaps barely fifteen feet square, and is lit only by two sash windows looking over the east roadway on to the back of the houses in Montagu Street. Such a cramped room was always quite unworthy to serve as an office for the head of one of the greatest collections of printed books in the world. Most of the centre was taken up by a very large double-sided desk, set at right angles to the windows and on the opposite, inner wall was a generous fire-place with a comfortable coal fire. Behind the desk, there was a door, with a small brass knob, which, I later learned, led to the Keeper's lavatory. (It was told of R. F. Sharp, Marsden's predecessor, that shortly before his retirement he posed standing behind his desk for a press-photographer, who asked him to relax and rest his hand on the knob of the door. The photo ultimately bore the caption: 'Mr. R. F. Sharp, Keeper of Printed Books, who is about to retire'.)

Wilfred Alexander Marsden, like all his successors in the next four decades except A. H. Chaplin, was of only medium height. When he rose from his desk, I noticed that he was wearing a spotted bow tie and spats, which, I soon discovered, was his dapper attire at almost all times of the year. The other thing that struck me was the unmistakable, strong odour of peppermint. Marsden was sucking a bulls-eye. Taking a bag from a top drawer, he offered me one, and then, for the next quarter of an hour or so, he repeated Hill's questions about my career, in a very friendly way, and explained the kind of work I should be doing, if I were appointed. I must confess that cataloguing and revision did not mean a great deal to me, but by the time my bulls-eye was dissolving I could talk more easily. Then the most extraordinary thing happened. Marsden leaned across the desk and said, in a rather depressed tone of voice: 'I suppose we shall have to take some women: it's an awful nuisance, isn't it?'. Before I could think of a suitable reply, Marsden rose, offered me another bulls-eye and shook my hand again as he ushered me out.

The competitive interview for the first five posts took place in November at Burlington Gardens, then the headquarters of the Civil Service Commission, and now (1990) the home of the British Museum's Department of Ethnography. I now recall little of it, apart from the great double staircase. I hardly noticed the preceding candidate when he came out, and was glad to see two familiar faces, Hill's and Marsden's, among the five interviewers. It lasted some forty minutes, and when I emerged, I noticed the next candidate at the waiting table, a round-faced man wearing a gold watch-chain across his waistcoat (who stood third in the following list). A few weeks later the result, in order of merit, reached me:

A. H. KING
G. L. CLUTTON
R. W. LADBOROUGH
N. M. KENYON
G. H. SPINNEY

Clutton, having friends in high places, knew what I did not – that the earliest vacancy caused by retirement of an established Assistant Keeper would ultimately (in fact, in 1939) be filled not according to the order of the competitive interview, but by the Assistant Cataloguer who began work first. Clutton contrived to start on 5 February 1934 and thus, by a mere three days, gain nearly two years' pensionable seniority over me. Spinney (with whom I had been at school) and I were summoned to start on 8 February.

There was a curious preliminary ritual. We were taken to see J. H. Witney, the pompous Assistant Secretary, in his room which was adjacent to the Director's. There, each successively holding a Bible, we swore an oath of loyalty to the Crown, and were joined soon afterwards by I. E. S. Edwards, a newly appointed Assistant Keeper in the Department of Egyptian and Assyrian Antiquities. (In 1955 he became Keeper of Egyptian Antiquities.) Then all three of us were taken back to the 'outer office' – a narrow corridor linking the West wing with the main building, and here the senior clerk, one H. H. E. Simmonds, gave us each a 'house key' for which we duly signed. I cannot recall the original number of mine, but it was high. Later, I was given key no.4, and after that no.265, a medium security key needed for access to the room, also my office, where the Royal Music Library was kept. (The term 'house key' reflects the Museum's character inherited from Montagu House. All staff were recorded in a 'house list': there was a senior 'house maid' who looked after all supplies of linen, towels and the like; the 'house men' were the invaluable people who kept the place clean and tidy.) Then Spinney and I were taken to the Ante-Room where Marsden greeted us, and summoned by telephone an Assistant Keeper, L. W. Hanson, who was to be our reviser. (Later he became Keeper of Printed Books in the Bodleian.) With him, we entered for the first time the Catalogue Room which lay behind the huge doors at the extreme north end of the King's Library. As I have explained elsewhere (p.190 above), this room had just been completely rebuilt and refitted. All round its walls ran the catalogue, on four shelves, the lower two projecting under the sort of desk top used for consulting these massive volumes. Down the centre of the room, out into the floor, ran an elegant iron-work grille through which warmth rose from the large water pipes laid beneath it, as built in 1838. On either side of the grille stood the work-tables, made of oak with a green composition inlay. Each place had an oak desk-chair with curved arms and a comfortable padded seat, and for each newcomer there was a large blotting pad, a pen-tray with several pens, an inkwell, pencils, a rubber, a pile of 'title-slips' and an unbound copy of the cataloguing rules. (Later, these rules were bound in cloth, with the owner's name on the upper cover.) There was also a full water-jug fitted with a stiffened linen cover and a tumbler – very welcome because in winter the floor heating made the air very dry. At the side of each working place stood a large, wheeled barrow, with a long iron handle, loaded with the books which were to be catalogued. All was neat and orderly, with natural light from tall windows on the north and east, and adequate electric light from a dozen or more pendants.

One was introduced to colleagues working in the Catalogue Room itself; one was taken to look at the Reading Room and some of the adjacent book stacks. After lunch there followed a brief outline of the basic principles of cataloguing and one was left to get on with the job and told to ask whenever in doubt. My diary records that on that first day, Thursday, 8 February 1934, during which I worked from 11 a.m. to 5 p.m., I wrote eleven 'titles', which increased gradually to a daily average of thirty-five. After three months or so, and more introductions to staff working elsewhere, the vast labyrinth became understandable, as did also the work done by the department as a whole. It is no part of this essay to describe the work and organisation of current cataloguing (GK I) and the revision of the catalogue (GK II). I have given a full account elsewhere, (pp.166–88 above), with all the necessary technical details. I believe it will be much more interesting if I try to describe the atmosphere of the department, its routine, and its general day to day management in some relation to the Museum as a whole.

In *The Observer* of 24 February 1974, Angus Wilson wrote an autobiographical article in which he referred to 'the extraordinary mummified late-Victorian world that still existed in the Museum', and went on to describe it in terms of derision and contempt. As Angus Frank Johnstone-Wilson, he had entered the Department of Printed Books in 1937 as a Temporary Assistant Cataloguer – not, as he later stated in *Who's Who,* as an Assistant Keeper – and worked there until 1942 when he joined the Foreign Office for the next four years. From 1946 to about 1950 he worked on the replacement of books destroyed in the war, and from 1951 until his resignation in 1955 he was Deputy to the Superintendent of the Reading Room. Sir Angus, as he became in 1980 (he had been appointed C.B.E. in 1968, despite his earlier scorn of the honours system), chose to exclude all his pre-1946 Museum service from his entries in *Who's Who* from 1956 onwards. His novel *The Old Men at the Zoo* (1961) is a satire on the Museum, with some clearly identifiable characters. Wilson (hereinafter always styled simply Angus Wilson) was not, of course, the first person of literary or scholarly distinction to have detested the Department of Printed Books. Edmund Gosse, who served briefly from 1867 to 1875, found it totally uncongenial. (*See* Esdaile, *The Library of the British Museum,* 1946 pp.123, 364–5.)

Perhaps the most contemptuous (and contemptible) of all was the noted geographer Sir John Abraham Jacob de Villiers, clearly a tiresome snob, who had entered the Department in 1887, retired as head of the Map Room in 1924, and published his vitriolic views in *My Memories,* 1931, pp.59–61. Such impatient people as these failed totally to understand that the essential work of a great library had long been maintained by cultured, dedicated, self-effacing men of high erudition and scholarship concerned with using their intellect for the public good, oblivious of the dingy surroundings to which a perpetually mean Treasury confined them, and quite unconcerned with their personal appearance.

Up to 1934, the Printed Books staff was wholly male, although as Marsden foresaw, change was imminent. Dark suits were generally worn by all the senior grades, contributing perhaps to some appearance of self-importance. The lower grades, too – the Attendants – had a rather similar air which is well described by William C. Smith in the first chapter of his *A Handelian's Notebook* (1965):

> Recruited without much regard to education, but carefully chosen largely from the families of servants of the Trustees, or other well-to-do people, the attendants as a class were distinct and exceptional. Most of them, very carefully dressed, endeavoured to carry themselves with a dignity of fussy importance intended to convey that they were not as other folk. As many of them had grown up familiar with domestic service, they seemed to bear the marks of their origins (worthy as they were) in the immaculate polish on their boots and a punctilious regard for their clothes. Some of them had grace and charm, and they were by no means all without knowledge of other than the three Rs. I believe that the ultimate salary of most of them was £120 per annum after many years of service, and to supplement this they did various jobs in their evenings or on off days. Waiting at restaurants and social functions, ushering of sorts at theatres and elsewhere, and other similar work came their way. They would be found as extras in the refreshment tents at the Eton and Harrow and other cricket matches, in the ornamental uniform of attendants at the Royal Opera, Covent Garden, or even occasio-nally as footmen complete with livery, riding high through the London streets behind the carriage of some distinguished person in a civic or other public procession.

(Smith omits to mention that Attendants had to pass an entrance examination.) Quaint though such general comportment and attire seemed to such people as Angus Wilson, they were little different from what other great libraries, such as the Bodleian or Cambridge University – or, for that matter Harrods – would have shown in the 1930s. Here may be quoted a letter from a member of the public who had strong views on the subject, faithfully reflecting contemporary attitudes:

R. A. Mess
Woolwich.
10/11/32.

Director
  B.M.

Dear Sir,

Must your officials in the Reading Room be so dowdily dressed?

When I first made use of it they dressed in accordance with the dignity and tradition of the place and wore top hats.

Today there was a callow youth in the sacred Inner Circle dressed in what looked like a brown 'Sports jacket', with dark trousers, a soft coloured collar which may or may not have been washed last week, and a loud tie.

What impression does this make on foreign visitors to what is as near as I am likely to get to the hub of the intellectual universe?

Yours faithfully,
Alfred H. Burne (Major R.A.)

P.S. A practical reason for having some uniformity in dress for your officials is that it would preclude the present possibility of addressing queries to fellow students in the belief that they are officials, and thus avoid a certain embarrassment! As it is a Government concern perhaps a question in the House would put it right.

A.H.B.

The writer was Lt. Col. Burne, R.A., educated at Winchester and Woolwich. He was awarded the D.S.O. in 1914, and Bar in 1918, and was the author of some sixteen books on military history. The Museum Director, Sir George Hill, passed the letter to A. I. Ellis, the Superintendent of the Reading Room, with a note: 'I should say "dowdy" was the wrong word'. The reply to Burne is unrecorded, but on 18 November he wrote again:

Dear Sir,

I am obliged for your letter, and am glad to have your assurance that the dress of officials in the Reading Room is being looked into. I presume some improvement will come about in due course. (None was appreciable today!)

[247]

But surely the job is such a sought after one that you could impose whatsoever Sartorial Regulations you wished.

Yours truly
Alfred H. Burne (Major)

The originals of this correspondence are preserved in the B.M. Archives.

Perhaps the absence of women added to the sombreness of Printed Books. There was, before 1934, only one female member of the senior staff, an Assistant Keeper in Manuscripts, and in the whole Museum only two typists who both worked in the Director's Office. (It was, incidentally, quite a sensation when in the later 1930s Norman Sainsbury, of Oriental Printed Books and a specialist in Turkish, brought his own typewriter to use for cataloguing: he added the diacritical marks by hand.)

For its routine security and various services the Department of Printed Books formed part of the Museum as a whole. Everyone had a house key which he drew daily, on arrival, in the Front Hall. All keys were hung on named and numbered hooks within a series of small oak cupboards which lined the wall immediately to the left of the entrance. The door of each cupboard was fitted with a dozen or so small racks, in which the Front Hall staff left most letters which the recipients picked up either on arrival or at lunch time. Only for senior staff were letters delivered by messengers, who also took all parcels. The Hall Superintendent's office stood right opposite the key-cupboards. It was a box-like structure, some fifteen feet by ten, built into the lower left wall of the staircase and extending just beyond the first free-standing column to the east. Into the brickwork of that column was built a small steel safe in which all departmental safe keys were hung at night. This safe was often open in the daytime, within easy view of the public. The upper part of this office was glazed, and its door faced the staff key-cupboard on the opposite wall. The office had a low wooden roof: working conditions were appalling, especially in warm humid weather. It served as a collecting and dispersal point for mail, and would sometimes sell stamps to the staff for their personal letters. It was the only place in the Front Hall where visitors could ask for information. Judged by modern standards, in an inevitably much changed world, all these arrangements were primitive. But they worked, and were hardly modified until the early 1960s.

The regulations in respect of hours of work, leave and the like, which bound senior graduate staff, applied also to Temporary Assistant Cataloguers. In Treasury jargon, we were 'conditioned' to a thirty-eight and a half hour week. On Mondays to Fridays the hours were nine to four or ten to five, and on Saturdays nine to twelve-thirty or ten to one-thirty. In 1938 Marsden circulated a stern memorandum to all senior staff reminding them that these hours of work must be strictly observed. (Other grades had different hours, based on a routine and some public service duties which started and ended earlier.) Lunchtime was a strict forty-five minutes and there was a small, cheap French restaurant named 'Randal et Aubin', which some of us used, only a few yards from where Centre Point now stands. A morning coffee break was unknown and junior staff never took tea, though their seniors might sometimes enjoy a cup in the small staff restaurant (off the east of the Egyptian gallery), ten minutes or so before they finished work. Printed Books had its own customs for taking vacation. The applicant wrote his name and the day or days requested on a small brown slip which he deposited in a tray on an Ante-Room table, and a clerk recorded the details. Two days' notice was required for anything more than a half day, which could be booked on the previous day. Emergency leave could be granted only by the Keeper, to whom everyone was required to report personally after any break of a fortnight or more. Marsden was always genuinely interested to learn where his staff had been, what they had seen and done. It was a delightful, paternal society.

Everyone had to keep a diary, in which were recorded the number of titles written or other work done; the languages of the books dealt with; daily hours; time of lunch; annual leave taken and any sick leave. The reviser might inspect the diary, which the Keeper signed at the end of each month. The Catalogue Room, like most other large rooms in the department, had only one telephone which was intended solely for official communications; except in a real emergency personal calls were never made. Distractions were therefore few. There were no retirement parties, no speeches, no farewell presentations. On the day, having confirmed his pension arrangements, the retiring officer tidied his desk, passed any unfinished work to a colleague, said goodbye to his personal friends and hung up his key for the last time.

The 'atmosphere' of the department was quite extraordinary, both in the literal and figurative sense of the word. Pressures such as developed from the 1950s onwards were almost unknown, and orderly concentration was taken for granted. Besides the absence of telephones already mentioned, there was a general sense of quiet, enhanced, until rebuilding began from 1932–33 onwards, by the great height of the original rooms in the North Wing. The Banksian Room, with all its books still in place; the Old Music Room, with its dark bays and lofty windows, almost empty and awaiting the builders; and the Arch Room, then the abode of incunabulists and no one else – all these soared to thirty-two feet. (Of these, only the Arch Room has remained intact.) Sounds moved upward and were soon lost in space. In the South-East Quadrant, the tallest of the bookstacks round the Reading Room, the light filtered down from the glass roof nearly forty feet above. There the silence was unbroken, save

[249]

by the thunderous metallic rumble of the heavy rolling presses as they moved on the horizontal steel cross-girders from which they were suspended on wheels. In the Keeper's Ante-Room the only intrusive noise was the hollow rattle of the wooden hoist, worked by a rope and pulley, on which books required for cataloguing were brought up after being stamped in the basement.

Everywhere, in stacks and workrooms, there was the strong odour from the leather or cloth bindings of books, and the fainter but all-pervasive smell from the millions upon millions of printed pages enclosed between their covers. Nowhere was this smell stronger than in the Copyright Receipt Office, which stood on the left of the entrance of the King Edward VII Building, with service entrance through a small door on the right of the North Gate. In addition to books, newspapers were delivered here, from all over the British Isles, in huge quantities. Accumulated, prior to despatch to Colindale, in hundreds of pigeon holes that ranged from floor to ceiling, they exuded an overpowering odour of fresh newsprint, enriched by the fragrance from the serried rows of elephantine leather-bound ledgers with thick web straps, in which every item received was recorded by hand.

Such was the milieu in which a multifarious routine proceeded entirely untroubled by the active intrusion of trade unions, and untrammelled by the disturbing, relentless traffic of books being moved about for photographic reproduction. And the continuous upheaval caused by the processes of xerox and microfilm were then as unimaginable as the triffid-like emergence of information science. There were, above all, no time-consuming promotion boards. The Keeper knew all his men, on each of whom he had submitted annual reports to the Trustees. When any vacancy occurred, anyone who thought himself suited for promotion could write to the Keeper, asking to be considered. He then made his recommendation in the venerable form (still used for all reports, on any topic, to the Trustees) – 'Mr. Marsden has the honour to report that a vacancy has occurred . . . .' Any unsuccessful candidate always had the right of appeal direct to the Trustees, who might occasionally overrule the Keeper.

The staff and its work seldom impinged on the readers. There was one rare occasion in the mid 1930s when those working on the Subject Index of Printed Books were moved to the gallery of the North Library while their room was being rebuilt. The raw material for this Index comprised large quantities of thin slips cut from the printed Accessions Parts. These slips were put in appropriate order and accumulated in piles before being pasted down in final sequence on to large sheets of paper. One of the staff, an eccentric Irishman named Philip Wilson, suffered from nasal trouble which sometimes caused him to sneeze violently. When this happened, readers working below that part of the gallery were astonished to find these slips, fluttering down from on high, accompanied by the muffled curses of the sneezer.

Even by the later 1930s, the entire staff of the Museum, taking account of all grades, only amounted to about 560, and of this total 161 were in the Department of Printed Books (Fig. 24). Its Keeper, like the Director and two other Keepers, lived in an official residence on the Trustees' premises. There was thus something of a collegiate atmosphere about the place which, for the graduate staff, was enhanced by the *British Museum Quarterly* which began in 1926 and was given to them *gratis*. Besides articles on important acquisitions, it included the full names and qualifications of all graduate recruits to every department. All Temporary Assistant Cataloguers were listed and it should not be forgotten that their influx – some twenty-five or more up to 1940, for not all the early entrants stayed, thus creating vacancies – was a phenomenon unprecedented anywhere in the whole of the Museum's previous history. (Annual vacancies, even in Printed Books, had rarely exceeded two a year, and were even less frequent in other departments.) This large, rapid intake might well have strained the resources of a less skilful management than that provided by Marsden and his senior men.

They all treated their new young colleagues with unfailing courtesy, friendliness and tolerance, and everyone, down to junior Assistant Keeper level, gave instruction and advice with remarkable patience. In return, the department asked – and generally received – steady, uninterrupted work of the most meticulous standard of accuracy. All this was made easier because most of the new staff accepted and understood a loyalty, bred of long tradition, which was essential to the smooth running of all the complex procedures required by the public service. Such loyalty was something which also mollified any personal animosities among the older staff: the newcomers were naturally unaware of them, and in any case gradually developed their own, but not to the detriment of the expected standard of their work.

I have already described Marsden's personal appearance. Apart from being an excellent all-round linguist, he made no claim to scholarship. But he was a wise and humane administrator, who, as his letters and reports show, went to endless pains with the difficulties, domestic and official, of all his staff, in any grade. His senior Deputy Keeper, Henry Thomas (later Sir Henry) was an internationally respected Hispanist, of rather quiet disposition, and was reputed not to see eye to eye with Marsden on various matters of policy. (Thomas's sister, Amy, died in 1981. In her will, published in *The Times* for 8 July, she bequeathed some £50,000 to the British Library Board to found the Sir Henry Thomas Trust, for the purchase of Spanish literature.) Arthur Ellis, the second of three Deputy Keepers and Superintendent of the Reading Room, was an unforgettable character, who had a rather plummy voice, and a somewhat vague, languid manner. This he might have cultivated as a defence against the readers' incessant demands which he met with unfailing courtesy however silly some of them were. It was an open secret that Ellis, out of his great kindness of heart, gave regular help from his own pocket to help some of those who were indigent – or posed as such. The third Deputy Keeper was J. V. Scholderer, a world-famous incunabulist.

There were some rare characters among the older Assistant Keepers. The most remarkable was surely L. C. Wharton, a delightful, gentle bachelor with a long, thin nose and a mass of white hair and a drooping moustache, which gave him the appearance of Lewis Carroll's White Knight and made him seem much older than his years. He was the last man to wear a top-hat when on duty in the Reading Room, and at all other times in the department kept a battered trilby on his head because (he said) he had a thin skull and any strong light gave him a headache. Benign and courteous, Wharton was rarely roused to anger, with a loud 'cha!' as its strongest expression. He was grossly overworked because, with only one assistant before 1936, he had to deal with the acquisition and cataloguing of books published throughout the Slavonic and Balkan countries. Usually at his own expense, he regularly attended conferences, and always left on his desk a fairly complete time-table of his movements: 'at 4.0 p.m. on 1 July I shall be on platform 3 at Krakow railway station'. Among his other desk notes was one which simply read: 'Gone to bed – influenza'. Though his several desks were understandably chaotic, he was in fact methodical and cautious. When invasion threatened early in the war, the staff was warned – rather foolishly, perhaps – to prepare for evacuation with a change of clothing. Wharton was only only one who acted on the warning and on two of his pegs in the cloakroom hung small parcels labelled 'L. C. Wharton vests and pants', and 'L. C. Wharton shirts'.

The Assistant Keeper nominally in charge of GK II (the revision of the catalogue) was Alan Grant Macfarlane, affectionately known as 'Mac'. He had a first-rate cataloguing brain, but was hampered by a tiresome stammer, which probably reflected a nervous disposition and was certainly in part due to his experiences in Flanders. Mac habitually wrote with a rather spluttery 'J' nib, his corrections were sometimes hard to read, but he was an excellent reviser of difficult 'copy', and during the process he would mutter fiercely to himself. We knew when he was near the end of a long, successful revision because he always began to hum the tune that opens the finale of Elgar's second symphony. Mac's stammer was the cause of a memorable incident in the Front Hall, where he happened to notice a visitor with a cigarette in his mouth. As this had escaped the warders' attention, Mac approached the man intending to ask him to put it out. But, like Billy Budd in Britten's opera, Mac was struck dumb and could only stand there mouthing voicelessly. The visitor, stopped

24 The Senior Staff of the Department of Printed Books, photographed in 1939.
Front row (from left): A. F. Johnstone-Wilson, Wendy Charles, Annie Gibson, Annie O'Donovan, S. J. E. Southgate, C. G. Allen, G. D. Painter, A. P. Sainton, F. K. Forrester, R. G. Lyde. *Second row:* A. F. Johnson, L. C. Wharton, W. C. Smith, A. G. Crawley, A. I. Ellis (Deputy Keeper), H. Thomas (Deputy Keeper), W. A. Marsden (Keeper), J. V. Scholderer (Deputy Keeper), G. D. R. Tucker, F. C. W. Hiley, F. G. Rendall, E. W. Lynam, A. G. Macfarlane. *Third row:* F. Fuller, H. F. M. Lee, J. L. Wood, G. A. F. Scheele, H. M. Nixon, C. F. Beckingham, D. Barrett, H. A. S. Kelham, F. C. Francis, F. D. Cooper, F. L. Kent, Audrey Brodhurst, C. B. Oldman, W. A. Smith, L. A. Sheppard, G. L. Clutton. *Fourth row:* A. H. Chaplin, R. A. Wilson, L. W. Hanson, R. A. Skelton, N. F. Sharp, H. Sellers, J. C. W. Horne. (Absent: B. H. U. L. Townshend, A. H. King, G. H. Spinney.)

in his tracks, was first bemused and then astonished when Mac, in despair, moved sideways and plucked out the cigarette. The visitor, still unaware of his error, then took it all quite well and walked away tapping his forehead. He was, one supposes, foreign. Macfarlane's remaining years were all too few. He was already developing symptoms of disseminated sclerosis which caused him to retire in 1942. He died in 1947 aged 59, much regretted by all who remembered him.

Of G. D. R. Tucker, his extraordinary versatility and his endless diligence as 'Incorporator', I have written elsewhere (pp.175–6 above). Another man central to the department's routine was A. G. Crawley, very tall, with a clipped moustache and upright bearing which suggested (though wrongly) a military connection. He had in fact risen from a clerical grade, by much hard work and application, to be put in charge of all expenditure on purchases, and strictly enforced the limits laid down for all languages and categories. His bluffness concealed a rather nervous temperament which became more marked after illness in his later years. He developed an extraordinary form of mania, and became extremely sensitive to certain sounds. He worked in the Banksian Room, his desk screened by a tall bookcase in front and another at the back. If anyone came through the room, humming or whistling to himself – and many did – Crawley would leap out and abuse the offending passer-by, whether he knew him or not, convinced that there was a plot to persecute him.

A contemporary who had gained similar promotion was H. S. Kelham, who was in charge of the binding, a task that he contrived to make as undemanding as possible. His ignorance of languages was sometimes glaringly revealed. On the spine of all rebound older books, there were five spaces, generally marked with gold lines: the fifth, and lowest, was by tradition, the 'imprint' panel, which bore the name of the place where the book was printed, and its date. Once, Kelham read on the titlepage such words as 'Hildesheim, widerum gedruckt 1635'. His binding order produced in the imprint panel 'Widerum 1635' ('Widerum' means 'again' or 'a second time'). Such error induced Marsden to appoint Tucker, whose German was first class, to inspect all old, rebound books before they were reshelved. As Kelham usually went home at 3.45 p.m., inspection could be done unobtrusively after that. Kelham anticipated the later mania for sun-drenched holidays. He saved up most of his annual leave until mid-December, so that he could add three weeks or so from the next year's entitlement. He always went to the same hotel in Marrakesh, at which he simply sat reading in the sun, and so avoided part of the English winter.

All large departments have a bore and Printed Books was no exception. He was F. D. Cooper, a burly, humourless, but immensely industrious man, who was in charge of 'State Papers' (i.e. government publications, world-wide). He was totally obsessed by his work, and would hold forth at great length about its importance – which was undisputed – to anyone who could bear to listen. He was also a great nuisance because he insisted on retrieving from bound volumes in the General Library all publications which were 'official' but had long ago been ignored as such. For instance, many 'Admiralty Orders' or 'Army Instructions' had been placed with general naval or military history. All such 'tract' volumes (i.e. half-a-dozen small items bound in one) had to be 'pulled' in the bindery and then rebound, after the unavoidable renumbering and its consequential alterations elsewhere. All this made a huge amount of extra work all round, and took up a lot of Cooper's time which should have been better spent. His great day came at his retirement, not long after the war, when an official presentation – probably the first of its kind – was to be made. Contributors crowded into the Keeper's room at 11 a.m. where Thomas had prepared a brief speech. Cooper then replied and went on and on through his long career (he had also been eminent in local government). After forty-five minutes people, myself included, began to edge uneasily towards the door, but Cooper, in full flow, was apparently quite unaware. By about 12.20 p.m. there were left only Thomas, Cooper and one other, the ever courteous J. C. W. Horne (Wharton's successor), who told me this himself. Cooper finished at 12.35 p.m.

The Temporary Assistant Cataloguers who came in before 1939 can be assessed in two groups – those who left before or during the war, and those who stayed and served after it. The former comprised some ambitious men who would probably not have stayed even without the war. George Clutton, for example, had come into the Museum as a 'pis aller', because poor eyesight had disqualified him from the Foreign Office. But through his contacts, he was soon able to procure a war-time transfer as the first step to what became a distinguished career. His last two postings were to the Philippines (1955–59) and, as Sir George Clutton, to Poland (1960–66). (By an odd coincidence, another ambitious Museum man, Duncan Wilson, left early in the war, and was British Ambassador to Russia during some of Clutton's time in Warsaw). After Clutton retired, in 1966, his tall, elegant figure, wearing a black polo-neck jersey, was regularly seen in the Reading Room where he did desultory research into sixteenth-century German woodcut initials. His London clubs were Boodles and the Beefsteak. Time had considerably mellowed his arrogance. It so happened that I then had dealings with a Madame Chomińska, a Polish musicologist, whose husband, the famous Jozef Chomiński, Clutton had known in Warsaw. She was doing research for her husband, and after she had left I asked Clutton about her progress. He replied that she had said: 'The Reading Room is wonderful: but the staff, they are all Afghans'. There is a curious footnote to Clutton's career. In the *Sunday Times* of 22 July 1984, there appeared an 'Insight' article by Barrie Penrose and Simon Freeman headed 'M.I.5 list reveals the 21 spy suspects'. The list is in four groups: '1. Known Defectors'; '2. Partially confessed'; 3. 'Confessed'; '4. Unresolved'. The last name in group 4 is 'Sir George Clutton/ex-ambassador, dead'.

A more agreeable entrant in the later 1930s was Frederick Fuller, a prodigiously gifted Irishman of immense charm. After graduating at Liverpool and further study at the universities of Paris, Munich and Harvard, he had an excellent command of German, French, Italian, Spanish and Portuguese. He also possessed a lovely high-baritone voice which he had developed under

[255]

such teachers as von Warlich and Claire Croiza. He left to join the staff of the British Council in Brazil where he became friendly with H. Villa-Lobos. There is a plum label record of Fuller singing two of Villa-Lobos's charming songs, accompanied by the composer. Fuller also had a complete mastery of all European song, of any period. Even more remarkable as a linguist was David Barrett who had taken a good classics degree at Cambridge, and then discovered that he could attain fluency in reading and sometimes speaking any of the more difficult European tongues. Russian, Polish, Czech and Albanian all came easily. Early in the war I heard him broadcast fluently to the Finns in their own language. A varied career led him ultimately to the Bodleian, where he catalogued their large collection of books in Georgian. A true academic was Charles Beckingham, whose work culminated in the chair of Islamic Studies in the University of London, which he held from 1965 to 1981. The literary world claimed Peter du Sautoy: he entered publishing, and ultimately became chairman of Faber's. The delightful and diffident Richard William ('Dick') Ladborough left in 1936 to become a lecturer in French at the University of Southampton; he ultimately returned to Cambridge in the same capacity, became a Fellow and later Dean and Pepysian Librarian at his old college, Magdalene. When I delivered the Sandars lectures in 1961, it was he who introduced me. At his funeral, held in Little St Mary's Church on 30 May 1972, the address was given by a friend of his undergraduate days, Michael Ramsey, then Archbishop of Canterbury. He spoke with a warmth and charm which those who knew only his formal public utterances could hardly have imagined.

A remarkable pair were Charles Geoffrey Allen and Sidney John Ernest Southgate, both classicists, the former from Bristol Grammar School and Brasenose, the latter, a short, pugnacious Australian from St Andrew's College, in the University of Sydney, and Balliol. They were natural rebels, who accepted gradually some degree of conformity. Somehow during their re-vision of the catalogue they discovered that throughout the forms of name chosen for the Roman Emperors were extremely inconsistent. They prevailed on Marsden to persuade the Trustees to sanction a complete revision of all such headings: the resulting 'Accession Part' was printed for internal use only, and it fell to me, both as 'Incorporator' and a classic, to remove all the old headings, incorporate the new ones, and make sure that all the numerous cross-references were altered in conformity. This I did throughout February 1938. Ultimately, Allen left to become librarian in what was then the University of Rhodesia in Salisbury (his career ended in the library of the London School of Economics) and Southgate entered the Colonial Office in 1947, and – if memory serves – found a later career in the British Sugar Corporation. (He makes a brief appearance as a lesser character in *The Old Men at the Zoo*.)

Angus Johnstone-Wilson I have already mentioned. Without doubt, the one of us who achieved the greatest all-round distinction in literature was George Duncan Painter. Not only was he famous for his official work as an incunabulist, but his biographies of Proust, of Chateaubriand (as far as it went) and his study of Caxton singled him out as a scholar of international repute. His life of Proust was based on the inferential dating of many undated letters: its easy style and insight, combined with sympathy and profound erudition, have made it a classic. Painter also published a little poetry. Three of the five female Assistant Cataloguers left to get married. By far the most colourful was Wendy Charles, diminutive of stature, known for her cheerful insouciance and erratic time-keeping. In this last respect, Marsden appointed Tucker to keep an eye on her. One day, when she arrived at about eleven, Tucker asked, in his irreproducible stammer, why she was so late. 'But Mr. Tucker', came the reply, 'I must have my hair done sometime, mustn't I?'. The keenest mind was certainly Audrey Brodhurst, who had won a first in Greats. She became an expert on the library's vast collection of imperfectly catalogued French Revolution tracts, and continued to work on them after she retired. Unfortunately, some dispute with the British Library management caused her to give it up prematurely. She who gave the most dedicated service to the Trustees and subsequently to the British Library, was Annie O'Donovan. After her degree in classics at Girton, she won an M. Litt. for a dissertation entitled 'Ancient Mining in Spain'. She became a brilliant, tenacious cataloguer at all levels, and a repository of immense knowledge of the development and application of continually changing rules, precedents and practices. After retirement she worked voluntarily almost up to the year of her death in 1987 on tidying up some of the numerous, large, rather confused headings in the unrevised later volumes of GK I, and the dreadful muddles due to its successive, over-hasty, ill-planned reprinting into GK III and repeated in GK IV.

Despite its rather austere appearance, the Museum was by no means an inhospitable place in itself. Before the first war the Kenyons used to give Christmas parties for the children of senior staff, both resident Keepers and others. Hill, a bachelor, entertained the younger staff either to sherry or tea, so that he could get to know them a little better. (It is worth recording that Hill persuaded the Office of Works to plant two rows of cherry trees at the back of the lawns in the Front Court. This attempt to brighten the area failed because the trees could not survive the polluted atmosphere.) Resident Keepers did likewise. Other senior staff offered different hospitality. Victor Scholderer and his wife once invited me to dine at their modest home in Wimbledon. 'By the way', he said when confirming the day, 'we usually dress on Sundays'. Macfarlane preferred to give little lunch parties at the rather splendid Holborn Restaurant which stood right opposite the Kingsway en-

[257]

trance to the Underground. It was always an omelette followed by cheese and coffee, with ample claret and extensive, civilised conversation, ranging from Vergil to Calverley, worthy of a well-read and kindly host. Tucker used to ask his younger colleagues to his house in Gipsy Lane, just off Barnes Common. It was said, rather unkindly, that Mrs Tucker hoped to find suitors for her daughters. Marsden and his wife used the fine rooms of the Museum's no.1 residence in the East Wing to give very pleasant lunches. In his urbane *Reminiscences* (1970) Scholderer recalls 'the tale that in the long ago days a Keeper of Printed Books asked a junior assistant to lunch in the residence and kept him in talk over coffee until he grew restless and hinted that perhaps he ought to be back at work – whereupon the Keeper took him to the window, pointed at the Museum and said: "It'll be there to-morrow".' There is a minor error here. There were *two* assistants, one being Spinney, the other myself. The Museum buildings did indeed survive the onslaught of Hitler's bombers, and the damage was repaired. But forty years later, there was nothing that could withstand the take-over of all its collections of manuscripts and printed books by the British Library.

At the time that I write this, it is little more than one hundred and sixty years since the King's Library was completed to house the library of King George III and one hundred and thirty years after the Reading Room opened its doors to the first of the many millions who have since found peace, knowledge and inspiration beneath its soaring dome. At the end of the twentieth century when the British Library has moved to the Euston Road and long after, people will still be walking through the King's Library, but whatever then fills its shelves will be alien. The tradition of the 1857 Reading Room likewise will then be a vanished memory and that immense, numinous space – so wonderful to walk through late in the evening, whether in midsummer or midwinter all quietly ready for the readers next morning – will have been converted to other uses. The unique situation whereby a comprehensive library stood within the greatest museum in the world will have come to an end, and this will be an unique loss. What the library has for so long represented is eloquently described by Arundell Esdaile, in his book *The British Museum Library* (1946, p.172.):

> The cumulative effect of such a Library as the Museum's is impossible to estimate. It has the function, at first its only function, of preserving the printed and written records of civilisation. But, beyond that, it is a seedbed from which grows the forest of modern knowledge, specially but not only in its historical field. No proof can well be offered, but surely the Library fulfils the second function as well as it fulfils the first, though not all its users nor all its servants be worthy. The end and essence of its work is to preserve and to disseminate truth. Hardly any other life-work can more thoroughly

imbue the mind with a patient respect for fact. It is a discipline for which no one who has been through it can fail to give thanks to the company of his predecessors who created it, or to be proud of the old title, 'a servant of the Trustees of the British Museum'.

II · THE WAR YEARS, 1939–1945

The concluding paragraphs of the last section were, of course, an anticipation of events which no one, however far-sighted, could possibly have imagined in 1939. Yet change was in the air, if only because quite a number of senior men were due to retire in the 1940s. Even before the war was half-way through, this sense of impending change became more ominous and somehow spread throughout the department. No one could tell what form it would take, but of its immensity there was no doubt: 1939 had marked the end of an era.

On the surface, however, work went on as normally as increasingly difficult and dangerous circumstances allowed. The staff soon shrank as the younger men were called up, and others, in middle age, were seconded to various government departments because their Museum work was inessential. One thing which had to be maintained was the current cataloguing and the revision of the catalogue (GK II). Because the latter had a high proportion of American subscribers, who paid in much-needed dollars, all production staff over twenty-eight years old were designated by the Ministry of Labour as one of various 'reserved occupations'. The advance plans for the evacuation of the Museum's collections, their execution, and the subsequent catastrophic bombing of the buildings have been fully described with illustrations by the wartime Director, Sir John Forsdyke ('The Museum in War-time', *British Museum Quarterly*, xv, 1952, pp.1–9), and need not be repeated here. (It is perhaps worth mentioning that the first warnings of trouble were received from the Home Office as early as 1933.) I give only my rather disjunct recollections – based to some extent on my official diaries – of what happened in the Department of Printed Books and of some other events, elsewhere in the Museum – all vignettes that have lingered in memory for nearly fifty years.

I played a negligible part in the first evacuation of the collections of printed books, apart from a little help in the early packing. For the other Museum departments such work was done by the expert staff. But I recall vividly the one occasion on which I was in charge of one load of antiquities (their nature now escapes me). It was, I think, in the winter of 1940–41 when, armed with a sheaf of documents, I had to find my way in the blackout and encumbered by a gas-mask, to a point in the goods yard at St Pancras Station (probably where the British Library building now stands) where a large sealed container was waiting. It had been shunted so that it stood immediately behind the guard's van which most unusually was coupled directly to the steam-engine. I was to travel with the guard in his van. We left about 1 a.m. The guard made tea, which was very welcome, over a spirit-lamp, and through the window in the front of his van I could see the glare from the fire in the engine's boiler. The train had many goods wagons behind the Museum's container, and clanked its way very slowly through the night. The noise and banging in the guard's van was violent, and seemed to go on for ever. In fact it lasted little more than three hours. There was a lot of stopping and shunting, and by daybreak the engine, with only the van and the Museum container attached to it, had stopped in a quiet siding somewhere in the Midlands. At about 6.30 a.m. I heard voices outside, and was relieved to see some familiar faces from one of the Antiquities departments. They countersigned my papers, gave me a receipt, unsealed the container and began to unload the boxes on to a waiting lorry. Where I had breakfast, I cannot now recall, but it was a great relief to find myself, unwashed and weary, on a London-bound train: it had been 'a hard day's night'.

Many of the most valuable printed books had been sent away to safety in the new, spacious National Library of Wales at Aberystwyth, where they were in the charge of J. V. Scholderer. Consequently, as work on revision of the catalogue progressed, it was impossible to check the entries for the outhoused volumes for exact titles and many other details. So we had to post the title-slips to Scholderer and ask him to verify all details and post the slips back – a slightly weird process. (Long-distance telephone calls were then quite impracticable.)

Plans to keep the library going had been drawn up well in advance. Because its glass dome rendered the Reading Room highly dangerous, it was closed at the outbreak of war and its services transferred, on a much reduced scale, to the North Library, where many refugee scholars from Europe were able to do some work. Among them were a number of Poles, who were understandably anxious because their country had been invaded. Space in the North Library was limited, the gangway between the tables narrow, and there was no tall ceiling – as in the Reading Room – to absorb conversations. On one occasion, when two Poles were pacing the gangway and talking with very audible agitation, the Officer superintending felt obliged to ask them to moderate their voices. He did so, and added, not perhaps very tactfully, 'Forgive me, gentlemen, but this is not the Polish Corridor'.

Air-raid precautions had been thoroughly planned: some of them are described by Forsdyke in his article already mentioned. Others are perhaps no less interesting. A day-time, gas-proof shelter for staff was provided in the East Basement under the King's Library. The immensely thick, vaulted brickwork was strengthened with large steel girders (still there today), and benches provided under them and in the adjacent store-rooms. When the sirens warned of an imminent day-time air-raid, staff were ordered to get readers out of the building (where to, I cannot now remember), and assemble in the East Basement with their gas masks. At first quite a number did, and on one occasion were joined by Forsdyke with his gas mask and wearing a steel hat – a splendid sight! But as the risk of day-time raids grew less, few staff observed this drill.

Night-time air-raid procedure was very different. In order to help the Museum's permanent firemen, all Printed Books staff were given lessons in fire drill, handling hoses and other fairly simple tasks. Every night there was a duty rota of six men who slept on bunks in a small, very stuffy room off the North Basement. One soon learned who, among one's colleagues, were the most stertorous sleepers: light sleepers regularly changed their rotas. There was at first nowhere to go or rest either in the early evening or when one came off duty at about 6 a.m. Ultimately, after some pressure, the Trustees provided a 'leisure' room, where tea could be made and where, in due course, a small billiard table was installed. (This was the origin of the Museum's social club which came into being soon after the war, and later led to much improved staff restaurant services.)

Printed Books sustained the first air-raid damage on 23 September 1940 when a small bomb fell sideways through a window in the east side of the northern half of the King's Library. Rather oddly, the explosion destroyed only 428 volumes in presses (139 to 145, 275 and 276) very near to the central square. Of about 1,400 volumes affected 124 were entirely lost, and 304 damaged beyond repair. Of the 266 works (428 volumes) destroyed 166 were replaced by copies elsewhere in the library. But the blast totally wrecked part of the Italianate plaster ceiling, and loosened a lot more. The dust hung in the air for some time, but it was found that unless the locked glass doors on the lower floor had been shaken on their hinges, very little dust penetrated to the books, so well did the frames fit. Besides the dust caused by the blast, much more was unavoidably created by the Museum's fire-staff who had the difficult task of getting up ladders to attach ropes to the dangerously loose parts of the ceiling, and then of pulling them down. Men heaving on long ropes provided a rousing – though rather depressing – spectacle, while it lasted. (Ultimately, almost the whole ceiling in the northern section of the King's Library had to be replaced.)

It was ironical that when the really disastrous raid hit the Museum on 10 May 1941, bombs struck a water main, and not long after fire bombs set light to the books in the South-West Quadrant. The hoses ran dry and all the staff on duty could only watch the blaze. Later raids did relatively minor damage: a small bomb which fell in the Front Court blew one of the huge entrance gates right off its hinges, and wrecked part of the low stone wall that surrounds the east lawn. Even today, other scars and deep holes caused by bomb fragments can be seen on the inner side of the main walls, below the tall railings. While the Museum suffered much physical damage – though far less than many other public buildings – there was personal sadness, too, among its staff. For Marsden, the Keeper of Printed Books, the losses of his department were heart-rending. On the morning after the bombing, he was seen picking his way among the fire-hoses and other debris that littered the Front Court, with a kettle in his hand, filling it at one of the stand pipes that had been set up. The water supply to his own residence had been cut off.

Grievous personal loss was sustained by F. G. Rendall, the assistant superintendent of the Reading Room. Because of chronic shortage of rooms for staff, he had no place of his own except an extraordinary glazed box-like structure fixed, at ground floor level, to the open triangle formed by the design of the iron-work book-stacks in the South-West Quadrant. Hot in summer under the glass roof twenty feet or so above, and cold in winter, it was the only place he had for writing letters, talking to staff and keeping his papers. Here too, because his home was cramped, he stored some of the best of his fine collection of woodwind instruments, and his notes about them. All were destroyed on the night of 10 May 1941.

Neither the text of Forsdyke's article in the *British Museum Quarterly* nor the photographs accompanying it, make clear what happened when the books blazed, and what work was later done to save such as could be saved. Nor is the last point explained by Angus Wilson in his valuable contribution to the same volume 'The Library's losses from bombardment'. The South-West Quadrant was one of the four areas for book-storage built simultaneously with the Reading Room which was completed in 1857. By 1939 the original North-East and North-West Quadrants had been demolished and replaced by ferro-concrete structure with more floors. The South-East Quadrant had been enlarged by the somewhat hazardous addition of an extra floor, still under-neath a glass roof. The South-West Quadrant remained unchanged, and comprised a basement, ground floor and one upper floor, all under the original glass roof, and so designed because in the 1850s gas lighting was unsafe, and electricity unavailable. Light came down from the roof, through the open ironwork of all the floors. consequently when the fire-bombs rained down, those which landed on the concrete roofs exploded harmlessly. None hit the South-East Quadrant, but the South-West roof was shattered, and a huge fire raged. So intense was the heat that the iron of the first floor buckled and everything, molten iron and burning books, collapsed onto the ground floor, like a huge, rather leaking umbrella. But by no means all this catastrophe fell into the basement, for much of the first floor remained intact, though smothered in debris much dampened by the water from the firemen's hoses, as long as it lasted.

When the huge piles of rubble were removed, it was very soon clear that the worst of the fire and flood had affected only part of the basement, and that many books were still on their shelves. But it was also clear that they could not possibly be examined where they stood. Staff of all grades were given brown overalls and gloves and began to load the books on to barrows, which had to be handled carefully through the debris to the far corner of the North-West Basement to a lift by which they could be brought to the empty Reading Room. There a lot of desks were covered with cloths, to receive the books, each on its foredge, shelf by shelf. Art books, which had plates on glazed paper, were worst affected, dampened into a sodden block. Many others, however, had fared better. Though the cloth spine or the boards were charred and crumbling, the sewing was often intact. Books in this state were stacked on separate desks. Those beyond repair were thrown away. It was surprising how many volumes, whose pages were slightly cockled by damp, had survived. The whole Reading Room smelt of charred, damp paper, cloth and leather. The smell gradually penetrated to other parts of the library and lingered for a long time. My diary records that I started work on 'salvage' on 12 May: it lasted, with only short respite, until the end of 1941.

The sorting was done by a team which included besides Angus Wilson a tall, very plump lady named Miss Mary Knight, who was then Deputy Head Saleswomen (she retired about 1952 as Head Saleswoman). She was a humorous person, but perpetually nervous and very fussy, and spoke in a high-pitched squeaky voice. We all liked her, but Angus Wilson found her voice irritating, and when she was away used to give a brilliant imitation of it. (His keen ear for speech and sharp dialogue is one of the features of his early novels.) This sort of thing enlivened what became a rather wearisome task. But in the end we did rescue hundreds of books. They were sent to the bindery and re-covered in plain red cloth, but without any lettering on the spine because there were very few men available for such work. Instead, the re-covered books were gradually sent to a typist who typed the author's surname and the title, as on the titlepage, on brown paper labels roughly to the width of the space. These labels were later pasted on to the upper spine, and in this guise the books are still in use today, though few people now know how and why they look so different from other volumes in the '7,000s' – the presses most affected by the bombing.

Several consequences of this disaster seem to have gone unrecorded. While salvage work continued, the North Library closed to all readers. Authority realised that the disaster in the South-West Quadrant could be repeated in the South-East. So it was decided to move as many books as possible from the top floor of the latter Quadrant. My diary records that from 22 May to 28 May, I was moving novels (I was, of course, part of a team) to the empty shelves that ran round the gallery of the North Library. This entailed quite a long journey from the South-East Quadrant to the North East, where the only lift was sited, and then snaking the heavy barrows through the book stacks on the first floor along to the North Library. As there were several thousand novels, many such journeys were needed.

The floor of the North Library gallery is some eight feet wide, and being then almost empty was the obvious place for more safe storage under the immense strength of the rebuilt galleries above. After tests for load-bearing, the gallery floor was pronounced safe to carry heavy free-standing presses to which the 'W.P.s' (works in progress) could now be moved from the Quadrant's top floor. The only problem was to find and erect the presses. The only ones available were those discarded some ten years before from the second Supplementary Room, which had been rebuilt in the 1930s. To gain space, the original presses were designed to hang from the ceiling which was built entirely of steel girders. The top of each press was fitted with flanged wheels which rolled easily along the rims of the girders. The theory was that mobility produced a fifty per cent gain in space because no floor space was needed between each row. Unfortunately it occurred to no one that though all the shelves were of uniform depth, the books (which had originally been moved from deeper presses elsewhere in the library) were not. Consequently when the staff moved the hanging presses to gain access, protruding spines on one press knocked against others on the nearest press. To avoid damage, one row in three of these presses had to be removed, dismantled and stored, in a basement. Hence their availability in 1941. My diary for 3–16 June, and again 19–26 June, reads 'Erecting presses'. Each consisted of two seven-foot tall end-pieces with numerous deep slots into which brackets and the shelf ends could be fitted. The difficulty lay in man-handling the end-pieces up from the basement through a narrow lift and on a short barrow designed for carrying books. Some 120 such presses were erected with immense effort. But this was not all. Each press when full would weigh about half a ton, and there was no natural rigidity, as the press was never intended to stand on a floor. (The openwork gallery railing was not strong enough to be used for any attachment.) So I had to obtain batons of two by four inches – six-foot lengths, if memory serves – and somehow bolt a length on to the outer top side of each press in order to secure four or five presses together, with batons overlapping from one group of four on to the next, and so right round the gallery. When the job was done, the 'W.P.s' were brought down from the Quadrant by other hands.

All this and much other work to protect and rescue the collection of printed books went on in a state of general apprehension. But though air-raids continued, the Museum buildings sustained no more damage, and by 1943 the danger seemed to have receded. When the Reading Room had been cleared of all the debris left by the sorting of burnt books, it was put to a new purpose. Because the rules of the Ministry of Information forbade the immediate publication of damage caused by air-raids, it was some time before the library's losses could be made known in the press. But once permission was given, the Museum published full details and issued an appeal for gifts of books to replace those destroyed, and stated all the categories in which the losses had occurred. This information, printed in the national press and professional journals, elicited an astonishing response. The first trickle became a torrent, and the now empty Reading Room became the reception centre. When the shelves on the ground floor were full, those in the first gallery were used. The books had to be sorted into categories, put into alphabetical order, checked first against the catalogue, and then against the two lists of destroyed books – subject and author – which were being laboriously compiled from the fourth copy cards (i.e. catalogue entries arranged as shelf-lists). All this took many months, and some staff, notably Oldman, worked late into the evenings to get it done. It was very interesting to find that besides replacing lost books, the gifts (which came from libraries and people all over the country) included quite a number of books, both new titles and important revised editions, which were not in the collections at all.

All this prolonged anxiety and extra work were not unrelieved by lighter moments. One of them was the extraordinary occasion of Forsdyke's wedding. A widower for many years, he had become privately engaged to Dea Gombrich, the sister of Dr Ernst (later Sir Ernst) Gombrich, the distinguished art historian. The Archbishop of Canterbury, chairman of the Trustees, offici-ated at a private ceremony in the Chapel of the Savoy in 1942. Because of the difficult times, no announcement was made, and when some senior staff and their wives were invited to a party in the Director's residence very few knew about the ceremony; in any case Forsdyke was known, despite his great administrative ability, to be slightly eccentric, and no introductions were made. The guests were nevertheless astonished when Lady Forsdyke, an excellent musician, stepped forward and began playing a violin solo. When she stopped as suddenly as she had begun, a hush fell on the company, and the voice of Mrs Allan, the outspoken wife of the Keeper of Coins and Medals, could be heard saying in a loud whisper: 'Who on earth might that woman be?'.

By the end of 1942 the age of reservation for those born, as I was, in 1911 had been altered and those aged thirty-one were no longer reserved. Having previously been graded C³ at a medical examination, I was ineligible for military service but was seconded at the end of January 1943 to a department of the Foreign Office in the country, to which other Museum staff had been or were about to be sent. Among them was Angus Wilson who stayed until 1946. His chronically nervous state was not improved by an accident in the blackout. Walking home one night he tripped and fell face down into a low-cut hedge which inflicted scars on his face but spared his eyes. On another occasion when on weekend leave in London he visited a restaurant with friends and had a *crise de nerfs* at supper. He leapt from the table, sending crockery flying, tore the tablecloth in half and rushed into the street, pursued in the blackout by wrathful waiters shouting: 'It isn't the money, it's the coupons'.

My own stay out of London was cut short by a curious illness. I contracted gingivitis, a highly contagious infection of the mouth which caused me to be barred from the staff canteen as a danger to my fellows. On 15 July I was returned empty, so to speak, to the Museum where staff numbers were running very low indeed. My diary recorded that for the last days of January I was 'packing books', that is 'case books', for belated despatch to additional places of safety in the country as they became available. Little more of this, however, was needed by the end of 1943 as the risk of air-raids decreased. But authority was still taking as few chances as possible. Because war-time shortages still denied all shelving to the North-East Quadrant, most of the valuable books still remaining in the library were moved from vulnerable storage and stacked in piles on the concrete floors covered with brown paper. There they stayed for some time, unavailable to readers, until a type of shelving made of asbestos encased in plywood (which proved far more durable than was expected) could be supplied.

Everyone had to put his hand to almost everything. Hours of work had been extended to eight and a half a day (and remained so until March 1946), and night-time fire-watching duty went on, both during the week and on Sundays. My diary shows that besides work on GK II, I did proof-reading of current accessions, checking purchase lists and incorporation. In addition, I had immediately been put in charge of the bindery, which entailed writing the orders, inspecting the bound volumes, doing occasional liaison work with people from a laboratory concerned with leather research, visiting the News-paper Library at Colindale (which had suffered severe damage from a large explosive bomb) and much else.

Among many later social experiences, one of the most valuable was an invitation to the Christmas party which was organised by the bindery and the catalogue shop, and was held on the latter's premises above the Banksian mezzanine on Christmas Eve. Its fund came from a small subscription – I think it was sixpence a week – which, with regular contribution from all the staff built up substantially over the year. The Father of the Chapel had an agreement with the Stationery Office (as the employers) that Christmas Eve was effectively an extra holiday. The party therefore started at about 10.30, with a huge supply of every imaginable drink. Most guests came and left fairly early, certainly before noon, after which pretty riotous behaviour set in. By three o'clock, the men began to stagger home. Their quickest way out, on a normal working day, was through the Reading Room, but after one Christmas on which their excited, voluble behaviour particularly offended the readers, they were persuaded to take a longer way through the King's Library. When, in the later 1960s, amplified music became available, the racket was fearful. I was only asked to one of these parties.

My diary shows that when I was transferred to the Music Room on 27 December 1944, on the retirement of William C. Smith, my first task was the incorporation of the large arrears of music accessions. I could not give my whole time to the music: my diary also shows that my supervision of the bindery and writing orders for it continued until October 1945. But by then at least I thought I could begin to give my undivided attention to the huge arrears of Music Room work. Events proved me wrong.

Very slowly, staff returned after 'demobilisation'. Among my pre-war contemporaries, three were to play a notable part in the development of the library's work. Howard Nixon was ultimately appointed superintendent of the North Library and won world-wide repute for his scholarly knowledge of book-binding: he secured some outstanding collections to add to the Museum's already fine holdings. (After his retirement in 1974 Nixon became Librarian at Westminster Abbey, where he had been an assistant over forty years earlier and whence he had joined the Museum. In 1983 his ashes were interred in the Cloisters at the foot of the Library staircase.) Less spectacular, perhaps, but no less important, was the work of G. H. Spinney who was put in charge of the collection of State Papers, and worked prodigiously to expand it on a global basis by perfecting an exchange system so that the library acquired documents issued by most governments in return for British publications. The Official Publications Library (as the collections were ulti- mately named) is Spinney's monument. The contribution of J. L. Wood was equally unspectacular but essential to the efficiency of the department. His linguistic gifts made him ideally suited to be in charge of purchasing, a job which required tact and patience. Having just such qualities, Wood made as great a success in this post as he did when promoted in 1966 to be Keeper in charge of staff, with the control of selection boards, liaison with the Director's Office and much other difficult work. (As to myself, precisely why I was selected to go to the Music Room, I never discovered. There were others as well equipped as I: I can only assume that my good angel was Oldman who appreciated the few things I had published.)

III · WIDER HORIZONS AND THE HIRSCH MUSIC LIBRARY

In the Music Room (Fig. 25), the transition was different, and equally difficult, though for different reasons. There was only time for me to spend two half-days with my predecessor William Charles Smith. Perhaps it was just as well. He was an impossible little man, cordially detested by his colleagues, and had been a disastrous choice to succeed Squire on his retirement in 1920. (Misguidedly, Squire backed him: many wanted to bring in a scholar from outside the Museum.) Smith had contrived to reduce the routine of the Music Room to the bare minimum; for instance, his average annual expenditure on purchases was £135 a year – the total departmental grant varied between £6,500 and £9,500. Smith left most of the cataloguing to Humphries (of whom more later), and contented himself with proof-reading (only some 4,000 entries in one Accessions Part a year) and incorporation. Later, I learned that he spent some of his ample official spare time in building up his collection of books about London. He did indeed make a small contribution to GK II by 'revising', in advance, the heading 'LONDON – Livery Companies', of which he professed some knowledge. (I had to correct many of his errors when I was assistant Incorporator.) Smith was also able to build up his fine collection (ultimately purchased by the late Gerald Coke) of first and early editions of Handel. His various publications – the Walsh bibliographies and, with Humphries, *Music Publishing in the British Isles* – are first rate of their kind. But it should not be forgotten that it was his official idleness that made them possible in the first place. It should also be pointed out that Smith's own description of his work, in the early pages of *A Handelian's Notebook* (1964) is tendentious and inaccurate. Humphries told me nothing about Smith, but George Cole, his successor as Higher Clerical Officer (later a Junior Research Assistant) felt no such inhibition. Smith used to spend a lot of his afternoons just reading novels.

Smith's desk stood at the west end of the Music Room, backing on to windows which overlooked the gardens of some houses in Bedford Square. His staff all worked some way off, at tables set along the north side of the room, which was separated from the west end by the inner walls of the room containing the King's Music Library (as it was then known). On the outer wall of this room, near Smith's desk, was a bell push wired to a bell set above the

25 The Music Room, photographed in 1966. Right to left: A. H. King, O. W. Neighbour, H. J. Parkinson.

staff's work tables. Smith used it frequently – one ring for Humphries, two for Cole and three for the most junior, H. E. Crossman. I had the bell removed.

So, early in 1945, when Smith had finally handed me over to Humphries, he was fully justified in saying 'Just ask him – he knows everything'. Charles Humphries was an extraordinary character. He had joined the department in 1908 as a boy attendant, and had early been assigned to help Squire when the latter was working on his two-volume catalogue of the Museum's pre-1800 music which appeared in 1912. Called up for military service, Humphries finished his career as a sergeant in the Rhine Occupation army: he continually reminded me of that fact. Tall, nervous and aquiline of feature, he was self-righteous, deferential and a bully. How his juniors loathed him! Though extraordinarily industrious, he was pedantic, yet of formidable accuracy. He it was who, when his official work was done, had spent many hours transcribing from newspapers, directories and the music itself, the vast quantity of advertisements which formed the essence of the books published by Smith alone, or in acknowledged collaboration with him.

But Humphries was also very loyal. Without him, I could never have got through my first years in the Music Room and I think he was grateful for the two long-overdue promotions which I ultimately secured for him. (At that time senior posts in the clerical and executive grades were very scarce.) Humphries was terrified of innovation, and Smith had never bothered to acquaint himself with the many improvements in cataloguing practice that had evolved in the General Library from 1920 onwards. They applied just as much to music as to books. But Humphries's mind was firmly anchored in the world of 1908. So I had much difficulty in explaining to him the reasons for the changes I wanted to introduce. Events were to show how necessary they were.

As the intake of copyright music began to increase, I was able to catalogue a higher proportion of it than had been done before the war. But the principles of selection and rejection remained absurd, and the arrears were huge. It was not until 1966 when Claud Sington O.B.E., a retired Civil Servant, offered his services free, that I could hope for any reduction. (My successors enjoyed similar help from R. J. Fulford, a retired Keeper of Printed Books, who began work in 1985, and completed the work for all uncatalogued music received up to 1919. This occupied him until 1990.) A number of interesting donations soon began to come in. Lord Vernon gave a lot of Italian music from the early nineteenth century. In June 1945 I was asked to go to Wynnstay near Ruabon, the home of Sir Watkin Williams Wynn, the 8th baronet, who offered a large collection of eighteenth-century rarities, both English and European. It was, alas, kept in an outhouse, looked after – if at all – by the butler, and so damp that only a fraction of it was useable. Through the Royal Music Library in Stockholm we received a handsome gift of a pretty complete set of all important music by Swedish composers published in the late nineteenth-century and early twentieth. Here I would also record, as a matter of convenience, another gift which dates from a few years later. It was about the summer of 1952 that an acquaintance of mine who was on the music staff at Ardingly College, near East Horsham in Sussex, told me that Lord Courthope, who lived not far away, at Whiligh, had some 'early' music that he wanted to give to the Museum. (Lord Courthope was a renowned expert in forestry and a friend of Churchill. I believe that Whiligh contributed some of the oak used in the postwar rebuilding of the House of Commons.)

So, with my go-between, I was duly invited to lunch, before which we inspected the music. It was hardly 'early', being of the 1730s and 1740s, but was in almost pristine condition. There were about fifty pieces, kept in a very dusty cupboard. After inspection we were invited to clean up and were conducted to a large cloakroom just off the dining room. It looked as if it had been converted from an outhouse or stables. Along one wall were four or five hand-basins, and right along the wall above them there ran, in huge capitals, the legend: DON'T FORGET DEEP BREATHING. Another excursion from about the same time was to Rustington, on the Sussex coast, whence came an offer of 'old' French music, from the Comtesse de Belleroche. Alas, the lady was living in distinctly reduced circumstances, in a very ordinary modern house but the music comprised some 300 French songs of the period 1780 to 1870. Among other notable gifts were the 1,232 books of psalms and hymns comprising the library of Church House, Westminster (1949) and the valuable collection of the Catch Club (1952).

One of the benefits of working in the Music Room was a widening of horizons. To the east, on the same mezzanine floor of the King Edward VII Building, lay the offices of the Department of Prints and Drawings. Its Keeper in 1946 was Arthur Mayger Hind, who was an enthusiastic amateur violinist. A kindly man with a prominent white moustache and a slightly grand manner, he often came to look at chamber music for the domestic string quartet which he was able to form with his three musical daughters. From the same department came the far more jovial Edward Croft Murray, then its senior Assistant Keeper and later to be its Keeper from 1954 to 1972. 'Teddy', as he was always known, was, like his Keeper, an enthusiastic violinist, though of rather slender talents, but an even more enthusiastic – indeed a brilliant – kettle drummer. He possessed a splendid pair of drums dating from the Regency, and owned many other fine period instruments. Though Teddy specialised in the eighteenth century, and hated any music later than Weber, his knowledge of all the musical material in his department was as prodigious as his help was unstinted in lending it to brighten our otherwise dreary exhibitions. His hospitality, both in the privacy of his departmental office, in the Students' Room parties and in his splendid Queen Anne house in Maids of Honour Row at Richmond, was legendary. Teddy was tall, of generous build, with rugged features and a kindly mien. It was recorded that at one of the Students' Room parties, Rosalind – the daughter of his second marriage – was present when a child of three or four. At one moment in a crowded gathering, when she felt the company of so many adults rather frightening, she turned for help to her father, flung herself round his knees and called out in a penetrating voice 'Pretty daddy'.

From what was then British and Mediaeval Antiquities there came another frequent visitor to the Music Room, William Augustus Henry ('Willie') King, the department's specialist in Bow china. His purpose was first to enquire after one's health, and then to look at the score of an opera. Willie went to Covent Garden almost every week, and rarely missed any interesting production elsewhere. He once had the distinction of being turned out of his seat in the front row of the stalls at the Garden, on the order of Sir Thomas Beecham, whom he criticised audibly and persistently. Willie was invariably drunk, in a gentlemanly way. He was very thin and stooping; he had a high-pitched drawl and walked very quickly with short steps. His nose and eyes stood out from his rather purple face and when in later life he grew a short beard, his profile was unforgettable. (It is wonderfuly preserved in a portrait included in his wife Viva's autobiography, *The Weeping and the Laughter* (1976).)

A true eccentric, Willie was immensely kind. It was he who introduced me, near the end of the war, to that inimitable writer Norman Douglas (with whom I had been in correspondence), then a guest at the Kings' house in Thurlow Square. Willie never wore a coat even in the coldest weather. It was a miracle that he lived as long as he did, but his death in his early sixties was a sad loss to his friends. He is said to have been the original of Matthew Price, Curator of Birds, in Angus Wilson's novel *The Old Men at the Zoo*. (It was, incidentally, partly because of Willie's musicality and partly because I shared two initials with him, that I used my Christian names in full, rather than just my initials, in connection with my published work. Another possible source of confusion was that there was an A. H. King contemporary with me at Cambridge.)

I must now return to the overwhelming event of the later 1940s – the Museum's acquisition of the Paul Hirsch Music Library. Of Hirsch himself I have written elsewhere, as also of the technical procedures that we had to adopt to catalogue his library. Here I need record only the event, and the immediate impact of the collection on the work of the Music Room. It was soon after Christmas 1945 that news leaked out about Hirsch's intention to sell his library. Because collecting and cataloguing the library had been the ruling passion of his life since 1895, it was also known that he was desperately anxious for it to stay in the country of his adoption rather than be sold for the far greater price he could have obtained in America. He reasoned, quite sensibly, that if it were purchased by the British Museum, he would be given some degree of access. But the price, £120,000, was far beyond the individual resources of the Museum, especially in a period of acute post-war austerity. After much anxious negotiation, during which E. J. Dent played a notable part behind the scenes, the Pilgrim Trust gave £60,000, the Treasury £50,000, and the Trustees £10,000 (to be found in five annual instalments). During these months Thomas and Forsdyke were in full collaboration, and arrangements for payment were concluded in the summer of 1946.

I then had to arrange the transport of the collection from the University Library in Cambridge where it had been stored and made freely available to all *bona fide* students. I went to Cambridge on 29 October for this purpose and checked the whole again on 3 December. The work necessitated two stays in Cambridge, the first from 6–10 January 1947, and the second on the 13th and 14th. Humphries, with the two Museum housemen seconded for the job was a tower of strength. I had arranged for the Museum to send in advance a large quantity of plywood boxes, strong cord and blank, open lead seals. The last I collected from H. H. Simmonds, the Staff Officer in charge of security, who also provided the double-ended instrument on the underside of which was embossed the Museum crown. After each box was packed and corded, and the open seal placed under the end of the cords, this instrument compressed cords and seal so that the crown appeared on the upper side. We used a similar process to seal the thick ropes and the padlocks with which the railway vans, when packed, were secured. Forsdyke himself negotiated all arrangements with the railway: his wartime knowledge was invaluable. In all, three large vans were required. When the last of them had been weighed at Cambridge goods yard, the checkweighman told me that the total weight of the load in the three vans was just over 13 tons. Unpacking lasted for six days, from 15 −21 January (excluding Sunday).

The one easy thing, at the beginning, was finding space. There were enough of the fine, locked, glazed cases in the King's Music Library (as the room was then called) to house all the contents of the books on theory, comprising vol.I of Hirsch's own catalogue, and a good many opera scores. For the remainder of them and for the first few hundred of his classical first editions (vol.III), there were the empty upper glazed cases along the south corridor (the sun was bad for the books, but they had to be used). The rest of the library had to go on the upper, empty three shelves all round the rest of the room. (These shelves had been left empty to minimise the danger of access by steep ladders.) Another six or seven years were to pass before I could get the special locked doors and steel plating in order to reorganise two whole bays at the east end of the room; this was to create a totally secure area where the whole Hirsch library could be kept behind locks, although more than half could never be glazed.

Throughout all the early years of work on the Hirsch collection, Paul Hirsch himself was very much in the picture. The Trustees gave him a house key so that he could have easy access to the Music Room, where we put the then unused desk in the King's Music Library at his disposal. He came from Cambridge once or twice a week, with some dealer's catalogue, already marked, which he thought we might not have seen. He himself bought rarities, which we could not afford, both through dealers and at auction, and gave them as additions to his former library. When our recataloguing of the music was done, he read the proofs. But when he contracted pneumonia in 1951, his already weak heart could not stand the strain. His death, on 23 November 1951, was a great loss. (I have given fuller details of all this in an article, 'The Hirsch Music Library: retrospect and conclusion', in *Notes* IX, 1952−3, pp.381−7.)

Work on the Hirsch library dominated the Music Room for well over four years. Humphries was again invaluable. He himself did most of the pressmarking – on both title-slips and the titlepages. He shared the cataloguing with me, though I did all the proof-reading, and wrote the orders for binding. The numerous works in parts, which Hirsch had grouped in boxes, had to be redistributed in sequence, and because there was so little money for binding, I had to be content with flimsy red cloth folders, each with protective flaps, provided in three sizes on one bulk order from a reluctant Stationery Office. Humphries also supervised the labelling, and, later, the despatch of the books (i.e. literature as distinct from music) to the General Library for cataloguing, checking them on return. These labours went on one way or another, until the late 1950s. It is certain that in the post-war years no other division of the library had to deal with such a huge accession, for which there was immediate public demand, with no increase in staff. Indeed when O. W. (Tim) Neighbour joined me in 1951, the arrears were so great and other demands on my time so numerous, that we were really only maintaining the *status quo ante*.

Of course, apart from Hirsch, some of the extra work was the consequence of rational changes in responsibility. Until 1945 all photographic orders for material in the Music Room were entirely the duty of a clerical officer working in the Keeper's Ante-Room. Henceforward, all the work – identification, clarification, copyright clearance and much else – devolved on the Music Room. (The immense post-war increase required more staff.) So too did security of keys and case books. Until 1945, again, the keys to the case books and to the Royal Music were kept in the North Library, so that if any one on the Music Room staff needed to consult any such 'secure' music, one had to go down and collect the appropriate key, whose withdrawal and return had to be twice-signed and countersigned. The Music Room key safe, when supplied, was screwed to my desk, and the key to it daily drawn and returned to the Ante Room which now had the safe for all departmental keys.

Minor changes such as these were a distraction from the main tasks facing a small section of the library in those hectic post-war years. The first one was to overtake the huge arrears of purchasing, and this could only be tackled as more money became available after the fall of the Labour government in 1951. Before that, I had to establish new agencies for different parts of the world – France, Germany and other European countries, and for the Americas, north and south. Gradually, the music came in, and the extra capacity for cataloguing afforded by Tim Neighbour allowed the intake to be dealt with fairly promptly. The general increase in departmental funds enabled us to buy, both from dealers and at auction, important music from the recent and from the more distant past. All this was a matter of hard work and application, and the new momentum soon showed results. The state of the music catalogues was a far more intractable problem, which had its roots in history.

IV · THE CATALOGUES OF PRINTED MUSIC

The General Catalogue of Printed Books had been an entity since its inception in 1787. It contained all books, whatever their date, in one sequence, as did also the catalogue of maps. The catalogue of music had likewise grown as an entity ever since its inception in 1840, but, as I have related elsewhere (in my *Printed Music in the British Museum* 1979), in the first decade of the twentieth century there was a wide demand for a published catalogue of the 'early' printed music, which was judged to be all before about 1800. Squire, the Assistant Keeper (then equivalent to the later 'Deputy Keeper') in charge of the music could only meet this demand by extracting all entries for pre-1800 music, published in two volumes in 1912, which had many differences in principles and arrangement from those which governed the parent catalogue. Thenceforth there were two catalogues, one described as 'old' music, the other as 'new' music – a patent absurdity and most inconvenient to readers. Many important composers were in both catalogues, under headings arranged on two different principles. To this confusion was added a third catalogue in 1929 when there appeared a separate catalogue of the printed music in the 'King's Music Library' – as its title then ran – which had been deposited on loan in 1911. This again was quite different from the other two catalogues in both typography and layout.

To analyse these ridiculous anomalies was far easier than to solve the problems they posed. Tim Neighbour and I had many discussions, and consulted senior colleagues both in the department and in the Director's Office. We drew up a plan as a basis for a report to the Trustees, but in the end it was never formally submitted because the immense job of unification could only be done by an increase in staff at several levels. For we knew that, even with the Trustees' approval, the Treasury would never sanction this. So the frustration remained until the mid-1970s, when all the catalogues of printed books became the object of commercial interest. Ultimately the Munich firm K. G. Saur published unrevised but amalgamated editions both of the *General Catalogue of Printed Books* and of the music catalogues. The latter was of unparalleled complexity. The outside staff hired for the work on the music were supervised and guided by Tim Neighbour, who sustained this immense burden for four years while he was still in office. He saw the job through to its conclusion in the first three years of his retirement. *The Catalogue of Printed Music in the British Library* was completed in sixty-two volumes, 1981 to 1987, and is the greatest of his many, little-known services to the collection of printed music, both when they were under the jurisdiction of the Trustees of the British Museum, and during the difficult years of transition to the British Library.

One episode during this long process may be of interest. In 1955 the Government established a typing pool at Newcastle upon Tyne, and it sent out a circular to many departments offering its free services. When a copy reached the British Museum, it was sent to all Keepers, and in the Department of Printed Books it received a particular welcome in connection with the music catalogue. For very much space was taken up by the so-called 'transcribed entries' – entries which had been made on carbon paper for some thirty years from about 1850 to 1880. As the movable slips bearing these entries measured about ten inches wide by a minimum of 1 inch high, and ran to many thousands, they took up an inordinate amount of space, which could be saved if each was typed and so replaced by a slip of less than one quarter the size. I was authorised to take a dozen of the bulky large folio catalogue volumes to Newcastle for a trial run, and one day in November 1956 went to King's Cross for the train journey north. Having stowed the crate of volumes in the luggage van, I found my reserved seat in an adjacent first class compartment, on the corridor side, and noted that the two window seats were also reserved. On looking out of the window, I saw a top-hatted figure, clearly the head station master, walking about in a state of some agitation with lesser staff hovering near. Five minutes before we were due to start, a Rolls Royce drew up on the roadway at the end of the platform, and there emerged Lady Eden, the wife of the Prime Minister, and a gentleman whom I soon identified from recollection of newspaper photographs, as Lord Lambton. They made straight for the corner seats in my compartment, where, during the journey – except for the time when I was in the dining car – my presence was clearly an embarrassment. They could hardly discuss in my hearing Suez and that Canal which in Lady Eden's words (as reported by the press) was still 'flowing through her drawing room'.

About a year later, I made another strange journey north, this time in connection with a loan of music made to America for an exhibition held to mark the 350th anniversary of the foundation of Jamestown, Virginia. The Trustees had agreed to lend a volume from the Royal Music Library which consisted entirely of sacred music in the hand of Henry Purcell. This magnificent folio, bound in full red morocco, had been sent out by diplomatic bag, and was returned by liner (I forget which) under special seal, to Liverpool. I was provided with extensive documents which had three purposes – first to prove that I was A. H. K., and in the employment of the Trustees; second, that the volume belonged to them (only since the spring of 1957, in fact; previously (*see* p.285) it had been part of the Queen's Music Library); third, that it was in Purcell's hand. I and the documents were escorted from my hotel to the Customs Office in the docks by a gentleman from the Waterguard, who seemed at once to regard me and my peculiar mission with as much suspicion as the Customs were soon to show. Indeed the Waterguard and Customs were, to say the least, incredulous. Though my identity was not in question, all else was. It needed a précis of English musical history, a disquisition on why the Museum really needed a music library and a lot more talk and form-filling before I was released from the Customs, lugging a very heavy volume in a large suitcase to the taxi in which the Waterguard accompanied me to the train. I had great difficulty in finding a first-class carriage with a partially empty luggage rack. Very soon, another passenger heaved his case on top of mine. And with that minimum of protection I had to leave Purcell unattended while I had a much needed wash and brush-up followed by a quick tea. At such times of solitary pressure, the security rules of uninterrupted warding do not apply.

V · THE TRADE UNIONS AND SUNDRY AFFAIRS

There were a few more such excursions: at least they had the merit of being short, with little time needed for planning and no aftermath. But other official business took up much more time, and in the early 1950s 'union affairs' began to come to life after being fairly sluggish in the post-war years. I had been elected a member of the committee of the First Division Association, and so one of its representatives on the Whitley Council, on which all grades were represented. I was elected its chairman, and this involved me in numerous meetings to discuss a great variety of matters, some trivial, some quite important. Among the latter were such things as properly organised selection boards for promotion in all grades (on which Bentley Bridgewater, the Secretary of the Museum, was an unfailing tower of strength because of his unique knowledge of the staff), and the need for pay-slips which, as elsewhere in the Civil Service, showed not only the net monthly salary but all deductions from it. (Previously, one received only a net cheque, delivered in the internal mail: soon, payment direct to bank was introduced!) The acme of the 'Whitley year' was the meeting between the representatives of the Staff Side and the Official Side, the latter then comprising the Director (Sir Thomas Kendrick), the Secretary (Bentley Bridgewater), the Assistant Secretary (John McIntyre), a Trustee and a Keeper. At the meeting which lingers most in my mind, the Trustee was Lord de L'Isle, V.C., and the Keeper F. C. Francis, from Printed Books. It was a warm summer afternoon, and the westering sun flooded through the tall window of the boardroom, a splendid apartment with a coffered ceiling, and furnished with cupboards along the walls and a huge mahogany table round which some twenty people could sit in comfort. Points of business droned back and forth: Lord De L'Isle, seated with his back to the sun, nodded off; interjections came from Francis as Kendrick (a much-loved man) ambled vaguely through the agenda, and began to sum up to bring the meeting to a close. But he reckoned without the Staff Side secretary, a senior fireman-warder named John Francis Sinclair. Sinclair (who was promoted to Chief Warden in 1967, holding the post until about 1969) was a skilled shorthand writer, and had been taking notes of what Kendrick had said. At one point, the latter fumbled, and misinterpreted such notes as Bridgewater had taken. Sinclair intervened: 'But, with respect, Sir Thomas, what you said was . . .' Tea again seemed a long way off.

My work on this committee had, of course, nothing to do with the Music Room. Indeed, we were fortunate in that we were only on the fringe of all the hideous politics of the General Library during that dire decade when Francis persuaded the Trustees to terminate all work on the proper revision of the General Catalogue so that the staff could ultimately be directed to its shoddy photomechanical reproduction. (All this was in fact a mere sideshow to the transfer of the Patent Office Library to be part of the British Museum library, which led ultimately but directly to its transfer away from the Trustees to the power of the Board of the British Library.) It lies beyond the scope of this chapter to give a full account of all this. Readers who are interested in the suppression of GK II and its consequence should consult the excellent article by A. H. Chaplin (Principal Keeper of Printed Books from 1966 to 1970), The General Catalogue of Printed Books, 1881–1981 which is in *The British Library Journal,* vol.7, no.2, autumn 1981.

There were other aspects to Whitley Council and Staff Side work, some lighter, some more serious. One of the most extraordinary was the matter of 'Thorrington's Canteen', which rumbled on for some time. Thorrington was, if memory serves, a general labourer on the Trustees' staff which included skilled men such as electricians, glaziers and carpenters. For a long time these excellent men had nowhere to go when they wanted a cup of tea and a cigarette. In his spare time, which was considerable, Thorrington set up a canteen in a large hut on the east roadway, had it fitted with electricity by his expert friends and there provided what they all wanted. But there was no proper plumbing, and in addition the wiring was run above ground from a mains supply. The hut was also near to building stores, and so was regarded as a risk both to safety and to health. Officialdom was not pleased, though it accepted the needs of the workmen. The matter was the subject of endless discussion on the Council, where it was reasonably pointed out that if the men could be given somewhere to change out of their working clothes, they could use the official staff restaurant, such as it was. In the end, the fire-services, who (though some of their members used Thorrington's 'facilities') were very concerned by the fire risk, won the day, his premises were demolished and a proper works canteen provided. All this, hilarious while it lasted, took up a lot of time; one of the final benefits, though a small one, was that Thorrington was free – probably against his wishes – to do a full day's work.

Here, a digression on the vexed problem of restaurants in the British Museum may not come amiss. As mentioned on p.249, the sole provision in the 1930s was the small room off the centre of the west side of the main Egyptian gallery. (Lunches were served by a glamorous waitress named Alice, notorious for her prolonged affair with a gentleman in the Director's Office.) This small restaurant was made available in the afternoon to the public so that they could at least get a cup of tea and a bun. In the 1950s the staff were given a gloomy, narrow basement room under the South-West Front of the colonnade, and adjacent to the large, but flimsy single-storey old structure used for the preparation and study of casts of Greek and Roman sculpture. This 'cast room' itself soon became the staff restaurant, and Kendrick had the good idea of using its inner part for what became known as 'Trustees' lunches'. These occasions, at which sandwiches, wine or beer and coffee were provided, were held on one Saturday in each month, after the Trustees' meeting. The Keepers attended as their guests, and were allowed to bring the Deputy Keeper of a department responsible for some important recent purchase. Thus, for the first time in Museum history, senior staff could meet their 'lords and masters' informally (though a few did this at The Athenaeum). The couple who ran this staff restaurant were named Corbett, and having ultimately obtained a limited licence, were able to supply drinks for the riotous staff parties which from the late 1950s onwards were held at Christmas and many other occasions. When the 'cast room' was reclaimed by the Museum, in order that a new wing might be built in the area, restaurant 'facilities' were moved to the old 'Drill Hall' (built in 1840 as a savings bank, and used during World War II by a Territorial Army unit). This is an elegant room near the South-East corner of the King's Library. When this too was reclaimed (for Library use), all that the staff had was a couple of 'Portakabins' on empty space at the side of the White Wing. The present staff and public restaurants were built, partly on the site of the old 'cast room' in 1979–80. All these successive developments took place under the guidance of a Restaurant Committee, in which I had no part.

Rather more important to me was the completion of the war memorial, which is inscribed on the wall of the colonnade just to the east of the main (south) entrance. It was rightly felt that the names of the four members of the staff who died on active service in the Second World War should be added, between those recorded from the First. With the help of the Director's Office, the Staff Side traced all the nearest surviving relatives, and brought them together for a short, intimate ceremony at which, as chairman, I was present. The main entrance doors of the Museum were closed for half an hour, and barriers erected so that the Archbishop of Canterbury, Lord Fisher, who was then Chairman of the Trustees, could conduct the brief ceremony without disturbance. He did so with great dignity; a wreath was laid and it then fell to me to introduce the relatives to him. The least pompous of men, Lord Fisher had a kindly word for each group. He then went to his waiting car: the barriers were taken away; the great doors swung open and the flow of life began again.

VI · OTHER CATALOGUES AND EXHIBITIONS

Interesting as were such work and occasions, they were intermittent and took up relatively little of my official time. Far more demanding and prolonged were the affairs of the *British Union Catalogue of Early Music* (known generally by its abridged acronym *BUC*). Though its contents comprised all the music printed before 1800 in well over 100 libraries throughout the British Isles, the holdings of the British Museum comprised some seventy per cent or so of the whole. I served as secretary to the executive committee from 1948 until the publication of the catalogue in 1957, and thereafter as secretary to the limited company into which the committee was legally required to turn itself, for the purpose of winding up its affairs a few years later. I was therefore at the centre of *BUC* which deserves mention here not so much for my part in it as for a curious, barely recorded episode in the life of that distinguished music bibliographer Otto Erich Deutsch, whose idea *BUC* was. (The initial of his surname, 'D', is now used to identify all Schubert's works.)

He first put the idea forward in an article in *The Journal of Documentation*, vol.1, 1945, and in 1946 a large meeting was held in the board room of the British Museum, chaired by Sir Frederick Kenyon, who had retired as Director and Principal Librarian in 1930. Though his younger daughter Norah had briefly been a colleague of mine, this was the only time I met that prodigious scholar. He reminded me somewhat of A. E. Housman, whose lectures I had once attended. Their voices, high and rather dry, were not dissimilar, and there was some likeness in their strong features and rather lugubrious countenances. Both the names of all those present and the subsequent technical and financial arrangements are given in the introduction to the catalogue, and need not be repeated here. A council was established and from it an executive committee, including myself, was appointed. By unanimous agreement Deutsch was appointed editor and began work with great enthusiasm. But he was then in his sixty-third year, and while well-organised libraries in London and others within easy distance of it did not make heavy demands on his energy, those further away proved very different. By the time Deutsch reached Dublin, he was, to say the least, not putting his back into the work, and from various contacts the committee learned that he was spending a good deal of its time transcribing from the eighteenth-century Irish newspapers much material relating to Handel. By 1950 it was clear that a parting of the ways was at hand. It would be incorrect to say that Deutsch was dismissed, but equally imprecise to say (as it had to be at the time) that he 'retired'. He was persuaded to resign, and this was arranged with some ceremony. An active member of the committee was H. M. Adams, the then librarian of Trinity College, Cambridge. His spendid Wren Library served as the appropriate place for Adams to meet Deutsch, myself and Edith Schnapper, whom the committee had chosen to succeed Deutsch. Deutsch came with all his correspondence and notes and formally handed them over, giving up, as it were, his seals of office. As his bulky boxes of cards were too numerous and heavy to be moved twice, and as both the outgoing editor and his successor lived in Cambridge, we arranged for Schnapper to collect the boxes later in her car. She was not only a musicologist of repute but also had the advantage of having worked with Paul Hirsch on volume IV of his great catalogue. (She gave an excellent address some sixteen years later at Olga Hirsch's funeral.) Schnapper proved a good cataloguer, and had the benefit of relative youth to enable her to cope with visits to remote places and some awkward hotels.

One of the things I learned from my association with such work was the richness of the Museum's collections of 'early' music and its exceptional wealth of later music. In my time, this richness proved a crucial factor in our capacity to mount exhibitions of every period, kind and extent – an activity which took up an amount of energy quite out of all proportion to the results achieved. If the reader interprets this to mean that I was strongly against exhibitions, that is correct, and I must take the opportunity of stating my case. The most important of these exhibitions over this period were:

1949 Goethe
1950 J. S. Bach
1951 Handel: Messiah
*1953 Bicentenary (one of a monthly series to mark the foundation of the Museum)
*1956 Mozart
1957 Selections from the Royal Music to mark the bicentenary of George II's gift of the Old Royal Library

1957 Elgar
1957 Domenico Scarlatti
*1959 Handel and Purcell
1962 Richard Strauss
*1966 Music printing
*1970 Beethoven
*1972 Vaughan Williams
(* = larger exhibitions)

There is a crucial difference between any exhibition of music and one of any other type, be it of the visual arts, of maps or of literature. Most art exhibitions (at least of material produced before the twentieth century) show images which in themselves are familiar to the average viewer. So too with most maps: the names and countries and their outlines are familiar in themselves. Exhibited texts of printed books, apart from those in such founts as cyrillic or gothic, do not cause the viewer difficulty. Manuscript texts, of course, are more complicated, but fundamentally the image is the message, and with good labels much becomes clear to the eye and mind.

But in the case of music, the images – i.e. the notes – are *not* the message, but rather a fairly complex sequence of instructions to a performer to create sound of a certain kind, duration and pitch. Of the visitors to any music exhibition, only a proportion is likely to be able to read and profitably interpret an open page unless it be of fairly simple music in modern notation. Fewer still are interested in the nice distinctions between the three principal categories of music printing – from moveable type, from engraved plates, or by sundry applications of lithographic processes. A lot of manuscript music is even more arcane, although, like literary manuscripts, it enjoys an adventitious visual attraction when illuminations or miniatures are present. There is a similar benefit when an exhibition of early books printed in, say, gothic type includes some illustrated with handsome decorative or illustrative woodcuts.

The interest in any music exhibition is therefore mostly not musical at all, but visual – an absurd paradox. Fortunately much music is illustrated; many engraved songbooks of the eighteenth century, such as George Bickham's *The Musical Entertainer,* or J. B. de Laborde's *Choix de chansons* have handsome integral pictures. Covers of sheet music too are often very attractive. But all this is fortuitous. Many large music exhibitions mounted in the Museum gained enormously from pictorial and topographical material borrowed from the Department of Prints and Drawings, and the Music Room owed a continual debt of gratitude to Edward Croft Murray (Deputy Keeper and later Keeper of that department) for his enthusiasm and help, all the greater because, as mentioned above (p.271), he was an enthusiastic musical amateur in every sense of the word. His invaluable, imperturbable assistant was Reginald Williams. Equally great was our debt to Pamela Willetts in the Department of Manuscripts (in which she was an Assistant Keeper and later a Deputy Keeper) and to Hugh Cobbe (her successor in my time) for all their help in enlivening the mechanical dullness of print with the richness and variety of manuscripts, and for providing the brilliant labels which gave such enlightenment to the beholder. Even if the musical notes in the hand of a Beethoven are hard to read, the document itself has an unmistakable immediacy and individuality.

The nature of the work involved in preparing and mounting any exhibition is governed by the extent of the space available, by any use of that space for general purposes, and by the kind of cases provided. Nearly all the exhibitions that I prepared were in the King's Library, an apartment of unique splendour, designed by Smirke to accommodate the library of George III. It is 300 feet long and forty-one feet wide except at the middle where the central rectangle is expanded to fifty-eight feet. Because this apartment is so narrow, and because it serves as a transit gallery for the public to reach the upper floor of the Museum, the cases must stand fairly close to the sides, and also be so spread that the public have a safe circulation area. These facts have to some extent dictated the type of cases and their layout, which moreover ought not to obscure the superb vista.

The cases are of four main types. There are flat, desk-type cases, with gently sloping tops, some single-sided, other double-sided. More suitable for very tall books are the so-called 'gable-cases' which rise to a sharp point, some two foot six inches above the base of the case under which, as with the double-sided desk cases, are cupboards used for the storage of books. Many of these fine cases, some of maple, others of oak, date from the nineteenth century. None has internal lighting. In the early 1950s there were added four cases some seven feet tall made of glass within phosphor bronze corners and with doors at each end. These stood on a solid base and were lit from above by a fluorescent tube from which the down-light comfortably illuminated all three shelves. These, for some unknown reason, were called 'director' cases.

Because the Music Room was so remote from the King's Library, planning and layout of exhibitions was always laborious and sometimes hazardous. We were told well in advance how many cases and of which types would be available, and what their present positions were. If, as often occurred, a change of layout was necessary, this was worked out on paper, and a 'requisition' was sent to the 'heavy gang' asking them to be on the spot, a day before the books were put in, to move the cases. This had to be done well in advance because the gang of half a dozen strong men was in theory controlled by the Department of Greek and Roman Antiquities, and their services were every-where there in great demand. Their great skill in moving huge stone objects, ponderous oak screens ten feet long by six feet wide, and our cumbrous cases, was legendary. Armed with thick ropes, and long skids made of thin oak strips, they performed wonders, with endless patience and good humour.

Once this preliminary 'requisition' was agreed, planning could begin. The books were selected, the openings decided and the labels drafted and typed. The layout was done on sheets of brown paper cut to the exact sizes of the area available in every type of case. Gradually lists of titles were drawn up, and if a published catalogue were intended, the final numbered sequence had to be decided at this point. Items from other contributing departments had to be measured and intercalated, and headboards for the cases requisitioned, sometimes to be executed by an outside calligrapher on contract. The desk-top cases (usually lined with blue velvet or later with sail-cloth) presented little difficulty. But for the others, book stands were essential. At first these were ordinary, intrusive reading slopes, and were later replaced by perspex stands; the little blocks for the labels were also of the valuable new substance. Thin perspex strips also came into use for securing the book open – a welcome replacement for obtrusive white tape.

On the day of mounting, all the books had to be assembled on barrows, carefully tied, as far as practicable, in bundles without disturbing the perspex strips, and numbered to correspond with the numbered sequence of the cases. The barrows were laboriously taken down via the main lift in the King Edward VII building to the ground floor and then through many doors to the King's Library. There, other contributors were waiting, and a few of the heavy gang were in attendance to lower the huge screens onto their side so that framed items could be screwed on to their exact place. Also on standby elsewhere were a carpenter, a glazier, an electrician, and a locksmith, the last being essential to repair or adjust the old locks and keys which, being flimsy, might break inside the case. Worst of all were the 'director' cases, which had two security locks at each end, one being a bolt type which could not be moved until the ward lock was completely secured – a difficult job because of the bronze frames. Those exhibitions which were accompanied by a published catalogue were always the most stressful, because no last-minute changes in layout or sequence could be made, and sometimes miscalculations led to some pretty desperate expedients. It was also ironical that the sale of catalogues which, unlike art catalogues, were dull things, was nearly always below estimate and so lost money, sometimes to the wrath of the Trustees.

The larger exhibitions demanded a lot of extras. Besides a catalogue, there might be a poster (with many problems of design and wording); certainly a lot of advance publicity – mostly quite ineffectual – ; and a private press view, which, as we could seldom offer 'refreshments', was but poorly attended. A free information sheet had to be drafted. If there was a reception, this involved the immense labour of compiling an invitation list, which was always the subject of much bickering because selection was invidious and unpopular. There was never enough money to ask all those who merited invitation.

Some details of the larger exhibitions may not come amiss. The one mounted in 1953 was one of twelve planned to mark the bicentenary of the Museum's foundation. It was decreed that each should last a month and that there should be no gaps. It was therefore arranged that the outgoing exhibition be withdrawn on Saturday evening after the Museum closed to the public, all the cases cleared, and the new exhibition be in place before the galleries opened on the Sunday afternoon. All security arrangements within the department were suspended so that the staff had access to the galleries and keys. Since each exhibition occupied almost the whole of the King's Library and amounted to some 300 items, this involved hours of work at high pressure.

The Mozart exhibition was extremely complicated, for it was the first exhibition held in the King's Library to be televised. The presenter was Richard Dimbleby, whose charm and easy manner made all the rehearsals easier to endure. The 'link-man' with the BBC was William Glock who, if truth be told, was not of much benefit because, fine Mozart player though he was, he had little grasp of the nature of Mozart sources, and his garrulity was a hindrance rather than a help. Because the programme, which lasted some forty minutes, was broadcast live, it was essential that all concerned should keep to a carefully timed script. Bertram Schofield, the Keeper of Manuscripts, and I both managed to do this in our respectively allotted fields of the manuscript and printed music. But Teddy Croft Murray, who was responsible for the visual material showing the background to Mozart's sojourn in London, became so enthusiastic that he overran by several minutes, and no silent gestures could stop his flow! On a subsequent evening, there was a reception for which the Amadeus Quartet was engaged. They played in the centre square of the King's Library, at the west side. The vile acoustic, due to the omnipresent glass doors of the bookcases, made Mozart sound like Berlioz.

The Music Room's contribution to the great exhibition of 1957, held to mark the bicentenary of George II's gift of the Old Royal Library, was a 'director' case packed with items from the Queen's Music Library. This was only fitting because it was this collection (deposited on loan since 1911) that the Queen was about to present to the Trustees as an outright gift. There was, after all, as some cynics pointed out, nothing else appropriate that she could give! The Queen and the Duke of Edinburgh attended the private view, and various members of the staff, all in white tie and (mostly hired) tails, were duly presented. Neither Her Majesty, when confronted for the first time with her own music, nor I, knew what to say. Other objects aroused more interest, especially the great manuscripts of the Old Royal Library, some bearing the royal arms on the binding. Seventeen years later, there was a curious twist to this royal occasion. In 1974 the Queen's Gallery at Buckingham Palace mounted an exhibition entitled 'George III; Collector and Patron'. Sir Robin Mackworth-Young, the royal archivist, requested the loan of the autograph score of one of George III's favourite Handel oratorios. As this manuscript by now belonged not to the Queen but to the British Library Board, I had to remind Sir Robin that it would have to be insured to its full value, which was a great deal of money. He saw the irony of my point.

Hardly was the Mozart exhibition over before we had to start planning for the Purcell–Handel exhibition of 1959, the three hundredth anniversary of the former's birth and the two hundredth of the latter's death. This was a national occasion, marked by many concerts and some operatic productions, as part of a festival co-ordinated by the Arts Council. This meant that the Museum's large exhibition did, for once, receive rather more publicity than usual. Such was certainly not so with the next large exhibition, of music printing held in 1966, and timed to follow the publication of a booklet on the subject which I had written in 1964. I was given enough cases to display nearly 300 items, which entailed a great deal of extra work. Public interest was almost nil.

Fortunately in 1970, Beethoven, the bicentenary of whose birth fell in that year, was a name to conjure with, and aided by the use of the evocative association pieces in the Royal Philharmonic Society's library (deposited on loan in the Department of Manuscripts), it was quite a good show. But it was ruined by the totally absurd presentation, or, as the pundits call it, 'design'. The centre and about half of each end of the King's Library were divided into sections, marked off by screens, and above all there floated continuous sheets of white muslin, whose purpose was unclear. All they did was to flutter and flap uneasily in the draught that blows continually along this gallery.

Even more bizarre was the Vaughan Williams exhibition of 1972. The hired designer, Christopher Hudson, was obsessed with the notion that, because the composer had been interested in English folk-song, and had written a 'pastoral' symphony, green was the appropriate colour to dominate the show-case backings, labels and so on. Even the little catalogue had to have a green border. The effect was ludicrously artificial. Hudson also insisted that there must be some taped music: so in the *Job* section (where we showed some of the cardboard figures from Gwen Raverat's mock-ups for the original production, loaned by Sir Geoffrey Keynes) music floated out repetitiously from on high to help the viewer's understanding of the open page of the music in the case below.

All these exhibitions, which were mostly on show for barely two months, and very occasionally for three, were endlessly distracting and demanded an enormous amount of time and energy. Much of it was wasted because enquiry revealed that no viewer or visitor cared tuppence about 'display' as long as the labels were clear, the cases adequately lit and the books and manuscripts not overcrowded.

Before I pass to other, external, distractions, perhaps a few episodes in lighter vein may not come amiss.

VII · READERS, ROUTINE, AND RECORDED SOUND

Every large library has its share of tiresome readers and the British Museum was no exception. One of ours was John Tobin, the conductor of the London Choral Society. It was he who persuaded us to mount a small exhibition of the sources of Handel's oratorio *The Messiah* in 1951, having conducted in March 1950 the first of many performances of that work in an attempt at what would now be called the authentic style. Tobin became totally obsessed with this work, and because so many of the primary sources for the music were in our collections I allowed him to come to the Music Room itself rather than have the continual burden of sending the autograph score and so many rarities (including early manuscript copies, various scarce editions and the libretto) to him in the North Library. I can date this episode to the early part of 1952, because it was only after Paul Hirsch's death on 23 November 1951 that the small room within the Music room itself known, from its contents, as the King's Music Library, became vacant. During Hirsch's lifetime, he had the sole use of the room for his regular, helpful visits to us, and I was working at a desk just outside its door. (Only some time after Tim Neighbour had arrived did I appropriate the King's Music Library and use it as my office.) It was therefore probably in February or March 1952 that Tobin emerged from the King's Music Library, where he had been surrounded by all his sources, in a state of total rapture. He had, if recollection serves, made some textual discovery which he regarded as of supreme importance. I recall his words vividly: 'I have felt', he exclaimed, in ecstasy, 'as if the old man himself were looking over my shoulder'. Unfortunately, although in the end Tobin edited *The Messiah* for the *Hällische Händel-Ausgabe*, his enthusiasm was not balanced by much sense of textual values. Of his editorial work, and the two books derived from it, *The New Grove* fairly said: 'He also wrote two books as affectionate, not strictly scholarly by-products of his Handel studies'. Although Tobin commanded the complete devotion of the London Choral Society, he was in fact rather self important and, like many conductors, of short stature.

Another episode from these years was the theft of the first edition of the

French national anthem, the *Marseillaise*. At the time this seemed very serious, but with hindsight can be seen as an extraordinary affair with some curious twists in it. The *Marseillaise* was first published in Strasbourg as a small oblong bifolium in 1792. As only two copies of it are known, the one in the Hirsch library was rightly regarded as a great treasure. Hirsch himself had had made for it a very fine box designed by Douglas Cockerell in which it lay unbound and in pristine state. Like all other rare music in Hirsch's collection and in our own, it was readily available to readers in the North Library, where the rules demanded that all items in boxes should be checked by the staff before issue and again on return. Now it so happened that in the autumn of 1954 I had on my staff a young clerical officer who showed rather limited interest in her work. As she was of partly French descent, I attempted one day to increase her interest by showing her the *Marseillaise* in its box (for at that time part of a clerical officer's duties in the Music Room was to issue and inspect on return all case books).

On 30 January 1955 she came to my room in some agitation with the 'Marseillaise' box and explained that what it now contained was not the first edition which I had happened to show her. Then the hue and cry began and it took some very anxious investigations before we finally established the sequence of events set in train by a very clever reader, one Thomas Gerald Bolitho, who had had a ticket of admission to the Reading Room since 1919. From our register of case books on issue (which Bolitho did not know we kept) it was found that he had sent for the first edition several times in the preceding months. Each time it had come back safely. His plan was clever. Two days before the theft he had sent for another, later, edition of the *Marseillaise* which dated from about 1800 and which, being only a single sheet of no great value, was bound in what was called a 'tract-volume' with some forty other pieces of French sheet music of similar size in upright folio. This volume, not being a case book, was delivered to Bolitho in the main Reading Room. There it would not have been difficult for him, using a sharp knife or a razor blade, to cut out the sheet of the *Marseillaise* and take it out in his brief-case, because at that time readers' bags were never searched.

Bolitho was also sure, from his knowledge of the Reading Room, that the staff would never have had had time to check right through a tract-volume to make sure that all items in it were present both on issue and return. A few days later Bolitho came back with the cut-out sheet, sent for the first edition in the box and, no doubt during the lunch period when the staff in the North Library was reduced, removed the first edition and substituted the sheet of the later one. Again, he banked on the staff being satisfied with the presence of *a* sheet in the box, and indeed, not being specialists, they could not possibly be blamed for not recognising that substitution had taken place.

But fortunately the little display to my clerical officer bore good fruit because, when she came to check the box and its contents on return, she had detected the substitution at once. But for this chance, the theft might well have gone unnoticed for an indefinite period. In the end, the police caught Bolitho through his address in the register of admissions to the Reading Room, and he confessed, leading them to the hiding place of the *Marseillaise* in a suitcase in the left-luggage office at Charing Cross station. At his trial held at the Old Bailey, Bolitho, aged sixty-four, was described – appropriately enough – as an 'exporter'. From the evidence, it appeared that he had formed some muddled plan to take the *Marseillaise* out of the country and sell it for a substantial sum to a foreign library, in order to relieve his chronic indigence. *The Times* report stated that 'he took it to call attention to an injustice'! He cut a very sad figure in court on 22 April 1955 when for this and a similar offence he was sentenced to twenty-one months in prison. In retrospect, I believe that the whole affair was caused by our month-long exhibition of 1953 which I mentioned above. For it had included the *Marseillaise* and made quite a feature of its rarity. Otherwise, Bolitho, not a specialist in music, would probably never have known of the sheet's existence.

Even before the Bolitho episode, I had discovered that there were, broadly speaking, three types of reader. John Tobin was one of the rare few who knew almost exactly what he wanted. There were quite a number of similar readers who also knew their requirements with some certainty, and who, because they made their application through the normal procedure in the Reading Room, had no reason to seek my advice. But many readers from abroad were often a different matter. As the floodgates of pent-up research began to open in the later 1940s, I had a continual stream of visitors from both Europe and America. Some wrote in advance and arranged to make an appointment by telephone when they reached London, while others simply arrived and rang the bell. All of them were surprised to find that the Music Room was not itself a reading room. (Tobin's use of the Music Room was then, as I have mentioned, a very rare exception.) A fair number of them quickly made it clear that what they needed was not printed music at all but material in the Department of Manuscripts, to whose Students' Room they could easily be redirected after an advance telephone call by myself. But there remained many others who really did not know what they wanted and regarded their visit to the Music Room and myself as a kind of free tutorial. This applied particularly, but by no means exclusively, to Americans. I soon learned that when the visitor had settled in the chair the other side of my desk and began to tell me his (or her) life history, it was going to be a long morning or afternoon. Quite often the visitor had not even organised his thoughts or ideas in advance and was relying on us to concentrate his mind.

This sort of thing took up a great deal of time which ought to have been devoted to more pressing daily concerns. So once I acquired a reliable secretary, I worked out a very necessary arrangement. This lady sat near the entrance to the Music Room, and duly noted the time of the visitor's arrival. After half an hour had passed she would ring me up with a hypothetical reminder that I had an appointment to see the Principal Keeper downstairs in ten minutes or so. This fairly harmless scheme of interruption never failed, and when the visitor heard me thank my secretary for the reminder he usually left, often escorted by myself, with a fairly good grace. There were other types of more difficult visitors such as emissaries from publishers who wanted to know why their applications for the supply of illustrative photographs had been apparently so long delayed. To solve such difficulties as these needed a good deal of quick thinking and extempore tergiversation. On the whole we were able to keep both visitors and readers fairly happy, and could sometimes truthfully remind them, when they complained of delay in book supply, that we were a great deal quicker than our opposite numbers in the Bibliothèque Nationale in Paris.

Such episodes, however tiresome and time-consuming, were short-lived, unlike other distractions of a semi-official nature. Without doubt the most continuously demanding of all during my whole career was the British Institute of Recorded Sound. This was really the creation of one man and one man alone – Patrick Saul, who was totally single-minded and of exceptional tenacity and vision. Saul's mission in life was to establish a national collection of recorded sound which would include not only music but a vast range of other subjects such as the spoken word, dialect, phonetics, what, for want of a better phrase, was then called 'animal noises' (later 'wildlife sounds'), and in fact everything of scientific, historical and artistic significance which could be stored in some sound-producing medium. Saul knew that Britain was the only major European country without such an archive and it must have been late in 1947 or early in 1948 that he came to see me with a view to enlisting the support of the Trustees of the British Museum.

Saul was an extraordinary personality, tall, heavily built with a quietly spoken manner and a delightful sense of humour. He had been educated at Dover College, then took a degree in Economics at the London School of Economics. I believe he later went into a bank, from which however he resigned in order to devote himself at first unpaid, on slender private means, to the great passion of his life. Saul approached many people, including Frank Howes, the influential music critic of *The Times*, who lent the full weight of his publicity to the idea in several articles. The matter was reported to the Trustees who gave it their blessing and appointed me as their official representative. In due course a meeting was convened by the Arts Council which was attended by its own representative and by many others from interested parties such as the BBC, the British Council, the recording industry, music publishers, the Public Record Office and the like. Those present as individuals included Lord Esher, Desmond Shawe-Taylor, Sir Edmund Compton, Frank Howes, Mr (later Sir) Robert Meyer, Professor Dennis Fry and Michael Rubinstein (who became ultimately the institute's invaluable honorary solicitor).

Gradually, the existence and aims of the institute became known and everyone without exception who heard of it agreed that it was a splendid idea, but no one was willing to give it the essential financial backing. Its collection had in fact started with piles of records in Patrick Saul's flat and the first thing was to find a home for the collection and provide it with offices. This ultimately I was able to do by persuading my senior colleagues to interest the Trustees in the Institute's well-being to the extent of granting it the lease, at a peppercorn rent, of the lower part of a splendid house which they owned, No. 38 Russell Square. With this benefit, the Institute felt able to approach various parties for different kinds of help. Saul and I visited a good many influential people. Among them was Sir Compton Mackenzie, formerly the editor of *The Gramophone* magazine, whom we tried to persuade to deposit its splendid archive with the Institute. Unfortunately he could not see his way to do this. We also called upon Mr (later Sir) Edward Lewis and Sir Joseph Lockwood, respectively the heads of Decca and HMV, hoping to induce them to give one copy of all records issued to the Institute. They likewise declined, and in 1955 organised a strong lobby within the record industry to oppose a clause suggested for inclusion in the new Copyright Act of 1956, whereby the Institute would enjoy the benefit to legal deposit of all published records exactly as, under the Copyright Act of 1911, publishers were obliged to send a copy of every book to the British Museum.

Through Desmond Shawe-Taylor, we also introduced ourselves to Sir Denis Rickett, one of the senior officers in the Treasury concerned with the funding of libraries and educational projects. But he made it pretty clear that the Treasury was very wary of such new enterprises, especially one like the Institute which, having virtually no limits to its immense scope, might make huge demands on the public purse. In the end, however, after the Institute became incorporated in 1951, it did receive a small amount of government funding and this, combined with such other help in the way of loans and Saul's genius for persuading private owners and others to give or bequeath their collections, was enough to keep things going for the next decade or so. At first Saul worked with practically no staff for at least fourteen hours a day, seven days a week. Gradually he organised the cataloguing of the collection and was particularly successful in the programme of lectures which he planned and executed, all given by people eminent in the world of music or drama to illustrate the Institute's huge potential. Saul was the kind of man who had at least a dozen new ideas every day before breakfast and wanted to pursue all of them irrespective of practical considerations. It was an essential part of my job as Chairman of the Executive Committee to meet him several times a week (this of course apart from numerous committees) and sort out those ideas which were immediately practicable from those which were not. As his office was barely one hundred yards from mine, at least I did not have to spend much time in travel. All this was in an infinitely worthwhile cause and great things were achieved, but because they cost me immense time and effort, it was much to my relief when my formal connection with the Institute ended in 1962, the time having then come for a complete reorganisation of its structure.

In that year Sir Adrian Boult took over as Chairman and shortly afterwards the Institute moved to much larger premises at 29 Exhibition Road where it continued to survive and indeed flourish until, with its name changed to The National Sound Archive, it became part of the British Library in 1983. The wheel had come full circle with a vengeance after some thirty years! For in the early 1950s the executive committee devoted much anxious thought to the question as to whether or not the Institute should become a part of the British Museum, in close and indeed logical connection with the collections of music. But at that time it was felt that the unavoidable changes in staff grading and various administrative matters would have entailed the Institute's loss of independence, and when the executive committee came to consider the probable conditions of amalgamation and their effect on staff and grading, it reluctantly decided not to pursue the matter any further. Patrick Saul retired in 1978 after some thirty years of selfless, dedicated effort. He was subsequently appointed O.B.E., an award which gave wide pleasure as just recognition of his notable service.

During all this time, and throughout the various distractions I have already mentioned, staff relations were a perpetual problem. For in a small division such as the Music Room and in a confined space – it measured barely forty yards long by some twelve yards wide – there were always likely to be clashes of personality. One of the more difficult ones occurred in the 1960s when I had on my staff at the same time a male senior library assistant and a female clerical officer (not the same one who was concerned with the *Marseillaise*) who disliked each other cordially. Although their duties were entirely separate – he being solely concerned with book-supply and she with a variety of clerical work – they never lost an opportunity of rubbing each other up the wrong way. She was of a devout nature and developed the maddening habit of writing out texts from the Bible with full references to book, chapter and verse of passages which she thought suitable to express her strong disapproval of his personality and his work. She would do this almost every other day, leaving the slips of paper on his desk either at lunchtime or in the very early morning. His only method of retaliation was sarcasm, which in this case had little effect. But as her persecution – for that is what it was – became more intense, it affected his attitude to his other colleagues and indeed to the Museum as a whole. Things became so bad that in the end he decided to take early retirement which he could just afford to do because he had a small pension from his previous employment as an assistant purser with a shipping company.

But on the day of his retirement he decided to leave his mark on the entire system of book supply by putting some essential machinery out of action. Then, as now, all application slips from readers were sent up to the Music Room by Lamson pneumatic tubes, each slip being encased in an oblong metal container propelled by suction. A similar method was used to send back to readers any slips which were inaccurate, unclearly filled in or otherwise defective. In the days before his retirement, the officer concerned had secretly accumulated as many spare containers as he could find. Just before his final departure and after the book supply had closed for the day, he inserted a score of them, one after the other in quick succession, so that the normal suction was unable to cope and both tubes came to a halt at one of the bends in their progress. This was not of course discovered until the next day, when engineers had to be sent for. They soon pronounced that the tubes would have to be taken apart at several points in their long descent to the Reading Room. Until the repairs were finished, which took about a week, all application slips had to be taken up and down seventy-six stairs and along various corridors by hand.

VIII · RESIDENTIAL DUTY

As the idea of 'residential duty' was (and presumably still is) unique to the British Museum among all the nation's museums, libraries and galleries, its origins, nature and circumstances deserve to be set out in some detail. From the very foundation of the Museum, the statutes required that at all times when it was closed to the public and at weekends, one of its senior officers should be responsible for the safety of all the collections. For the first ninety years or so, while the Museum was small, the Principal Librarian (who from 1898 to 1973 bore the title 'Director and Principal Librarian') and all the Keepers, lived in the east and west wings of Montagu House. This practice continued throughout the nineteenth century after the new residences were constructed, nearly on the site of the old wings, from 1844 to 1849. Thus, up to 1921, it was not difficult for the needs of overall safety to be met by a rota of the senior officers in residence, who could easily arrange the duty among themselves. But as circumstances changed, far fewer Keepers wished to reside, and only the Director was required to do so. (The Statutes of 1871 required Deputy Keepers to live within one mile of the Museum, but this gradually fell into abeyance.) The Statutes of 1932 required the senior officers to have their usual abode within such distance of the Museum as the Standing Committee might require: but this too must soon have proved impracticable.

As the Director and two or (at the most) three of his Keepers residing could not be expected to share the duty all the time, a new arrangement came into being in 1921 (described in a minute of 9 July). The Trustees decided that the names of the Director, the Keepers and Deputy Keepers should be placed on a rota by which each in succession became 'duty officer' for a week at a time. In the early years of this system, the relatively small number of senior officers (sixteen in all) meant that the duty came round every three to four months. But after 1959, when a dozen or so new Deputy Keepers were created (the present writer being one of them), the frequency of the duty dropped, and averaged once in about every eight to nine months.

The Director, and any still resident Keepers, were able to do their turn from their own comfortable residences. Their obligation was merely to remain at home for seven successive evenings. For their colleagues, a residential flat and housekeeper were provided at public expense. The flat was a bizarre apartment, situated right in the centre of the west face of the East Wing, immediately opposite the Director's residence in the West Wing, the two wings being about 150 yards apart (Fig. 26). Like all the residences, the flat was not on ground level, but up a flight of six steps. This elevation gave a splendid view of the whole courtyard and much of the wings of the colonnades, from the tall windows of the sitting room, which was reached from a door in the spacious hallway. Another door led to the bedroom and bathroom at the back. The flat was generously though plainly furnished. It had a rather hard three-piece suite, in green rexine; an extending oak dining-table, with chairs to match; a heavy side-board, and an upright piano (the property of Bentley Bridgewater). Above this, the mantel-shelf and the sideboard were three portraits, of obscure benefactors. Heating was provided by a gas-fire supplemented by a low radiator in each window bay. A gas ring was fitted to the pipe of the fire. The windows were of the sash type, and so heavy that they had to be opened by long ropes: both sashes were hung on chains which jangled in operation. Each bay was fitted with tall dusty shutters. Though the high ceiling made the room cool in summer, there was always a fusty smell: after all, the building was over a century old, and had seen many residents.

26 The former Rota Flat, photographed in 1990. To the left of the door are the two windows of the sitting room.

On a table by the fireplace was a telephone and battered folder which contained a full list of the duty officer's responsibilities, hours, routine, and so on, with a sheet giving the names, addresses and phone numbers of all the Keepers and Deputy Keepers – essential in an emergency. In the corner by the other side of the fireplace was a shuttered opening that concealed a service hoist, of which more below.

The bedroom, with a capacious bathroom off it, backed due east, on to Montagu Street. Adequately furnished, it had one large window with shutters, a radiator at the bottom and some rather tattered curtains. The essential telephone stood on a table by the bed. For a light sleeper this room was an ordeal because all night long, with some respite only between about 2 a.m. and 4 a.m., taxis ground and roared their way up to Euston and King's Cross Stations. As they hurtled round the corner from Great Russell Street all the drivers changed gear and accelerated. The duty officer could keep some of the noise out if he closed both the window and the shutters in both bedroom and bathroom, but much of the continuous roar still came through. If, of course, one needed fresh air and opened the window, sleep was quite impossible.

The officer's welfare depended much on the housekeeper, who lived in the basement flat. Its sitting room too faced west, and because its area was generous, its windows caught some light in the afternoon. Otherwise, it was a gloomy place, and it was not easy to find someone to fill the post for any length of time, although the duties were mostly not onerous. The housekeeper had to provide the duty officer with breakfast and dinner on week days, and in addition with lunch on Sundays. She kept an account and the officer paid for what he had. In 1959, his allowance was fifteen shillings per night, and this sufficed for most. But the flat was the officer's to do what he liked with, and some used to bring in their wives and entertain quite lavishly. Edward Croft Murray used the flat's ample cellars to store wine, and gave dinner parties for which the housekeeper expected to be suitably recompensed in respect of the extra work. These being Trustees' premises, the officer could bring to the flat any movable Museum property. A Keeper could decorate the room with choice objects from the collections, or bring in large quantities of books to get on with his research. Some had special tastes in food. One officer always liked shepherd's pie for lunch on Sunday, and had his own recipe which he had explained to the housekeeper who understood its peculiar flavourings. Unfortunately on one occasion this understanding lady had just retired and her successor, unversed in this special dish, made such a complete hash of it that the Keeper (and his resident wife) found the result quite inedible. Rather than offend the lady by sending the pie back uneaten, they scraped it out of the dish and put the lot down the lavatory. The result was a complete blockage for which a plumber had to be requisitioned next day.

On the whole, the officers were well pleased and all those of the post-war years were grateful to Bentley Bridgewater, who countered Treasury indifference and meanness and secured such money as he could from central funds to make the flat habitable and above all see that the successive housekeepers were as content as possible. After all, the housekeeper's only time off was when the Director or a resident Keeper was the duty officer.

The great value of the flat was that, besides entertainment of family and friends, it could be used for any social purpose. Thus, in the early 1960s, it chanced that one of my periods of residence coincided with the week during which the joint committee of the International Association of Music Libraries and the International Society for Musicology was meeting in London to discuss its vast project, the International Inventory of Musical Sources. It so happened that one of its morning meetings had to continue well into the afternoon on a day in which the room we had been using at the Library Association's offices was not available. But I was able to say 'come to the British Museum, and just ask the Front Gate warder for the duty officer's flat'. To their utter astonishment, a dozen foreign visitors were directed to the East Wing and the spacious room where, at a small extra charge to myself, the housekeeper provided tea and cake to fortify our long discussion. The idea of private hospitality in a public place like the Museum was an unfailing source of wonder and delight.

Perhaps the most extraordinary feature of the flat was the arrangement for the delivery of meals – almost a ritual in itself. The above-mentioned hoist and its shaft were probably designed when the wing was built, intended for regular domestic use at the time when what became the duty officer's sitting room was the dining room of the residence and situated immediately above the kitchen. (The apparatus was identical to the hoist used for books in the Keeper's Ante-Room, fitted later in the nineteenth century.) The officer agreed in advance with the housekeeper the time when he would like his meals, and she came upstairs beforehand to lay the table. At the time agreed, the officer was generally waiting by the upper opening of the shaft, and could hear his dishes being loaded on to the hoist. Then came the rumble of rope on pulley as the housekeeper pulled, the clanking of the hoist against the walls, and the banging of the counterweight as the hoist creaked upwards. Finally the housekeeper used her bellpush which was connected to a loud bell at the top of the shaft, in case the officer was in the bedroom. If anything were missing, he could ring his bell, which sounded in the kitchen, call down the shaft, and up it would come. His main course done, he put the dishes on the hoist, rang and down it went, soon to return with (in the evening) his pudding and coffee. Presumably, over the years, the rope had been renewed, but otherwise this apparatus was a true Victorian relic, used twice a day on weekdays, thrice on Sundays.

Housekeeping apart, the officer's duties were straightforward enough, at least on paper. He had to be at his post in the flat from 6 p.m. to 9 a.m. Monday to Friday, and at the weekend his charge lasted from 1 p.m. Saturday until 9 a.m. Monday. At one time the turn of duty began on Monday, but as this meant that a rather wearisome weekend was its conclusion, the starting day was changed to Friday evening. At the weekend the officer was required to walk right through all the public galleries on Saturday afternoon and again on the Sunday. During the week he had to go on night patrol at least twice, once on a short patrol lasting about an hour, and again on a full patrol which might take some two and a half hours. These patrols, in which he accompanied a two-man team (equipped with strong lamps and full sets of keys which jangled from a long chain) comprised a police-warder and a fireman-warder. In their company he would go through numerous remote staff offices and a labyrinth of basement store rooms with which he was totally unfamiliar, up and down numerous staircases in turrets and passages. Every door was unlocked, relocked and checked, after many a thunderous clang. At the first patrol, any lights left burning had to be switched off, and dangerous things like electric kettles disconnected. All these patrols took place in the main building: the King Edward VII building was under a separate, different arrangement.

All departmental key safes had to be inspected to make sure they were locked. If any Keeper had omitted to sign back his safe key, he had to be rung up and reminded: if he lived within a reasonable distance, he was expected to come in person and return the key forthwith. Otherwise, its absence was noted as a black mark against him. It was not astonishing, especially in an aging building, how many things could and did go wrong, and so require the duty officer's attention. In harsh weather water pipes might burst with a dangerous flood as the result. Air ducts could become blocked and dirt-filled smoke blow out through the wrong vents. Often during violent storms roofs leaked and cases near a wall had to be emptied and moved, and the appropriate Keeper told by phone, sometimes in the early hours of the morning. The duty officer had to expect to be called out, at any time of the evening or night, by a ring on the telephone from the nearby Control Room. He also had to act, on occasion, as a press officer to deal with phone calls about some 'exciting' acquisition, having been briefed about this in advance.

One turn of duty might be totally uneventful: on the next there might be an incident every night, and the unfortunate officer emerged on Friday morning worn out by a succession of seven broken nights. By the later 1960s the frequency of residential duty was, as already mentioned, considerably reduced from what it had been even twenty years or so before. Nevertheless its very continuance did produce a certain coherence within the Museum. For apart from joint service on various committees, senior men in the antiquities departments seldom saw much of their counterparts in the library. But the succession of rota duty or incidents arising from it often put them in touch with each other. There was thus an unspoken feeling of unity born of the unique shared responsibility for the sole charge of the Museum and its multifarious collections. Moreover, whatever the attitude of the participants at the time, when their term of duty was over, they mostly felt some satisfaction in having done it.

INDEX